CO-AUY-779

EMORY UNIVERSITY STUDIES IN LAW AND RELIGION

John Witte Jr., General Editor

The Peril and Promise of Christian Liberty

*Richard Hooker, the Puritans, and
Protestant Political Theology*

W. Bradford Littlejohn

WILLIAM B. EERDMANS PUBLISHING COMPANY
GRAND RAPIDS, MICHIGAN

Wm. B. Eerdmans Publishing Co.
2140 Oak Industrial Drive N.E., Grand Rapids, Michigan 49505
www.eerdmans.com

23 22 21 20 19 18 17   1 2 3 4 5 6 7

ISBN 978-0-8028-7256-2

Library of Congress Cataloging-in-Publication Data

Names: Littlejohn, W. Bradford, author.
Title: The peril and promise of Christian liberty : Richard Hooker, the Puritans, and
    Protestant political theology / W. Bradford Littlejohn.
Description: Grand Rapids : Eerdmans Publishing Co., 2017. |
    Series: Emory University studies in law and religion |
    Includes bibliographical references and index.
Identifiers: LCCN 2016058804 | ISBN 9780802872562 (pbk.)
Subjects: LCSH: Liberty—Religious aspects—Christianity—History of doctrines. |
    Hooker, Richard, 1553 or 1554-1600. | Christianity and politics. |
    Protestant churches—Doctrines.
Classification: LCC BT809 .L58 2017 | DDC 261.709—dc23
    LC record available at https://lccn.loc.gov/2016058804

Contents

Contents

Acknowledgments

Like perhaps many other things in life, a book is a disconcerting combination of, on the one hand, meticulous planning and disciplined execution, and, on the other hand, the completely unforeseen and fortuitous: the chance meeting and conversation at a conference or (more often perhaps nowadays) online, the curious footnote pursued into a treasure-trove of exciting discoveries, an offhand suggestion by your supervisor that blossoms into an important new line of inquiry, the epiphany that comes during the morning walk to your desk or over your third coffee as you muse on Rachmaninov's Third. Unfortunately, it is only the first of these categories, by far the less consequential contribution, that the lowly writer can take any credit for. For the rest, he can only say, *non nobis, Domine, sed Nomini Tuo da gloriam*! However, it smacks suspiciously of false modesty to wax eloquent thanking God on an Acknowledgments page, a way of not-so-subtly insinuating to one's readers that everything before them has God's personal stamp of approval, being his own handiwork. Thankfully, however, God works mostly through strange and fallible secondary causes, especially those that walk on two legs, and to these it is appropriate to indulge in effusions of gratitude.

Many of these (some long dead) have made their contribution primarily through the written word, sealed up between two covers of a book; these are honored in the appropriate (though depressingly formal) way in the footnotes and bibliography that accompany this work, so there is little point listing them here. I will make an exception of three only. David VanDrunen deserves a word of thanks here. His book *Natural Law and the Two Kingdoms* fortuitously came my way six years ago and set me on a quest of refutation that led me unexpectedly to write the dissertation that led to the present book. In the process, of course, the nature of the refutation changed dramatically, and I learned a great deal from him; indeed, by the end it was clear that the points I wished to make could be argued without needing a sustained polemical foil, so you will find relatively little of VanDrunen's work in these pages. In any case, I am grateful to Dr. VanDrunen, who was polite enough to meet me for a beer and a somewhat confusing argument about Calvin even after I had intemperately savaged him in print—and has been just as gracious when our paths have crossed since. In a very different way, my debt to Torrance Kirby in various ways is evident all over the pages that follow, although he will no doubt find much to quibble with. The rich insights I have mined from his books and articles have been complemented by his patient correspondence and feedback over the past few years, during the early part of which he displayed great perseverance in trying to drill the Reformational two-kingdoms concept into my thick head. Third, of course, I must thank Richard Hooker, "of blessed memory" (as Paul Stanwood likes to always add), who has been far more to me during the years of writing this book than merely its subject. I hope it will not sound like sacrilege to say that his words have been a lamp for my feet and a light unto my path in more ways than I can count, many of them well beyond the scope of this research.

For introducing me to Hooker (or reintroducing, as I had made a passing though passionate acquaintance with him during a summer study at Oxford some years ago), I must thank of course my PhD dissertation supervisor Oliver O'Donovan, who throughout the process of my doctoral studies guided me with a gentle but judicious hand. His suggestions have been few but carefully chosen, and have usually yielded abundant fruit—none more so than his absurd insistence that I spend my Christmas break five and a half years ago toiling through the eight books of the *Ecclesiastical Polity*, which had, I thought, little bearing on my anticipated topic. The reader will find that when I came to write the conclusion of this book, his influence on me proved deeper than even I had realized, as I could not help circling back to his many insightful formulations of related problems in his own works over the past few decades. His wife, Joan, proved an extraordinary (though again, an unforeseen) secondary supervisor, meticulously flagging the least grammatical transgression or conceptual ambiguity throughout the process, and bringing to bear a rare mastery of the key texts and concepts with which I was wrestling. I have missed both of them dearly since leaving Edinburgh nearly three years ago, and I hope they will forgive my long procrastination in bringing this work to print. Susan Hardman Moore and Paul Avis served as gracious but attentive examiners for my dissertation defense, offering several useful suggestions on how to improve the text for publication.

Perhaps just as important as their formal supervision has been the quirky but unfailing advice of my friend and mentor, Peter Escalante. I had the uncanny experience, at various times since stumbling upon the topic and argument of this book, that I was simply unfolding ideas that he had somehow planted in my head sometime in autumn 2010. I appreciate also Peter's willingness to read over each chapter draft as it appeared. Many other friends (some of them friends formed along the way) also helped by their suggestions, conversations, feedback on drafts, and penetrating questions. Steven Wedgeworth, Jordan Ballor, and Eric Parker in particular, gave me many helpful ideas and put a number of key resources in my path; the opportunity to work with Jordan on a project on sixteenth-century Calvinist church discipline was especially fruitful. My dear friend Andrew Fulford read over several bits at the crucial revising stage, helping me ensure that they were polished and comprehensible enough, and has also given valuable feedback on the revisions. His own doctoral work on Richard Hooker, which I have enjoyed discussing with him these past couple of years, promises to add greatly to what I have tried to achieve in my own writing. I also owe a great debt of gratitude to my old and brilliant friend Davey Henreckson, who will no doubt be the secure occupant of a professorial chair at Yale Divinity while I'm still trying to jerry-rig my own personal theological-pedagogical revolution a few years hence. Throughout the process, he has asked many challenging but penetrating questions, and made a number of suggestions, many of which turned out to be very useful indeed—putting me onto John Perry's *Pretenses of Loyalty*, for instance. His read-through of the entire finished manuscript and of the rewritten first chapter of this book last year was particularly helpful. Matthew Tuininga, with whom I was so fortunate as to spar repeatedly during the time I was working on my dissertation, and with whom I have been even more fortunate to become friends since, also offered very valuable feedback on the entire project. And of course my faithful friend Brad Belschner has always been there to talk through ideas with me and reassure me that I was not crazy to get excited about the things that I got excited about. More recently, conversations about Richard Hooker with Ryan Handermann and Brian Marr have helped me improve some passages and highlight some key themes.

Although I dared to be rather pleased with how the original dissertation turned out, this book, I hope, is considerably improved. In particular, the first and last chapters are almost entirely rewritten and expanded, and various other points in the argument have been filled out or nuanced by the insights of subsequent research, conversations, and feedback. I am grateful to the O'Donovans for pointing me to Jon Pott at Eerdmans as a publisher for this study, and to Jon for his enthusiasm for the project, valuable suggestions, and great patience as an editor. I am grateful also to David Bratt, who took over the editorship of this project when Jon retired, and who was also gracious enough to allow me to let a couple of deadlines slip when other responsibilities piled up in the way of finishing the revised manuscript. John Witte Jr., the editor of the series in which this book appears, was good enough to take a liking to the text, and even better to suggest some much-needed improvements. He will certainly not agree with everything in the resulting final product, but the argument, I hope, is now clearer, stronger, and more accessible than it might otherwise have been.

When a pile-up of seemingly impossible deadlines threatened to postpone once more my finalization of this manuscript, Brian Marr, my research assistant, was good enough to do some wonderful editorial work on checking and standardizing the text that saved me many hours and much stress. For all the faults that remain in the text, whether minor typos or massive lapses in argument, the responsibility remains of course fully my own.

Even the rare reader inquisitive enough to read through an Acknowledgments section is likely to skip ahead when he encounters the section thanking family, as it is sure to be sentimental, and almost entirely unrelated to the matter of the book. And yet for the writer, no section could be more important. In particular, the bit where the author thanks his wife for her extraordinary patience and longsuffering over years of penniless and seemingly pointless toil (often in a foreign land, no less) can seem quite perfunctory, and yet it is anything but. To my wife, Rachel, I am indescribably and eternally grateful for her unfailing support at every stage of the way. It may sound trivial, clichéd, or maybe even sexist to single out for gratitude the extraordinarily fine dinners that I could look forward to at the end of a day of study and writing, but few things contributed so much to the relative ease and efficiency of my work. "An army can't move except on its stomach," said Napoleon, and the same is true of an academic. My seven-year-old son Soren was a source of frustration as well as delight along the way, but even the former was invaluable in keeping me grounded—such as his resort to the blunt expedient of slamming my laptop shut and saying "Don't work!" when it was high time to call it a day. My now three-year-old angel Pippa provided constant joy and inspiration on the crucial last leg of the dissertation (and to think I was afraid she would slow it down with sleepless nights!). Dear little Oliver arrived after the heavy-lifting was done, but his good cheer and mischievous grin have been another encouragement in my work of revision since. To thank one's mother may seem acceptable at a high school graduation speech, but frankly embarrassing at later stages of life. And yet I must thank her once more for teaching me to write—to write essays clearly, quickly, and effectively, from a young age. Too many scholars must labor simultaneously with forming their ideas and forming their words; I have been fortunate enough to be able to focus on the former and let the latter take care of themselves, thanks in large part to that training many years ago. My dad too has provided an ever-ready ear, to chat about things Hooker-related, or not-so-related, throughout my PhD work and beyond, keeping my morale up with his humor and his uncanny willingness to agree with me.

Finally, I will thank God directly—not for the content of this book, but for the joy it has brought me. For too many PhD students, it seems, a dissertation has become stale and lukewarm by the date of submission, and they are only too happy to do to it what God wanted to do to the Laodiceans. I am happy to say it was not so for me, and even if I occasionally tired of returning to it for publication revisions, it is still with a very fond farewell that I send this manuscript forth upon its voyage of publication.

Abbreviations and Notes on Citations

Abbreviations

Answere	John Whitgift. *An Answere to a certen libell intituled, An Admonition to Parliament.* London: Henrie Bynneman, 1573. Reprinted in *Whitgift's Works.* Edited by John Ayre. 3 vols. Cambridge: Parker Society, 1849–51.
CR	*Corpus Reformatorum.* Edited by C. B. Bretschneider and H. E. Bindseil. Halle and Brunswick: C. A. Schwetschke, 1834–.
FLE 1	W. Speed Hill and Georges Edelen, eds. *The Folger Library Edition of the Works of Richard Hooker,* vol. 1: *The Laws of Ecclesiastical Polity: Pref., Books I to IV.* Cambridge, MA: Belknap Press of Harvard University Press, 1977.
FLE 2	W. Speed Hill, ed. *The Folger Library Edition of the Works of Richard Hooker,* vol. 2: *The Laws of Ecclesiastical Polity, Book V.* Cambridge, MA: Belknap Press of Harvard University Press, 1977.
FLE 3	W. Speed Hill and P. G. Stanwood, eds. *The Folger Library Edition of the Works of Richard Hooker,* vol. 3: *The Laws of Ecclesiastical Polity: Books VI, VII, VIII.* Cambridge, MA: Belknap Press of Harvard University Press, 1981.
FLE 4	W. Speed Hill and John E. Booty, eds. *The Folger Library Edition of the Works of Richard Hooker,* vol. 4: *Of the Lawes of Ecclesiasticall Politie: Attack and Response.* Cambridge, MA: Belknap Press of Harvard University Press, 1982.
FLE 5	W. Speed Hill and Laetitia Yeandle, eds. *The Folger Library Edition of the Works of Richard Hooker,* vol. 5: *Tractates and Sermons.*

	Cambridge, MA: Belknap Press of Harvard University Press, 1990.
FLE 6	W. Speed Hill, ed. *The Folger Library Edition of the Works of Richard Hooker*, vol. 6: *Of the Lawes of Ecclesiastical Politie, Books I–VIII: Introductions and Commentary*. Binghamton, NY: Medieval & Renaissance Texts & Studies, 1993.
LEP	Richard Hooker. *Of the Lawes of Ecclesiastical Politie. Eyght Bookes*. London: John Windet, 1593, 1597; Richard Bishop, 1648; J. Best, 1662.
LW	Martin Luther. *Luther's Works: American Edition*. Edited by Jaroslav Pelikan and Helmut T. Lehmann. St. Louis: Concordia, and Philadelphia: Muhlenberg, 1955–1970.
Replye	Thomas Cartwright. *A Replye to an Answere Made of M. Doctor Whitgift . . . Agaynste the Admonition*. s.l., 1574. Reprinted in *Whitgift's Works*. Edited by John Ayre. 3 vols. Cambridge: Parker Society, 1849–51.
RSR	Thomas Cartwright. *The Reste of the Second Replie: Agaynst Master Doctor Whitgifts Second Answer Touching the Church Discipline*. Basel, 1577.
SR	Thomas Cartwright. *The Second Replie of Thomas Cartwright: Agaynst Master Doctor Whitgifts Second Answer Touching the Church Discipline*. Heidelberg, 1575.
ST	Thomas Aquinas. *Summa Theologiae*. Translated by the Fathers of the English Dominican Province. At New Advent, www.newadvent.org.
WW	John Whitgift. *Whitgift's Works*. Edited by John Ayre. 3 vols. Cambridge: Parker Society, 1849–51.

Notes on Citations

Since both Whitgift's *Answere* and Cartwright's *Replye* were reprinted as part of the text of Whitgift's 1574 *Defense of an Answere*, which comprises the Parker Society edition of *Whitgift's Works*, I have simply used that edition for citations of all three sources. So, where the *Answere* or *Replye* is cited, I provide the original page #, followed by the *Whitgift's Works* page #: so, for instance, "Whitgift, *Answere*, 61 (*WW* II:44)," or "Cartwright, *Replye*, 14 (*WW* I:190)"; however, when the citation is from the *Defense*, you will see only, e.g., *WW* I:235.

All quotations or citations of Richard Hooker are assumed to be from the *Lawes* unless otherwise specified. They will generally be given by parenthetical references in the main body text (unlike all other citations, which will be footnoted), which will give first the book (in roman numeral), chapter, and paragraph from the *Lawes*, and then the volume (in arabic numeral), page, and line number from the *Folger Library Edition*. So, for instance, the citation "(II.4.3; *FLE* 1:153.30–154.5)" denotes that the quotation is taken from Book II, ch. 4, par. 3 of the *Lawes*, which can be found in vol. 1, beginning on p. 153, line 30, and ending on p. 154, line 5 of the *Folger Library Edition*. The same format of *FLE* citations will be used for Hooker's other works.

A Note on Spelling and Punctuation

Although it is the current preference among academic historians to faithfully reproduce the spelling and punctuation of early modern English sources, however anomalous and frankly bewildering they may be at times, I have deliberately eschewed this approach here. When nonspecialist English readers read early modern sources from writers such as John Calvin or Martin Luther, they have the pleasure of reading them in standardly spelled modern English prose, thanks to the labors of translators, who are wise enough not to impose on their translated texts the English of five centuries ago. It seems curious indeed that we should find sixteenth-century German and French texts easier to read than those in our own native tongue! While this difficulty cannot be entirely removed without transgressively modernizing the word choice and style of the early English writings, there seems to be no reason to perpetuate additional obstacles to comprehension by retaining archaic spelling. The sixteenth century is alien enough as it is.

Accordingly, I (or rather my esteemed assistant, Brian Marr) have taken the liberty of changing all spelling of quotations from early English texts, including Hooker's, to contemporary American English. The only exceptions are (a) in the titles of texts and (b) in cases where I am quoting from secondary scholarship that itself quotes the primary sources in their original spelling. Additionally, I have made the following two changes in matters of punctuation: (1) Where the slash mark (/) is used in earlier sources to signify a comma, I have replaced it with a comma; likewise, in some cases where a colon is used for functions we would not denote with a semicolon or period, I have amended accordingly. (2) Where quotations within quoted text were denoted in the original by italicizing the text, I have replaced with inverted commas or (in block quotes) with quotation marks.

CHAPTER ONE

"Different Kings and Different Laws"

Christian Liberty and the Conflict of Loyalties
since the Reformation

We may call the one the spiritual, the other the civil kingdom. Now, these two, as we have divided them, are always to be viewed apart from each other. When the one is considered, we should call off our minds, and not allow them to think of the other. For there exists in man a kind of two worlds, over which different kings and different laws can preside. By attending to this distinction, we will not erroneously transfer the doctrine of the gospel concerning spiritual liberty to civil order, as if in regard to external government Christians were less subject to human laws, because their consciences are unbound before God, as if they were exempted from all carnal service, because in regard to the Spirit they are free.

John Calvin, *Institutes*[1]

Truly, we must take good heed that we bring not the Church of Christ into such bondage, that it may not use anything that the Pope used. . . . How shall we debar the Church of this liberty, that it cannot signify some good thing, in setting forth their rites and ceremonies?

Peter Martyr Vermigli, Letter to John Hooper[2]

1. John Calvin, *Institutes of the Christian Religion*, ed. John T. McNeill, trans. Ford Lewis Battles (Louisville: Westminster John Knox, 1960), 1:847 [III.19.15].

2. Letter to Hooper, in Matthew Parker (?), ed., *A Briefe Examination for the tyme, of a certaine declaration, lately put in print in the name and defence of certaine Ministers in Lon-*

From the moment that Christ enigmatically rebuffed Herod's political theologians with the words "Render unto Caesar the things that are Caesar's, and to God the things that are God's," his followers have had to grapple with the challenge of living under "different kings and different laws." At various times and places, some have been so bold as to imagine they had removed the sting from Christ's statement, whether by bringing God and Caesar into alliance, by restricting their kingdoms to different worlds, or by ensuring that Caesar would adopt pluralistic policies that would grant free rein to any religious conscience. Each such solution has in due course been exposed as an overoptimistic illusion, leaving Christians to grapple anew with the tensions of their dual citizenship. Whatever the failures of Reformation political thought, it must at least be credited with its refusal to blithely dismiss the problem; indeed, fewer questions, as I hope this study will show, were more central to early Protestant theology and churchmanship.

The first of the quotes above can claim to be something of a classic text when it comes to Reformation political thought, appearing constantly in the secondary literature—although this ubiquity of citation hardly guarantees any unanimity of interpretation. The second quote, although coming from a reformer almost as renowned in his day as Calvin, is almost entirely obscure. Together, as I hope shall be clear by the end of this chapter (or at least by the end of this book) they mark out the profound tensions that attended the understanding of liberty and authority in the sixteenth-century European reformations, and which indeed remain with us right down to the present.

Let us begin with the first. Why is Calvin so concerned to warn us against a "transfer" of spiritual liberty to civil order? Why does he insist that we "call off our minds" from political issues when we consider this doctrine of Christian liberty? Certainly, most of those who have written on the topic of Protestantism and modern political thought have tended to ignore this warning. A host of preachers, writers, and scholars throughout the past three centuries have been busy making just this transfer, the so-called "Whig history" of liberty, in which Protestantism, with its protest against papal authority, unleashed an unstoppable impulse toward individual freedom, toppling tyrannical governments, establishing constitutional order, separating church and state, and eventually (for many of its twentieth-century advocates at least) generating human rights.[3] Even if spiritual liberty and civil liberty ought not to

---

don, refusyng to weare the apparell prescribed by the lawes and orders of the Realme (London: Richard Jugge, 1566), 32v, 33v.

3. Different versions of this narrative shall be considered below, though for a particu-

be conflated, such historians argue, one cannot deny the historical fact that the proclamation of the latter closely succeeded the former, with a geographical as well as a temporal correlation to the centers of the Protestant Reformation. Are we to dismiss this as a historical accident or is there some inward connection, by which Protestantism served as the "midwife"[4] for civil liberties and the separation of church and state? And if there is some connection, why is Calvin so eager to deny it; what is so bad about this "transfer"?

One answer is to say simply that Calvin was a reactionary conservative, fearful of losing the support of the Genevan magistrates if the Reformation threatened to upend the social order. Although it might be a stretch to label Calvin in such terms, given his obvious willingness to go toe-to-toe with the authorities when his convictions were on the line, it is standard to see such charges lodged at many of the magisterial Reformers, from Luther to Cranmer. And to be sure, they did rely heavily on the support of Protestant princes, did sincerely believe in the divine calling of such rulers, and were deeply suspicious of any doctrines that tended toward anarchy. Indeed, even the most fervent modern liberal can prove just as suspicious of ideologues who refuse their loyalty to the values that sustain the public order—as the backlash against conservative Christians in the wake of the marriage equality revolution has shown.

But perhaps more is at stake for Calvin. If we consider his words in light of sixteenth-century polemics against the Anabaptists as both seditious libertines and legalistic purists, it seems plausible that he meant "transfer" in the strong sense of the word. Taken literally, to "transfer" something from point A to point B generally means that it is no longer in point A, where it started;

---

larly clear (because crudely drawn and popularized) version see Douglas F. Kelly, *The Emergence of Liberty in the Modern World: The Influence of Calvin on Five Governments from the 16th through 18th Centuries* (Phillipsburg, NJ: P&R Publishing, 1992). It is worth noting that this narrative is not remotely new; one of its most famous proponents was Abraham Kuyper more than a century ago (see "Calvinism, the Source and Stronghold of Our Constitutional Liberties," in *Abraham Kuyper: A Centennial Reader*, ed. James Bratt [Grand Rapids: Eerdmans, 1998], 279–317). And Glenn Moots has recently documented how in mid-eighteenth-century sermons, for instance, the equation of "popery" with "tyranny"—in the sense of anything that subverts the rule of constitutional law—had become so commonplace that the two terms were virtually interchangeable, and similarly with the opposite equation of "Protestantism" and "constitutionalism" ("Searching for Christian America," in *For Law and for Liberty: Essays on the Trans-Atlantic Legacy of Protestant Political Thought*, ed. W. Bradford Littlejohn, Proceedings of the Third Annual Convivium Irenicum (Moscow, ID: Davenant, 2016).

4. The phrase comes from John E. Witte Jr., *Reformation of Rights: Law, Religion, and Human Rights in Early Modern Calvinism* (Cambridge: Cambridge University Press, 2007), 2.

the transfer thus accomplishes an inversion. We could thus read Calvin here as warning that, by attributing to the civil realm a liberty that was properly spiritual, we might find ourselves no longer possessing such liberty in its original proper arena, the spiritual realm, and might find ourselves outwardly free while inwardly in bondage. Were this the case, it would be reason to worry indeed, since any outward liberty worth having would be unlikely to last in circumstances of spiritual bondage.

In this book, I hope to both challenge and defend the notion that Protestantism's proclamation of "freedom of conscience" helped give birth to the modern liberal version. The challenge can be posed on multiple fronts. First we must face the obvious difficulty that whereas Luther's ideal of the liberated conscience was one in bondage to the word of God, modern liberalism's seems inherently pluralistic—it is the freedom of every individual to worship any God or none, and reflect that worship in their lives as fully or minimally as they like. This difference at the individual level is mirrored at the political level: modern liberalism's *sine qua non* is its insistence that this freedom of conscience must be guarded as an inviolable political right, with apparent corollaries about the inappropriateness of religious establishment of any kind; Luther and his followers, however, had little hesitation in retaining and indeed insisting upon a Christendom model, in which orthodoxy was defended and indeed imposed by political authority.

Indeed, I will argue in this opening chapter that this reflects not so much a difference between Luther and modern liberalism, but a tension that runs right through any account of liberty of conscience, premodern or modern. If individual conscience is not to be aimless and anarchistic, must it not be bound to a higher law, and if so, must it not seek to remake the political order in obedience to that law, actively overthrowing injustice rather than quietly pursuing its own freedom of worship? Without such an activist idea of conscience, oriented toward some universal law, an appeal to liberty of conscience seems a call for the disintegration of society into an interminable conflict of myriad self-justifying preferences (the paralysis that grips late modern consumer society). If such an activist conscience dominates, however, the social order is always in danger of being overthrown by a band of zealots, whose campaign for justice and righteousness threatens to trample underfoot the liberty of any consciences that might beg to differ (the danger that religious traditionalists today fear from the successive waves of social justice crusades that have reshaped Western liberalism in recent decades). In either case, it should be noted, freedom of conscience seems to be pitted against the freedom of a commonwealth to *be* or act as a commonwealth rather than a mere collection of individuals or as the executive agent of the higher law.

The second quotation above, from Peter Martyr Vermigli, accordingly reflects a concern for some concept of corporate liberty over against a fissiparous demand for individual liberty. In the context of his argument, the appeal is to the liberty of the institutional church, but he and other sixteenth-century Protestants were also concerned to defend the liberty of the political state against both an overreaching church authority (the Catholic threat) and a seditious libertinism (the Anabaptist threat, at least as they saw it). The relation between these two institutional liberties threatens to add another wrinkle to any account of liberty in the shadow of the Reformation. For many Protestants, such as John Calvin and more so the English presbyterians who invoked his authority, the corporate liberty of the church and the corporate liberty of the state stood in a tense dialectic, always prone to break out in open rivalry. Perhaps due to our Puritan founding, Americans have always tended to think of the problem in such terms, often with a tendency to correlate the two kinds of liberty of conscience just noted to these two institutions: the state is the domain of a laissez-faire liberty of conscience, the church the domain of the activist conscience, captive to the word of God. Indeed, this is precisely how Reformed ethicist David VanDrunen describes the matter, together with a sophisticated new version of the "Whig narrative" of Protestantism and political liberty, in his recent book *Natural Law and the Two Kingdoms*. Such a construal, of course, threatens (or promises, depending on your perspective) to secularize the political realm and to burden the ecclesiastical realm with legalism. An alternative account, as we shall see in this book, was offered by Protestants such as Richard Hooker, for whom the institutional liberty of church and state, and the obedience of both to the law of God, were constituted together. Hooker's account also challenges, as we shall see, our modern assumption that individual liberty and institutional liberty are a zero-sum game, such that one must choose between the freedom of a Christian conscience and the freedom of a Christian commonwealth; again, he argues, the two stand or fall together.

Perhaps more fundamental than all these issues, however, as a challenge to the Luther-to-liberalism narrative, is the essential inwardness of Luther and Calvin's concept of spiritual liberty. When we speak of the liberty of individual conscience, for us the stress is likely to fall on the word *individual*, rather than *conscience*, so much so that we unproblematically assume that inward liberty of belief automatically entails outward liberty of action—if you are not constrained to believe in God, by the same token you must not be constrained to act out that belief in visible worship. Luther, however, as we shall see in

Chapter Two, was well aware that the constraints that limit internal freedom are markedly different from, and much more profound than, those that limit external freedom, and the former were his chief concern. The "freedom of a Christian" that chiefly concerned him was not the freedom of a Christian to act as he saw fit (even if he frequently asserted this against burdensome ecclesiastical regulations), but the inward freedom of a conscience liberated from fear and animated by love thanks to the justifying grace of Christ. This central theological concern was never far from the surface in the tumultuous sixteenth-century debates about the freedom of a Christian man, the freedom of a Christian church, and the freedom of a Christian commonwealth. Indeed, I shall argue, a reassertion of this concern was crucial to Richard Hooker's strategy for reconciling these rival liberties. With such a distinctively theological account of freedom as our sixteenth-century starting point, it should be clear that the road to a modern secularized political account of freedom will be, if it still exists at all, a long and tortuous one, and one in great danger of running afoul of Calvin's warning about a "transfer."

And yet I do not intend to altogether dismiss the relevance of the Reformation, and the achievements of Luther and Hooker, for the emergence of modern liberalism. While I hope that my arguments in this book will chasten any subsequent efforts to draw straight lines from Luther or Calvin to Jefferson or Rawls, I hope that they will also prove generative for new insights about the legacy of the Reformation in modern political thought.

I. "Captive to the Word of God": Loyalties in Conflict

Let us begin, then, by tracing the legacy of Protestantism's proclamation of freedom in relation to Western political order, and see if we can gain insight into Calvin's worry. Certainly, few deny that a central contribution of Protestantism, what Alister McGrath calls its "dangerous idea," was an epistemological revolution: the insistence on the freedom of individual Christian consciences to determine Scripture's meaning for themselves.[5] Luther's famous words at Worms offer a memorable summary of this freedom:

> Unless I am convinced by Scripture and plain reason—I do not accept the authority of popes and councils, for they have contradicted each other—

---

5. Alister McGrath, *Christianity's Dangerous Idea: The Protestant Revolution—A History from the Sixteenth Century to the Twenty-First* (New York: HarperOne, 2007), 2.

my conscience is captive to the Word of God. I cannot and I will not recant anything for to go against conscience is neither right nor safe. God help me. Amen.[6]

From this right of "religious conscience," argues John Witte, flowed "attendant rights to assemble, speak, worship, evangelize, educate, parent, travel, and more on the basis of their beliefs." And from these flowed, in due course, rights of constitutional order.[7] Thus did spiritual freedom give birth to civil freedom. But obviously, this spiritual freedom was not a freedom to do just anything, but even in Luther's formulation, goes hand-in-hand with obedience. We are free in relation to human authority because we are bound in relation to God; God has spoken in his Word, and "we must obey God rather than men" (Acts 5:29), as the apostles said. On the basis of this subjection, the Protestant could stand against all the demands of earthly authorities who might overstep their bounds, whether in church or in state.

Viewed in this light, then, Luther's declaration that his "conscience is captive to the Word of God," and the freedom this entails, is simply a manifestation, or an intensification, of the conflict of loyalties that is a recurrent feature of human society.[8] The potential for such a conflict, between loyalty to God and man, conscience and community, is probably as old as humankind. Indeed, it is famously represented in the ancient Greek tragedy *Antigone*, which presents the possibility that a higher law than that of the state might demand civil disobedience by a pious individual. But the dilemma thus generated is not yet by any means the modern dilemma of conscience and authority. For *Antigone* represents the clash of two publicly available value claims, both of which would have been easily recognized by the play's audience: the claims of piety toward the gods and loyalty toward the fatherland. The clash between these two equally ultimate claims is tragic, but not terribly destabilizing to the social order. For Antigone is not Kierkegaard's Abraham, called to a lonely journey of faithfulness that none can understand; she remains firmly within the universal, as he would have put it, a tragedy but not an enigma. Creon may rage against her act of treason, but he can hardly have been mystified by

6. Quoted in Roland Bainton, *Here I Stand: A Life of Martin Luther* (New York: Abingdon-Cokesbury, 1950), 185.

7. Witte, *Reformation of Rights*, 2.

8. For the framework of a "conflict of loyalties" and the need for political-theological strategies to "harmonize loyalties," here and throughout, I am profoundly indebted to John Perry's excellent book *The Pretenses of Loyalty: Locke, Liberal Theory, and American Political Theology* (Oxford: Oxford University Press, 2011).

it; the religious rites on which she insists are part and parcel of the state cult that sustained the social order over which Creon presided.

When a Greek two generations later, Socrates, did dare to claim individual insight that stood in some tension with the state cult, he denied that this gave him any license to disobey the laws of Athens, to which he submitted unto death. Although the Christian martyrs five centuries later were similarly to submit to their Roman executioners, something has clearly changed between Socrates's "I am that gadfly which God has attached to the state . . . arousing and persuading and reproaching you,"[9] and Polycarp's "Fourscore and six years have I been serving him and he hath done me no wrong; how then can I blaspheme my King who saved me?"[10] something important has changed. For Polycarp and the early Christian martyrs, the God for whom they died was described as another King to whom they owed an allegiance that trumped any that Caesar could claim, a declaration that confused and enraged the Roman authorities. Christ himself may have offered a distinction of the just bounds of the different jurisdictions when he said, "Render unto Caesar the things that are Caesar's, and unto God the things that are God's" (Mark 12:17 ASV), and most of the early Christians were sincere in their protestations of civic loyalty. But the possibility of conflict could not be denied, and that mere possibility destabilized the entire Roman public order. For a brief triumphal season under Constantine, it may have seemed that the conflict of loyalties could be resolved under a godly emperor, but the ambiguities of the Arian controversies soon dispelled that illusion, and for Western Christendom at least, Augustine's doctrine of the "two cities" would confirm the incommensurability of the reign of God and the reign of earthly rulers in this present age.

To this extent, Christianity itself could be said to have announced a spiritual liberty that could not avoid some kind of transfer to civic polity; the mere presence of the faithful within the commonwealth, and their allegiance to a different king, demanded some kind of public recognition and adjustment of the legal order, if that order was not to crumble altogether. In point of fact, the Western Roman political order did crumble, though not under the weight of Christianity, and the power vacuum it left postponed for several centuries much of the conflict between earthly kings and the heavenly King that might otherwise have seemed inevitable. When a resurgence of political power did occur in the eleventh century, it was in an environment less like that of Polycarp and more like that of Antigone. That is to say, the long leavening

---

9. Plato, *Apology* 31a (in Jowett's translation).
10. Eusebius, *Church History* 4.15.20 (in McGiffert's translation).

of Christianity throughout the European social order meant that the claims of piety, just as much as those of political loyalty, had an assured public status. Indeed, the institutional consolidation of the papacy in this same period meant the claims of piety had a *more assured* public status than did the claims of the civil power. If Antigone was no Abraham, Gregory VII most certainly was not.

As conflicts of loyalty then proliferated between the high and late medieval monarchs and pontiffs, these, unlike the conflicts of the early church, could in principle be adjudicated within a common frame of reference, within the terms of the Christian faith and the duties it demanded of clergy and laity, subjects and rulers. However sharp their contentions, the papal legates and imperial publicists never felt they had collapsed into mutual incomprehension.[11] Indeed, although their ambition was never fully realized, the popes certainly aspired to render all conflicts of loyalty completely tractable by means of their supreme epistemological authority. That is, if the spiritual and temporal orders were part of one Christian society under one king, Christ, who had fully revealed his will to his people, then in principle no conflict was necessary, so long as that will was fully understood. As the popes claimed ever more emphatically to be able to declare that will to the world, they hoped to define beyond all ambiguity the Christian's many duties to his several authorities in their several hierarchies, with the pope at the top of it all. All loyalties could in principle be harmonized underneath this one visible authority.

Protestantism, as part of its doctrine of Christian liberty, shattered this synthesis (which had never worked very well in practice anyway). By depriving the pope—indeed, any human authority—of the power to authoritatively declare the voice of God, the reformers liberated the Christian conscience from any absolute human epistemological authority, the authority to determine truth.[12] Henceforth, Scripture alone could infallibly declare to believers the will of God, and although other authorities might make claims upon the outward conduct of believers, only God could bind the heart.[13]

---

11. For a good introduction to these contentions, see Oliver O'Donovan and Joan Lockwood O'Donovan, eds., *From Irenaeus to Grotius: A Sourcebook in Christian Political Thought, 100–1625* (Grand Rapids: Eerdmans, 1999), parts 3 and 4.

12. To be sure, the doctrine of papal infallibility was still a long way off from crystallization in this period, and the precise *de jure* authority asserted, and *de facto* authority realized, by the papacy ebbed and flowed from the thirteenth century to the sixteenth. Such authority was certainly on the rise again, however, by the time Luther lodged his protest, quickly showing him that any meaningful reform would require a fundamental reconception of the nature of the church's authority.

13. For a particularly full statement, see Article XXVIII of the Augsburg Confession. For

Of course, this dialectic was hardly a stable one; the possibility of a conflict of loyalties had returned with a vengeance. How could a believer be sure that her loyalty to God, the supreme and final good, might not come into conflict with her loyalty to the magistrate, the fallible guardian of the temporal common good? No human authority could finally dictate what God demanded, and what God demanded, human authority could not demand. Once such a wedge had been introduced, spiritual liberty demanded some recognition in civil order, some limit on how much obedience civil authorities could require. A "transfer" of some kind seemed inevitable.

II. Two Tales of Two Cities: Calvinism and the "Transfer" of Liberty

There are many different narratives as to how this transfer played out, but I want to highlight two main forms of the narrative, which I will call the "quietist" and the "activist" versions. Note that these two labels are merely heuristic; in practice, they function more as poles along a spectrum, and indeed, as we shall see at various points, can readily blur into one another. To oversimplify radically, the *quietist* forms are perhaps more concerned with Isaiah Berlin's "negative liberty"—in this case, the freedom of the religious conscience to be left alone to its religious activities—while the *activist* forms are more interested in the development of "positive liberty"—in this case, the freedom of the religious conscience to empower individuals or societies through putting its convictions into action. The quietist forms thus attempt to defang the conflict of loyalties by using liberty of conscience itself as the means to adjudicate the boundaries of each set of loyalties. Indeed, Calvin's quote above could be read as doing just this: assigning the just bounds of civil authority to prevent it from meddling in affairs of conscience.

The great historian of political thought, Quentin Skinner, offered an influential version of the quietist form of the narrative in his *Foundations of Modern Political Thought: The Age of Reformation*. Essential to the modern idea of politics, he says, is the idea "that political society is held to exist solely for political purposes. The endorsement of this secularized viewpoint remained impossible as long as it was assumed that all temporal rulers had a duty to

---

a discussion of the knots into which this claim of individual hermeneutical authority tied the reformers, see Susan Schreiner, *Are You Alone Wise? The Quest for Certainty in the Early Modern Era* (Oxford: Oxford University Press, 2011), ch. 3.

uphold godly as well as peaceable government."[14] Of course, Skinner unhesitatingly acknowledges that the Protestant Reformers hardly abandoned this medieval assumption; rather, they consistently upheld the ideal of the godly prince, even if he thinks their theology tended in directions that would sever the medieval synthesis of theology and political philosophy. Nonetheless, the circumstances of persecution and the need to assert their freedom of conscience against ungodly magistrates led to a key shift, he argues. Within Skinner's narrative, the key moment was the move by Protestant resistance theorists from the language of a *duty* to resist idolatrous tyrants (grounded in religious obligations to protect right worship) to the language of a *right* to resist tyrants in the face of their violation of constitutional laws and norms of civil justice:

> They were able, that is, to make the epoch-making move from a purely religious theory of resistance, depending on the idea of a covenant to uphold the laws of God, to a genuinely political theory of revolution, based on the idea of a contract which gives rise to a moral right (and not merely a religious duty) to resist any ruler who fails in his corresponding obligation to pursue the welfare of the people in all his public acts.[15]

In other words, under pressure of persecution, and faced with rapid changes in policy by successions of more favorable and more hostile regimes, Protestants quickly adopted the notion of a general political right to freedom of worship and assembly, which any just regime must protect. Any regime, whether Protestant or Catholic, could be equally compelled by the same arguments to honor this right, grounded as it was in the nature of political society itself. It may seem odd to label a view forged in the fires of religious war "quietist," but the point is that for Skinner, the endpoint of the conflict was a conscience left alone in an increasingly private sphere, recognized by the political realm, but buffered from it. Modern political liberalism, of course, does not spring fully formed out of this transition; nonetheless, thinks Skinner, this emergence of an autonomous sphere of political rationality was necessary and essential for the development of liberal order. And while he denies that this development emerges directly out of the Reformers' teachings, he does see it as the natural fruit of the political crises the Reformation generated, and the Reformers' firm removal of temporal authority from ecclesiastical control.

14. Quentin Skinner, *The Age of Reformation*, vol. 2 of *Foundations of Modern Political Thought* (Cambridge: Cambridge University Press, 1978), 352.

15. Skinner, *Age of Reformation*, 335.

John Witte's *Reformation of Rights*, as the title suggests, also focuses on the emergence of rights-language within the early Reformed tradition (among the resistance theorists particularly but also, he thinks, proleptically within Calvin himself), as seminal to the development of liberal political order. Unlike Skinner, he is less concerned about how the Reformation might lead to an autonomous political order than he is about how it might lead to a pluralistic one dedicated to individual freedom, and though he recognizes the journey is a long one, he believes that it begins, not in unintended consequences, but in the theological teaching of the Reformers. Although he acknowledges Calvin's firm distinction between spiritual and political liberty and his warnings against a transfer, Witte is confident that the distinction itself grounds a progressive development of political liberty. How? Witte's argument is subtle, acknowledging that the relevant threads in Calvin's thought are tenuous and not always consistent, but two points at least stand out. By sharply contrasting the two kingdoms, Calvin staunchly denies any attempt for civil authority (indeed, any human authority) to coerce the conscience; whatever obedience civil magistrates may demand of their subjects, they cannot in the nature of the case touch the conscience, which is in the hand of God alone. Witte, indeed, might have dwelt more insistently on this point than he does; although we have come to take the non-coerceability of conscience as a virtual truism, we forget the extent to which we owe the notion to the Protestant Reformation. Indeed, even today after Vatican II, many Catholics will argue that their church has never actually conceded this principle, and maintains that church authorities can and should coerce erring consciences, and can in principle call upon secular authorities to add some teeth to this coercion.[16] Even the most minimal right to an inviolable freedom of conscience, then, was an important contribution of the first Protestants.

Witte also draws attention to the way that Calvin's two-kingdoms distinction undergirded a "two-track morality"—a spiritual morality of true faith and obedience which the church sought to cultivate, and which answered ultimately to God alone, and a civic morality of outward virtue and good order which it was the state's responsibility to cultivate.[17] This laid the groundwork for an anti-perfectionism in the civic realm, in which political authorities

16. See Thomas Pink, "Conscience and Coercion," *First Things* 225 (August 2012): 45–51; also Thomas Pink, "The Right to Religious Liberty and the Coercion of Belief: A Note on *Dignitatis Humanae*," in *Reason, Morality, and Law: The Philosophy of John Finnis*, ed. John Keown and Robert P. George (Oxford: Oxford University Press, 2013), 427–42.

17. See also Matthew Tuininga, "Remembering the Two Kingdoms," *Christian Renewal* 30, no. 8 (Feb. 2012), for a development of similar arguments.

could allow their subjects freedom in matters irrelevant to the commonwealth. Of course, Witte is the first to admit that the actual practice of Calvin's Geneva was far from liberal in this respect, but he insists that the principle laid important groundwork. By means of these two factors, argues Witte, this first right of freedom of conscience became, over the course of a lengthy historical development, both the "mother" and the "midwife" of the many other civil liberties we now enjoy.[18]

David VanDrunen, in his *Natural Law and the Two Kingdoms*, has recently offered a longer and more theologically complex narrative that shares some similar themes. For him too, the very wall that Calvin erects between the spiritual and temporal kingdoms is the means by which a certain transfer of liberty takes place. Largely equating Calvin's two-kingdoms distinction with that of "church" and "state" in institutional terms,[19] VanDrunen traces at least

---

18. I should add that in singling out Witte's *Reformation of Rights* as an example of the "quietist" version of the narrative, I am knowingly abstracting it from Witte's work as a whole, which has often given attention to the ways in which Protestant jurisprudence actively transformed political order in response to theological ideals (see, for instance, *Law and Protestantism: The Legal Teachings of the Lutheran Reformation* [Cambridge and New York: Cambridge University Press, 2002]).

19. See for instance David VanDrunen, *Natural Law and the Two Kingdoms: A Study in the Development of Reformed Social Thought*, Emory University Studies in Law and Religion (Grand Rapids: Eerdmans, 2010), 79, 81. This misunderstanding, or at the very least oversimplification, greatly impairs the value of VanDrunen's otherwise illuminating study. Darren R. Walhof explains the importance of this issue: "The key thing to note about Calvin's distinction is that it is *not* equivalent to a distinction between church and state, despite the language of 'spiritual' and 'political' which might suggest otherwise. To draw the spiritual/temporal distinction along the same lines as the church/state distinction would have been, for Calvin, a major concession to the Roman Catholic hierarchy, which claimed exclusive and complete authority over the spiritual lives of its subjects. His claim, rather, is that 'human laws, whether made by magistrate or by church . . . do not of themselves bind conscience' and, therefore, cannot claim such authority (2:1183–84 [IV.10.5]). The 'life of the soul' or the 'spiritual' aspect of human beings, which Calvin also calls the 'forum of conscience,' is not subject to governance by others; instead, 'conscience refers to God,' and, 'properly speaking, it has respect to God alone' (1:847–49 [III.19.15]). External actions and obedience to human laws, whether of the church or of civil government, do not have any bearing on the state of one's soul in relation to God nor on the possibility of eternal salvation. This is solely a matter between the individual and God, mediated by conscience" ("The Accusations of Conscience and the Christian Polity in John Calvin's Political Thought," *History of Political Thought* 24, no. 3 [Autumn 2003]: 410). For a full consideration of this question and the relevant literature, see Matthew Tuininga, *Calvin's Political Theology and the Public Engagement of the Church: Christ's Two Kingdoms* (Cambridge: CUP, forthcoming 2017), esp. chs. 3 and 4. While acknowledging the institutional implications of Calvin's doctrine in church and state, Tuininga notes that at its heart, it is an eschatological contrast.

two key developments, which in many ways parallel those which Witte identifies. First, argues VanDrunen, Calvin's distinction, especially as developed and refined by his followers, carved out an autonomous sphere within which the church, obedient to the laws of God in Scripture, was therefore free from the authority of civil laws. This ensured (or at least should have ensured) the nonintervention of civil magistrates in religious affairs, guaranteeing the civil liberties of subjects in such matters, and encouraging the understanding of politics as a secular order. (Note that this is something of a mirror image of Skinner's narrative; whether the key contribution of Protestantism was liberating the state from the church, or liberating the church from the state, the upshot ends up quite similar.) This understanding was encouraged by the firmly subordinate and anti-perfectionist account of the temporal kingdom that this distinction generated. Although created and governed by God and good in its place, the whole world of politics and culture was, according to VanDrunen, separated from the redemptive rule of God in Christ, which is found only in the spiritual kingdom, the church. Rather than Scripture, then, the norms for this realm were to be a relatively minimalist standard of natural law, which, as the moral order of the Noahic covenant, is concerned merely with the restraint of evil and preservation of civil order.[20] It is not difficult to see how VanDrunen's narrative, with these two principles of strict separation of church and state and of an anti-perfectionist "traffic cop" theory of civil government, both culminates in and theologically supports something like modern liberal pluralism.

One thing that each of these three narratives share in common is the relatively passive role that Protestant clergy and citizens play in them—although I must stress the word *relatively* here. Certainly, Skinner, Witte, and VanDrunen all have a great deal to say about the resistance theorists, and the important role played by their stand against tyrannical authorities who transgressed the bounds of religious liberty. But still, heroic and hard-won though these changes may have been, the basic mindset is still essentially one of *laissez-faire*, of a certain kind of quietism. That is to say, on narratives such as these, the way that Protestantism upset the medieval political order was simply by demanding a sphere of immunity for its religious principles, a sphere in which

---

20. For VanDrunen's fuller constructive development of this natural law as Noahic covenant argument, see *A Biblical Case for Natural Law* (Grand Rapids: Acton Institute, 2006), and at much greater length, *Divine Covenants and Moral Order: A Biblical Theology of Natural Law* (Grand Rapids: Eerdmans, 2014).

to obey God, rather than man, thus effecting a slow transformation of the civil order so as to protect the pursuit of godliness, without itself being directly concerned with this pursuit.

This common feature becomes more apparent when we examine some other, more "activist" accounts of the development from spiritual to civil liberty in Protestant, and particularly Calvinist, communities. These lay much more stress on the other side of the "freedom of conscience" that we noted above—the freedom to obey God's word. To obey God's word was to put it into practice, and often in the social sphere just as much as the individual sphere. Needless to say, on this narrative, the more theocratic manifestations of the Calvinist tradition (which for Witte and VanDrunen must be treated as outliers, the results of Protestants not really following through on their principles) look like much more natural fruitions of the liberated individual Protestant conscience.

The noted political theorists, Michael Walzer and Eric Voegelin, each in their own ways saw the fundamental legacy of the Protestant Reformation as one of radicalism and activism, reform and revolution in the political sphere. On this account, Calvin's warning against a transfer was quite directly ignored, with a quasi-Anabaptistic radicalism the legacy of many of his followers, and of course, as with most cases of radical reform, the line between freedom and totalitarianism proving a tenuous one. Walzer claims to discern in the English Puritans in particular a model for the origins of radical politics. Calvinism was, contra VanDrunen's narrative, "anchored in this-worldly endeavor; it appropriated worldly means and usages: magistracy, legislation, warfare. The struggle for a new human community, replacing the lost Eden, was made a matter of concrete political activity." Animated by the "anxiety and alienation"[21] that Walzer sees as central to Calvin's theology, these saints sought obedience and discipline above all, creating in the process voluntary communities of activists that would aspire to remake the social order from below. The conflict of loyalties, far from being adjudicated, is intensified: "The band of the chosen confronts the existing world as if in war. Its members interpret the strains and tensions of social change in terms of conflict and contention."[22] Accordingly, far from being apolitical, "the band of the saints is a political movement aiming at social reconstruction. It is the saints who lead the final attack upon the old order and their destructiveness is all the more total because they have

---

21. Michael Walzer, *The Revolution of the Saints: A Study in the Origins of Radical Politics* (Cambridge, MA: Harvard University Press, 1965), 28.

22. Walzer, *Revolution of the Saints*, 317.

a total view of the new world."[23] None of this, of course, transitions readily into liberalism as we now know and (mostly) enjoy it. On the contrary, the Puritan, in Walzer's reading, can never be at home in the liberal order. Yet the revolutionary attack on the old theopolitical order it undertakes, and the revolutionary mindset it engenders, is a necessary prerequisite for the emergence of liberal order.

For Voegelin on the other hand, the key development is closer to what we identified above in the tension between the testimony of private conscience and the truth to which the public order witnesses. Not that Voegelin thinks that the Reformation marked a fundamentally new departure. Rather, he discerns in it, and in the Calvinist movement in particular, a version of the "Gnosticism" that he identifies as a perennial temptation within Christianity. For Voegelin, the essence of the Gnostic is not contempt of the material world (the sense in which the term is most frequently tossed around nowadays), but the claim to secret knowledge, knowledge that gives him the key to the meaning of history. By virtue of their private revelation, opaque to the surrounding society, Gnostic groups will lay claim to the mantle of being called by God to usher in the next age of history, whether that be one in which all God's people are prophets or one in which private property and finally the state are abolished (Voegelin considers the modern world to be a string of experiments in secularized Gnosticism, with communism but the most pronounced example). In this paradigm, freedom of conscience hardly leads to pluralism, except as an eventual unintended by-product of the revolutions it ignites. Rather, the freedom of the conscience to obey God (or the *Zeitgeist*) rather than man demands the transformation of human authority structures to conform to the divine order. The Reformation did not introduce the possibility of such movements, but it did make them more likely and more natural; Calvin and especially his English followers, the Puritans, argues Voegelin, did more than anyone to bring the Gnostic spirit into the modern world.[24]

It is not difficult to see that these narratives contrast rather sharply with those of Skinner, Witte, and VanDrunen; indeed, Voegelin's would seem to be almost the polar opposite—here is the Calvinist not as anti-perfectionist, but as arch-perfectionist, not as separationist, but as arch-transformationalist.

23. Walzer, *Revolution of the Saints*, 319.

24. See Voegelin's initial analysis of Gnosticism in medieval and subsequently modern thought in *The New Science of Politics: An Introduction* (1952; repr., Chicago: University of Chicago Press, 1987), 106–32. On the importance of the Reformation as "the successful invasion of Western institutions by Gnostic movements," see p. 134. On the English Puritans as paradigmatic Gnostics, see pp. 135–50; on Calvin, pp. 138–39.

Of course, both Walzer and Voegelin were political theorists who enjoyed painting with a broad brush, not Reformation historians, and what history they do draw on is a half-century out of date. But we should not be too quick to dismiss them on that account. On the contrary, any honest look at the historical evidence suggests that there is every bit as much an activist legacy to Protestantism, and perhaps Calvinism in particular, as there is a quietist one. Philip Benedict's magisterial survey of the Reformed tradition, *Christ's Churches Purely Reformed*, highlights this impulse—not political revolution per se, but certainly aggressive social reform—as lying at its heart.[25] This reformist impulse may not always have taken on the form of freedom as we tend to imagine it; indeed, it was often downright oppressive. But inasmuch as Reformed churches and communities were ready to challenge the *status quo* in favor of the will of God, as they understood it, they signaled an awareness of the possibility of a clash of loyalties, in which obedience to God demanded a remaking of the social and political order.

This sort of freedom, the fervent obedience of the conscience to a "higher law" than that of the state, was accordingly to become a powerful force for reform in England and America through the succeeding centuries, even as it lost some of its distinctly Reformational flavor. In his recent book *Weird John Brown*, Ted Smith traces how the language of the "higher law" to which conscience must yield, even at the cost of civil disobedience, came to animate the abolitionist movement in America in the mid-nineteenth century. He cites the declaration of the American Moral Reform Society in 1843: "Therefore, under whatever pretext or authority these laws have been promulgated or executed, whether under parliamentary, colonial, or American legislation, *we declare* them in the sight of Heaven wholly *null* and *void*, and should be *immediately abrogated*."[26] He shows that such language could be grounded, in more theologically orthodox fashion, in the demands of Scripture (as in the rhetoric of Presbyterian minister Henry Highland Garnet), or in a generic theism (as in

---

25. "They repeatedly unsettled the political order by sparking a rejection of established rituals, the formation of illegal new churches, and resistance to princely innovations in worship believed to threaten the purity of God's ordinances. The political history of later sixteenth- and seventeenth-century Europe is incomprehensible without an understanding of the history of Calvinism and the reasons its spread proved so unsettling. One reason the faith proved so compelling to many was that it inspired dreams of a dramatic transformation of manners, morals, and the social order" (Philip Benedict, *Christ's Churches Purely Reformed: A Social History of Calvinism* [New Haven: Yale University Press, 2002], xvi).

26. Ted A. Smith, *Weird John Brown: Divine Violence and the Limits of Ethics* (Stanford: Stanford University Press, 2015), 92.

the rousing Senate speeches of William Seward). But perhaps most representative of the age was the use to which the language of conscience and the higher law was put by Methodist bishop Gilbert Haven:

> What Haven called the "moral law," though, arose as an expression of a higher human faculty, Conscience. Conscience was the "viceregent" of God (7), Haven said, and while it could be "rendered imperfect and obtuse by reason of sin," it retained a "force that is ever pressing it against all temptations" toward right discernment of an unchanging moral law (9). As Conscience was higher than the social element in humans, the moral law was higher than the civil law in society. Haven's language was unmistakably theological. But at the heart of his argument was not a string of biblical texts but individual conscience.[27]

A subtle shift was well under way in how the language of conscience was used. In the older way of speaking, "conscience" was *con-scientia*, a way of "knowing-with." But what was the "higher law" that it knew? The unchanging moral law of God, revealed in nature and then corroborated and further revealed by Scripture. As Darren Walhof summarizes, for Calvin at least, "conscience is that aspect of human nature that innately apprehends the natural law."[28] Conscience, then, points beyond itself, laying hold of an object to which it then submits. Conscience is an inner and hidden means of knowing, a faculty that belongs to each individual, and yet the truth it lays hold of is a publicly available one, the law to which it submits is the one to which everyone's conscience witnesses, or ought to witness. The appeal to conscience, from this standpoint, does not seem like such a radical notion. But once one entertains a strong enough view of human depravity, it is easy to imagine that in reality, very few people's consciences are laying hold of the higher law; it lies hidden beyond their grasp. Only those who have received special illumination (and who does not like to count themselves among this number?) have rightly functioning consciences that can apply the higher law against the near-universal convictions of their contemporaries. This is the essence of Voegelin's "Gnosticism," which, whether or not he rightly diagnoses it in Calvin, is indeed a recurrent feature of modernity.

27. Smith, *Weird John Brown*, 94, quoting from Gilbert Haven, "The Higher Law," preached in Amenia, New York, in November 1850, in *National Sermons: Sermons, Speeches, and Letters on Slavery and Its War: From the Passage of the Fugitive Slave Bill to the Election of President Grant* (Boston: Lee & Shepard, 1869), vi.
28. Walhof, "Accusations of Conscience," 402.

In this way of thinking about conscience, although the appeal to a "higher law" remains, it is not hard to see that the conscience itself becomes effectively not the *pointer* to this law, but its *source*, a sacrosanct seat of authority that cannot be challenged. Orestes Brownson, though himself also an abolitionist, challenged this new way of thinking about conscience in the 1850s:

> "The appeal to the supreme Lawgiver is compatible with civil government," Brownson wrote in 1851, "but the appeal to private judgment, or conviction, as to a higher law than that of the state, is not; for it virtually denies government itself, by making the individual paramount to it." Brownson argued that relying on individual conscience as a guide to the higher law could end only in anarchy or tyranny. If every individual was left free to follow his or her own conscience, there could be no civil order.[29]

If conscience did not entail a right to private judgment, then, was the law of the state paramount? Brownson did not want to say this either, so he found refuge in the authority of the Catholic Church, to which he was the most noted American convert of this era. His contemporary American theologian, John Williamson Nevin, reached a similar conclusion of the necessity of an authoritative church as the only solution to the scourge of private judgment that Protestantism had unleashed, although he stopped short of converting to Rome. Nevin's critique of the principle is instructive. Although, he says, the sects that make up American religious life are "loud for liberty, in the more outward sense, and seem to be raised up in their own imagination for the express purpose of asserting in some new way what they call liberty of conscience," in fact "they are bold for liberty only in their own favor, and not at all in favor of others."[30] "Every sect is ready to magnify the freedom of the individual judgment and the right of all men to read and interpret the Bible for themselves; and yet there is not one among them, that allows in reality anything of the sort."[31] If we believe Walzer and Voegelin, Protestantism could not have been otherwise from the beginning; if its freedom was freedom only to obey God, then how could it permit freedom to others *not* to obey God?

With such losses of faith in Protestantism, we seem to have come full circle. The tyranny of an authoritative church as interpreter of God's law is

---

29. Smith, *Weird John Brown*, 95–96, quoting from Orestes A. Brownson, "The Fugitive Slave Law" (1851), in *The Works of Orestes A. Brownson*, ed. Henry Francis Brownson (Detroit: Thorndike Nourse, 1884), 17:34.

30. John Williamson Nevin, "The Sect System," *Mercersburg Review* 1, no. 5 (1849): 497.

31. Nevin, "Sect System," 494.

cast off, and Scripture, God's written law, as interpreted by conscience, the law written on the heart, is put in its place. Initially no one doubts that Scripture, perspicacious as it is, will speak clearly and publicly, but in the presence of profound and persistent disagreements, the seat of authority recedes into the inward recesses of the heart. A "law" that is purely private is no law at all, merely a recipe for anarchy, and yet no one wants the tyranny of a state Leviathan that will legislate in place of conscience. So a backlash emerges, in which the public interpretive authority of the church is called back in to avoid the dangers of either anarchy or tyranny—or at least state tyranny. Is this then the "transfer" that Calvin was worried about? I pause here to note this cycle because it does not, in fact, take three centuries to play out. In fact, it can take just a few short years, and was manifest already in the sixteenth century itself, as we shall soon return to see.

III. An Uneasy Legacy: Liberty of Conscience in a Liberal Age

Both the "quietist" and the "activist" narratives of the legacy of Protestantism's declaration of Christian liberty have much to be said for them, for clearly both impulses were operative within the first decades of the Reformation itself. Indeed, the demand for the freedom to obey the higher law of Scripture could go in either direction, even in very similar faith communities. The Swiss Anabaptists signed the Schleitheim Confession in 1527, eschewing all use of the sword and calling for withdrawal into quietistic communities; but by 1534, some of their brethren were busy trying to usher in the millennium by the sword in Münster. In seventeenth-century France, presbyterian Calvinists accepted their minority position in society and sought only the freedom to organize and worship, while in nearby England, they campaigned vigorously (and in the 1640s, violently) for the comprehensive reform of society. Nor, of course, can the two impulses be neatly separated; even the quietistic demand for freedom of conscience, and the many other liberties that grow out of it, can itself be quite revolutionary. To be sure, there are times and places where the two ends of the spectrum could stand in rather stark opposition. Consider the contrast in 1850s America between John Brown, who appealed to a higher law in favor of slave rebellion, and James Henley Thornwell, who invoked the doctrine of Christian liberty to preserve the neutrality of the church from anti-slavery agitation, lest consciences be imposed upon beyond Scripture. Indeed, although certainly not endorsing his views on slavery, David Van-Drunen highlights Thornwell as a paragon of this "separationist" version of

Christian liberty. However, it is also worth noting that this opposition is an unstable one; in our further discussion of Thornwell below, we will find that there is little in the logic of his position to keep it from morphing into a form of legalistic activism.

In any case, we moderns, heirs to both legacies, find ourselves increasingly torn between them; we have a love/hate relationship with the increasingly individualized notion of freedom of conscience that Brownson complained about, and the revolutionary impulses it can unleash. On the one hand, we laud the stirring appeals of William Seward and even the abolitionist preachers of that era to the "higher law" of conscience that requires civil disobedience to the Fugitive Slave Act. On the other hand, we are inclined to shift uneasily in our seats before John Brown's invocation of a "higher law" in support of his abortive slave rebellion in 1859. As Ted Smith chronicles, the halo of martyrdom that surrounded Brown in the years after the war turned gradually to suspicion and fear in the early twentieth century, as Brown appeared like the quintessential "religious fanatic," a Bible-thumping zealot ready to kill and overturn the social order in obedience to his crazed conscience.[32] Even those modern liberals who might be willing to forgive Brown his indiscretions for the sake of the sanctity of his cause might change their tune in evaluating a more recent would-be John Brown, Paul Hill, who killed a Pensacola abortion doctor in 1994. Hill, like Brown, appealed to the Bible in defense of his actions, with complete sincerity and with not-implausible exegesis.[33] In the face of such violent, anarchistic appeals to the "higher law" to trump the current civil laws, many liberals have called passionately for a strict religious neutrality when it comes to political action. Mark Lilla's *The Stillborn God* is simply the most academically respectable of a long series of recent attacks on religion as the chief source of violence and accordingly calling for the abolition of all appeals to religion in public life.[34] And yet those same liberals most concerned about the intrusion of destabilizing religious appeals into the political process are likely to be profoundly grateful, despite themselves, for the contributions of such religious discourse to the many profound reforms that our societies now look back on with pride, from Wilberforce's abolition of the slave trade to Martin Luther King Jr.'s campaign against segregation. Ted Smith notes how King's worst enemies were the lukewarm white liberals who acknowledged

32. See Smith, *Weird John Brown*, 24–29.

33. See Smith, *Weird John Brown*, 101–2.

34. Mark Lilla, *The Stillborn God: Religion, Politics, and the Modern West* (New York: Knopf, 2007). See Smith's discussion in *Weird John Brown*, 43–46.

the justice of his complaints, but winced at his radical invocation of a "higher law," mounting instead "An Appeal for Law and Order and Common Sense." And yet, says Smith, "Contrary to their expectations, a politics of the higher law did not underwrite violent action but faithful witness."[35]

Despite its debt to the crusaders of conscience like King, however, modern liberalism remains quite nervous about the kind of activist freedom of conscience that gave it birth and nourished it. Having used the language of *obedience to God*, filtered increasingly through the prism of individual conscience, as the means by which to resist servile obedience to princes, Western society hopes now to bury this disquieting legacy, lest conscience find in Scripture reason to disobey, and even actively subvert, the norms of liberal society. We would much prefer to draw upon the more quietist kind of conscientious freedom that we find in narratives such as Witte's and VanDrunen's: Christian liberty as carving out a sphere of immunity for faith, rather than underwriting a campaign to remake society in obedience to Scripture. "You can be free to believe whatever you want, so long as it doesn't hurt anyone else, or force anyone else to change"—that is the motto of the modern ideal of freedom of conscience, for which theorists such as John Rawls attempted to supply an adequate theoretical scaffolding. Despite the triumph of Rawlsian rhetoric in much public thinking about religion, politics, and individual freedom, however, that scaffolding has been under attack ever since Rawls tried to erect it, and has proven increasingly unworkable in the courts, as John Perry has chronicled recently in his *Pretenses of Loyalty*.[36] Aside from the ambivalence we already mentioned—that we secretly want the fruits of an activist freedom of conscience even while formally demanding a merely passive freedom—it is not at all clear where the lines between the two might fall. Just because someone maintains that they are merely trying to be faithful to their own personal beliefs, not laying any claims on others or challenging the social order, that doesn't mean that others will perceive their actions accordingly.

Consider the celebrated cases of burqa-wearing in France or cake-baking for same-sex marriages in the United States. In both cases, the defendants appealed, in good liberal fashion, to the freedom of religion and the sanctity of their individual consciences, asking only the liberty to live out their fundamental beliefs without impinging upon others. And yet in both cases, courts ruled that others *were* in some way impinged upon, and the public order of justice threatened, by the apparently benign actions of wearing a head cov-

---

35. Smith, *Weird John Brown*, 108.
36. See chapter 1 in particular.

ering and not baking a cake. Even if we think that the courts were obviously wrong in these cases, there are plenty of cases in which the appeal to religious freedom does come into profound conflict not just with the individual rights of others, but more seriously, with the responsibility of the state to protect the public good. Consider "conscientious objectors" to military service, who have rarely been so numerous as to pose a serious threat of national weakness in time of war, but theoretically could do so. And why, for that matter, can we simply assume that citizens' personal religious convictions will not include, as part and parcel of those convictions, a responsibility to remake the public order in accordance with them, as did John Brown's or Paul Hill's? For many Christians, there is no such thing as a merely private conviction that abortion is wrong. You cannot say, "you are free to that individual belief, but not free to try to impose it on others," since it is of the very nature of the belief, as a fundamental principle of moral law, that it must be imposed on others (even if most would stop short of such radical activism as Paul Hill's). Indeed, if you believe that religious unfaithfulness will bring down God's temporal judgment on the nation, then for you, there is no distinction between "your private belief" and "the public good," and if you are free to your belief, who's to say you aren't free to take all the actions implied by it?[37]

The conflict of loyalties, then, although certainly rendered more acute by such radical programs of reform as that of the Münster Anabaptists in 1534 or John Brown in 1859, is hardly done away with by espousing a more modest, quietist, and "liberal" concept of freedom of conscience.

Indeed, what makes this conflict of loyalty even more problematic is that one cannot simply count on all religious believers being sincere. After all, if freedom of religion gives one an exemption from some civil duty that one considers onerous, what is to prevent anyone from claiming such religious beliefs? The conscientious objector mentioned above has long posed this problem in particularly pointed form. If some are allowed to opt out of military service so they can obey the higher law to which they feel a higher loyalty, what's to prevent everyone from claiming such loyalty? It is this problem to which the title of Perry's book (drawn from Locke) alludes—the *pretenses* of loyalty. Indeed, it should be noted that to those who do not share these particular religious convictions, any protestation of them is likely to seem a matter of

---

37. Perry illustrates this dilemma pointedly through the example of Henry Blackaby, a Southern Baptist pastor who argued that the adoption of same-sex marriage and other anti-Christian stances would bring divine judgment upon America (*Pretenses of Loyalty*, 51–53).

"pretense," a mask for other more selfish and sinister motives. One can see this, in fact, in the recent controversies over the Christian cake-bakers and same-sex marriage: from incredulous commentators on the left, one frequently hears the suggestion that religion is simply being invoked as a mask for base feelings of prejudice.

Perry's book is a sustained polemic against any who might imagine that these conflicts can be easily adjudicated by more patient and careful boundary-drawing. Such a jurisdictional approach, he says, often looks to Locke, but Locke himself knew better. For Locke, argues Perry, the drawing of the "just bounds" between faith and politics could only be undertaken after a prior har-monization of loyalties, that is, after first convincing believers that obedience to their God was not at odds with an embrace of toleration in the state. After all, it's not as if a good Rawlsian could simply have walked up to the abortionist murderer Paul Hill and dissuaded him from his actions by patiently explaining to him the appropriate boundaries between his faith and his duties to the polit-ical society in which he found himself. He does not so much *fail to understand* the distinction thus proposed as *refuse to accept* its assumptions. The Rawlsian wants to claim that since his faith commitments are private ones, they can be set aside when fashioning and submitting to the laws of public order, but his faith, in this case, includes the conviction that it is extremely relevant for public order. Perry himself takes the example of evangelical opposition to homo-sexuality or same-sex marriage; far from trying to implement a theocracy, as its opponents shrilly declare, leaders such as Jerry Falwell and Pat Robertson can and do make their case on arguments for the public good; they are simply convinced, at least in large part due to their faith, that public endorsement of homosexuality will indeed be bad for the civic order.[38]

In all such cases, persuasion depends on first showing that, in point of fact, the believer's theological convictions do not in fact compel the conclusion that the public good is at stake in the way he believes; or, at the very least, that *more* harm will arise to his neighbors whom he is to love if he cannot tolerate for the time the infidelity or injustice he so decries. And such persuasion can only be effected by a sympathetic interlocutor who takes the believer's theo-logical convictions seriously and is prepared to argue from within them. Such, contends Perry, was John Locke, but we have simply accepted for so long the conclusions of his argument that we have forgotten its theological underpin-nings. These underpinnings, though, depended on a particularly Protestant conception of ecclesiology and authority, one that Locke himself recognized

38. See Perry, *Pretenses of Loyalty*, 135–39.

could hardly be shared by atheists or Catholics. Modern liberalism thus finds itself today in a curious conundrum, having, like Wittgenstein, thrown away the ladder once it has climbed up it:[39] now that the wall of liberty has been scaled by means of Protestant ideas about the individual conscience, the authority of God, and the role of human authorities and institutions, we may now, to bring the project to its conclusion, cast them aside in favor of a neutral concept of public reason, even if it is not clear that we are left with any sure ground beneath our feet.

IV. "Into Such Bondage": The Clash of Two Liberties in Protestant Thought

In surveying the tensions above, we have tended to frame the problem exclusively in terms of individual liberty in relation to the authority of God and the authority of the state. Indeed, from our modern vantage point, we are liable to think of "individual liberty" as almost a redundant phrase, since what other liberties are there worth considering? To our ears, then, the second quotation with which this chapter began, invoking a notion of corporate or institutional *liberty*, sounds a discordant note:

> Truly, we must take good heed that we bring not the Church of Christ into such bondage, that it may not use any thing that the Pope used. . . . How shall we debar the Church of this liberty, that it cannot signify some good thing, in setting forth their rites and ceremonies?[40]

The liberty to which Vermigli appeals here is the liberty of the church, which was indeed in the particular context of his argument interchangeable with the liberty of the state, since at issue were particular laws the English crown was making for the maintenance of good order in the church—specifically, clerical vestments. Against what was Vermigli asserting this liberty? What was it that threatened to bring the church into bondage? Ironically, the principle of Christian liberty, as we described it above: we must obey God, not human authority. As we shall see in much more detail in the next chapter, Vermigli faced a challenge from English Protestants who, asserting the sole

---

39. The reference is to the famous cryptic Proposition 6.54 at the end of the *Tractatus Logico-Philosophicus*.

40. Vermigli, "Letter to Hooper," 32v, 33v.

authority of Scripture over the consciences of believers, wanted to deprive human authorities of prescribing anything outside Scripture. Such a protest was couched in terms of preserving the liberty of the church, but Vermigli here argues the opposite; the liberty of the church as an institution to pursue its own common good is in fact infringed upon by this overreaching grant of liberty to its individual members. Given contemporary liberalism's preference to dissolve the common good into the aggregate sum of individual goods, restricting institutional liberty accordingly, this early Protestant concern introduces an additional complication into any Luther-to-Rawls narrative.

Indeed, we shall find that there was no general agreement at all among sixteenth-century Protestants that Christian liberty should leave everything to the discretion of the individual conscience. Quite apart from the fact that all of the Reformers gave strong authority to the traditional Christian creeds, and their elaborations in more contemporary confessions, many also contended that even in those matters ancillary to the true faith, and left free by Scripture, discretion did not necessarily belong to each individual believer. These were the so-called adiaphora, or "things indifferent," about which Calvin said in his discussion of Christian liberty that "regarding outward things that are of themselves 'indifferent,' we are not bound before God by any religious obligation preventing us from sometimes using them and other times not using them, indifferently."[41] Such a formulation naturally invited the question as to what counted, after all, as indifferent, a thorny question indeed in the sixteenth century, as we shall see throughout the coming chapters. But alongside that was perhaps an even more fundamental question—who is the "us" in Calvin's statement here? "Us" as individuals, or as communities, churches, even polities? Whatever Calvin's own view on this question, which is complex and disputed,[42] there was no unanimity among his followers or contemporaries.

The issue here was what came to be called the "regulative principle of worship," which was seen by many in the sixteenth century and afterward, particularly in the Presbyterian tradition, as part and parcel of the doctrine of Christian liberty described above. Indeed, in David VanDrunen's account of the contribution of Reformed political thought to contemporary liberalism, the principle looms large as an essential implication of the Protestant claim

---

41. Calvin, *Institutes*, 1:838 [III.19.7].

42. Witte argues for a significant evolution in Calvin's view from a more individualist account to a more institutionalizing account as his career proceeded (*Reformation of Rights*, ch. 1). See however the helpful treatment in Tuininga, *Calvin's Political Theology*, ch. 5, where he argues that Calvin clearly supports the legitimacy of discretionary ecclesiastical legislation to regulate extrabiblical details of worship and polity.

to liberty of conscience. However, to its critics, it was an example of just the sort of "transfer" that Calvin was worried about—externalizing the essentially inward liberty of the individual Christian in such a way as to compromise its foundation. Let us then take a few moments to trace the logic of this principle, as the debates it engendered illustrate just how elusive and slippery the concept of Christian liberty could be.

The slipperiness is evident in VanDrunen's reformulation of Calvin's statement just quoted: that we are "freed from obligation to do or not to do external things that are in themselves morally indifferent."[43] This formulation appears far more sweeping than Calvin's by its omission of "before God" and "religious obligation." What precisely Calvin might mean by these qualifiers, we shall investigate later, but for now we should note that, taken at face value, VanDrunen's formulation would seem to deprive civil government of nearly all basis of authority. For if individuals can never be obliged to do or not do things in themselves morally indifferent, then governments may never make laws in such matters. But it would seem that these are precisely the matters over which governments *are* necessarily making laws. Which side of the road to drive on, what form of identification voters must possess, what percentage sales tax one should pay—all of these things have moral implications, to be sure, and must be directed to the pursuit of justice, but in themselves they are morally indifferent. Are governments then left only to legislate those things already expressly commanded or forbidden by God—i.e., to be executioners of divine law? Again, we will find that some drew this implication, or something very close to it, in the sixteenth century. VanDrunen himself certainly does not want to, however; on the contrary, one of his purposes is to liberate civil government from such religious constraints. Accordingly, having glossed Calvin's principle in such a sweeping way, he goes on to argue that it applies only within *the church*.

By positing the Christian's "spiritual liberty" as an external liberty within the visible church, VanDrunen draws the corollary that "the officers of the church have authority to do and command only those things prescribed in Scripture, and Christians in the spiritual kingdom are thus free in conscience from anything *beyond* this."[44] This is, as VanDrunen is well aware, a restatement of the regulative principle of worship that emerged among some of the sixteenth-century English Reformed, which Walter Lowrie summarizes as, "that nothing is lawful in the church which is not expressly or implicitly sanc-

43. VanDrunen, *Natural Law and the Two Kingdoms*, 73.
44. VanDrunen, *Natural Law and the Two Kingdoms*, 73.

tioned in the word of God."[45] Although formulated and often defended as an amplification of the Christian liberty doctrine, it is in fact, as Lowrie argues, "its express logical contrary," as can be seen by comparison with a classic creedal formulation of the third principle of Christian liberty, Article VI of the Thirty-Nine Articles: "Holy Scripture containeth all things necessary to salvation: so that whatsoever is not read therein, nor may be proved thereby, is not to be required of any man, that it should be believed as an article of the faith or be thought requisite or necessary to salvation." Lowrie continues: "[I]n so far as it [the regulative principle] extended the operation of this principle from what is to be believed to what is to be done, it transformed a guarantee of freedom into a bond of scruple."[46]

Let us pause to make sure we understand Lowrie here, for the relationship of Christian liberty in *what is to be believed* and liberty in *what is to be done* was to prove exceedingly thorny in the sixteenth century, as indeed it must in every age. On the one hand, liberty of belief without liberty of action would seem to be worth rather little. If you are told, "Don't worry, you are free to believe in the God of the Bible alone, and to deny all idols," but in the next breath, "Nonetheless, you will be compelled to bow down and worship these idols," you would probably feel rather cheated. So, in the sixteenth-century context, many Protestants insisted that their protest against the truth of the doctrine of transubstantiation entailed also a refusal to outwardly venerate the elements. On the other hand, to demand that just as Scripture alone could bind our beliefs, so Scripture alone can command our actions, would seem to legalistically *prevent* all extrascriptural action. Why? Does not Lowrie go too far too quick in glossing "nothing can be required outside of Scripture" as "nothing can be done outside of Scripture"? Could we not simply say that "nothing can be *required to be done* outside of Scripture," that ministers cannot *compel* worshipers to sing some hymn, or engage in some liturgical action, outside of Scripture; the individual worshipers may still do what they like? The problem is that this ignores the social context of action. To say that every individual must be left free to drive on whichever side of the road they prefer is, in many cases, equivalent to saying that no one can drive at all. Likewise, to say that every individual must be left free to sing whatever hymn they want

45. Walter Lowrie, *The Church and Its Organization in Primitive and Catholic Times: An Interpretation of Rudolph Sohm's Kirchenrecht*, vol. 1 (New York: Longmans, 1904), 64.

46. Lowrie, *Church and Its Organization*, 66. Whereas Christian liberty meant that nothing beyond Scripture "may be exacted as an article of faith," says Lowrie, "the Dissenters asserted that nothing but this may be permitted in the Church—either to be believed or to be done" (67).

is equivalent to saying that no one can effectively sing at all in public worship. In such cases, the *freedom of each* not to have to do anything beyond Scripture becomes the *requirement for all*, at least when assembled corporately, to do nothing beyond Scripture. And when it comes to the actions of the minister, who stands representatively in place of all, the liberty of each not to do things outside Scripture likewise must become a requirement for the minister to restrict himself to scriptural precedent (thus the heated sixteenth-century debates about something so apparently innocuous as clerical vestments). Hence VanDrunen's formulation, "the officers of the church have authority *to do* and command only those things prescribed in Scripture," and Lowrie's more blunt "that nothing is lawful in the church which is not expressly or implicitly sanctioned in the word of God."

One can quickly see how on this construal, to safeguard the liberty of each individual within the institution, the institution itself must be deprived of liberty of action. The preservation of Christian liberty in the church means that the church is in fact bound—it has no liberty to speak or command anything on its own accord, and should it attempt to do so, believers *must* disobey it. The liberty left to individual believers is a curious one, for it is a liberty that cannot extend to any corporate action; as *the church*, the liberty of believers would appear to mean its opposite. Hence Vermigli's complaint, "Truly, we must take good heed that we bring not the Church of Christ into such bondage, that it may not use anything that the Pope used . . . how shall we debar the Church of this liberty, that it cannot signify some good thing, in setting forth their rites and ceremonies?"[47]

Vermigli's complaint was to be taken up and elaborated by Richard Hooker at the close of the sixteenth century, and then again by none other than John Locke late in the seventeenth (along with many others in between). Although we know Locke as the great defender of religious liberty, advocating official government toleration for all Protestant sects, this is not how he began his career. Very little Locke scholarship has taken much note of this background, instead focusing almost entirely on his later work, but John Perry insists that we cannot understand the later Locke without it. Accordingly, he invites us to first attend to Locke's early *First Tract on Government* (1660), written in response to nonconformist Edward Bagshaw's *The Great Question Concerning Things Indifferent*.

The Anglican attempt to crack down on nonconformity after the Restoration rested, as it had for more than a century, on the concept of adiaphora.

47. Letter to Hooper, 32v, 33v.

For conformists, the Christian's liberty in matters indifferent was exercised by their representative, the magistrate, who was free to make policies regarding such rites and orders, and to demand uniformity in them. This uniformity was no violation of Christian liberty, since it was imposed as a matter of *civil* necessity, not *spiritual* necessity. Thus conformists would argue that although in themselves indifferent, the rites in question ceased to be so contingently once the magistrate established a particular usage. Although not among those Puritans who so insisted on the regulative principle that there were no adiaphora left, Bagshaw opposed this conformism with his own concept of contingent indifference. Many of the disputed rites were indifferent per se, he acknowledged, but ceased to be so contingently once they became a stumbling block, a source of superstition; then, it was necessary for Christians to avoid them.[48] Conformists responded that this source of offense could be removed by proper instruction regarding purpose of the rites, whereas the offense of disobeying the magistrate could not.

However, Bagshaw argued that there was another way in which adiaphora could cease to be indifferent—if they were commanded by the civil authority:

> So long as a thing is left Indifferent, though there be some suspicion of superstition in it, we may lawfully practice it, as Paul did circumcision. But when any shall take upon them to make it Necessary then the thing so imposed presently loses not its Liberty only, but likewise its Lawfulness; and we may not without breach of the Apostles' Precept submit to it.[49]

Bagshaw does not here oppose merely making such rites necessary *to salvation*, or articles of faith, as did Article VI of the *Thirty-Nine Articles*, but necessary in any sense. In Bagshaw's view, if such matters are made necessary by law, Christian freedom in adiaphora is violated, and civil authority has demanded a loyalty that only God can claim. Far from being original with Bagshaw (as Perry seems to suggest), this line of argument appears repeatedly in English Puritan polemics and can be found in other Protestant controversies over adiaphora, such as the Lutheran Matthias Flacius's 1548 *Liber de veris et falsis*

---

48. Examples of such superstitious rites were "bowing at the name of Jesus, the [sign of] the cross in baptism, pictures in churches, surplices in preaching, kneeling at the sacrament" (Perry, *Pretenses of Loyalty*, 89, quoting from Edward Bagshaw, *The Great Question concerning Things Indifferent* [Oxford: 1660], 2).

49. Bagshaw, *Great Question*, 9–10, quoted in Perry, *Pretenses of Loyalty*, 90.

adiaphoris.[50] The basic reasoning is the same as that which underlies the regulative principle: individual freedom of conscience is automatically abridged when a norm is prescribed for corporate action. Thus institutions cannot have the freedom to establish standards regarding the use of such rites for the sake of order and the common good.

In his *First Tract on Government*, however, John Locke saw the Protestant doctrine of adiaphora as the means by which to rightly distinguish and harmonize the loyalties of believers. He argued that all matters left adiaphorous by God's Word are by that very fact made subject to the oversight of the civil magistrate, who has care, not over the souls, beliefs, and salvation of his subjects, but over their external actions, so far as he is not limited by the Word of God (as he is not, by definition, in adiaphora).[51] He thus does not bother to quibble with Bagshaw about whether certain rites are or are not superstitious, but simply affirms that they are fundamentally civil and not religious matters, and that maintaining Christian liberty in such matters thereby transgresses on the liberty of the magistrate.[52] Again, although Perry sees this "thoroughly political" rather than religious argument for uniformity as a new departure,[53] Locke too is in fact treading well-worn ground. The equation of religious and civil adiaphora, and the consequent argument for religious uniformity on the basis of civil peace, can be found in English conformist writers from the very decade of Henry VIII's separation from Rome. For the early Locke, as for many of his conformist predecessors, this subjection of adiaphora to civil oversight is in fact the best way to ensure they remain adiaphora. Without uniformity in adiaphora, summarizes Perry, "the only liberty we would achieve is 'liberty for contention, censure and persecution [turning loose] the tyranny of religious rage; were every indifferent thing left unlimited nothing would be lawful.'"[54] This was no idle fear, since as we have seen, the Puritan regulative principle did move from denying that adiaphora could be *enforced on* the church to denying that they could be *practiced in* the church, leading to bitter strife and even schism. Uniformity seemed the only way the magistrate could keep in check the intolerance of his subjects for one another's practices.

Accordingly, the early Locke contends that although the magistrate must

50. See full discussion in Chapter Two below.

51. See Locke, "First Tract on Government," in *Political Essays*, ed. Mark Goldie (Cambridge: Cambridge University Press, 1997), 15.

52. Perry, *Pretenses of Loyalty*, 90–91.

53. Perry, *Pretenses of Loyalty*, 90. See also Jacqueline Rose, "John Locke, 'Matters Indifferent,' and the Restoration of the Church of England," *Historical Journal* 48, no. 3 (2005): 611.

54. Perry, *Pretenses of Loyalty*, 91, quoting from Locke, "First Tract," 65.

make no attempt to command his subjects' beliefs, he may command their actions—those actions acknowledged by Protestant theology to be inessential. Although the permissibility of such uniformity is established on theological grounds, its advisability is established on grounds of political prudence,[55] in line with earlier conformist writers such as Richard Hooker. When Locke later concluded that imposed uniformity was incapable of bringing civil peace, and toleration was the more prudent course,[56] he had to find a way of showing tolerated sects why they should tolerate one another. He sought to achieve this harmonization of loyalties by drawing on his earlier distinction between things indifferent and things essential to salvation; it is because the differences between Protestant groups concern the former, rather than the latter, and that the latter, in any case, cannot be coerced, that Christians should not worry that loyalty to God requires them to persecute or quarrel with those who differ.[57] Those who would not accept the relegation of their differences to the category of adiaphora, like some of the stricter Puritans, could hardly accept Locke's argument for toleration any more than his earlier argument for uniformity.

The ambiguity here was to persist in the Reformed tradition, manifesting itself particularly vividly in a high-profile 1860 debate between the two giants of American Presbyterianism, Charles Hodge and James Henley Thornwell, which VanDrunen too highlights as a test case for the legacy of Christian liberty. The question at stake (a typically Presbyterian one) was whether the denomination was permitted to create a mission board.[58] Charles Hodge ar-

55. Perry, *Pretenses of Loyalty*, 93, 98–99.

56. Of course, his transition was not that seamless, for his other early argument against toleration was principled, not merely prudential. It seemed clear to him that the magistrate rightfully has authority over all indifferent matters, that the liberty that naturally belongs to individuals is ceded to the public authority upon the formation of a political society. So far as he could see, then, there was no logical way to draw a line around which indifferent matters the magistrate may regulate, and which he cannot. It was to provide such a criterion that Locke later developed his concept of rights, offering a new account that strictly limits the legitimate powers of civil government, and excludes matters of religious conviction, as Locke defines it, from those powers (see Perry, *Pretenses of Loyalty*, 99–101).

57. See John Locke, *Letter Concerning Toleration*, ed. Mario Montuori (1689; repr., The Hague: Martinus Nijhoff, 1963), 23–27.

58. Hodge's chief contribution to the discussion may be found in "Presbyterianism," in *Discussions in Church Polity* (New York: Charles Scribner's Sons, 1878), 118–33; Thornwell's, in *The Collected Writings of James Henley Thornwell*, ed. B. M. Palmer (Richmond, VA: Presbyterian Committee of Publication, 1873), 4:145–296. For a recent analysis, see A. Craig Troxel, "Charles Hodge on Church Boards: A Case Study in Ecclesiology," *Westminster Theological Journal* 58 (1996): 183–207.

gued a resounding "Yes," appealing to the doctrine of Christian liberty, and complaining, in terms reminiscent of Vermigli, that Thornwell's doctrine "'ties down' the government and action of the Church," and is as good as a new popery, substituting "the mummified forms of mediaeval Christianity" for "this free, exultant Church of ours."[59] Thornwell, for his part, returns the charge upon Hodge, identifying him with another defender of the liberty of the church, the Elizabethan theologian Richard Hooker:

> These are astounding pretensions; they carry in their bosoms the deadly tyranny of Prelacy and Popery. Dr. Hodge maintains the very same principles—only a little more extravagantly—which were maintained by Hooker in his Ecclesiastical Polity; and he parades against us the same objections against us which Hooker paraded against the Puritans of his day.[60]

As Thornwell's reference to Hooker suggests, this is far from the first time that we find Reformed Protestants lobbing the charge of popish tyranny against one another over perceived infringements of the doctrine of Christian liberty. Nor is this empty polemical rhetoric; on the contrary, so central was the doctrine of Christian liberty to the Reformation that to forsake it *would* be to resurrect papal tyranny. But clearly the doctrine could be taken in very different directions. So who were the true heirs of Luther and Calvin? Those, like Vermigli, Hooker, and Hodge, who defended the right of believers, acting corporately *as the church*, to choose their rituals within certain biblical constraints? Or those, like the Puritans and Thornwell, who insisted the church could never act without scriptural warrant, for fear of trampling on liberated consciences? David VanDrunen insists that Thornwell is the better guardian of the Protestant heritage here; in the chapters that follow, I will suggest otherwise.

In any case, Thornwell's position entailed two further difficulties. First, if scriptural precedent and prescription alone governed the actions of the church, this would seem to require a way of authoritatively determining what Scripture did and did not prescribe. Let us recall Orestes Brownson's worries, contemporary with the Hodge-Thornwell debate, about the language of the "higher law" in nineteenth-century American Protestantism. Troubled by the disorder and anarchy unleashed by individual appeals to conscience, Brownson had rejected

---

59. VanDrunen, *Natural Law and the Two Kingdoms*, 258; quoting from Hodge, "Presbyterianism," 118–19, 133.

60. Thornwell, *Collected Writings*, 4:251.

the American idea of the church as a voluntary society gathered for spiritual purposes, and had turned to the Catholic idea of the church as authoritative mediator of divine law to believers. Thornwell was to do much the same, even while protesting against "the deadly tyranny of Prelacy and Popery":

> The laws of the church are the authoritative injunctions of Christ, and not the covenants, however benevolent in their origin and aim, which men have instituted of their own will; and the ground of obligation which the Church, *as such*, inculcates is the authority of God speaking in His Word, and not pledges of honour which create, measure, and define all voluntary associations.[61]

Of course, just as Thornwell's strict biblicism helped generate the need for such authoritative clerical interpreters, so it was in turn exacerbated by it; for the only way to maintain any claim to Christian liberty in the face of such conscience-binding was to confine all their pronouncements and actions to Scripture alone.

A second problem, though, was that this way of thinking would seem to require a very clear dividing line between church and state. For as we have already noted, such a strict biblicism would seem to be crippling if applied to any civil polity. If believers could never be required to take actions not directly authorized by Scripture, then many of the laws that order civil society would be untenable. If ministers necessarily bound consciences by their teaching, then any instruction they gave on civil affairs would subject the state to the authority of church officers, much as the late medieval popes had sought to do. This, in fact, is how VanDrunen reads Calvin's warning about a transfer; clearly this sort of "Christian liberty" could not be applied in the civil sphere without disastrous consequences. But whereas VanDrunen therefore wants this concept of Christian liberty, and the attendant regulative principle, to be the means by which we distinguish the just bounds of church and state, in fact, it would seem to depend on such a distinction already being in place. Thornwell could make his case for a strict regulative principle in nineteenth-century America without threatening the civil order, because he had the relatively

61. "Speech on African Colonization," in *Collected Writings*, 469; italics original. It is perhaps worth noting in passing how great a distance there was between the legacy of "Christian liberty" in John Brown's anarchistic abolitionism, on the one hand, and on the other, Thornwell's almost exactly contemporary appeal to Christian liberty against any meddling with the *status quo* of slavery (which, he insisted, would be to impose upon believers' consciences beyond the dictates of Scripture).

novel advantage of a legal structure that defined churches as disestablished voluntary societies, whose internal conduct had nothing to do with the affairs of state. But in the early modern period, where such a distinction was far from apparent, the regulative principle could not but lead to profound conflicts of loyalty. It was far from obvious to civil authorities, for instance, that regulating ministerial vestments or public prayers was not integral to their responsibility of maintaining good order in the commonwealth, and it was far from obvious to Puritan clerics, for instance, that magistrates were any more free to permit idolatry in their realms than ministers were to permit it in their parishes.

We have thus witnessed the startling irony (to modern eyes at least) that Protestants who most adopted the language of individual liberty of conscience often ended up being the most illiberal, committed as they were only to a liberty within the dictates of divine law as they interpreted it. By comparison, those who limited individual liberty within the boundaries of human law, even to the extent of regulating religious uniformity, look decidedly more amenable to liberal toleration, since freedom of belief is openly asserted, and freedom of action curtailed only where necessary to protect the common good. This ought not really surprise us given our observation above about the limits of a "jurisdictional approach" for safeguarding liberty of conscience. In any attempt to draw the "just bounds" between human law and the "higher law," one's conception of the higher law itself must determine the nature of the boundaries; for the anti-abortionist who is convinced that abortion is murder and there is no higher demand than the demand to prevent murder, violent action against abortionists is no transgression of the boundaries of religion and politics, but a religious duty and therefore a political one. Indeed, those tempted to try to resolve the conflicts by trying to define the "higher law" with ever more rigidity and precision, like the "regulative principle" Puritans, found their efforts backfiring. By framing the relationship of the Christian to society ever more legalistically, they invited potential jurisdictional quarrels arising at every point. Is there any way around such conflict, or is it simply an inevitable feature of the relationship of religion and politics?

V. Law in the Indicative Mood: Another Look at "Spiritual Liberty"

In fact, what we have witnessed with the clash between institutional and individual liberties, and the various attempts to resolve the conflict of loyalties via a proper jurisdictional definition, is perhaps an illustration of what Ted Smith, following Charles Taylor, calls the "code fetishism" that has dominated much of Western and particularly modern Western thought. In this way of thinking, a clash between the higher law of God and the human laws of church or state is inevitable because the higher law is seen "as *the same kind of thing* as positive, earthly law. Such higher laws take the form of codes of obligations and prohibitions."[62] One can see this most vividly in the legalism of a Thornwell, for whom obedience to the higher law of Scripture entails the strict application of an exhaustive code, mediated by ecclesiastical lawmakers and courts, whose jurisdiction must be carefully defined and constantly policed in order to prevent conflict with the laws of civil society.

In response to this "code fetishism," Smith suggests a different understanding of the "higher law" that is "marked by four qualities: an *indicative* mood that serves to *negate* absolute obligations in this age in ways that invite a *free response* in history that is *permeated by the presence of God*." "The indicative of the higher law," Smith says,

> is not present as a simple description; it is present through its negation of earthly law. It breaks the structures of obligation of earthly laws not just by proposing better content for those laws but by declaring an indicative of fulfillment that undoes the absolute quality of the whole category of earthly law. . . . The proclamation of the Reign of God . . . relativizes the full spectrum of people's obligations.[63]

This "higher law" is first and foremost one of liberation, not obligation, and so does not, at least *prima facie*, butt up against the demands of earthly law.

Although Smith's particular conception of this "higher law" is informed more by Walter Benjamin and Giorgio Agamben than by Luther and Calvin, it perhaps gives us a helpful push in the direction of what Calvin originally had in mind in his warning about the "transfer" of spiritual liberty. Calvin was not worried that this liberty described a particular jurisdictional space of authority or immunity (church), which might be wrongly confused with a different jurisdictional space (state), thus disordering both. Rather, he was worried that this liberty, which was of *another order altogether* than any earthly jurisdictions, might be confused fundamentally with a qualitatively lower form of liberty, thus returning us to a kind of spiritual bondage (without guaranteeing a stable earthly liberty either). We can see this if we turn at

---

62. Smith, *Weird John Brown*, 109.
63. Smith, *Weird John Brown*, 118.

last to consider his full definition of Christian liberty. You might think that I ought to have done this right at the beginning, but I think that we can only grasp the surprisingness and the profound implications of Calvin's definition if we have first observed the conundrums created by a misconstrual of the doctrine.

Calvin begins his chapter on Christian freedom by calling it "a thing of prime necessity," apart from which "consciences dare undertake almost nothing without doubting." Indeed, the doctrine is an "appendage of justification and is of no little avail in understanding its power."[64] Already it is clear that we are in somewhat different soil than that to which we are accustomed in considering this doctrine. Recall that we considered it above in light of Luther's declaration that his conscience was "captive to the Word of God," in other words, as an essentially epistemological doctrine: the freedom of a Christian was the freedom to submit his beliefs to the revelation of God's word alone, eschewing or at least relativizing other epistemic authorities that might make a claim upon him. But here, the context is soteriological; Christian liberty has to do with the believer's *justification*, his freedom from the bondage of external works.

Calvin expounds three different elements to the doctrine:

The first: that the consciences of believers, in seeking assurance of their justification before God, should rise above and advance beyond the law, forgetting all law righteousness. . . .

The second part, dependent upon the first, is that consciences observe the law, not as if constrained by the necessity of the law, but that freed from the law's yoke they willingly obey God's will. For since they dwell in perpetual dread so long as they remain under the sway of the law, they will never be disposed with eager readiness to obey God unless they have already been given this sort of freedom . . .

The third part of Christian freedom lies in this: regarding outward things that are of themselves "indifferent" [*adiaphora*], we are not bound before God by any religious obligation preventing us from sometimes using them and other times not using them, indifferently.[65]

(Throughout this book, I will designate these the principles of *justification*, *voluntariety*, and *indifference*, respectively.)

64. Calvin, *Institutes*, 1:833 [III.19.1].
65. Calvin, *Institutes*, 1:834, 836, 838 [III.19.2, 4, 7].

Several things are striking about this exposition. First, Calvin begins with a higher law that is, as Ted Smith puts it (following Benjamin and Agamben), the "'relief' of law . . . a fulfilled, delivered, and renewed law";[66] it is the negation of the burden of law, the call to "rise above and advance beyond" it, "forgetting all law righteousness." It is, in other words, the doctrine of justification by faith, in which the consciences of believers are set free by the realization that they are already accepted by God in Christ, and need no longer fear the inadequacy of their own works. Of course, Calvin is no antinomian; believers are still summoned to obey God, as he has revealed himself in his works and in his Word; there is still a law that consciences should observe, but the mode of this observance has totally changed. It is no longer one of being "constrained by necessity" but of "willingly obey[ing] God's will" with "eager readiness" rather than "perpetual dread." In other words, we ought not have to prod and drag ourselves, as if under a sense of compulsion and fear of the consequences, to obey this law; to the conscience mindful of the first element of Christian freedom, this obedience ought to come willingly, almost spontaneously; even the "imperative" elements of the law do not really confront the conscience as imperatives.

From this standpoint, it appears that the way in which we described the Protestant proclamation of freedom of conscience at the beginning of this chapter was precisely backward. There we suggested that the spiritual liberty that seemed so obviously to point toward political liberty was the idea that "we are free in relation to human authority because we are bound in relation to God." I suspect that this way of expressing the matter seems so natural to most readers that you did not notice the blatant contradiction between it and what Calvin actually says in the quote that headlined this chapter: "as if in regard to external government Christians were less subject to human laws, because their consciences are unbound before God, as if they were exempted from all carnal service, because in regard to the Spirit they are free."[67] In other words, for Calvin, the doctrine of Christian liberty is that "we are still bound in relation to human authority although [or because?] we are free in relation to God." No wonder, then, that he could warn so strongly against a "transfer." On this reading (which seems the only one true to the text), "Jesus does not squeeze himself into Caesar's throne," in Smith's words, demanding disobedience to human authorities in loyalty to divine law, because Jesus's summons is first and foremost of another order.

66. Smith, *Weird John Brown*, 116.
67. Calvin, *Institutes*, 1:847 [III.19.15].

However, clearly this cannot be the whole story, can it? After all, even if the first part of the doctrine of Christian liberty is wholly indicative, a tension emerges already with the second part, and further ambiguities arise at the third part. For even if our posture toward the law of God is transformed, it is still there to be obeyed, and this obedience certainly may bring us into some kind of conflict with earthly authorities. It certainly may help to lower the stakes of such conflict, and render it more readily navigable, if the sphere of conflict is displaced from the realm of *justification* to that of *sanctification*, as it clearly is in Calvin's formulation, but the conflict remains. We were wrong, it appears, to imagine *sola Scriptura* as the starting point and ground of the Protestant doctrine of Christian liberty—that place clearly belongs to *sola fide*. But inasmuch as Scripture alone governed the liberated conscience, it could still clash with other norms.

This tension spills over into our interpretation of the third part of Calvin's doctrine, the principle of indifference. Here too it appears that we will misread Calvin disastrously if we fail to read the principle in light of the *first* part of the doctrine of Christian liberty. This liberty too is a liberty first and foremost vis-à-vis God, not an obedience to God that generates liberty vis-à-vis human authorities (as Thornwell and VanDrunen read it, for instance): "we are not bound *before God* . . . by any *religious obligation*." The point here was that, whatever these indifferent things are, our souls need not fear God's wrath in our conduct of them. Of course, we saw that this was true also of those things in the second part of the doctrine, the principles of the law. The logic of the three parts together, taking justification *sola fide* as their fundamental orientation, thus seems to be: (1) you have been freed from fear of God by knowing his gracious justification; (2) therefore, where his will is manifest, you obey it out of spontaneous gratitude, rather than fear, and (3) where his will is not manifest, you live all the more without fear, and without a sense of religious obligation, conducting yourself as circumstances seem to dictate.

If we fail to maintain *sola fide* as the fundamental orientation, and by focusing on the epistemological question, elevate *sola Scriptura* from a background condition of Christian liberty to its starting point, we are liable to run into trouble. We saw this in VanDrunen's exposition, or Thornwell's, which placed little or no emphasis on a fear of works-righteousness; indeed, we find Thornwell accused of reinstating a papal tyranny, only one that consists in the *proscription* rather than the *prescription* of particular works. Christian liberty, on this view, is fundamentally about the conscience being bound to Scripture alone, and free outside of it. This view requires the doctrine of the two kingdoms as a way of distinguishing the sphere over which scriptural authority operates to the exclusion of human laws (on VanDrunen's view, the institutional church) from that in which liberty to make and obligation to obey human laws still pertains. As we have seen, this has the paradoxical effect that the believer *is not* at liberty within the "spiritual kingdom" of the church, but *is* within the "civil kingdom," apparently contrary to Calvin's exposition. On this reading, adiaphora, whatever they were, could not be the subject of human legislation, without violating the principle of Christian freedom.

When the principle is read in a more soteriological rather than epistemological key, however, it is not hard to see how many Protestants, from Vermigli to Hooker to Locke to Hodge, could conclude that adiaphora fell well within the bounds of human authority to legislate, at least so long as human authorities did not go beyond prudential rationales for such laws. Such civic obligations hardly counted as a "religious obligation" "before God." From this perspective, it is the freedom of the conscience from all bondage to external works, the inwardness of the Christian's relation to Christ by faith, that ensures, not that Christians *ought not* to be conscientiously bound in adiaphora (as VanDrunen reads it), but that Christians simply *cannot* be conscientiously bound in adiaphora.[68] Since the Christian lives by faith *coram Deo*, his conscience is not determined by works *coram hominibus*. On this understanding, the doctrine of the two kingdoms is thus not an attempt to control the implications of the doctrine of Christian liberty with an institutional separation of church and state, as some have read it, but is part and parcel of the doctrine. The "spiritual kingdom" properly speaking describes the inner realm *coram Deo* in which the believer is subject immediately to Christ alone, while the "civil kingdom" refers not merely to civil government or what we might call "secular" matters, but to the life of the Christian *coram hominibus*, mediately governed by human authorities.[69] The church exists in both realms, and most

---

68. This is made quite clear in Calvin's exposition in *Institutes*, 1:846–49 [III.19.14–16]: "[W]e conclude that they [consciences] are released from the power of all men. . . . They have surely fallen away from it if they can, at men's good pleasure, be ensnared by the bonds of laws and constitutions" (1:846–47 [III.19.14]). He goes on to contend that if consciences could be bound by civil laws [which chiefly concern adiaphora], "all that we said a little while ago and are now going to say about spiritual government would fall" (1:848 [III.19.15]). He concludes that "however necessary it may be with respect to his brother for him to abstain from it," speaking concerning eating meat, a matter in which the believer has adiaphorous liberty, "he still does not cease to keep freedom of conscience. We see how this law, while binding outward actions, leaves the conscience free" (1:849 [III.19.16]).

69. As a matter of fact, the development of Luther's two-kingdoms doctrine, at least, does quite clearly proceed in this latter way—out of his doctrine of justification by faith alone, not his doctrine of Scripture. See F. Edward Cranz, *An Essay on the Development of Luther's*

matters of liturgy and polity were in the latter realm; to say otherwise was to make the juridical and liturgical form of the church constitutive of the kingdom of Christ, which was the pope's error. On this latter understanding, the Puritan attempt to make the avoidance of particular ceremonies *obligatory* was indeed, as Hodge accused Thornwell, a return to "the mummified forms of mediaeval Christianity"; the conscience-binding *proscription* of works was as bad as its *prescription*. The regulation of such ceremonies as a civil matter that English conformists advocated was then, far from a violation of the distinction of the two kingdoms, a way of protecting it, preventing an unhealthy fixation on externals. From this standpoint, however, the question remained: Assuming that Scripture had something to say about matters of liturgy and polity, how did it inform or limit such civil regulation?

After all, it was not at all immediately clear where the boundary between the second and third parts of Christian liberty fell. When did we move from those things where we were *free to obey God's will* to where we were *free because his will had not been revealed*? To be sure, both spheres must be maintained as spheres of freedom; we ought to remember that in either case, we should trust God's grace rather than fear his wrath. But still, divine commands were not to be lightly ignored, and so presumably we must make it a priority to discover which things were and which were not indifferent.

Even when a distinction could be maintained in the abstract, contingent circumstances may render it difficult to sustain. After all, if a believer is convinced that particular ceremonies will lead to superstition or will cause his brother to stumble, they are not indifferent for him, and his loyalty to God is brought into conflict with his loyalty to the magistrate. The possibility of such crises of conscience, in an age that, as Susan Schreiner has documented, was particularly consumed with the quest for certainty,[70] demanded the provision

---

Thought on Law, Justice, and Society (Cambridge, MA: Harvard University Press, 1959). For a fuller exposition of Luther's doctrine of the "two kingdoms" and "two regiments," along the lines described in this paragraph, see W. D. J. Cargill Thompson, "The 'Two Kingdoms' and the 'Two Regiments': Some Problems of Luther's *Zwei-Reiche-Lehre*," *Journal of Theological Studies* 20, no. 1 (1969): 164–85, and John Witte Jr., *Law and Protestantism*, 89–115. Note that there is considerable complexity and variation in the terminology, with Luther's *Zwei Reiche*, distinguishing domains, being translated as either "two kingdoms" or "two realms," and his *Zwei Regimente*, distinguishing modes of rule, being rendered as either "two regiments" or "two governments." Although I will generally stick with the most familiar term—"two kingdoms"—in this book, I will occasionally make use of the others when helpful or when authors I am discussing do so.

70. See *Are You Alone Wise?* Schreiner gives particular attention to the late medieval struggles to achieve philosophical certainty, the existential struggles to achieve certainty of

of a certain standard for adjudicating such dilemmas. I will argue that it was primarily in answer to this demand that Scripture came to take on such a central role, particularly in the English Reformation, for defining the scope and nature of Christian liberty. However, in the absence of a consensus about how Scripture was to be used in ecclesiology and politics, and how it was to be interpreted, the biblicist turn served simply to heighten the conflict of loyalties, impinging upon the institutional liberty of church and state even as it altered the character of individual conscientious liberty.

The question, then, that was urgently posed by the Reformation's proclamation of the freedom of a Christian was this: How can the liberty of human authorities to seek the common good be reconciled with the liberty of individual consciences to serve God? How can the freedom of a Christian person coexist with the freedom of a Christian commonwealth?

Clearly a full engagement with this question would require extensive consideration of multiple leading reformers, and the emergence of tensions between churches and civil authorities in Germany, Switzerland, France, the Netherlands, Scotland, and England in the decades following the Reformation. Thankfully, however, the tumultuous debates of the Elizabethan period serve as a convenient and reliable proxy for such a study; although idiosyncratic in many regards, I shall argue in Chapter Two that the English Reformation was thoroughly engaged with developments in the continental Reformation when it came to issues of Christian liberty and the two kingdoms. In particular, I shall turn to the magisterial political-theological synthesis of Richard Hooker as one of the most convincing sixteenth-century attempts to answer this question and to harmonize the loyalties to God and prince within the terms of orthodox Protestant theology. His synthesis, I shall argue, seeks to establish the Christian subject's duty to submit to the determinations of the prince, while at the same protecting all three dimensions of Christian liberty, and clarifying the relation of scriptural authority to the doctrine. The answer he provides, I shall argue, can enable us to offer a more coherent *descriptive* account than most offered to date of how the fundamental tenets of Protestant theology did and did not impact their understanding of civil government, laying the groundwork for modern civil liberties in important ways, but not

---

salvation that helped launch the Reformation, and the hermeneutical struggles to achieve certainty in the interpretation of Scripture that the Reformation unleashed. A significant missing theme in her book is the struggles for certainty over matters of ethics (i.e., debates over the adiaphora), a *lacuna* that the present study perhaps makes some contribution to filling.

necessarily the ways we would expect. Moreover, it also provides resources for a valuable *prescriptive* account of how a Protestant political theology for our day might attempt to reconcile these clashing loyalties, one that offers a more integrated account of the function of divine law, natural law, and human law, than most modern Protestants possess, and thus a stronger foundation for Christian political engagement in our own day.

The choice of Hooker for such an inquiry is a natural one. He stands, as it were, midway between Calvin and Locke—not quite temporally, to be sure, but in the development of the history of ideas. And he constructed his work in conscious dialogue with and often opposition to the Puritan and presbyterian reformers who played such a central and paradigmatic role in several of the narratives we canvassed above. In particular, he addresses head-on the questions of liberty and authority—divine authority, civil authority, and ecclesiastical authority—that created such tensions in their thought and in many of their modern heirs. His *Of the Lawes of Ecclesiasticall Politie* has of course long been renowned for its systematic coherence and thoroughness, far surpassing the other English polemical literature of this period, and for its creative synthesis of Reformed Protestantism with the categories of medieval scholasticism, especially Thomism. Hooker's rejection of Puritan legal voluntarism and his defense of consensual government have often earned him respect as a defender of liberty, despite his role as unyielding apologist for the *status quo*. Hooker also exerted an enormous influence on the political and religious thinkers of seventeenth-century England, especially Locke (although scholars have largely ignored this influence until recently).[71]

That said, several elements of the argument to follow in these pages may require some justification in light of long-entrenched historiographical assertions. For one, I have already in this opening chapter referred to the "Protestant doctrine" of Christian liberty, or of adiaphora, even while acknowledging inner tensions and conflicting receptions of that doctrine within the first decades of the Reformation. Some historians may still be suspicious of

---

71. Diarmaid MacCulloch provides a good survey of the seventeenth-century reception of Hooker, demonstrating how widely his influence was disseminated, in "Richard Hooker's Reputation," in *A Companion to Richard Hooker*, ed. W. J. Torrance Kirby (Leiden: Brill, 2008), 563–99. The fullest survey is Michael A. Brydon, *The Evolving Reputation of Richard Hooker: An Examination of Responses 1600–1714* (Oxford: Oxford University Press, 2006). Alexander Rosenthal traces his influence on a wide range of seventeenth-century English political theorists in ch. 4 of *Crown under Law: Richard Hooker, John Locke, and the Ascent of Modern Constitutionalism* (Plymouth, UK: Lexington Books, 2008), before analyzing Locke's use of him extensively in ch. 5.

such indiscriminate lumping. In particular, so stubborn has the retrospective dualism between "Lutheran" and "Reformed" proved within Reformation scholarship, that my attempts to move (in this chapter and the next one) back and forth from Luther and Melanchthon to Calvin and Vermigli may still seem to some inexcusably transgressive. Thankfully, however, modern scholarship has increasingly demonstrated the anachronism of erecting such hard-and-fast borders in this early period, and has drawn attention to the unimpeded cross-pollination of ideas between different reformers during the first several decades of the Reformation.[72]

The same must be said, all the more so, of the relationship of the English Reformation to the Continental context. Until very recently, much English Reformation and especially Hooker scholarship remained captive to the old myth that the Protestant church that emerged on the west side of the English Channel was *sui generis* and could be narrated on its own terms. Of course, a glimpse at the primary sources of the period reveals no such sense among the leading actors of the time, on either side of the Channel (and indeed, many of them spent plenty of time on both sides). Indeed, modern scholarship has progressively broken down this barrier to understanding.[73] Although in the Henrician period, the reformation in England undoubtedly held a middle course between full-blown Protestantism and the old church, historians have found it impossible to ignore the immense traffic, both in people and ideas, between the continent and England during the Edwardian reformation, and the tremendous influence of continental Reformed ideas on the Puritan wing within the Elizabethan Church. Harder to shake, however, has been the prejudice that the architects of the Elizabethan Church—the queen and her bishops—had only a tenuous loyalty

---

72. Benedict's *Christ's Churches Purely Reformed* and Diarmaid MacCulloch's *Reformation: Europe's House Divided, 1490-1700* (London: Allen Lane, 2003) are two recent overviews that give an excellent sense of the fluidity of the early decades of the Reformation. Although Benedict remains methodologically wedded to the Lutheran/Reformed dichotomy by the nature of the task he has set, several points in his narrative reveal its anachronism (see particularly pp. 55, 225-26, 289-90). François Wendel, in his sketch of Calvin's theology, *Calvin: The Origins and Development of His Religious Thought*, trans. Philip Mairet (New York: Harper & Row, 1963), draws repeated attention to the basic kinship between his theology and Luther's (see especially pp. 133, 220-25).

73. See especially Patrick Collinson, "The Fog in the Channel Clears: The Rediscovery of the Continental Dimension to the British Reformations," in *The Reception of the Continental Reformation in Britain*, ed. Polly Ha and Patrick Collinson, xxvii–xxxvii, Proceedings of the British Academy 164 (Oxford: Oxford University Press, 2010), and indeed all the essays in this fine volume.

to Protestant theology, and sought to chart their own *via media* course.[74] It is only within the past three decades that this thesis has been decisively refuted, with Torrance Kirby's monograph *The Zurich Connection and Tudor Political Theology* demonstrating this continuity even on the controversial issue of the relation of church and state.[75] Needless to say, however, this debate is still far from fully resolved, and the present work necessarily constitutes a contribution to it. Indeed, perhaps the most resilient feature of the old *via media* idea of the Church of England is the conviction that Richard Hooker's theology constitutes a unique synthesis midway between Geneva and Rome.[76] By bringing him into my narrative as the heir and indeed in many respects the champion of Luther's doctrine of the freedom of a Christian, I am consciously contesting this narrative, which has been perpetuated by poor readings of Hooker himself and chronic inattention to his third-generation international Reformed contemporaries.[77] My hope is that by positioning him within this broader narrative, I will be able to shed new light on areas of Hooker's thought—natural law and human law, church and state, Scripture and reason—that have already been the subject of hundreds of articles and monographs over the past century. Whether I succeed enough to justify my methodological choices, I will leave you to decide.

---

74. Sir John Neale offered one of the most influential statements of this thesis in his *Elizabeth I and Her Parliaments*, 2 vols. (London: Jonathan Cape, 1957), and its presence can be felt, although in a qualified form, in the work of his student, Patrick Collinson, *The Elizabethan Puritan Movement* (Berkeley: University of California Press, 1967).

75. W. J. Torrance Kirby, *The Zurich Connection and Tudor Political Theology* (Leiden: Brill, 2007). For a broad sketch of the "Calvinist consensus" in Elizabethan and Jacobean England see Patrick Collinson's *The Religion of Protestants: The Church in English Society, 1559–1625* (Oxford: Clarendon, 1982). For good summaries of the development and current state of the historiography of this period see Peter Lake, "The Historiography of Puritanism," in *The Cambridge Companion to Puritanism*, ed. John Coffey and Paul C. H. Lim (Cambridge: Cambridge University Press, 2008), 346–72, and Peter Marshall, "(Re)defining the English Reformation," *Journal of British Studies* 48, no. 3 (July 2009): 564–86.

76. See especially Peter Lake, *Anglicans and Puritans? Presbyterianism and English Conformist Thought from Whitgift to Hooker* (London: Unwin Hyman, 1988).

77. For more on this question, see my article, "Search for a Reformed Hooker," *Reformation & Renaissance Review* 16, no. 1 (2014): 68–82, and my book, *Richard Hooker: A Companion to His Life and Work* (Eugene, OR: Cascade, 2015), and the collection of essays in the new volume, edited by Scott Kindred-Barnes and me, *Richard Hooker and Reformed Orthodoxy* (Göttingen: Vandenhoeck & Ruprecht, 2017).

VI. Structure of the Argument

The argument that follows will consist of six chapters, two of which will set the stage for Hooker's contribution, and three of which will examine in detail his treatments of the relevant issues in the *Lawes of Ecclesiasticall Politie*; the final chapter will seek to draw together what we have learned from the study and how it might enrich both our understanding of the sixteenth century and the political-theological questions of our own day.

Chapter Two will be the most wide-ranging chapter, as I seek to provide an overview of how the doctrines of the two kingdoms, Christian liberty, and adiaphora were understood and debated during the first fifty years of the Reformation, both on the continent and in England. I shall begin with Luther's classic statement of the doctrine in *The Freedom of a Christian* and seek to sketch its implications, ambiguities, and tensions with relation to the issues we have highlighted here already—its inward and outward dimensions, its soteriological and epistemological contexts, and its individual and institutional implications. We shall then travel to 1530s England to see how a similar bundle of concepts could be applied with a rather different emphasis to undergird an ecclesiological arrangement that might seem quite distant from Luther's ideal. However, by examining in tandem two nearly contemporary conflicts over adiaphora—the 1548 Adiaphora Controversy in Germany and the 1550 Vestiarian Controversy in England, we will find that in fact very similar dynamics were at work among Luther's followers on both sides of the channel, bringing to the surface similar tensions in the understanding of Christian liberty. Finally, we will see how these conflicts intensified in the Second Vestiarian Controversy, with demands for conformity in adiaphora proving such a strain on the consciences of some English Protestants that they were driven into open opposition to the church hierarchy.

Chapter Three will attempt to discern the logic by which this protest for liberty in adiaphora became, in the disciplinarian movement, a functional rejection of adiaphora, as a "code fetishism" took hold in an attempt to resolve the conflict of loyalties that merely heightened it. As believers acted upon their liberty of conscience to discern the will of God, they applied increasingly precise, detailed scriptural regulation to all matters of ecclesiastical polity (and in some cases, civil polity as well). I will suggest that this shift reflected a general "precisianist" impulse to reduce the gap between the inward and the outward, the invisible and the visible, with a consequent need to achieve the same level of certainty in the realm of action as Protestantism had sought to establish in the realm of faith. By discerning the logic of this shift, we can arrive at a more nuanced understanding of Puritan biblicism than the stereotypes found in most of the secondary literature (and therefore prepare the ground for a more nuanced understanding of Hooker's response). Along with this shift came a divergent understanding of the two kingdoms; no longer were they distinguished as inward and outward, but rather as two outward bodies, church and state, ruled by distinct laws and governors. We will trace these themes, and the alternative logic of conformism, by following the Admonition Controversy, the literary exchange of Thomas Cartwright and John Whitgift. In particular, we shall see how the theme of edification came to dominate such debates—whereas Puritans contended that adiaphora must be used for the spiritual edification of believers, conformists contended that commonwealth's institutional liberty to impose uniformity for the sake of civil order was a form of edification, and indeed trumped other considerations. I shall argue that, although avoiding some of the doctrinal problems created by the emerging disciplinarians, the Elizabethan conformists by and large failed to adequately preserve the full dimensions of the doctrine of Christian liberty, putting severe strains on the consciences of Puritan dissenters.

In the course of tracing the emergence of these conflicts of conscience, and rival versions of the two kingdoms, we shall encounter at least three sets of questions that are central to ecclesiology and political theology. First, we find Protestants wrestling with such questions as, to what extent does the Word of God leave us at liberty in the management of ecclesial and civil affairs? Is this liberty reserved to individuals, so that liberty of conscience is protected, or does it belong to institutions, so that anarchy may be avoided, order preserved, and the common good pursued? Second, having drawn attention to this tension between individual and institutional liberty, we may then ask whether these two need be opposed to one another, and whether it suffices to make a rigid distinction between inner freedom, which is inalienable from the individual, and outward freedom, which may be constrained by institutional laws. Or can we achieve a deeper reconciliation through a conception of corporate moral agency? Third, if individual and institutional freedom are to be somehow harmonized, mustn't the community itself exercise its freedom in obedience to the authority of God? And if so, how can it do so without reinstating theocracy? Should civil and religious affairs be radically distinguished in order to preserve freedom of conscience, or may they remain married together? In Chapters Four through Six, I will accordingly consider in turn how Hooker seeks to address each of these clusters of questions, and in ways that safeguard the three dimensions of Christian liberty.

In Chapter Four, I seek to establish the relevance of Richard Hooker's contribution to these debates. I will show that Hooker clearly situates his apology for the Elizabethan church within the tradition of debates on liberty, adiaphora, and edification. He clearly recognizes the tension that has arisen between individual liberty and institutional liberty, and clearly, along with other conformists, considers the latter to be most important. However, strikingly, he recognizes that the preservation of the latter, through an emphasis on the spiritual quality of Christian liberty, is actually necessary to ensure the preservation of the former. It is Puritan doctrine, he contends, that undermines true liberty of conscience, endangering the centrality of justification by faith and overthrowing the principle of indifference through its demand for scriptural justification for moral and political actions. He also recognizes the need to provide a thorough conceptual grounding for the concept of adiaphora, and to clarify the relation between its *soteriological* and *epistemological* senses, both of which must be distinguished from its *moral* sense, as some Puritans had failed to do. His definition of adiaphora, I shall argue, depends heavily on a two-kingdoms schema that decisively locates those matters of ecclesiastical polity that are indifferent within the "civil kingdom." It is on this basis that he can argue for the church's regulation of such matters through the instruments of civil authority.

Chapter Five attempts to show how the preceding argument, which is in many ways simply an elaboration and clarification of those offered by previous conformists, avoids trampling on Puritan consciences. Indeed, Hooker explicitly sets up his argument as one intended to "resolve the consciences" of his opponents, recognizing that a summons to obedience can only be authentically Protestant if it honors the principle of voluntariety and seeks to elicit a free, conscientious obedience. Hooker's strategy for ensuring such a free obedience is three-pronged. First, unlike many earlier conformists, Hooker recognizes that even adiaphorous ceremonies must still be ordered toward the positive edification of believers. His attempt to explain how such ceremonies, which he has clearly classified as *civil*, may yet be *spiritually* edifying, involves a remarkable nuancing of his doctrine of the two kingdoms, demonstrating how the radical distinction between the two realms, far from pitting them against one another, allows them to work in closest harmony. Second, Hooker, unlike many of his predecessors, seeks to respond to the Puritan demand for certainty by rehabilitating the probable authority of reason in discerning the goodness of established laws and ceremonies; by encouraging his Puritan opponents to apply the test of reasonability, rather than narrow biblical fidelity, to debated ordinances, he hopes to persuade them to a free embrace of such laws. Finally, however, he argues that even in the absence of individual conviction that a pre-scribed ceremony is reasonable or edifying, free consent to such a ceremony may still be understood to have been given through established representatives. Hooker accordingly uses a sophisticated concept of corporate rationality and corporate moral agency in order to characterize the legal imposition of church orders as a free act of self-limitation on the part of the English people. By these means, Hooker seeks to reconcile the inward and outward, individual and institutional elements of Christian liberty.

In Chapter Six, I shall turn to consider more precisely how such reconciliation could possibly be achieved without either wholly privatizing religious expression, in the manner of the "quietist" understanding of freedom of conscience analyzed earlier in this chapter, or else sacralizing the state as the executor of the divine law, in the manner of the activist liberated conscience that Walzer and Voegelin described. Key to Hooker's endeavor is a rehabilitation of *reason* that is neither an arrogant rationalism nor a minimalist "public reason." Rather, Hooker offers a nuanced account of natural law and divine law as intimately related and mutually interpretive. His constant fidelity to the principle that "grace does not destroy nature, but perfects it" leads him to argue that the best political community is a self-consciously Christian political community, in which the reign of Christ over the commonwealth is explicitly acknowledged, though it does not require that all positive law be derived from Scripture. In this he offers an explicit rebuttal to Cartwright's separation of the commonwealth from the kingdom of Christ, and the de-Christianization of the political order that this implies. By this means, Hooker's argument offers a direct rejoinder to modern versions of the two-kingdoms paradigm that would similarly seek to separate the state from the rule of Christ and empty the civic order of any public Christian identity.

The final chapter will seek to draw out and analyze the problems in the conceptualization of liberty that have been traced in this narrative. By juxtaposing the rival accounts of liberty offered by liberal theorist Isaiah Berlin and those of Christian ethicists Richard Bauckham and Oliver O'Donovan, I argue that the disconnect between modern liberal and sixteenth-century conceptions of "freedom of conscience" is not just historical, but theological. I go on to argue, however, that there are at least two distinct theological accounts of liberty, corresponding to the epistemological and soteriological emphases introduced above and highlighted throughout this book. Although both stand in considerable tension with contemporary ideals of liberty, and are thus sure to generate clashes of loyalty, I argue that the soteriological emphasis, particularly as developed in Richard Hooker's political theology, has much more to offer contemporary Christian political theory. Indeed, this approach to Christian liberty offers just what scholars like VanDrunen and Witte had sought to find, though by a rather more indirect route than they pursued: a precursor and midwife of modern liberal freedoms that remains distinctively Christian and theologically grounded.

CHAPTER TWO

Freedom for the Neighbor

....

Christian Liberty and the Demand for Edification

> A man does not live for himself alone in this mortal body to work
> for it alone, but he lives also for all men on earth; rather he lives
> only for others and not for himself.
>
> Martin Luther, *The Freedom of a Christian*[1]

> This persuasion a godly man must always retain and kepe safe in
> his mind: but when he cometh to the use and action of them, then
> must he moderate and qualify his liberty, according to charity to-
> ward his neighbor, and obedience to his Prince. So though by this
> knowledge his mind and conscience is always free; yet his doing
> is as it were tied or limited by law or love.
>
> Matthew Parker, *A Briefe Examination for the Tyme*[2]

In February of 1589, Richard Bancroft, chaplain to the lord chancellor and the
future archbishop of Canterbury, preached one of the most audacious sermons
that the celebrated pulpit of Paul's Cross had witnessed: "Dearly beloved, believe not every spirit, but try the spirits whether they be of God." The sermon
launched a direct attack on Puritan dissenters as seditious libertines, a threat
to both church and state. At the heart of their threat to good Protestant orthodoxy and social stability, Bancroft would charge, was their exhortation to their
followers to "Search, examine, try, and seek: bringing them thereby into a great

---

1. *Freedom of a Christian*, in *LW* 31:364.
2. *Briefe Examination*, 15v.

uncertainty."[3] To be sure, he does not wish to commit the popish error of "forbid[ding] the children of God to prove anything"[4] and he grants that believers ought to "read the Scriptures, *but with sobriety*."[5] "Sobriety" meant submission, recognizing that "God hath bound himself by his promise unto his church of purpose, that men by her good direction might in this point be relieved. To whose godly determination in matters of question, her dutiful children ought to submit themselves without any curious or willful contradiction."[6]

The Puritan radical John Penry cried foul to this remarkable constriction of Christian liberty, but his own solution to the problem of uncertain interpretation was scarcely better. Rather, he vests all authority in the presbyterian ministers, from whom no layperson, not even the queen herself, has any right of dissent: "[H]er majesty and the Parliament are bound to establish and erect amongst their subjects, all such laws and ceremonies, as the true ministers of the word, shall prove by the Scriptures of God, to be meet and necessary."[7] Both sides had been brought to this impasse by the seemingly insoluble problem of adiaphora: Just what sorts of things were indifferent, and as for those that were, who was to decide what we were to do with them? Leaving the Christian conscience free before God seemed a recipe for disaster, since his Word was proving so pliable in the hands of various disputants. Better to seek some definitive sentence from human authority, whether it be magistrate or minister.

I. The Freedom of a Christian: Adiaphora in the Lutheran Reformation

Things had certainly come a long way from Luther's 1520 proclamation of the "freedom of a Christian," intended to liberate the Christian conscience from

---

3. *A Sermon preached at Paules Crosse the 8. of Februarie, being the first Sunday in the Parleament, Anno. 1588. by Richard Bancroft D. of Divinitie, and Chaplaine to the right Honorable Sir Christopher Hatton Knight L. Chancelor of England* (London: E. B. [Edward Bollifant] for Gregorie Seton, 1588, i.e. 1589), 39. For a discussion of the audacity of the sermon, see Mary Morrissey, *Politics and the Paul's Cross Sermons, 1558–1642* (Oxford: Oxford University Press, 2011), 208–14.

4. Bancroft, *A Sermon*, 33.

5. Bancroft, *A Sermon*, 42.

6. Bancroft, *A Sermon*, 42.

7. Penry, *A Briefe Discovery of the Untruthes, and Slanders Against Reformation, and the favourers thereof, contained in D. Bancroft's Sermon [. . .]* (Edinburgh: Robert Waldegrave, 1589/90), 41. For a fuller discussion, see W. Bradford Littlejohn, "Bancroft v. Penry: Conscience and Authority in Elizabethan Polemics," in *Paul's Cross and the Culture of Persuasion in England, 1520–1640*, ed. W. J. Torrance Kirby and P. G. Stanwood (Leiden: Brill, 2014), 327–42.

any such tyranny by human authority. Luther's attempt to demote the whole heavy burden of ecclesiastical ceremonies that had accumulated in the medieval church to the level of adiaphora was in itself nothing new; many would-be reformers had said as much, most notably Erasmus. In themselves, Erasmus contended, these ceremonies were neither pleasing nor displeasing to God, but were valuable only if taken up as a means of true devotion by a God-fearing conscience.[8] Luther, however, by coupling the notion of adiaphora with his central doctrines of *sola fide* and *sola Scriptura*, achieved an explosive new theological synthesis, the doctrine of Christian liberty, which struck at the heart of late medieval authority structures.

Luther sets forth the doctrine in *The Freedom of a Christian* in terms of his familiar binary division between the inward and the outward man, evident in the famous paradox, "A Christian is a perfectly free lord of all, subject to none. A Christian is a perfectly dutiful servant of all, subject to all."[9] Luther goes on to explain that in his inward character, before God, the Christian is entirely free because justified by faith; outwardly, before men, he is enslaved by love to serve all. Only by virtue of such a radical distinction between the inward and the outward, Luther believes, can the freedom of a Christian conscience before God be guaranteed, for if the Christian is led to believe that his justification before God depends on any outward works, rather than the free gift of faith, he is in bondage.[10] By this means Luther attacks the whole array of Catholic ceremonies, saying,

> It does not help the soul if the body is adorned with the sacred robes of priests or dwells in sacred places or is occupied with sacred duties or prays, fasts, abstains from certain kinds of food, or does any work that can be done by the body and in the body. The righteousness and the freedom of the soul require something far different.

---

8. Bernard J. Verkamp, *The Indifferent Mean: Adiaphorism in the English Reformation to 1554* (Athens: Ohio University Press, 1977), 24–25, 36–40. Verkamp offers a helpful introduction to the history of the concept adiaphora, which derived originally from the Cynics and Stoics, in ancient and medieval thought. The earlier usage, he argues, differs from the Reformational usage in that the term was used in a philosophical sense, designating actions that had no intrinsic moral value in themselves, but became good or evil depending on intention (21–26).

9. *LW* 31:344.

10. "First, let us consider the inner man to see how a righteous, free, and pious Christian, that is, a spiritual, new, and inner man, becomes what he is. It is evident that no external thing has any influence in producing Christian righteousness or freedom, or in producing unrighteousness or servitude" (*LW* 31:344–45).

That something, he says, is the "the most holy Word of God, the gospel of Christ."[11]

It is crucial to understand that the purpose of this radical distinction is not to attack outward works per se, but merely to establish the priority of the inward, which is faith: the outward must never determine the inward, grace must never be conditioned upon works, but the inward life of grace will determine the outward, issuing forth in good works. Thus it is that the principle of justification issues into the principle of voluntariety: moral laws, and precepts of Scripture are obeyed, but out of an overflow of love, not a spirit of bondage. Likewise, it grounds the principle of indifference: outward things are indifferent to the life of faith inasmuch as they do not determine it, and their practice has no necessary relation to the conscience. Yet because the Christian lives outwardly before others as well as inwardly before God, their indifference for one's own conscience does not mean they are indifferent to one's neighbor. Freed by faith from having such works reign over the conscience, the believer remains bound by love to let the needs of the neighbor reign over his outward conduct:

> A man does not live for himself alone in this mortal body to work for it alone, but he lives also for all men on earth; rather he lives only for others and not for himself. To this end he brings his body into subjection that he may the more sincerely and freely serve others. . . . Man, however, needs none of these things for his righteousness and salvation. Therefore he should be guided in all his works by this thought and contemplate this one thing alone, that he may serve and benefit others in all that he does, considering nothing except the need and advantage of his neighbor. . . . This is a truly Christian life. Here faith is truly active through love, that is, it finds expression in works of the freest service, cheerfully and lovingly done, with which a man willingly serves another without hope of reward; and for himself he is satisfied with the fullness and wealth of his faith.[12]

The freedom of a Christian is thus not so much a freedom *for* oneself, but a freedom *from* oneself, a liberation from the preoccupation with one's own salvation and merit, from fear that one is not toeing the line and meeting the standards; instead, he can actually focus on serving his neighbor. "No longer does he need to use his neighbor as party to some moralistic scheme of proving

11. *LW* 31:345.
12. *Freedom of a Christian*, in *LW* 31:364–65.

himself worthy," explains Bernard Verkamp. "Now instead, his love of neighbor can be genuinely altruistic."[13]

This focus on freedom for the neighbor protects Luther's teaching against the radical individualism for which he might seem to have opened the way. Indeed, precisely because the Christian man justified by faith understands the indifference of outward works, he should often feel no need to assert his inward freedom outwardly. If existing laws or circumstances constrain his outward behavior, he happily complies, knowing that he remains free before God. Since Christian freedom is an inner freedom that expresses itself in outward servitude, it is not nullified by external bondage, as Luther is careful to explain. "For a Christian, as a free man, will say, 'I will fast, pray, do this and that as men command, not because it is necessary to my righteousness or salvation; but that I may show due respect to the pope, the bishop, the community, a magistrate, or my neighbour, and give them an example."[14] Calvin later puts it even more sharply, asserting that if someone is obliged to abstain from meat for their entire life out of regard for their neighbor's weakness, they are not on that account any less free.[15]

In principle, then, the designation of a matter as adiaphorous did not mean that it must remain entirely unregulated by authorities in church or state, as we shall see in a moment, but merely that regulations must be based on the demands of order, decency, or love for the neighbor, not duty toward God or salvation of the soul. This was still a radical claim, however, directly undermining the medieval church's claims to make liturgical ceremonies necessary *media* of grace, and to withhold salvation on the basis of sins committed or penance omitted. Human rulers could still require certain conduct for temporal ends, but they could no longer insist that it was necessarily what God required. Any obligations with respect to adiaphora were contingent, not necessary.

This shows that although the leading reformers did undoubtedly protest against the quantitative multiplication of superfluous ecclesiastical ceremonies, their chief concern was with the qualitative claims about the status of such ceremonies. The call for freedom *in* things indifferent was thus not a call for freedom *from* things indifferent. This was not always clearly understood by their followers, however. Luther's colleague Andreas von Karlstadt quickly

13. Bernard J. Verkamp, "The Limits upon Adiaphoristic Freedom: Luther and Melanchthon," *Journal of Theological Studies* 36, no. 1 (1975): 57.

14. *Freedom of a Christian*, in *LW* 31:370.

15. Calvin, *Institutes*, 1:842 [III.19.10].

took the clarion call of Christian liberty much further than Luther intended, insisting that all impositions beyond Scripture must be rejected outright, a view we have already met with above in the strong regulative principle of worship advocated by Presbyterians like J. H. Thornwell. And just as Charles Hodge would complain that this kind of "liberty" was actually a new legalism, so Luther charged that Karlstadt destroyed freedom just as clearly as the papists did, only by forbidding instead of commanding in things indifferent.[16] The very indifference of the adiaphora, then, meant that to insist on one's external liberty in them would be to attribute to them more significance than they actually possessed, to make one's faith dependent again on externals. Of course, the Henrician conservative bishop Stephen Gardiner would complain that the magisterial reformers themselves erred just as surely as Karlstadt in this respect when they insisted on evangelical freedom for priests to marry:

> Tell me I pray you how these things agree in constancy and continuity of doctrine: we are by only faith justified and made acceptable to God, according to your doctrine, and yet a large part of our controversy bears upon food and wives. If those things do not pertain to justification, why do you who are reclaimed from the elements of the world contend about them, as if without them no happiness could find place in a Christian man?[17]

Karlstadt's example and Gardiner's complaint show just how difficult it was, from the very beginning, to hold the dynamic tension of Luther's doctrine in balance. For it was not the case that Luther was willing to deny that Christian liberty had any external expression—far from it. In *The Freedom of a Christian* he argued that toward "wolves" who urge ceremonies upon us as necessary, we "must resist, do the very opposite, and offend them boldly lest by their impious views they drag many with them into error. In the presence of such men it is good to eat meat, break the fasts, and for the sake of liberty of faith do other things which they regard as the greatest of sins."[18] He himself was soon to provide a particularly shocking example of this behavior in his marriage to Katerina von Bora. But then, in this same passage, Luther went

---

16. Verkamp, "Limits," 70.

17. Stephen Gardiner, *Contemptum humanae legis* (1541), in *Obedience in Church and State: Three Political Tracts*, ed. and trans. Pierre Janelle (Cambridge: Cambridge University Press, 1930), 195.

18. *LW* 31:373. See also Philipp Melanchthon, *Loci Communes* (1521 edition) in *CR* XXI:226; Calvin, *Institutes*, 1:843–45 [III.19.11–12].

on to advise just the opposite course of action before the weak in faith who needed to be initiated slowly into gospel liberty, just as Calvin spoke of the need to observe traditional fasts for the sake of the weaker brother.

This was precisely the difficulty with the doctrine—there were no fixed rules! The whole point, after all, was to be ready to respond as love demanded in concrete circumstances. Luther cites the example of St. Paul circumcising Timothy, so as not to offend the weak, while later refusing to circumcise Titus, so as not to give in to Judaizers.[19] Therefore, although he might issue some general guidelines, Luther could not establish *a priori* which response in the adiaphora would be right or wrong.

To this extent, it seems difficult to deny that Luther's teaching could have a tendency to favor individual liberty at the cost of institutional liberty; while the individual Christian's freedom may not be a freedom for himself, but one to be used on behalf of others, he alone remains the arbiter of how best to use it on behalf of others. Although Luther thought he had averted a clash of loyalties toward God and toward man by clearly distinguishing the inward relation to God from the outward relation to man, a new clash had now arisen within the outward realm: when to defer to authoritative determination about what is best for the community or institution, and when to insist on liberty to judge the concrete needs of one's neighbor. The magisterial Reformers would frequently attack Karlstadt and other radical Reformers as unprincipled, self-serving libertines, who perverted the doctrine of Christian liberty for their own pleasure, failing to understand that it was not a freedom *for* oneself. No doubt this was sometimes true, and many Protestants quickly twisted liberty into license. But this need not be the explanation for every form of radicalism. As we shall see with the Puritans, many who sought to assert their liberty externally did so with Luther's concern about "wolves" in mind, or else with the fear that weak Christians would be led into superstition; they were, as Luther taught, subordinating adiaphora to their desire to love and edify the neighbor. However, what about those weaker brothers who would be offended by such hasty rejection? How could one do justice to both? Far from removing the problem of uncertainty that dogged the late medieval conscience, Luther had merely displaced it from the realm of justification to that of sanctification. Faced with such uncertainty, the urge was to find a set of fixed rules to guide Christian conduct, even if such rules might tend to hinder the believer's ability to freely respond as circumstances seemed to dictate.

19. *Freedom of a Christian*, in *LW* 3:368–69.

There were two places to look for such rules: to God or to man. The former possibility has appeared already in an ambiguous line from *The Freedom of a Christian* quoted above, where Luther said that Christian liberty was grounded in submission to "the most holy word of God, the Gospel of Christ." While for Luther, the gospel is the substance of Scripture, so that even its moral laws serve chiefly to drive the believer to faith in Christ and free submission to him alone, other reformers were to increasingly emphasize the didactic function of Scripture as a moral guide for the believer's whole life.[20] Or to put it in other terms, for Luther faith embraced the gospel, and love embraced the law, whereas later reformers, and especially the Puritans, would tend to make the law itself, as part of Scripture, an object of faith. This shifting emphasis would tend to move the focus from Luther's soteriological construal of adiaphora, in which anything not essential for justification could be considered indifferent, to an epistemological construal, in which it was only those things left undetermined by Scripture that were indifferent.[21] Although this epistemological

20. The radicalism of the early Lutheran understanding of freedom in relation to the law is well displayed in Melanchthon's 1521 *Loci Communes* (*CR* XXI:194–206), where he speaks of the Decalogue itself having been abrogated (although the Spirit leads the believer to freely embrace the same things the Decalogue commands). Such an emphasis was absent from the Zwinglian reformation from the beginning, which always accented the need for moral reform based on rigorous obedience to Scripture (see Philip Benedict, *Christ's Churches Purely Reformed: A Social History of Calvinism* [New Haven: Yale University Press, 2002], 23–28; Bernard J. Verkamp, "The Zwinglians and Adiaphorism," *Church History* 42, no. 4 [1973]: 489–90), and a heavy accent on the *tertius usus legis*—the positive role of Scripture in the moral life of the believer—was to be an enduring distinctive of the Reformed branch of Protestantism. However, the emphasis could be found in Melanchthon as well from the 1530s on (John E. Witte Jr. and Thomas C. Arthur, "The Three Uses of the Law: A Protestant Source of the Purposes of Capital Punishment?" *Journal of Law and Religion* 10 [1993–1994]: 434–36; John Witte Jr., *Law and Protestantism: The Legal Teachings of the Lutheran Reformation* [Cambridge and New York: Cambridge University Press, 2002], 128–29).

21. Verkamp argues that to attribute to Luther this strong, solfidian doctrine of adiaphora, as did Clyde Manschreck, "The Role of Melanchthon in the Adiaphora Controversy," *Archiv für Reformationsgeschichte* 49 (1957): 165, and T. W. Street, "John Calvin on Adiaphora: An Exposition" (unpublished PhD dissertation, Union Theological Seminary, NYC, 1954), 255–56, is not strictly accurate, because Luther and Melanchthon did in fact insist on the necessity of good works for sanctification, good works that responded to what was commanded and forbidden in Scripture ("Limits," 53–58). Accordingly, Verkamp wants to restrict the definition of adiaphora, even for the early Luther, to those things "neither commanded nor forbidden" in Scripture, i.e., my "epistemological construal" ("Limits," 59–60). However, this is perhaps to be overly precise and miss the salient point about the Lutheran understanding of Christian liberty (even though Verkamp elsewhere shows a good understanding of the logic of the doctrine): justification meant that all works besides faith were to flow out of a free response

language could be used fairly innocuously, it could also take on a potentially radical dimension. After all, if Scripture tells us all that is necessary, and it is necessary for the believer to know what is edifying in the church and what is not, Scripture must provide guidance on all disputed matters, so that very little, if anything, can be said to be strictly "indifferent" in this sense.

The latter possibility, of seeking for rules in the decrees of human legislation, might seem to contradict the spirit of Luther's reform altogether. However, even if in his earliest reforming enthusiasm Luther had hoped for a purely voluntary community of true Christians, he very soon conceded the necessity of coercive authority in external church administration, and most of the other Reformers never doubted it. Although this has often been treated as a betrayal of the original genius of his two-kingdoms theology,[22] it was in fact a thoroughly consistent development of it, particularly given his strong emphasis on the believer as *simul justus et peccator*. For Luther, there would never be in the world a community of true Christians who were only true Christians—they would also be gross sinners, and as such, subject to the government of God's "left hand," exercised by force.[23] In all matters of the earthly regiment, within which of course adiaphora necessarily fell, the Christian might find himself subject to the constraint of law, even while remaining spiritually free before God. As the government of the visible church was taken to be part of the

---

of love, so that one was not bound by scriptural commands or prohibitions *as law*, but only as specifications of the law of love, to be applied as circumstances demanded. That is to say, both externals commanded by Scripture and those left free by Scripture were treated not as good in themselves, but good in respect of their end; the relationship of the conscience to them is the same. See for instance Luther, *Treatise on Good Works*, in *LW* 44:26. However, it is certainly the case that Zwingli's concept of adiaphora functioned more within the epistemological key from the beginning (Verkamp, "Zwinglians and Adiaphorism"), and this becomes the dominant articulation in the English Reformation (Verkamp, *Indifferent Mean*, 28–29).

22. Indeed, one of the chief burdens of Johannes Heckel's *Lex Charitatis: A Juristic Disquisition on Law in the Theology of Martin Luther*, ed. Martin Heckel, trans. Gottfried G. Krodel (Grand Rapids: Eerdmans, 2010), is to dispute the notion that the development of Lutheran state churches was an appropriate development of Luther's two-kingdoms doctrine. Cargill Thompson, *Political Thought of Martin Luther*, ed. Philip Broadhead (Brighton, UK: Harvester, 1984), ch. 8, offers a more qualified assessment, but with some of the same concerns. However, James Estes unequivocally puts this old claim to rest in his *Peace, Order, and the Glory of God: Secular Authority and the Church in the Thought of Luther and Melanchthon, 1518–1559* (Leiden: Brill, 2005), esp. 40–41, 66–68, 105–9, 202–4.

23. Cargill Thompson makes this point quite effectively against Heckel ("The 'Two Kingdoms' and the 'Two Regiments': Some Problems of Luther's *Zwei-Reiche-Lehre*," *Journal of Theological Studies* 20, no. 1 [1969]: 177–82).

worldly regiment, it would seem to have need of laws as well.[24] Such laws could indeed flow quite logically out of the demand to use adiaphora for edification, for as the reformers were quick to realize, peace and order were blessings not to be undervalued, and far more edifying than discord. So, although John Milton, like his fellow seventeenth-century dissenter Edward Bagshaw, was to ask "by what right the Conformists had changed the nature of adiaphora by submitting them to legislation,"[25] their conformist opponents were on firm ground in deeming adiaphora fit subjects of legislation. Luther's colleague, Melanchthon, had clearly argued as much,[26] and the nearly universal early Protestant practice of promulgating official liturgies and church ordinances, often backed by secular authority, confirms this conviction.[27]

The more difficult questions, which were to create substantial tensions as the Reformation wore on, were *by whom* and *with what authority* such ordinances were to be established. Many reformers were caught in a tension between their initial anti-clericalism, which saw as one of Rome's chief errors its granting of political and coercive authority to ecclesiastics, and their desire for an authentically evangelical church, directed by the ministry of the word rather than political machinations. The preference of many continental reformers, then, was for most "human precepts in the church" to be promulgated by ecclesiastical authorities with no strictly coercive force, but only as rules of good order, which it was rarely godly to flout, but which did not directly bind the conscience.[28] Nonetheless, they did not deny that some

---

24. See F. Edward Cranz, *An Essay on the Development of Luther's Thought on Law, Justice, and Society* (Cambridge, MA: Harvard University Press, 1959), 144–55; Witte, *Law and Protestantism*, 7, 110; Estes, *Peace, Order, and the Glory of God*, 41, 66–67, 107–8. More generally, see P. D. L. Avis, *The Church in the Theology of the Reformers* (Atlanta: John Knox, 1981), chs. 9–10.

25. Verkamp, *Indifferent Mean*, 132.

26. See Estes, *Peace, Order, and the Glory of God*, 65–68; Verkamp, "Limits," 172–74 (especially footnote 134, where he critiques Manschreck for attempting to drive a wedge between Melanchthon and the English reformers on this point), and Melanchthon, *Loci Communes* (1555 edition), ch. 34.

27. Verkamp has an excellent endnote (*Indifferent Mean*, 152n8) in which he offers citations from every major reformer, as well as a number of confessions, in defense of the idea of legislation of ecclesiastical adiaphora. For an overview of the promulgation of *Kirchenordnungen* (church ordinances) by political authorities during this period, see Michael S. Springer, *Restoring Christ's Church: John à Lasco and the Forma ac Ratio* (Aldershot, UK: Ashgate, 2007), 23–39.

28. See Melanchthon's *Loci Communes* (1555 edition), in *Melanchthon on Christian Doctrine*, trans. and ed. Clyde L. Manschreck (New York: Oxford University Press, 1965), ch. 34, and *Whether it be a mortall sinne to transgresse civil lawes which be the commaundements*

ecclesiastical precepts would require coercive imposition, and such force could only come from the magistrate. Melanchthon, indeed, would speak of the Christian magistrate as the *summus episcopus* in the church,[29] and by the 1530s and 1540s, this position of honor had been codified in many Lutheran cities, where civil authorities oversaw a wide array of ecclesiastical legislation.[30] Other continental reformers such as Bucer, Zwingli, Bullinger, and Vermigli showed much less reluctance at this point,[31] and even Calvin's position is rather more "Erastian" than is usually acknowledged.[32] To this extent, the difference between the continental and English reformers on the magistrate's authority over adiaphora, as we shall see, is more one of emphasis than of fundamental principle.

If ecclesiastical laws could be backed by civil authority, however, this endangered a key tenet of Luther's doctrine of Christian liberty, which had been to deny to ceremonies not only a "necessity of means" (an intrinsic necessity to salvation) but a "necessity of precept" (in which positive law could render them

---

of civill magistrates. The judgement of Philip Melancthon in his Epitome of morall Philosophie. The resolution of D. Henry Bullinger and D. Rod[olph] Gaulter, of D. Martin Bucer, and D. Peter Martyr, concerning thapparel of Ministers, and other indifferent things (London: Richard Jugge, Printer to the Queenes Maiestie, 1566), 3–16 (taken from his *Moralis Philosophiae Epitome* [1541], in *CR* XVI:109–16). Verkamp traces the tension on this point in the Lutheran and English reformations in *Indifferent Mean*, ch. 7.

29. Witte, *Law and Protestantism*, 137.

30. Witte, *Law and Protestantism*, 182–96.

31. For Zwingli, see Robert Walton, *Zwingli's Theocracy* (Toronto: University of Toronto Press, 1967), or Bucer, Bk. II of his *De Regno Christi*; for Vermigli and Bullinger, see W. J. Torrance Kirby, *The Zurich Connection and Tudor Political Theology* (Leiden: Brill, 2007).

32. Carrie Euler observes that the lack of conflict between Bullinger and Calvin on church government owes not merely to diplomacy, but to the fact that "he [Bullinger] and Calvin actually had much in common in their attitudes toward church polity and discipline. In fact, the structures of discipline in Zurich and Geneva were not that different. . . . [B]oth the Zurich and Genevan consistories reflected an overlapping of the secular and spiritual spheres" (*Couriers of the Gospel: England and Zurich, 1531–1558* [Zurich: Theologischer Verlag, 2006], 48–49). See also Jordan J. Ballor and W. Bradford Littlejohn, "European Calvinism: Church Discipline," in *European History Online*, ed. Irene Dingel and Johannes Paulmann (Mainz: Institute of European History, 2013). See Matthew Tuininga, *Calvin's Political Theology and the Public Engagement of the Church: Christ's Two Kingdoms* (Cambridge: CUP, forthcoming 2017), ch. 1, for a good survey of the various approaches to magisterial reform in the early Reformation, and ch. 2 for Calvin's approach in Geneva. Although Tuininga is at pains to stress the distinctiveness of Calvin's approach, he shows that the chief point at issue concerned the power of excommunication, which Calvin considered an extension of the ministry of the word; on ecclesiastical laws more generally, Calvin was much more flexible on the relative role of magistrates and church authorities (see ch. 5).

necessary to salvation).[33] For the reformers were unanimous in preaching a very high doctrine of civil authority and the Christian's duty before God to obey the magistrate. Romans 13:5, many argued, meant that the believer was conscience-bound to obey any laws commanded by the civil magistrate that were not contrary to Scripture, even to the point that disobedience was mortal sin.[34] More careful Protestant thinkers could thread the needle by emphasizing that it was only the end of the law, the divine rule of charity, that bound the conscience per se; the particular law, as a specification of charity in particular circumstances, bound only *per accidens*.[35] But the potential for tension at this point was undeniable, particularly when the demands of charity seemed to run counter to the demands of law, and the more forceful apologists for magistratical authority whom we shall soon encounter did little to ease troubled consciences with their peremptory declarations.

The concept of adiaphora, then, held great promise and great peril. On the one hand, it seemed a promising foundation on which to maintain a large space for corporate and institutional freedom, buffering the body politic against the fissiparous logic of the individual liberty of each Christian in the spiritual kingdom, and maintaining loyalty to the common good alongside loyalty to God. The Christian was free inwardly, but bound outwardly. However, although not automatically nullified by external constraint, this internal liberty clearly required some space for external expression, a freedom to act as love seemed to demand in the situation. By making Christian liberty a liberty to be exercised in charity, *for the common good*, Luther's reform left room for a renewed clash of loyalties. For who was to determine the common good? Prudence alone seemed a weak reed on which to rest contentious judgments on questions that soon engulfed the young Reformation churches. If Scripture was to be the guide, was it left to be interpreted by each individual believer, thus pitting individual liberty against institutional? Or was it to be interpreted by the proper authorities, the ministers, raising the specter of new papal tyranny? In either case, there was the risk that Scripture be reconceived as an exhaustive law-book, rather than a proclamation of the good news of forgiveness, shackling the conscience again to a new legalism. Some might instead

---

33. See the careful discussion by Verkamp, *Indifferent Mean*, 38–54.

34. See for instance Melanchthon, *Loci Communes* (1555), in Manschreck, *Melanchthon on Christian Doctrine*, 334; *Whether it be a mortall sinne*, 4–5, 9–10 (*CR* XVI:110, 112–14). For more examples see Verkamp, *Indifferent Mean*, 58n71.

35. Such appears to be Calvin's reasoning in *Institutes*, 1:847–49, 2:1193–94 [III.19.15 and IV.10.5]. Verkamp suggests that Calvin may have been unique, however, in recognizing the need for this sort of qualification (*Indifferent Mean*, 49–50).

insist that civil authority was to be the guide, even if it seemed sometimes to thwart the quest for godliness. To a certain point, it would be easy to argue that Christian love equaled submission to civil authority, since in a chaotic age, few things were more loving than the maintenance of peace and order. But in the end, must not human laws serve only as rules of thumb about what love might require in particular circumstances? No human ruler, according to Protestant teaching, wielded final epistemological authority over the conscience, so must not Christian liberty allow some room for the believer to disagree with and even disobey his ruler?

These tensions, I will argue in what follows, repeatedly reached a boiling point in the course of the English reformations. Although the conflict was starker here, due to the particularly forceful doctrine of royal supremacy and the duty of obedience that many English reformers articulated, similar tensions and conflicts were liable to emerge throughout Protestant Europe.

II. The Freedom of a Christian Prince: Adiaphora in the Early English Reformation

From its outset, the Henrician Reformation, the product of calculating royal policy rather than a monk's troubled conscience, was not overly interested in the freedom of an individual Christian, a doctrine that hardly seemed conducive to the safety of the state. It was a telling indicator of the future tenor of reform in England that Tyndale entitled his 1526 outline of Protestant theology *The Obedience of a Christian Man*, and Henry VIII's protest against papal domination was lodged on behalf of the freedom of a Christian prince, not so much his subjects. However, these obvious differences have led many scholars to underestimate the continuities between Lutheran and English treatments of liberty and authority, church and state; and as the conservatism of Henry's reign gives way to the more forthrightly Reformed churches of Edward and Elizabeth, we find striking parallels between debates on Christian liberty in England and those on the continent. In what follows we shall survey first the fairly authoritarian concepts of adiaphora voiced by Henrician theorists Thomas Starkey and Stephen Gardiner, and then turn to see how the tensions thus generated spawned conflict in the successive Vestiarian controversies of Edward and Elizabeth's reigns. In particular, we shall discern an increasing strain between the believer's liberty in adiaphora and the magistrate's liberty to compel obedience in adiaphora. We will also find a tension between different understandings of what Christian charity demands in the use of adiaphora, with some equating charity with civil peace and order, and others conceiving it in more dynamic and ecclesiological terms. Meanwhile, the ambiguity between a soteriological conception of adiaphora, concerned chiefly with what is indifferent *to salvation*, and the more narrow epistemological conception that focused on the limits of scriptural commands, was to help heighten the tensions.

The concept of adiaphora clearly played a central role in the theological defense of the Henrician reform, but scholars dispute just how much the concept owes to Lutheran sources. Whereas W. Gordon Zeeveld, followed by Quentin Skinner,[36] argued for political-theological continuity between the Lutheran and the Henrician Reformations, others have argued for sharp contrast. T. F. Mayer, followed by Glenn Burgess, has insisted that Henrician theorist Thomas Starkey's concept of adiaphora differed radically from the Lutherans.[37] When Starkey describes adiaphora as "all such things which by God's word are neither prohibited nor commanded, but left to worldly policy, whereof they take their full authority,"[38] Burgess contrasts this with the Lutherans, who used the concept "to indicate a sphere of liberty for Christians," not "an area where the civil authority was free to regulate matters as it chose. Indeed, Starkey goes so far as to say that, once adiaphora are determined by civil authority, then the people 'are to them bound, yea by the virtue of God's own word.'"[39] As we have already seen, however, this is not so contrary to Luther and Melanchthon as Mayer and Burgess suppose, given that they too recognized that the magistrate may have to take order in many adiaphora, and Christians are bound to obey the magistrate. However, the tension we noted above—that Christian consciences had been freed from clerical authorities in the adiaphora only to be bound again by civil authorities—is considerably sharpened in Starkey's exposition.

In fact, prominent conservatives such as Starkey and Gardiner were explicit in affirming that while adiaphora did not have a necessity of means, they

---

36. W. Gordon Zeeveld, *Foundations of Tudor Policy* (Cambridge, MA: Harvard University Press, 1948), 128–49; Quentin Skinner, *The Age of Reformation*, vol. 2 of *Foundations of Modern Political Thought* (Cambridge: Cambridge University Press, 1978), 88–108.

37. Thomas F. Mayer, "Starkey and Melanchthon on Adiaphora: A Critique of W. Gordon Zeeveld," *Sixteenth Century Journal* 11, no. 1 (Spring 1980): 39–50.

38. Thomas Starkey, *Exhortation to Unitie and Obedience* (London, 1540; facsimile repr., Amsterdam: Theatrum Orbis Terrarum, 1972), 6v.

39. Glenn Burgess, *British Political Thought: 1500–1660: The Politics of the Postreformation* (Basingstoke, UK: Palgrave Macmillan, 2009), 50–51, quoting Starkey, *Exhortation*, 6v. (I have modernized the language here.) But see Verkamp, *Indifferent Mean*, 132–33.

did have a necessity of precept, to the extent that they were not even soterio-logically indifferent once the king enacted them into law.[40] Starkey would go so far as to say, "For to the obedience of princes and of all other common orders and politic we are bound, after they be ones received, by God's own word and commandment. And such things as by their own nature be indifferent, are made thereby to our salvation necessary."[41] Gardiner, while not quite so forthright, argues the same against Martin Bucer in his *Contemptum humanae legis*: "But he who contemns [human law], what else does he do but rise up against the divine power, and fight with God?"[42] Bucer was protesting Henry VIII's reactionary *Six Articles* of 1539,[43] in which he decreed in no uncertain terms the continuance of traditional Catholic practice on key issues such as clerical celibacy, and went so far as to assert, as robustly as any Catholic might, that these things were binding by divine law. After this, Gardiner would not hesitate to tell Bucer that "by me marriage of priests was no sin before God till the King's Majesty made it sin before God."[44] Such a declaration would appear to collapse Luther's distinction between the two kingdoms, allowing tempo-ral laws to have eternal consequences, giving to man the power to change a believer's standing before God, a key part of what the doctrine of Christian liberty denied.

To be sure, Starkey and Gardiner could both employ very Lutheran lan-guage in their treatises, speaking of justification by faith alone, of Scripture's sole authority over things necessary to salvation, of the indifference of all external ceremonies and the hypocrisy and superstition that characterized so

40. Indeed, Daniel Eppley has argued that Christopher St. German ended up going even further, giving to the King-in-Parliament not merely the power to issue binding com-mands within the realm of things by nature indifferent, but to determine what was by nature indifferent in the first place (*Defending Royal Supremacy and Discerning God's Will in Tudor England* [Aldershot, UK: Ashgate, 2007], 61–141).

41. Starkey, *Exhortation*, 8v.

42. Stephen Gardiner, *Contemptum humanae legis* (1541), in *Obedience in Church and State: Three Political Tracts*, ed. and trans. Pierre Janelle (Cambridge: Cambridge University Press, 1930), 187.

43. For discussion of Gardiner's controversy with Bucer see Janelle's introduction to *Obedience*, xli–l.

44. *The Letters of Stephen Gardiner*, ed. James A. Muller (Cambridge: Cambridge Uni-versity Press, 1933), 491, quoted in Verkamp, *Indifferent Mean*, 50. Note that Eppley argues that Gardiner does not give to the ruler any power over the conscience (*Defending Royal Suprem-acy*, 32–41), but this appears to result from his failure to attend to the *Contemptum humanae legis* and his insistence on reading Gardiner's later conscientious protest against the policies of Edward VI back into his Henrician arguments.

many of them. Not only that, but perhaps more surprisingly, we find in both Starkey and Gardiner's works a heavy accent laid upon the principle of charity as the rule of all Christian conduct, the surest guide for the right exercise of liberty. But unlike Luther, these Henrician theorists see charity exercised primarily in passivity, rather than activity. To be sure, we must always use our liberty to edification, but for Starkey and Gardiner, nothing is so conducive to edification as peace, order, and decorum, and this means firmly subordinating individual judgment to authoritative determination.[45] Accordingly, in the *Exhortation*, having declared that the prince has divine authority to determine what ought to be done in adiaphora, Starkey admonishes believers to content themselves with clinging to the essential truths of the Christian religion laid down in the Creeds, and, apart from this, not to trouble themselves with trying to understand the justifications for various doctrines or practices, but instead to meekly follow the laws in such matters.[46] Like Luther, we have here a conscience freed of fear and worry about indifferent things, and called to subject itself in externals for the sake of charity. But while Luther would say that "O it is a living, busy, active, mighty thing, this faith,"[47] Starkey will tell us that faith consists in meek, passive humility. Luther's conscience never rests secure in its freedom, but uses it indefatigably to seek out how the neighbor can be served in every circumstance, thinking creatively about the right way to show charity as each situation demands, even if this risks impinging on loyalty to the prince. Starkey's conscience, however, passively contents itself with the decree of the prince, heedless of any offense caused to its neighbors, who have only themselves to blame for their lack of submission.

This might be a more stable basis for governing a commonwealth than Luther's version of Christian liberty, and does promise the believer greater certainty for how to act than Luther's paradoxical prescriptions. However, it is worryingly reminiscent of the Catholic doctrine of "implicit faith," in which believers did not need to understand biblical teaching themselves, but merely to trust in church authorities, who exercised intelligent faith on their behalf.

---

45. See for instance Starkey, *Exhortation*, 40v, 82r–82v; Gardiner, *De Vera Obedientia: The Oration of True Obedience* (1535), in *Obedience in Church and State*, ed. Janelle, 161.

46. Starkey, *Exhortation*, 7r–8v. This passage highlights the minimalist direction in which a soteriologically oriented conception of adiaphora could go, encouraging believers to concern themselves with little else once they had believed those things necessary for salvation. Incidentally, it also highlights the equivocation between such a soteriological conception and an epistemological one (which Starkey has just given two pages before, defining adiaphora as "all such things which by God's word are neither prohibited nor commanded").

47. Luther, *Preface to the Epistle of St. Paul to the Romans* (1546) in *LW* 35:370.

We will recall that Bancroft, in professing fifty years later to steer a golden mean between this doctrine and libertinism, had failed to clearly differentiate his position from the former. Inasmuch as the principle of voluntariety seemed to demand that to be genuinely free, Christian liberty must be intelligent and rational, grasping the goodness of a course of action and embracing it of its own accord, Starkey's recommended posture of default submission seems an inadequate exercise of liberty, even if motivated by charity.

As willing, then, as Luther and the other reformers were to admit the need for authority, law, and obedience in the midst of Christian liberty, these had remained secondary, necessary to help govern a liberty that had its seat in the individual. We may discern in Lutheran doctrine a dynamic tension between the liberty of the individual and the institution, a tension that could perhaps collapse into outright contradiction. The Henrician theorists, by using the doctrine of adiaphora to put institutional liberty front and center, achieved greater stability and consistency, perhaps, but at the risk of eviscerating evangelical doctrine. The liberty of the individual believer in adiaphora, although asserted at times, is never a central concern. Rather, we find a sense that the English church must be well ordered, that reform has to proceed from the top down by statute, and the leaders will decide what is edifying and what is not. This core difference in spirit, we shall discover, persists as we move through the English reformations, even though Gardiner and Starkey proved to be outliers, opposed by more Protestant-minded reformers in England, and soon superseded. Cranmer, Cromwell, and others articulated a more evangelical concept of Christian liberty, and denied the power of the king's laws in adiaphora over conscience (although precisely how this related to their understanding of Romans 13:5 remained unclear).[48] Nonetheless, even though the more evangelical strain gains strength and becomes increasingly explicit, the English taste for good order, civil concord, and lawful authority, and the conviction that these are edifying above all else, remains.

The ambiguity thus introduced, although it would come to dominate Elizabethan debates on adiaphora, could arise for any Protestant. For if one allows, as the Lutheran reformers did, that laws can be made regarding ecclesiastical ceremonies, and if the laws cannot be made on the basis that they are necessary to salvation or especially honoring to God, as the Reformers were keen to deny, then they must be made on the basis that they conduce to public good, civil order, etc.[49] But this ran the risk of instrumentalizing the church,

---

48. See Verkamp, *Indifferent Mean*, 50–53.

49. Gardiner mocked this distinction in his debate with Bucer, insisting that it was

completely subjecting it to political ends, as had often been the case in Henry VIII's reign and as Starkey and Gardiner seemed prepared to justify. However, if more positive and specific content is to be given to the concept of edification—e.g., that vestments encourage more reverent worship—this merely invites dispute over whether they are in fact edifying, and invites disobedience from those who beg to differ. In addition, if a rite is prescribed because it is particularly edifying, this might be taken as saying it has a particular spiritual efficacy, which in the minds of many, was too close for comfort to the Roman doctrine of ceremonies that had just been rejected. The two horns of this dilemma, coupled with the tensions we already observed above in the doctrine of adiaphora, were to lead to an anti-adiaphorist reaction, which although hinted at in Henrician writings such as those of William Turner and John Bale,[50] first boiled to the surface in the Edwardian period.

III. The Christian Man vs. the Christian Prince: Controversies over Adiaphora

The Edwardian Vestiarian Controversy

Under the boy-king Edward VI, who unsurprisingly proved much less self-willed than his obstreperous father, the pace of reform accelerated. With firmly Protestant leaders like Cranmer and Ridley at the helm, no longer could things like prayers to the saints be considered "things indifferent," things potentially edifying for the churches, as they were for Starkey and Gardiner. Although the initial struggles of the new regime were against conservatives who considered the pace of reform too fast, this was soon to change, as an influx of Protestant exiles from the continent and Scotland (Martin Bucer, Peter Martyr Vermigli, John à Lasco, John Knox, and others) brought a more advanced version of the Reformation with them. Many of these were men who of necessity bore more allegiance to the cause of Reformation than to any homeland or nation, who did not entirely share the English Reformation's overriding concern for civility, order, and structure.

However, the conflicts over liturgy, polity, and magisterial authority in the church that were to play out in the reigns of Edward and Elizabeth were

---

unworkable: "as if . . . subjects might ask from their prince, and inquire, why he decides this or that" (*Contemptum* in *Obedience*, ed. Janelle, 195).

50. Verkamp, *Indifferent Mean*, 68–71.

not, as is often implied, a uniquely English problem, the result of its hybrid liturgy and its Erastian polity. Rather, they reflected theological tensions and concerns shared by continental reformers, whose input was frequently solicited and frequently offered in debates over adiaphora, Christian liberty, and the *cura religionis*. Nowhere were the issues at stake more sharply outlined than in the successive Vestiarian Controversies, first in 1550 under Edward and then in 1565–66 under Elizabeth. In each case, it was in fact overenthusiastic Englishmen who raised the trouble, and the foreign reformers, rather than leading the radical charge, by and large sided with the authorities. In each case, the seemingly trivial question of what liturgical vestments should be worn became the occasion for profound tensions on the relation of conscience to authority, of the church to the civil magistrate, and of Scripture to both, to rise to the surface. In each case, the authorities readily enough won their case on the narrow question at stake, but by failing to entirely resolve the theoretical tensions, they enabled the seeds of further and more radical dissent to take root.

The first major "Puritan" test for the reforming government appeared in 1550 in the person of John Hooper. Hooper had spent several years in exile, having been dangerously in advance of the pace of reform during Henry's reign, and in the course of his peregrinations to centers of continental Reform, had imbibed a more thoroughgoing opposition to anything that looked like "popery" and a conviction that purity took priority over peace and order. When in 1550 he was offered the bishopric of Gloucester and refused to wear the prescribed episcopal vestments, the ensuing First Vestiarian Controversy brought the question of the nature and use of adiaphora to the fore. The government relied on foreign reformers such as Bucer and Vermigli, who shared Hooper's distaste for vestments, to convince him that they were nonetheless adiaphora, and should be patiently borne as such.[51] Of course, this did not entirely resolve the problem, for adiaphora, all agreed, ought to be used in accord with Christian charity, with the goal of edifying other believers; if a minister was convinced that they were not on the whole edifying, did he not have a duty to abstain from them? And if they were adiaphora, ought not the conscience to be free in these matters from the compulsion of law? The uncertainty that surrounded adiaphora allowed a seemingly trivial matter to become the stage on which the clash of loyalties, to God and to prince, would

---

51. See Verkamp, *Indifferent Mean*, 66–78, 149–51 for a brief narrative of the controversy and a thorough discussion of the issues at stake, and John Primus, *The Vestments Controversy: An Historical Study of the Earliest Tensions within the Church of England in the Reigns of Edward VI and Elizabeth* (Kampen: J. H. Kok, 1960), 3–67, for a fuller analysis. Torrance Kirby analyzes Vermigli's role in both Vestiarian controversies in *Zurich Connection*, 204–7.

play out. The Henrician theorists had emphasized the decree of the prince as the surest resolution to such uncertainty. But Hooper, with his more advanced Protestant sentiments, thought it better to fall back on the supreme authority of the Word of God, to which the reformers had taught that the church ought to conform itself, as much as possible, in its worship and discipline. But if directed by the Word of God, were these things really indifferent?

In explaining his position, Hooper highlighted the tensions. While acknowledging the existence of adiaphora in principle, John Primus observes that "he sets up demands which seem to nearly exclude the whole sphere of indifferent things."[52] To qualify as adiaphora, something must meet four criteria: (1) they must have their "origin and foundation in God's word"; (2) they must have the implicit sanction of Scripture; (3) they must have "manifest and open utility," and be "edifying"; (4) they "must be instituted with levity and without tyranny, and those that are not, are no more indifferent."[53]

In each case, we may note, as Verkamp does, that Hooper has transformed what were considered principles for the right *use* of adiaphora into principles for their *definition*. Accordingly, while Hooper denies that things indifferent have the "express sanction" of Scripture,[54] he insists in the first two conditions that we must be able to positively derive their indifference from Scripture, rather than treating scriptural silence on the issue as sufficient proof of indifference. (We will meet this argument again in Thomas Cartwright.) Likewise in the third condition, Hooper argues not merely that adiaphora must be *used* to edification, but that, if unedifying, they do not qualify as indifferent in the first place.[55] This point invites the question of what was to count as "utility" and "edification"—certainly for Hooper's opponent Nicholas Ridley, speaking for the magistrates and many of the bishops, the good order, stability, and continuity provided by maintaining the old vestments were of great utility and edifying to the people.[56] Yet such

52. Primus, *Vestments Controversy*, 17.

53. Verkamp, *Indifferent Mean*, 72–73.

54. "Expressum Dei verbum habeat quo se tueatur" (Constantin Hopf, ed., "Bishop Hooper's 'Notes' to the King's Council," *Journal of Theological Studies* 175-76 [1943]: 196).

55. As Verkamp points out, this condition involves Hooper in a contradiction, since he began by defining adiaphora as "a thing whose use is not profitable and whose non-use is not harmful" (*Indifferent Mean*, 72–73). Although John Primus tries to rescue Hooper from contradiction by suggesting that Hooper must in fact mean that edification is a condition for right *use* (*Vestments Controversy*, 26–27), Verkamp insists this misses the point that for Hooper, along with his ally John à Lasco, and Flacius in Germany, the usefulness of adiaphora became integral to their definition, and thus *prima facie*, rather than *ultima facie*, permissibility (*Indifferent Mean*, 73–76).

56. Primus, *Vestments Controversy*, 27–28.

merely civil edification was not what Hooper had in mind; ceremonies in the church must be spiritually upbuilding. In the fourth point, Hooper appears to insist that adiaphora must be free from legal compulsion; internal freedom must find external expression, and adiaphora be left to the decision of the individual conscience.[57] If so, then we find here the dynamic tension between inward and outward in Luther's statement of Christian liberty beginning to collapse.

Hooper's ideas, however, were certainly not new or unique. On the contrary, they had been voiced already in the midst of Lutheran Germany, by hardline reformer Matthias Flacius Illyricus, in opposition to Philipp Melanchthon. The context of the Lutheran debate was the imposition of the 1548 Leipzig Interim on Saxony in the aftermath of Charles V's triumph the previous year over the Lutheran princes at the Battle of Mühlberg. Although it appeared at first that Lutheran doctrine would be wholly proscribed, the Interim represented a victory of sorts for Melanchthon and other Wittenberg leaders, preserving inviolate the basic tenets of Lutheran doctrine, while consenting to the imposition of a wide array of traditional liturgical practices. Although Melanchthon disapproved of these and considered them a "harsh servitude," he accepted the ceremonies as in themselves indifferent, and hence subject to the prudential calculus of edification, which in this case required accepting the practices for the time being that the church might be preserved and the gospel still preached.[58]

It was not long before Melanchthon and the other conformists were denounced as traitors to the cause of the Reformation by Lutherans in other parts of Germany, some of whom had forsaken their home churches in refusal to submit to the "popish tyranny." Many insisted that the Interim "meant an end to Christian liberty,"[59] suggesting that Christian liberty *could* be nullified by mere externals, which Luther and Melanchthon had always denied. Flacius led the opposition to Melanchthon, and developed this claim about Christian liberty in the *Liber de veris et falsis adiaphoris* (1549).[60] In it he argued (antici-

---

57. See Primus, *Vestments Controversy*, 23–24, 29–30.

58. Manschreck summarizes the background of the controversy in "The Role of Melanchthon," 166–71. See also Verkamp, *Indifferent Mean*, 87–88; Verkamp, "Limits," 66. The fullest account of the controversy, though one that suffers from a rather partisan reading in favor of Flacius, can be found in Oliver K. Olson, *Matthias Flacius and the Survival of Luther's Reform* (Wiesbaden: Harrassowitz Verlag, 2002), 68–167.

59. Manschreck, "The Role of Melanchthon," 171.

60. Flacius's arguments are analyzed in Manschreck, "The Role of Melanchthon," 173–75, Verkamp, *Indifferent Mean*, 71, and Verkamp, "Limits," 66–68.

pating Hooper's fourth condition) "that all rites and ceremonies, regardless of how non-essential they are by nature, cease to be adiaphora when they become compulsory. Compulsion undercuts Christian liberty and destroys the church of God."[61] He also argued that "[i]n the present situation it is necessary to reject ceremonies and rites otherwise non-essential, for adiaphora in certain circumstances cease to be indifferent, *in casu confessionis et scandali*."[62] This was plausible as an application of Luther's teaching that before "Pharisees," those who cause Christians to stumble by making adiaphorous ceremonies necessary to salvation, it will often be necessary to openly disobey in order to demonstrate our liberty to those who would deny it; however, Melanchthon insisted that the authorities had not Pharisaically proclaimed these ceremonies necessary for salvation, but for civil order.[63] In any case, Flacius went beyond Luther in saying that with such Pharisaical imposition, these ceremonies had ceased to be adiaphora, so that defiance was *necessary*. We see here the impulse to simplify into universal rules what Luther had been content to leave as guidelines for conscience to apply as particular circumstances seemed to demand. Flacius was to take this further, arguing that we must distinguish between true and false adiaphora, the former being intrinsically edifying, and the latter unedifying.[64] Here we see the elevation of edification from a condition for the right *use* of the adiaphora into a condition for the *definition* of adiaphora.[65] This meant that the concept of "edification" no longer functioned within a prudential calculus on a case-by-case basis, on which individual Christians might differ, and in which concerns of civil order might be prominent. The effect of this was to attempt to remove the uncertainty surrounding the right use of adiaphora, an uncertainty that called forth a free and creative exercise of prudence, and to replace it with a rule-governed certainty that would circumscribe our options in advance. For Flacius, things are either edifying in themselves or they are not; God's Word provides us direction as to which are which; and only if they meet this condition are they permissible in principle. Of course, if they are edifying and are suggested in God's Word, are they really adiaphora, or are they in fact required? To be sure, while retaining the term, Flacius does render it largely obsolete, and it is perhaps no coincidence that

61. Manschreck, "The Role of Melanchthon," 173.

62. Manschreck, "The Role of Melanchthon," 173.

63. The difficulty of discerning whether the prince imposed a particular rite for "civil" or "religious" purposes, highlighted by Gardiner in his letter to Bucer, was to prove intractable here.

64. Verkamp, *Indifferent Mean*, 71.

65. See Verkamp, *Indifferent Mean*, 71–76 for a full discussion.

much of Flacius's support came from Lutherans such as John Epinus, who denied the notion in the first place.[66]

Flacius thus offered a threefold distinction—things prohibited *in se*, things prohibited by virtue of being unedifying ("false adiaphora"), and things that are edifying and therefore true adiaphora. A group of Hamburg pastors, influenced by Flacius's polemics, wrote a concerned letter to Melanchthon during the controversy, outlining the same understanding of three categories and asking him which category certain practices fell into.[67] Melanchthon's reply is brief and circumspect, but in listing what are and are not adiaphora he sticks with two categories only, leaving out the so-called "false adiaphora."[68] The ceremonies in question might be unedifying, he says, but that does not in itself compel their rejection, for it would be even more unedifying for pastors to desert their churches. In the use of adiaphora, prudence calls us to weigh all such factors in the balance before determining the course that love of neighbor and loyalty to God demand, even if that means living with uncertainty and disagreement.[69]

The controversy loomed large in the backdrop of Hooper's showdown with the Edwardian authorities. Verkamp has argued that Hooper (as well as John à Lasco, his ally in the First Vestiarian Controversy) had probably encountered Flacius during their time in Germany in 1547–49, while the controversy was raging.[70] Flacius's *Liber* would likely have been known by Hooper, and in fact would exert a significant influence on Elizabethan nonconformists, by whom it was reprinted fifteen years later at the height of the Second Vestiarian Controversy.[71] Hooper's establishment opponents also seem to have been aware of the relevance of the controversy, as the letter from the Hamburg pastors and Melanchthon's reply appeared in English translation in 1549.[72]

66. Verkamp, "Limits," 69.

67. *De Rebus Adiaphoris: Epistola Concionatorum Hambergensium ad D. Philippum Melanthonem, et Responsio Eiusdem* (1549), in Anthony Sparrow, ed., *A Collection of Articles, Injunctions, Canons, Orders, Ordinances, and Canons Ecclesiastical: With Other Publick Records of the Church of England, Chiefly in the Times of K. Edward VI., Q. Elizabeth, K. James, and K. Charles I* (London: Printed for Robert Cutler and Joseph Clarke, 1671), 9–19.

68. *De Rebus Adiaphoris*, 23–25.

69. *De Rebus Adiaphoris*, 27.

70. Verkamp, *Indifferent Mean*, 71.

71. Verkamp, *Indifferent Mean*, 71–72. Verkamp offers evidence that following its republication, the book was widely read and cited by Elizabethan nonconformists. See also Primus, *Vestments Controversy*, 138–39.

72. This is the *De Rebus Adiaphoris* cited above. The circumstances surrounding the

In any case, Hooper's protest revealed the presence of serious divergences in how the Protestant doctrine of Christian liberty and the adiaphora was to be understood. Was Christian liberty to mean primarily the liberty of each believer to determine what was edifying in the church (i.e., what was according to Scripture), without any external requirement, and to act accordingly, as Hooper believed? Or did it mean the liberty of the church (-state) to determine what the body on the whole required, which was most urgently unity and peace? Peter Martyr Vermigli, a continental reformer of impeccable Protestant credentials, defended the latter against Hooper, as we have seen already: "Truly, we must take good heed that we bring not the Church of Christ into such bondage, that it may not use anything that the Pope used . . . how shall we debar the Church of this liberty, that it cannot signify some good thing, in setting forth their rites and ceremonies?"[73] Hooper's conception of liberty thus opposes the Henrician doctrine of passive submission, which preserved corporate freedom at the cost of an authentically free individual agent. However, aware that an anarchy of individual convictions would seem to make common action in the church impossible, Hooper seeks to establish a certain rule for action in the Word of God. The danger here is that by invoking Scripture as a self-interpreting law code that will determine in advance our exercise of freedom, those of Hooper's persuasion substitute heteronomy for authentic liberty as surely as Starkey does. The full development of this biblicism, however, would have to wait for another round of controversy that would bring the tensions in the doctrine of Christian liberty into sharper relief.

The Elizabethan Vestiarian Controversy

Although Hooper himself relented after a few months, other such conflicts would surely have emerged in the Edwardian church if the nascent Reformation had not been suddenly cut short by Edward's death and Mary's accession. And indeed, exile did not put an end to conflicts over adiaphora, but inten-

---

translation and publication of this text are obscure, but the title page dates it in 1549, and Anthony Sparrow, editor of the *Collection of Articles*, has placed it between Cranmer's 1548 Articles of Visitation, and Ridley's 1550 Articles of Visitation, suggesting that it was published with official backing, for purposes of addressing similar debates in the Edwardian church.

73. Vermigli, letter to Hooper in Parker (?), ed., *A Briefe Examination for the tyme, of a certaine declaration, lately put in print in the name and defence of certaine Ministers in London, refusyng to weare the apparell prescribed by the lawes and orders of the Realme* (London: Richard Jugge, 1566), 32v, 33v.

sified them; many scholars have argued that the "troubles at Frankfurt," in which the exile church split over differences regarding the Prayer Book, can be regarded as the crucible of what was to become Elizabethan Puritanism.[74] On Elizabeth's accession, however, differences were temporarily put aside as exiles hurried home from Frankfurt, Zurich, Geneva, Emden, and other continental refuges, all hoping that Elizabeth's settlement would legally establish their concept of a "church purely reformed." Elizabeth, however, while probably of genuinely Protestant convictions, took rather more seriously than these zealous exiles the need to placate Catholic subjects at home and Catholic enemies abroad; this concern, coupled with her own taste for more ceremonial worship, meant that the resulting settlement disappointed the aspirations of nearly all her churchmen. Those with close ties to Zurich, however (who received most of the high-level ecclesiastical appointments), were on the whole more willing to adapt to these remaining imperfections than those who had resided in Geneva (who were largely excluded from preferment[75]), conceding indifferency of the unsatisfactory orders and ceremonies and the broad prerogatives of the magistrate in such matters.

However, it was former Zurich exiles Lawrence Humphrey and Thomas Sampson who were to take the lead among those opposing the imposition of the "relics of the Amorites," the popish vestments that Elizabeth and her archbishop Matthew Parker had prescribed in 1564. Hundreds of lower churchmen, unable to accept this apparel as indifferent, and certainly not as edifying, balked at the prescription. Elizabeth, wary of incurring the personal hostility of so many of her subjects, left it to her bishops to propound, enforce, and defend the vestments regulations. They undertook this task with some reluctance, but ultimately held their line. Although excoriated at the time and by many since as pragmatic and ambitious time-servers, willing to compromise their beliefs to maintain their position, a closer look at the writings of the period tells a different story.

In fact we find among the bishops of the 1560s an earnest attempt to grapple with the tensions of the principle of adiaphora, which required them to subordinate their own personal preferences, largely against the vestments, to their acceptance of the magistrate's right to command in things indifferent,

---

74. See for instance M. M. Knappen, *Tudor Puritanism: A Chapter in the History of Idealism* (Gloucester, MA: Peter Smith, 1963), ch. 6.

75. This was largely due to the politically disastrous timing of John Knox and Christopher Goodman's precipitous calls to revolution published in Geneva in 1558, just before Mary's death; Calvin's earnest protests that he had never endorsed such publications or ideas proved vain.

as Vermigli had done in the First Vestiarian Controversy. In this, they sought to privilege Reformed doctrine, maintaining the indifference of such outward ceremonies, over prevailing continental Reformed practice, which largely eschewed them. The disjunction between doctrine and practice meant that both sides in the Elizabethan controversy were able to portray leading reformers as being on their side, and both sides quickly took to the printing presses to publicize these testimonies. As none of the Edwardian foreigners had returned after Elizabeth's accession—Lasco and Bucer now dead, Vermigli and Ochino happily ensconced at Zurich—these opinions had to be mined from earlier writings or sought by correspondence.[76] We have already mentioned how Flacius's *Liber* was reprinted at this time; so was all the literature from the earlier Vestiarian dispute, including Hooper's, Ridley's, Vermigli's, and Bucer's contributions, and counsel was sought from Reformed leaders at Zurich, Geneva, and elsewhere.

The most decisive continental intervention was Heinrich Bullinger's answer to the letters of Humphrey and Sampson, who had expected him to endorse their cause. "Bullinger's reply," says Torrance Kirby, "landed like a bombshell"; "he sided unequivocally with [Archbishop] Parker and the Queen."[77] Bullinger sent a copy of the letter to his friends who were conformist leaders as well, and they promptly published it to score a propaganda victory against the nonconformists. This elicited another letter from a rather miffed Rudolph Gualter, Bullinger's assistant, who was keen to emphasize that neither he nor Bullinger was at all in favor of the vestments, nor of the harsh treatment that nonconformists had received; they would certainly prefer that such vestments be done away with, and that in any case, those pastors who objected should be allowed to follow their own consciences.[78] However, this preference did not change their stance on the key questions: Were the vestments in question adiaphora, and could they be legitimately required? Yes and yes.

In his letter, Bullinger staunchly resisted the Flacian logic that made its appearance in Sampson and Humphrey's questions.[79] When they worried that

76. The most thorough discussion, which analyzes all the major publications of the controversy, is to be found in Primus, *Vestments Controversy*, 71–147. See also D. J. McGinn, *The Admonition Controversy* (New Brunswick, NJ: Rutgers University Press, 1949), 14–23, and for a more recent discussion, Kirby, *Zurich Connection*, 203–20.

77. Kirby, *Zurich Connection*, 209–10.

78. This letter is reprinted in W. H. Frere and C. E. Douglas, eds., *Puritan Manifestoes: A Study of the Origins of the Puritan Revolt* (London: Society for Promoting Christian Knowledge, 1954), 41–43. See discussion in Patrick Collinson, *The Elizabethan Puritan Movement* (Berkeley: University of California Press, 1967), 80.

79. I have used here Kirby's reprint of Bullinger's letter in *Zurich Connection*, 221–33. It

any legal compulsion in the adiaphora meant an abridgement of Christian liberty, Bullinger replied by distinguishing the inward liberty of conscience regarding the necessity of a practice, and the outward constraint regarding its use:

> I answer that indiffering things may sometimes be prescribed, yea, and also constrained too, as I may term it, as touching the use, but not as of necessity, that is, that any indifferent thing of his own nature should be forced to a man's conscience, and thereby a kind of religion charged to his conscience. The times and places of holy assemblies, are rightly accounted to be indifferent: and yet if there be no order prescribed therein, I pray you what confusion and misorder would rise hereby?[80]

Bullinger granted that ceremonies must be used unto edification, but like Melanchthon, he worried that failure to submit to legitimate, even if misguided and oppressive, laws would prove more harmful than any use of the offending vestments could: "weigh with your selves, if ye refuse to wear a thing mere[ly] politic and indifferent . . . do you set your churches at liberty, when you minister occasion to oppress them with more and with greater burdens?"[81] In a situation where refusal to wear the vestments meant deprivation from their pulpits, surely they should recognize that edifying their flocks should mean accepting the vestments.[82]

When they wondered, again following the Flacian logic, whether something unedifying like vestments could even be indifferent in the first place, Bullinger seemed almost puzzled by the question: "Surely it seemeth to be an indifferent thing, insomuch as it is a mere civil thing, appointed for decency, seemliness, and for order, wherein is put no religion."[83] And when they asked, betraying the increasing biblicism in the nonconformist attitude toward ceremonies, "whether any new ceremonies may be increased, besides the express word of God?"[84] Bullinger replied, despite his own Swiss preference for a biblical minimalism in ceremonies, "I would have no ceremonies brought into

---

first appeared in English translation as part of the pamphlet, most likely assembled by Archbishop Matthew Parker, *Whether it be a mortall sinne*, 27–46.

80. Heinrich Bullinger, *Concerning thapparel of Ministers*, in Kirby, *Zurich Connection*, 229–30. See also his response to their first question, p. 225.

81. Kirby, *Zurich Connection*, 228.

82. Kirby, *Zurich Connection*, 231, 232.

83. Kirby, *Zurich Connection*, 228.

84. Kirby, *Zurich Connection*, 230.

the Church, but such as are necessary: yet in the mean season I confess that the laws touching these ceremonies, which perchance are not necessary, and sometime[s] unprofitable, may not by and by be condemned of wickedness."[85]

The final question they raise, however, highlights growing tensions within Reformed theology over the relationship of magistracy and ministry that the next few years of controversy in England would bring to a boiling point. Sampson had asked "whether the prince may prescribe anything touching ceremonies, without the will and free consent of the Clergy."[86] Bullinger, who had always been one of the foremost apologists for the Christian magistrate's *cura religionis*, his duty to oversee and reform the church, notes that if the prince had always waited for the consent of the clergy, then reformation might never have happened, and he cites Old Testament examples for the right of princes to reform religion. He would prefer that bishops be consulted, of course, but only in an advisory role; they must not claim for themselves any legislative authority: "Neither would I again have them challenge unto themselves that power, which they usurped against princes and magistrates in time of popery."[87] Bullinger's worry here presages the recurrent polemic of English conformists in the 1570s and 1580s that the Puritan assertion of clerical prerogative to prescribe ecclesiastical laws would result in a new popery.

It also reflects the growing tensions between Bullinger's Zurich and Geneva, where Theodore Beza was increasingly asserting the autonomy of the presbyterian ministry. Unsurprisingly, the anti-Vestiarians found a more sympathetic ear when they wrote to Beza asking for support.[88] His response, sent directly to Bishop Edmund Grindal in London, granted, like Bullinger, the *prima facie* indifference of the ceremonies under dispute, but he argued rather more strenuously that in the present case they could only be unedifying,[89] and he exhorted the bishops not to oppress their brothers' consciences. Most significantly, however, he ended by saying, "by what right . . . may either the civil Magistrate by himself . . . or the Bishops without the judgment and consent of their Eldership, of duty ordain anything, I have not yet learned."[90]

---

85. Kirby, *Zurich Connection*, 230.

86. Kirby, *Zurich Connection*, 232.

87. Kirby, *Zurich Connection*, 232.

88. See Collinson, *Elizabethan Puritan Movement*, 81.

89. Frere and Douglas, eds., *Puritan Manifestoes*, 47–52.

90. Frere and Douglas, eds., *Puritan Manifestoes*, 54.

IV. Unresolved Tensions

These growing ambiguities regarding the relative role of civil and ecclesiastical authorities can be discerned beneath the surface of conformist publications in the 1560s, despite the presence of common themes on the basic shape of Christian liberty and civil obedience. In 1566, Archbishop Matthew Parker had responded to a prominent anti-Vestiarian pamphlet by Robert Crowley with *A Briefe Examination for the tyme*.[91] That same year, he edited and published a collection of writings by continental Reformers relevant to the adiaphora dispute, which was headlined by a *scholium* from Melanchthon's 1541 *Moralis Philosophiae Epitome*, entitled "Whether it be a mortall sinne to transgresse civill lawes."[92] Around the same time also appeared a remarkable document, a set of theses on the subject of Christian liberty and related doctrines, generated by disputes within the Dutch Strangers' Church in London.[93] This raised fundamental questions about Christian liberty, adiaphora, and both ecclesiastical and civil authority, and led ultimately to a schism. The party who drew up the articles, led by Gottfried van Wingen, argued strongly for the spiritual nature of Christian liberty and the responsibility of individual Christians to submit to ecclesiastical and civil authorities when it came to the regulation of adiaphora. Van Wingen submitted it to the review of the leaders of Reformed churches in Heidelberg, Bern, Lausanne, Zurich, and Geneva, from which it received general, though not unanimous approval; Theodore Beza in particular suggested some extensive clarifying amendments. The final draft, incorporating many of these suggestions, was submitted to Grindal, who, as Bishop of London had jurisdiction over the Strangers' Churches. Pleased at its contents, seeing its relevance to the ongoing Vestiarian disputes, and recognizing its value as a pan-Reformed consen-

91. The attribution to Parker, it should be noted, is likely but not certain.

92. This text occupies pp. 3–16 of the pamphlet *Whether it be a mortall sinne*, and the original appears in *CR* XVI:109–16.

93. This was a church consisting of refugees from the persecution and fighting in the Netherlands. They were affiliated with a congregation of French refugees as well, under the leadership of Nicholas des Gallars, and maintained close ties to Beza in Geneva. The conflict that gave rise to the articles seems to have been complex, involving both disputes over baptismal liturgy and church government, and rising tensions, against the backdrop of the Dutch war of rebellion against Spain, on the legitimacy of resistance to magistrates. See Martin van Gelderen, *The Political Thought of the Dutch Revolt, 1555–1590*, Ideas in Context 23 (Cambridge: Cambridge University Press, 2002), 99–101, and J. Lindeboom, *Austin Friars: History of the Dutch Reformed Church in London, 1550–1950* (The Hague: Martinus Nijhoff, 1950), for a fuller account.

sus statement on these issues, he had it published.[94] Although both Thomas Cartwright and John Whitgift later refer to it in the Admonition Controversy of the following decade,[95] it has been neglected by historians of these English ecclesiastical disputes.[96]

On a great many points, it coheres closely with Parker's doctrine of Christian liberty in *A Briefe Examination*, and with Bullinger's response to Sampson and Humphrey. First, it clearly emphasizes the essentially inward character of Christian liberty, the freedom of a conscience justified before God by faith alone, rather than a license to do whatever we want in the sphere of outward action.[97] In this outward sphere, the designation of a matter as indifferent does not mean it is morally inconsequential, only that its rightness or wrongness is circumstantially dependent.[98] Accordingly, our outward liberty

94. At least, so claims John Strype, in his *Life and Acts of Archbishop Edmund Grindal* (1710; repr., Oxford: Clarendon, 1821). He explains that Grindal encouraged the Dutch congregation to make these propositions public, recognizing that they "might serve to satisfy those of the English Church in these days, that scrupled submission in the ecclesiastical appointments about the ceremonies. They were printed by Jugg, printer to the Queen's Majesty, in Latin and English" (190). However, I have only succeeded in locating the edition that appeared in 1647: *XXXII Propositions or Articles, Subscribed By severall Reformed Churches, and Concurred in by divers godly Ministers of the City of London* (London: Robert Ibbitson, 1647). Strype reprints the articles in Appendix XVIII to his *Life and Acts* (pp. 519–27), and I used his version in the quotations here. Noting that this version represents the articles after the incorporation of proposed amendments from Theodore Beza, R. W. Dixon offers the originals in Latin, with Beza's comments interspersed in translation (taken from Epistle 24 of Beza's *Letters*), in *History of the Church of England from the Abolition of the Roman Jurisdiction*, vol. 6, *Elizabeth, A.D. 1564–1570* (Oxford: Clarendon, 1902), 186–89.

95. *WW* 1:209; *SR* 65.

96. Although frequently noted by scholars of the early Dutch Reformed churches, the latest reference to this document, and the controversy behind it, that I found among English church historians is Dixon's discussion in *History of the Church of England*, 6:184–92.

97. Article I declares: "Christian liberty is not a wandering and unruly licence, by which we may do or leave undone whatsoever we list at our pleasure; but it is a free gift bestowed upon us by Christ our Lord; by the which, the children of God (that is, all the faithful), being delivered from the curse of the law, or eternal death, and from the heavy yoke of the ceremonial law, and being endowed with the Holy Ghost, begin willingly of their own accord to serve God in holiness and righteousness" (Strype, *Life and Acts*, 519).

98. Article V: "Indifferent things are called those, which by themselves, being simply considered in their own nature, are neither good nor bad, as meat and drink, and such like; in the which therefore, it is said, that the kingdom of God consisteth not; and that therefore a man may use them well or evil: wherefore it followeth, that they are marvelously deceived, which suppose they are called indifferent, as though without any exception we may omit them, or use them as often as we list, without any sin" (Strype, *Life and Acts*, 520).

must be used for the love of neighbor, and is limited accordingly. Parker argues similarly in *A Briefe Examination*, noting,

> As touching Christian liberty, the faithful man must know, that it is altogether spiritual, and pertaineth only to the conscience, which must be pacified concerning the law of God, and next well stayed in things indifferent. This liberty consisteth herein, not to be [held] and tied with any religion in external things: but that it may be lawful before God to use them or omit them, as occasion shall serve. This persuasion a godly man must always retain and keep safe in his mind: but when he commeth to the use and action of them, then must he moderate and qualify his liberty, according to charity toward his neighbour, and obedience to his Prince. So though by this knowledge his minde and conscience is always free; yet his doing is as it were tied or limited by law or love.[99]

This little conjunction, *or*, however, becomes the source of considerable tension and ambiguity. Are "law" and "love" two different considerations that may each constrain our actions for different reasons? The Dutch articles initially seem to suggest so,[100] and provide a separate discussion of each constraint. Article VIII begins, "Generally, the use of these indifferent things is restrained by the law of charity, which is universal," and makes this duty paramount, that "nothing, otherwise indifferent and lawful, be done, whereby thy neighbour is destroyed; or that anything be omitted, whereby he may be edified." Of course, as we have already seen, this raised the question of how the believer was to judge, in uncertain circumstances, how the neighbor was to be edified. The Dutch articles, unsurprisingly, point us to Scripture: "[J]udgment [must] be taken out of the word of God, what may or ought to be done, or not done."[101] This, however, raises the specter of

99. Parker, *A Briefe Examination*, 15v. He follows this passage with quotations from John Calvin and Peter Martyr Vermigli to demonstrate his continuity with the continental reformers on this point.

100. Article II: "Therefore, sith that he which is the Son of God is ruled by the Spirit of God, and that the same Spirit commandeth us, we should obey all ordinances of man (that is, all politic order, whereof the magistrate is the guardian), and all superiors, which watch for the health of our souls; yea, and that according to our vocation we should diligently procure the safeguard of our neighbour; it followeth, that that man abuseth the benefit of Christian liberty, or rather, is yet sold under sin, who doth not willingly obey either his magistrate or superior in the Lord, or doth not endeavour to edify the conscience of his brother" (Strype, *Life and Acts*, 519).

101. Strype, *Life and Acts*, 521.

private judgment, whereby individual liberty to judge what Scripture requires will clash with institutional liberty when the demands of love seem to come into conflict with those of law. This was certainly Parker's concern in response to Crowley: "Upon this universal sentence, 'That Christ's Ministers must build up and not pull down,' you determine that Vicars, Curates, and parish priests ought to admit no orders which may not manifestly appear unto them that they do edify; giving every man in his parish an absolute authority."[102]

Parker's solution was to argue, sounding a characteristically Lutheran note (and one we have seen also in Starkey and Gardiner), that the laws of the magistrate in adiaphora are in fact derived from the law of charity; law is a specification of love, and on this basis, carries divine authority:

> Whatsoever man shall decree, which by any means may make to the use of his neighbours, for that the same is derived from the rule of charity, as be laws civil, [domestic] statutes, ceremonies and rites which Christian men use, thereby to teach or hear God's word more commodiously, or to prayer, and about the Lord's Supper and Baptism, yea, and whatsoever shall be a furtherance to pass our life here more profitably and decently: that thing ought not to be esteemed as a tradition or precept of man, though by men it be commanded, but as the tradition or precept of God.[103]

Article IX of the Dutch articles proceeds in a similar vein, declaring that, "Specially, the use of these things is forbidden by ecclesiastical or civil decree." Clearly mindful of the need to explain how such human decrees can bind the conscience without abridging Christian liberty, the article goes on to say that although "only God doth properly bind the conscience of man," the magistrate or church may impose orders for the sake of edification that "do so far forth bind the conscience, that no man wittingly and willingly, with a stubborn mind, may, without sin, either do those things which are forbidden, or omit those things which are commanded."[104]

Of course, the implication of this line of reasoning, in which the law of love serves as the basis for the authority of civil laws, is that such laws cease to bind when, by virtue of circumstances, they no longer serve the cause of edification, and the believer may disobey them without sin. The Dutch

102. *A Briefe Examination*, 7r.
103. *A Briefe Examination*, 10r.
104. Strype, *Life and Acts*, 521.

article X draws this implication,[105] and article XI emphasizes strongly that human authorities must *only* make laws in adiaphora for the purposes of "edifying," "policy," or "ecclesiastical order."[106] Naturally, Parker is not so keen to endorse the logic of article X, warning against "perilous authority granted to every subject, to determine upon the Prince's laws, proclamations, and ordinances, that when they shall see them (many times otherwise than they are indeed) unprofitable, then shall they, nay they must not do and accomplish the same."[107] Accordingly, the subject must consider that once a law has been made, the offense that will come from disobeying it outweighs any other concerns of offense:

> In indifferent things, if law, for common tranquility have prescribed no order what ought to be done, a Christian man ought to have a great regard of his neighbour's conscience, according to S. Paul's doctrine. But if law foreseeing harms and providing quietness, have taken lawful order therein, offence is taken, and not given, when the subject doth his duty in obedience.[108]

Melanchthon, as a matter of fact, had argued similarly in his "Whether it be a mortall sinne," the text Parker had recently reprinted, contending that breaking civil laws "doth hurt, and troubleth common quietness; therefore in civil laws, respect of charity and offence is always of force."[109] But could the same be said of ecclesiastical laws? Given that the original function of the doctrine of Christian liberty was to restrain clerical tyranny and ease the burden of conscience in ecclesiastical ceremonies, some Protestants were clearly reticent to say so. Melanchthon had in fact expressly insisted that "the binding is unlike":[110] whereas ecclesiastical laws bound *only inasmuch* as circumstances dictated, and could be disobeyed without sin if there was no offense or stub-

---

105. "And sith these things are not ordained simply for themselves, but in respect of certain circumstances, not as though the things themselves were of their own nature unlawful things (for it belongeth only to God to determine this) in case those circumstances do cease, and so be that offence be avoided as near as we can, and that there be no stubborn will of resisting; no man is to be reproved of sin, which shall do otherwise than those ordinances" (Strype, *Life and Acts*, 521).

106. Strype, *Life and Acts*, 522.

107. *A Briefe Examination*, 14r.

108. *A Briefe Examination*, 10v.

109. *Whether it be a mortall sinne* 12 (CR XVI:114).

110. *Whether it be a mortall sinne*, 11 (CR XVI:113).

bornness (precisely the standard given in the tenth Dutch article), civil laws, it seemed, always bound the conscience. But why? Although he later suggests that in the case of civil laws, disobedience would always, as a matter of fact, cause offense, he initially states: "Touching obedience due to the civil laws, Paul sayeth, we must obey, not only for fear of vengeance, but also for conscience' sake. This commandment bindeth us even without matter of offence; for we must obey the authority of God, though no offence be given."[111] The voice of the magistrate is the voice of God, full stop. Melanchthon certainly does not wish to say the same of the minister, and therefore takes a more moderate line on ecclesiastical laws; however, he does not explain in this text how the believer is to understand laws proceeding from *civil* authority, imposed for *civil* reasons, but regulating *ecclesiastical* matters. This was the dilemma he was to face seven years later in the Adiaphora Controversy, and of course the dilemma that Elizabethan churchmen were facing.

As Parker reprinted Melanchthon's *scholium* without commentary, we can only guess at how he intended to apply it. Unlike Melanchthon, Parker does not seem to have viewed ecclesiastical ceremonies and laws of civil order as fundamentally different in nature; both can bind the believer for the sake of good order.[112] Although he reasons more along the lines that Melanchthon uses for ecclesiastical law (emphasizing that these laws indirectly bind the conscience by virtue of the demands of charity, rather than appealing directly to Romans 13:5), he does not seem to contemplate the possibility of occasional disobedience, as Melanchthon and the Dutch articles do.

The ambiguity here was fatal, given the conviction we have already seen from Sampson, Humphrey, and Beza of a certain clerical autonomy in the matter of ecclesiastical ceremonies.[113] For, although we have discussed the problem thus far in terms of individual vs. institutional liberty, and this is clearly how figures like Parker saw it, we have now seen the emergence of rhetoric that suggests a clash of institutions. The concern for "*eutaxia*, that is, seemly order,"[114] after all, was one that could be found just as much in John Calvin as in Tudor bishops. None of the reformers wanted individual freedom

---

111. *Whether it be a mortall sinne*, 9–10 (CR XVI:112).

112. He draws an express analogy between the way they function in *A Briefe Examination*, 12r–12v. Primus draws attention to the ambiguity in Parker's use of Melanchthon in *Vestments Controversy*, 140.

113. Indeed, Primus notes that in their response to Bullinger's letter, Humphrey and Sampson "objected strenuously to Bullinger's regarding the vestments issue as a mere *civil* matter when it so obviously relates to *ecclesiastical* polity" (*Vestments Controversy*, 131n60).

114. Parker, *A Briefe Examination*, 12v.

for every believer to do as he or she liked in matters of worship or discipline; this was self-evidently unedifying. In his *Institutes*, accordingly, Calvin makes very clear that in its external form as part of the civil kingdom, the church, like any human society, requires a "form of organization . . . to foster the common peace and maintain concord."[115] In explaining the authority of such rules, he argues very similarly to the Dutch articles, explaining that in framing such laws, ministers do not lay down new laws binding on the conscience before God, but rather "the divine and eternal command of God not to violate love,"[116] specified for particular circumstances, beyond which it does not bind. Unlike Melanchthon, Calvin extends the same kind of reasoning to civil laws, recognizing the need to carefully navigate the relationship between Romans 13:5 and the principle of Christian liberty: "Moreover, the difficulty [of defining conscience] is increased by the fact that Paul enjoins obedience toward the magistrate, not only for fear of punishment, but for conscience' sake. From this it follows that consciences are bound by civil laws. But if this were so, all that we said a little while ago and are now going to say about spiritual government would fall."[117] Therefore, the same restrictions must reply to both: "[H]uman laws, whether made by magistrate or by church, even though they have to be observed (I speak of good and just laws), still do not of themselves bind the conscience. For all obligation to observe laws looks to the general purpose, but does not consist in the things enjoined."[118] But when he spells out this "general purpose" by reference to "God's general command, which commends to us the authority of magistrate,"[119] we have to ask whether God similarly ratifies the authority of the minister. Calvin himself suggests the two are parallel, and the Dutch articles on Christian liberty had, quite strikingly, put God's command to obey "all superiors which watch for the health of our souls" on the same par as his command to obey "all politic order, whereof the magistrate is the guardian,"[120] and it was, after all, a protest against the *ministers* of the Strangers' Church that had prompted these articles. Indeed, in Article XX, we find the parallelism made explicit: "In the Church of Christ, that is to say, in the house or city of the living God, the Consistory, or fellowship of governors, con-

---

115. Calvin, *Institutes*, 2:1205 [IV.10.27]. It should be noted that this line of argument contradicts VanDrunen's reading of Calvin, in which the visible church, *qua* institution, is identified with the spiritual kingdom, such that all its laws must derive directly from Scripture.

116. Calvin, *Institutes*, 2:1200–1201 [IV.10.22].

117. Calvin, *Institutes*, 1:848 [III.19.15].

118. Calvin, *Institutes*, 2:1183 [IV.10.5].

119. Calvin, *Institutes*, 2:1183–84 [IV.10.5].

120. Article II (Strype, *Life and Acts*, 519).

sisting of the Ministers of the word, and of Seniors lawfully called, sustaineth the person of the universal Church in ecclesiastical government, even as every magistrate in his commonwealth."[121]

With such tensions evident within the very documents that were employed by conformist leaders to quell the anti-Vestiarian dissenters, it is not surprising that the controversy was not long resolved. Although most of the dissenting ministers conformed, the murmurings of discontent were soon to lead in a more radical direction, one presaged by the more clericalist strand of the Reformed that we have here encountered. In pitting the institutional liberty of the ministers against that of the prince, however, these dissenters would increasingly deemphasize it as an adiaphoristic liberty. After all, the Protestant polemic against arbitrary clerical authority to make new laws for the church was not soon forgotten. The authority of ministers was to be an interpretive authority, bound to the word of God, which was the only sure guide as to what should or should not be done in the adiaphora. Yet increasingly, this authority was to acquire judicial, rather than merely epistemic weight. The need for certainty, confronted with the contradictory demands upon the believer to use the adiaphora to edification, rather than to destruction, had prompted the call for a new authority who would adjudicate the conflict of loyalties by recourse to Scripture, which could, after all, be relied upon to tell us all that was necessary. Of course, it also followed then that if such a judging authority was itself necessary, Scripture must have told us about it. It was thus possible to argue that church polity was not a matter of indifference after all, that divine law in fact required an autonomous, scripturally regulated clerical jurisdiction with responsibility for all ecclesiastical affairs. Needless to say, such a resolution, far from resolving the conflict of loyalties, simply transposed the locus of the conflict and heightened the stakes.

121. Strype, *Life and Acts*, 524.

CHAPTER THREE

"Exact Precise Severity"

The Puritan Challenge to Prince and Conscience

> The greatest liberty and freedom of Christians is to serve the Lord
> according to his revealed will, and in all things to hang upon his
> mouth.
>
> Thomas Cartwright, "Second Replie to Whitgift"[1]

I. The Beginnings of a New Movement

Between 1567 and 1572, the Elizabethan Church entered upon a decisive new
stage, engendering a movement that was to leave a wide and lasting legacy
on the Reformed world over succeeding centuries, particularly in Britain
and America, a movement traditionally known as "Puritanism." Although a
number of scholars have quite helpfully traced lines of development for the
Puritan movement back to the Marian exile, or the Edwardian reform, or even
the Henrician period (lines we have to some extent followed in the previous
chapter),[2] there is wisdom in the preference among contemporary scholars to

---

1. *SR* 442.30–32.

2. Among older scholarship, M. M. Knappen's *Tudor Puritanism: A Chapter in the
History of Idealism* (Gloucester, MA: Peter Smith, 1963) sees fit to begin the story with William Tyndale back in 1524, thus losing for the term in clarity what it gains in context. More
careful, and quite helpful, is Verkamp's *Indifferent Mean*, which traces the roots of the Puritan
attitude toward adiaphora back into the reigns of Edward and Henry. The connection between
Elizabethan Puritanism and some of the radicalism engendered during the Marian exile is
undeniable, and is particularly helpfully treated in Joan Lockwood O'Donovan, *Theology of
Law and Authority in the English Reformation*, Emory University Studies in Law and Religion
1 (Atlanta: Scholars, 1991), 91–108.

confine the term to the Elizabethan era and beyond. Indeed, even the Elizabethan Vestiarian Controversy, despite its central importance to the development of the new movement, represents more of a prologue to "Puritanism" than its first chapter. A great deal seems to have changed between the conclusion of this controversy in 1567 and the outbreak of the Admonition Controversy in 1572, when young radicals John Field and Thomas Wilcox, frustrated by the lack of official response to reforming overtures and complaints, published and disseminated a scandalously rancorous *Admonition to Parliament*.

The document, clearly intended (despite its name) as a piece of public propaganda,[3] ignited a firestorm of controversy: Field and Wilcox were imprisoned, an official *Answere* by John Whitgift was commissioned, and battle lines were drawn as pamphlets and counter-pamphlets, treatises and counter-treatises, began to multiply. The immediate literary controversy, in which Whitgift emerged as the spokesman for the establishment, and Thomas Cartwright as the spokesman for the Puritans, lasted until 1577, but the movement that the *Admonition* called into being lasted in organized form until the early 1590s, when it had grown so militant that the bishops and Privy Council took dramatic steps to quash it. The cast of this new act in the drama, however, were quite different from those who had fought it out with the bishops over vestments in 1565–67, most of whom had grudgingly submitted when it was clear the policy was inflexible. Of the twenty scrupulous Protestants who presented a supplication to the bishops over vestments in 1565, only three, says Patrick Collinson, "remained staunch to the radical cause until their deaths," and most "at once dissociated themselves from the new extremism." So much so, in fact, that from 1572 on, "we are evidently witnessing the beginnings of a new movement rather than the conversion of the old."[4]

And indeed, the issues at stake in the Admonition Controversy are far different, and broader, than those in the Vestiarian. No longer is the question one of the legitimate scope for resisting imposition of certain ceremonies that troubled scrupulous consciences, a dispute on the margins of the Elizabethan settlement, but it concerns the basic validity of that settlement in its essential features. "We in England are so far off from having a church rightly reformed, according to the prescript of God's word, that as yet we are not come to the outward face of the same," the *Admonition* fulminates,

3. See the discussion in W. H. Frere and C. E. Douglas, eds., *Puritan Manifestoes: A Study of the Origins of the Puritan Revolt* (London: Society for Promoting Christian Knowledge, 1954), xii–xvii; Patrick Collinson, *The Elizabethan Puritan Movement* (Berkeley: University of California Press, 1967), 118–20.

4. Collinson, *The Elizabethan Puritan Movement*, 75, 120.

throwing down a gauntlet to the bishops and the government.[5] At stake now is not whether the bishops should enforce strict conformity, but whether the bishops have power to govern the church at all; not whether civil law should presume to bind ministers to wear the cap and surplice, but whether civil authority has any role in determining ceremonies. A fundamental platform of the *Admonition* is the presbyterian doctrine of church government, which, aside from a general sense that lower clergy ought to have more authority in determining church affairs, had been nowhere on the radar in the earlier controversy. This system of polity is not presented as a suggestion, as that best suited to the edification and good government of the churches, but as a biblical requirement. This emphasis reflects a shift in attitudes toward adiaphora across the board, with the new admonitionists suggesting not so much that indifferent ceremonies were being used unedifyingly, but that they were not indifferent in the first place.[6] Earlier protests against tyranny in adiaphora, and suggestions that only Scripture could guide us to their right use, hardly seem to provide a basis for these aggressive new claims. So how do we account for this shift?

We have seen in the last chapter how dissenters in the 1560s, faced with insoluble crises of conscience, began to gravitate toward the idea of an independent ministry with final interpretive authority. Beza's presbyterian Geneva was a natural place to draw support for such a conception, all the more so given that the bishops, as unwilling but seemingly tyrannical enforcers of Elizabeth's policy, had completely lost their credibility during the Second Vestiarian Controversy. Passionately loyal to their sovereign and seeking a scapegoat, the dissenters grew increasingly hostile to the very idea of episcopacy, and began to look to presbyterianism as an attractive alternative.[7] The intense need for certainty, for authoritative guidance that would dictate the shape of the church, meant that the justification for this presbyterianism must be sought directly in Scripture. Accordingly, Beza's doctrine, a hardened and

---

5. John Field and Thomas Wilcox, *An Admonition to Parliament*, in *Puritan Manifestoes*, 9. This sentence was quickly amended in the second edition of the *Admonition* to the somewhat more moderate, "as yet we are *scarce* come to the outward face of the same"; but the damage was done—conformists would hereafter charge the Presbyterians with denying that the church of England was a true church.

6. Collinson, *Elizabethan Puritan Movement*, 105.

7. On the bishops' reluctance to enforce the Queen's policies, see Diarmaid MacCulloch, *The Later Reformation in England, 1547–1603* (Basingstoke, UK: Palgrave Macmillan, 2001), 30–31. On the resulting scapegoating of the bishops, see Frere and Douglas, *Manifestoes*, x; Collinson, *Elizabethan Puritan Movement*, 115.

doctrinaire version of that which Calvin had pioneered,[8] was taken up by some of those dissatisfied with the ineffectual protests of the 1560s. Its chief exponent was Thomas Cartwright, who made a name for himself by expounding the presbyterian system in a series of lectures on Acts at Cambridge in 1570. However, it is not enough to explain Cartwright's presbyterianism simply as the application of Genevan ideas to England, as has been customary among many historians.[9] On the contrary, with Cartwright and his associate Walter Travers, we find a systematic development of presbyterianism, along with a distinctive version of the two-kingdoms doctrine, that went beyond anything Beza had yet articulated and indeed likely exerted an influence on his own crystallization of presbyterian doctrine.[10] Certainly, as we shall see at points, Cartwright's views on adiaphora, law in Scripture, and the two kingdoms go well beyond those of his hero Calvin, with whom he has too often been simply equated.

To be sure, such men as Cartwright and Travers represented a fairly radical point (although certainly not the most radical) along a spectrum of advanced Protestant dissent in Elizabethan England, and we must avoid casting all of Elizabethan Puritanism in their mold. However, conformist apologists such as Whitgift and Hooker were hardly being arbitrary in singling out their works for critique, recognizing in these writings a logic dangerous to the liberty of the English church. So we find that in Cartwright's exchange with Whitgift we can discern the theological anxieties at the root of the Puritan protest in this period. These anxieties manifest themselves in part in the biblicism so often seen as a hallmark of Puritanism, and also in the Puritan erosion of magisterial authority in favor of an independent presbyterian jurisdiction, commonly noted by historians of political thought. But these are merely symptoms. Nearer to the heart of the problem was the Puritan concern

8. That Beza, rather than Calvin, is responsible for the emergence of a *jure divino* concept of presbyterianism, has been increasingly recognized by scholars; the fullest exposition can be found in Tadataka Maruyama, *The Ecclesiology of Theodore Beza: The Reform of the True Church* (Geneva: Librairie Droz, 1978).

9. So we find Knappen in *Tudor Puritanism* setting the stage with a chapter entitled "The Genevan Model and Its Propagandists" (134–48). See also Stephen Brachlow, *The Communion of Saints: Radical Puritan and Separatist Ecclesiology, 1570–1625* (Oxford: Oxford University Press, 1988), 36–37, and more nuanced statements in Collinson, *Elizabethan Puritan Movement*, 109–13 and Peter Lake, *Anglicans and Puritans? Presbyterianism and English Conformist Thought from Whitgift to Hooker* (London: Unwin Hyman, 1988), 3–4.

10. Anthony Milton, "Puritanism and the Continental Reformed Churches," in *The Cambridge Companion to Puritanism*, ed. John Coffey and Paul C. H. Lim (Cambridge: Cambridge University Press, 2008), 116.

for "visible saints," a zeal to move beyond an understanding of justification by faith alone that seemed to license apathy and complacency and in its place to cultivate a more dynamic spirituality.[11]

I will suggest in section II, therefore, that this concern served to intensify the crisis of conscience posed by adiaphora by again vesting temporal matters with eternal significance. Underlying all of this, however, are the tensions regarding the doctrines of Christian liberty and the adiaphora, the clash of loyalties and the quest for certainty, that we have discerned in the previous two chapters. Understanding this will enable us to see the conformist critique of Puritanism as motivated, in part at least, by a desire to protect their own understanding of the magisterial Protestant doctrine of Christian liberty.

From this standpoint, I will argue in section III, we can gain a new clarity about the exact motivation and nature of Puritan biblicism, which is best understood not as a distinctive concept of *how authoritative Scripture was*, but of *how Scripture exercised its authority*—namely, in such a way as to minimize the need for human prudence. The new understanding was to be summed up by Thomas Cartwright at the conclusion of his *Second Replie*: "It is the virtue of a good law to leave as little as may be in the discretion of the judge."[12] Dwight Bozeman has captured this emphasis in his book *The Precisianist Strain*, where he identifies the theme of "preciseness," a "zest for regulation," as lying at the heart of both Puritan theology and piety:

> A primary attribute of the deity they served, "exact precise severitie" was equally a habit and credential of his people. "Walke precisely, or exactly, or strictly in all things," enjoined John Preston in a sermon, "Exact Walking."
> ... To *"walk exactly*," this eminent preacher and college head explained, is

---

11. See Brachlow, *Communion of Saints*, ch. 3; Edmund Morgan, *Visible Saints: The History of a Puritan Idea* (New York: New York University Press, 1963), ch. 1.

12. *SR*, Appendix, i.21–22 (cf. p. 94). Classics scholars will recognize this as a quotation from Aristotle's *Rhetoric* I.1.7, which might seem rather jarring given Hooker's commitment to an Aristotelian theory of action and judgment in his critique of Puritan ideas of law. However, the irony of Cartwright's reference to Aristotle here is that it has the opposite effect of what Aristotle intended, for whereas Aristotle aims to vest authority in human *legislators*, rather than in judges applying legislation, Cartwright intends to remove authority from human legislators to vest it in divine legislation: "Whereupon the argument of authority of the Scripture is good; but naught from men" (i.25–26). See also Aristotle's discussion of equity in *Nicomachean Ethics* V.10, and his famous introductory pronouncement that "it is the mark of an educated man to look for precision in each class of things just so far as the nature of the subject admits" (*NE* I.3), a theme central to Hooker's attack on precisianism. Thanks to my assistant Brian Marr for highlighting this allusion for me.

to "go to the extremity." It is "so to keepe the commandements . . . that a man goes to the utmost of them, . . . lookeing to every particle of them."[13]

To be sure, such generalizations about Puritanism have become hotly contested in the scholarship of the past few decades, with some arguing against the usefulness of the term altogether and insisting that Puritanism is little more than a polemical construct by paranoid opponents.[14] Most have retained the term, while acknowledging that the distinctiveness of Puritanism lay less in definable doctrinal distinctive, more in its "culture," an "ethos," or "*mentalité*"—one dominated by a conviction of the transformative power of God's law in individual, church, and society.[15] But of course, such an ethos naturally existed along a spectrum, and recent scholars have preferred to emphasize the more moderate and mainstream points along that spectrum, rather than the troublemakers who preoccupied Whitgift, Hooker, Bancroft, and earlier generations of historians.[16] This study constitutes something of a corrective

13. Dwight Bozeman, *The Precisianist Strain: Disciplinary Religion & Antinomian Backlash in Puritanism to 1638* (Chapel Hill: University of North Carolina Press, 2004), 5, quoting Preston, *Sermons Preached before His Maiestie* . . . (London: Eliot's Court Press and R. Young, 1630), 108–9. Bozeman does not mean by this to resurrect the stereotype of Puritan as mere nitpicker, preoccupied by a merely negative agenda of removing offenses that trouble his trivial scruples. John Coolidge, echoed by Peter Lake, has rightly attacked this image, emphasizing the very positive vision of reform that drove precisians of all stripes (Coolidge, *The Pauline Renaissance in England: Puritanism and the Bible* [Oxford: Clarendon, 1970], especially ch. 2; Peter Lake, *Moderate Puritans and the Elizabethan Church* [Cambridge: Cambridge University Press, 1982], 2–3). But contrary to Coolidge's sometimes rosy-spectacled revisionism, this positive reform was to be conducted at every point according to strictly predefined rules, under the watchful eye of a rule-loving God.

14. Foremost among these has been Patrick Collinson, though in more recent writings such as "Antipuritanism," in *Cambridge Companion to Puritanism*, and in *Richard Bancroft and Elizabethan Anti-Puritanism* (Cambridge: Cambridge University Press, 2013), he has softened these claims somewhat. For good surveys of recent developments in this debate over terminology, see especially Lake and Fincham's "Introduction: Puritanism, Arminianism, and Nicholas Tyacke" to *Religious Politics in Post-Reformation England* (Woodbridge: Boydell, 2006), Lake's article "Antipuritanism: The Structure of a Prejudice," in the same volume, and Lake's essay, "The Historiography of Puritanism," in *Cambridge Companion to Puritanism*, 346–72.

15. These terms are proffered by Christopher Durston and Jacqueline Eales in "The Puritan Ethos, 1560–1700," in *The Culture of English Puritanism: 1560–1700*, ed. Durston and Eales (New York: St. Martin's, 1996), 9. The essays in this volume are an excellent example of the new emphasis. See also Francis J. Bremer, *Puritanism: A Very Short Introduction* (Oxford: Oxford University Press, 2009).

16. This emphasis has gone so far that astonishingly, the controversy between Whitgift and Cartwright receives not a single reference in *The Culture of English Puritanism, 1560–1700*

to this overreaction, arguing that even when writings like Cartwright's Admonition Controversy polemics represent more extreme perspectives that not all "Puritans" shared, they can help us understand the theological anxieties at the root of the Elizabethan Puritan protest. However, to focus attention on the core anxiety that Bozeman highlights—"preciseness"—I shall dispense with the slippery word "Puritanism" in the rest of this chapter and adopt the term "precisianism," which was in fact initially the more common designation in Elizabethan polemics.[17]

For those preoccupied with such preciseness, there was naturally a need to find authoritative interpreters of God's commandments, lest the believer go astray. From this, therefore, I will suggest in section IV that we can gain a clearer understanding of the nature of the precisianist challenge to civil authority, which consisted not chiefly in a boundary-dispute over jurisdictions, but in an arrogation of supreme epistemological authority to the presbyterian ministers. Such an assertion of clerical authority to make conscience-binding determinations of God's will invited the challenge from conformists that the precisianists were reversing the Reformation and resurrecting popish tyranny. Even aside from this, however, it is easy to see how the precisianist outlook was bound to create deep theological rifts in a church formed by the Protestant spirit of adiaphorism, which contended both that a great deal of the Christian life was left underdetermined by God's commandments, and that, by virtue of the doctrine of justification by faith, failures to walk exactly were readily pardonable. The doctrine of Christian liberty, with which the precisianist protest began, was at risk of being lost in a thicket of legalism.

II. "A Shifting View of Redemption Itself": The Precisianist Rejection of Invisible Grace

Adiaphora in Three Dimensions

We began in Chapter One with John Perry's concept of the "clash of loyalties," and the recurrent sense in the Reformation that there was an urgent need to determine the "just bounds" of a Christian's political and religious duties. In

---

(1996), and merits only the most fleeting mentions in the *Cambridge Companion to Puritanism* (2008), and Lake and Fincham's *Religious Politics in Post-Reformation England* (2006).

17. Patrick Collinson, "Antipuritanism," in *The Cambridge Companion to Puritanism*, ed. John Coffey and Paul C. H. Lim (Cambridge: Cambridge University Press, 2008), 21.

depriving the Christian conscience of any authoritative human arbiter of these duties, Luther had opened the door for various human authorities to jostle for position, potentially leaving the believer suspended in perpetual doubt, torn by different loyalties. Yet so sweeping was Luther's two-kingdoms doctrine that it sought to render this loss of certainty unproblematic, by insisting it could never touch the conscience. Because justified by faith in Christ alone, not by any outward works, the Christian's conscience belonged to God alone, and could confidently face any uncertainties that confronted him in the external forum, sure that his standing before God was not in jeopardy should he err. The radical freedom thus unleashed, freedom to "make new Decalogues" even,[18] proved too much for most reformers, and was increasingly fenced in by strict adherence to the Word of God.

As mentioned above, there was an ambiguity in the concept of adiaphora. While Luther and others could sometimes speak from a soteriological standpoint, as if everything but faith was indifferent, there was an increasing preference to define adiaphora as those things neither commanded nor forbidden in Scripture. Scripture, after all, had a great deal to say not merely about justification but about sanctification, about how the justified Christian must live out his freedom in obedience to God and for the blessing of his neighbor. In this context, then, the concept of adiaphora functioned primarily as an epistemological rather than a soteriological distinction—it distinguished those duties of which we have certain knowledge by special revelation (whether essential to salvation or not) from those duties of which we have uncertain knowledge, deriving from natural revelation or human authority. This difference between these two eroded, however, with an increasing stress on the "third use of the law," Scripture's guidance for the process of sanctification, which was an integral part of salvation, even if not its basis.[19] "Things necessary to salvation," then, could encompass all things required in Scripture, which are part of the life of sanctification, leaving a much smaller sphere of adiaphora. But the emphasis on sanctification, on the conformity of the visible realm of outward behavior to the invisible realm

18. Martin Luther, *Theses Concerning Faith and Law*, in *LW* 34:112.

19. While noting that the concept of the "third use" could be found in Lutheranism as well, Witte summarizes, "Among sixteenth century Protestant reformers, Lutherans tended to emphasize the theological use of the moral law consistent with their emphasis on the doctrine of justification. Calvinists tended to emphasize the educational use of the moral law, consistent with their emphasis on sanctification" (John E. Witte Jr. and Thomas C. Arthur, "The Three Uses of the Law: A Protestant Source of the Purposes of Capital Punishment?" *Journal of Law and Religion* 10 [1993–1994], 436n8; see full discussion on pp. 434–43).

of grace,[20] also rendered increasingly problematic the realm of uncertainty regarding moral questions that lay outside special revelation. For, from the *soteriological* and the *epistemological*, we might also distinguish a *moral* sense of adiaphora, which is indeed probably the first that comes to our own minds if we hear of "things indifferent." When something was designated "indifferent," did that mean it was morally neutral or irrelevant? While the early Luther at times spoke as if all things but faith were morally inconsequential,[21] he and later adiaphorists were generally clear to distinguish that this was not what the term *adiaphoron* meant.[22] There were plenty of deeds indifferent to salvation that still had moral weight, requiring deliberation according to Scripture and natural law. Or were there?

Such a distinction depended on maintaining a barrier between justification and sanctification, the hidden and the visible. If this were eroded, if failure to conform to the will of God could exclude one from the community of the saved and thus perhaps from salvation itself, then anything not morally indifferent was potentially of eternal significance. From this standpoint, it was no longer a viable option to leave large swaths of the realm of moral conduct shrouded in uncertainty. The clash of loyalties precipitated by disputes over adiaphora had already made it clear that Calvin's dictum, "Let love be our guide, and all will be safe,"[23] simply would not be sufficient. "To walk exactly" was necessary for the believer who wanted to please God, and to walk exactly, one needed exact and certain guidance, which could be afforded by Scripture alone. Accordingly, the conviction arose that "the word of God containeth the direction of all things pertaining to the church, *yea, of whatsoever things*

---

20. This shift of emphasis can be seen in the increasing drive for ecclesiastical discipline that came to dominate particularly Reformed (but many Lutheran as well) churches from the mid-1530s on, to the extent that some added "a third mark"—the right practice of ecclesiastical discipline—to the Lutheran definition of a true church as one that maintains the pure preaching of the gospel and the sacraments. By this means, the outward moral purity of professing Christians was made into an essential component of what it meant to be a Christian, and of what it meant for a fellowship of Christians to be a genuine church. See Jordan J. Ballor and W. Bradford Littlejohn, "European Calvinism: Church Discipline," in *European History Online*, ed. Irene Dingel and Johannes Paulmann (Mainz: Institute of European History, 2013).

21. For instance, *Treatise on Good Works*, in LW 44:26.

22. See Clyde Manschreck, "The Role of Melanchthon in the Adiaphora Controversy," *Archiv für Reformationsgeschichte* 49 [1957]: 165; Bernard J. Verkamp, "The Limits upon Adiaphoristic Freedom: Luther and Melanchthon," *Journal of Theological Studies* 36, no. 1 (1975): 52–59. Indeed, we have seen this clearly stated above in Art. II of the Dutch propositions on Christian liberty as well.

23. Calvin, *Institutes*, 2:1208 [IV.10.30].

can fall into any part of man's life," as Cartwright so succinctly put it.[24] By this means, the distinct conceptions of adiaphora—soteriological, epistemological, and moral—were collapsed into one another, with destructive consequences for the doctrine of Christian liberty.

The problem was not the idea that Scripture should rule our lives; this in itself was not inimical to freedom. As Cartwright would say, in words offensive perhaps to modern sensibilities but impeccably Protestant, "[T]he greatest liberty and freedom of Christians is to serve the Lord according to his revealed will, and in all things to hang upon his mouth."[25] The problem, as we shall see, was the way in which Scripture was taken to rule, "to leave as little as may be in the discretion off the judge."[26] Prudence was to be eliminated, eroding the extent to which the believer could be seen as a rational and active participant in God's work, as the principle of voluntariety—the second part of Calvin's formulation of Christian liberty—would seem to call for.

Before proceeding to examine how this comprehensive concept of biblical authority functioned for precisianists, let us first examine the tendency toward this elision of justification and sanctification, hidden and visible, in precisianist thought.

Eliding Sanctification and Justification

In *The Communion of Saints*, Stephen Brachlow describes how radical precisianists increasingly looked for *"visible* evidence of true, saving faith by means of what they called an 'open' or 'outward' profession of faith that issued in a visibly active and obedient membership."[27] While constantly fighting shy of the temptation to make such good works *constitutive* of salvation, they laid enormous stress on them as necessary for assurance of salvation. Good works may not get the believer into heaven, but they were the best guarantee for knowing that one had a ticket there. Dwight Bozeman concurs, noting how in the emerging Puritan divinity, in sharp contrast to Luther, "Ethical activity was to flow toward, not away from, religious security. . . . [T]he quest for assurance—despite regular appeals to free pardon and the Spirit's inward witness—led squarely into the realm of behavior."[28] In his study *The Precisianist*

24. Cartwright, *Replye*, 14 (*WW* 1:190); italics mine.
25. *SR* 442.30–32.
26. *SR*, Appendix, i.21–22.
27. Brachlow, *Communion of Saints*, 120.
28. Bozeman, *Precisianist Strain*, 12–27. Of course, it should be noted that, to some

Strain, Bozeman chronicles how this obsession increasingly worked to subvert Puritan commitment to justification by faith alone, eventually generating an antinomian backlash. "They spoke of Christian freedom," he says, "but usually had in mind freedom to obey."[29] "One can imagine," he goes on,

> the irascible Luther's reaction to Cartwright's flat statements that the "Gospell" aims to "perswade [men] to submit themselves to the kingdome of Christ, and to obey his laws." . . . [W]hen we find a figure like John Udall (1560–1592) . . . suggesting that "Amend your lives" is "a sentence . . . containing the very substance of all religion, and the whole sum of Christianity," we may infer that advocacy of formal church discipline was but one expression of a shifting view of redemption itself.[30]

The contrast can be well illustrated by one of Cartwright's most (in)famous lines, which we shall return to below. When Whitgift asks whether the guidance of Scripture is needed for any action whatsoever, even "to take up a straw,"[31] Cartwright answers in the affirmative, explaining that "as no man can glorify God but by obedience, and there is no obedience but where there is a word, it must follow that there is a word" to guide us even in such matters.[32] It is likely that Whitgift was here alluding to Luther's statement in *A*

---

extent, English Protestant thought had never adopted Luther's thoroughgoing solfidianism, but had tempered it with a vision of moral reformation informed by humanist and perhaps Lollard emphases (Bozeman, *Precisianist Strain*, 13–23). Nonetheless, Elizabethan and Jacobean Puritanism undoubtedly displayed an intensification in this theme, as both Bozeman and Brachlow chronicle at length. This may be attributed to the volatile synthesis of this native English moralism with several strains in Reformed continental divinity at this time: the general Bucerian/Calvinist disciplinary drive that had distinguished the Reformed since the 1540s but was finally coming to full expression by 1560 (Bozeman, *Precisianist Strain*, 17–18; Brachlow, *Communion of Saints*, 114–17); the emergence of covenant theology, in particular the concept of a bilateral covenant in which blessings were contingent on obedience (Bozeman, *Precisianist Strain*, 32–39; Brachlow, *Communion of Saints*, 31–35, 50–55); and the hardened predestinarianism of Beza and Zanchi, which, as R. T. Kendall has argued, led to the development of a distinctively English "experimental predestinarianism" concerned with "making one's calling and election sure" (*Calvin and English Calvinism to 1649* [Oxford: Oxford University Press, 1979]; Brachlow, *Communion of Saints*, 30–39, 118–19). Kendall, to be sure, has been criticized for overplaying the rupture between Calvin and English Calvinists on this last point, but at least a shift in emphasis is apparent.

29. Bozeman, *Precisianist Strain*, 30.

30. Bozeman, *Precisianist Strain*, 31–32.

31. *WW* I:193.

32. *SR* 59.33–36.

Treatise on Good Works: "Now everyone can notice and feel for himself when he does what is good and what is not good. If he finds his heart confident that it pleases God, then the work is good, even if it were so small a thing as picking up a straw."[33] Indeed, given the similarity of Luther's statement to Cartwright's statement, "we cannot otherwise be assured that they please God," and the fact that both Cartwright and Luther go on to refer to Romans 14:23, "Whatsoever is not of faith is sin," Cartwright likely had this passage in mind as well. If so, it provides a striking example of the soteriological-to-epistemological shift we have highlighted. For Luther, the security that one pleases God proceeds from justifying faith, so a believer can undertake any action, however trivial, with confidence of divine approval; for Cartwright, precisely because the stakes of salvation are so high, the believer must not undertake even the most trivial action without scriptural guidance, lest he lack such confidence.

Whitgift is well attuned to this shifting view, and when Cartwright goes so far as to say that "all the commandments of God, and of the apostles, are needful for our salvation,"[34] he cries foul: "What is to lay an intolerable yoke and burden upon the necks of men, if this be not? or whereby could you more directly bring us into the bondage of the law, from the which 'we are made free,' than by this assertion?"[35] Whitgift is convinced that the confusion of the soteriological and epistemological dimensions here, and the concomitant blurring of justification and sanctification, hidden and visible, results in the destruction of evangelical ecclesiology, playing into the hands of the two great enemies of the evangelical Reformation, the papists and the Anabaptists.[36] The latter in particular had sought, like the precisianists, to make the pure community of the godly visible in separated churches. They had insisted that without discipline and "the ban," by which ungodly members were cut off from the fellowship of the saved, there could be no church.[37]

---

33. *LW* 44:25.

34. Cartwright, *Replye*, 18 (*WW* I:231).

35. *WW* I:235.

36. *WW* I:181–87.

37. For an excellent discussion of this Anabaptist theme, and its relation to early Reformed ecclesiology, see Kenneth R. Davis, "No Discipline, No Church: An Anabaptist Contribution to the Reformed Tradition," *Sixteenth Century Journal* 13, no. 4 (1982): 43–58. Of course, modern scholarship has increasingly recognized the difficulty of making generalizations about the myriad of different Anabaptist groups, even if the emphasis on separated visible purity was, in one form or another, a fairly common element. For a full overview, see John D. Roth and James M. Stayer, eds., *A Companion to Anabaptism and Spiritualism, 1521–1700* (Leiden: Brill, 2007).

Although perhaps influenced by this Anabaptist emphasis on discipline, considering it to be crucial for the health of the church, Calvin had repudiated the idea that it was essential to the being of a church, and consistently maintained that the visible church remained a "mixed multitude," in which tares remained inseparable from the wheat—there was a limit to how much even the best-reformed visible church would approximate the invisible.[38] The precisianists, however, had no qualms in adopting discipline as a third mark of the church, and laying considerable stress upon it: "The outward marks whereby a true Christian church is known, are preaching of the word purely, ministering of the sacraments sincerely, and ecclesiastical discipline which consisteth in admonition and correction of faults severely."[39] Indeed, they went further, insisting not merely that some practice of discipline was essential, but that *"the discipline"*—by which they referred to the presbyterian model of polity and discipline—was essential, indeed, part of the gospel. Brachlow chronicles extensively how for many radical Puritans, soteriology and ecclesiology became closely linked, such that "the practice of a biblical discipline was as necessary for salvation as a confession of doctrinal orthodoxy."[40] In his *Replye to an Answere*, Cartwright specifically repudiated the idea that matters of discipline "were not matters necessary to salvation, and of faith"; on the contrary, "Excommunication, and other censures of the church, which are

38. See John Calvin, *Treatises Against the Anabaptists and the Libertines*, ed. Benjamin Wirt Farley (Grand Rapids: Baker, 1982), 57–66, and Willem Balke, *Calvin and the Anabaptist Radicals* (Grand Rapids: Eerdmans, 1981), 230. Despite a recurrent emphasis on the importance of discipline for the health of the church, Calvin self-consciously resists making it part of the essence of the church, retaining just the two Lutheran marks of the word and sacraments (see Paul D. L. Avis, "'The True Church' in Reformation Theology," *Scottish Journal of Theology* 30, no. 4 [1977]: 327–32).

39. Field and Wilcox, *Admonition*, in *Puritan Manifestoes*, 9. The subject of the "marks of the church" or *notae ecclesiae* has often been a focal point of Reformation scholarship seeking to identify a distinction between Lutheran and Reformed (e.g., Robert Kingdon, "Peter Martyr Vermigli on Church Discipline," in *Peter Martyr Vermigli: Humanism, Republicanism, Reformation*, ed. Emidio Campi [Geneva: Librairie Droz, 2002], 67–76), or magisterial and radical Protestant ecclesiologies (W. J. Torrance Kirby, *Richard Hooker's Doctrine of the Royal Supremacy* [Leiden: Brill, 1990], 81–86; Avis, "True Church"). However, given that one can find two-mark and three-mark formulations comfortably existing side-by-side in nearly every branch of the Reformation from the 1530s on, the language itself matters less than what is meant by "discipline" (see Glenn Sunshine, "Discipline as the Third Mark of the Church: Three Views," *Calvin Theological Journal* 33 [1998]: 469–80) and whether the *notae* are being used descriptively or constitutively. See Ballor and Littlejohn, "European Calvinism: Church Discipline," for a full discussion.

40. Brachlow, *Communion of Saints*, 35. See further pp. 35–67.

forerunners unto excommunication, are matters of discipline, and the same are also of faith and salvation."[41]

For Whitgift, this was clear evidence of both popery and Anabaptistry. The pope, too, he reminds Cartwright, had insisted that his outward government was necessary to salvation, and like Cartwright, he had done so without scriptural justification.[42] Whitgift rejects Cartwright's assertion on three grounds. The first is that "I find no one certain and perfect kind of government prescribed or commanded in the scriptures to the church of Christ; which no doubt should have been done, if it had been a matter necessary unto the salvation of the church."[43] The second is his commitment to Luther and Calvin's two-mark ecclesiology. Whitgift quotes Calvin's writings against the Anabaptists on this point, and concludes that although government "may be a part of the church, touching the outward form and perfection of it," it is not so essential that a church ceases to be the body of Christ if it lacks the proper form of government; in other words "the 'kind of government' of the church is not 'necessary to salvation.'"[44]

To these first two points, Cartwright's response in the *Second Replie* helps clarify his motivations. He rebukes Whitgift for a reductionism interested only in the bare minimum that is necessary to qualify as a church: "As though the question were what things the church (of those which be prescribed by the word of God) may want and yet be the church of God, and not what things it ought to have by the prescript of the word off God."[45] Perhaps the church could exist without discipline, so that from a soteriological standpoint discipline could conceivably be classed among the adiaphora, but that is hardly the point. For the precisian, the emphasis has shifted toward conforming as fully as possible to all the words of God, which are all *necessary* for the believer to obey; if God has made his will clear regarding a matter, it is certainly not indifferent from the epistemological perspective. This raises the stakes immensely for

---

41. Cartwright, *Replye*, 14 in *WW* I:181. See also *SR* 5. Naturally, this was one of those points where precisianists were prone to rhetorical overreach in the midst of polemics, and Cartwright would later qualify such remarks, admitting that discipline was not quite so essential as word and sacrament—was, perhaps, part of the *bene esse* as well. Nonetheless, it is part of the contention of this study that differences of rhetoric and emphasis mattered a great deal, even where the formal principles espoused, as articulated in the most sober moments, were quite close to those of the conformists.

42. *WW* I:182.

43. *WW* I:184.

44. *WW* I:185.

45. *SR* 52.21–24.

the believer's conscience; at every point of the Christian life, it is necessary to grasp rightly the will of God, and only certainty that one has done so can yield a conscience at peace with God. Of course, Whitgift will dispute, as a matter of empirical fact, that God has spoken to the matter of ecclesiastical discipline, so at this point, he contends, soteriological and epistemological indifference quite overlap. For Cartwright, however, the conclusion that God *has* in fact spoken is less an empirical observation about Scripture than an *a priori* conviction about how revelation functions, as we shall see below.

Whitgift's third objection is also a staple anti-Anabaptist argument. If the practice of excommunication is necessary to salvation, as Cartwright seems to contend, "then any man may separate himself from every church wherein is no excommunication."[46] Against this, Whitgift has no difficulty summoning up a barrage of writings from Reformed heavyweights (Calvin, Bullinger, and Gualter) opposing the Anabaptists on just this point. To this, Cartwright will insist in the *Second Replie* that he is not speaking to the duty of individual Christians, as if they ought to take matters into their own hands when discipline is not practiced rightly, but to the duty of ministers to excommunicate.[47] This, however, misses part of the point of Whitgift's objection, and those he has quoted from other Reformed authorities: that, if the *Admonition* and its defenders are going to speak of discipline as of such fundamental necessity, it will be difficult to resist the Anabaptist conclusion that churches that lack it are not true churches, and true Christians should separate from them and erect their own. Of course, this was no idle concern, given that a number of precisianists would do just this, particularly in the 1580s and the 1590s, forming the Separatist movement. Tellingly, the Separatists berated Cartwright, Travers, and other nonseparating precisians for inconsistency, insisting that they were simply acting on the principles articulated by these writers in the 1570s. Apologists for conformity naturally seized upon such statements,[48] and modern scholars have generally admitted that they certainly seem to have had a point.[49] Brachlow in

---

46. *WW* I:185.

47. *SR* 247.7–18.

48. Hooker: "Thus the foolish Barrowist deriveth his schism by way of conclusion, as to him it seemeth, directly and plainly out of your principles" (Pref. 8.1; *FLE* 1:39). For more on the separatist Henry Barrow's importance as background for Hooker's work, see Scott N. Kindred Barnes, *Richard Hooker's Use of History in His Defense of Public Worship: His Anglican Critique of Calvin, Barrow, and the Puritans* (Lewiston, NY: Edwin Mellen, 2011), esp. 60–65.

49. See especially Morgan, *Visible Saints*, 16–28; Collinson, *Godly People: Essays on English Protestantism and Puritanism* (London: Hambledon, 1983), 539–44; David Como, "Radical Puritanism," in *The Cambridge Companion to Puritanism*, 241–58.

particular, as mentioned above, has argued compellingly that between separatists and "radical Puritans" such as Cartwright, there was little difference of principle: "[T]he breach between separatists and non-separating radical Puritans is not to be explained as a difference of ecclesiology but as a difference of strategy, timing, and the extent to which each was willing (or unwilling) to disavow their allegiance to the church as constituted by English law."[50]

Accordingly Hooker is justified later on in reproaching Cartwright for the separatist logic of his position, even if he never followed through on it. If the conscience could only be assured by following Scripture at every point, then English Christians would have to depart from a church that was not so thoroughly aligned with Scripture.

Visible and Invisible Saints

In any case, Cartwright clearly shares the later separatist and precisianist stress on "visible saints"—a desire to make the purity of the invisible church clear already in the godliness of those making up the visible. By means of right discipline, the kingship of Christ might be made apparent here on earth, so that "our saviour Christ sitteth wholly and fully not only in his chair to teach but also in his throne to rule, not alone in the hearts of everyone by his spirit, but also generally and in the visible government of his church, by those laws of discipline he hath prescribed."[51] Peter Lake notes that in such passages, we discern a shift in the use of standard Protestant terminology, such that "language normally applied to the internal process of individual salvation was being applied to the collective cause of national reformation," thus describing the visible church in terms usually reserved for the invisible.[52]

Indeed, Cartwright has no patience for Whitgift's characterization of the church as simultaneously visible and invisible; on the contrary, he argues, these are separate bodies altogether, with the invisible church simply designating those elect from all eternity that have not yet been outwardly called. Thus one is either a member of the invisible church, or of the visible, but never of both at the same time: "For seeing the invisible church upon earth is of those only which either are not called, or lie hid and ungathered, unto any known fellowship where the word

50. Brachlow, *Communion of Saints*, 6.

51. Cartwright, *Replye*, 155 (*WW* III:315). See also Brachlow, *Communion of Saints*, 119: "The purity of the church triumphant should, they [radical Puritans] believed, be reflected in the church militant."

52. Lake, *Anglicans and Puritans?* 31.

of God is preached and the sacraments administered, he which by repentance joineth himself to the visible church of God, cannot be said to be a member of the invisible church."[53] Although not going so far as to deny that there are no false members of the visible church, "for Cartwright," notes Lake, "there was a practical assumption that the elect and the godly were roughly coterminous."[54] Thus when Whitgift questions popular election of ministers on the basis that the church contains many ignorant, ungodly, and papists, unfit to make such elections, Cartwright is indignant: "[T]he A[nswerer] imagineth of the church as of dogs . . . and not as sheep which hear the voice of their pastor."[55] If there are such ignorant, ungodly, and papists in an assembly, they are to be cut off by discipline, not granted to be members of the church, so that "such ignorance as you speak of, cannot fall into any which are of the visible church of God."[56]

To all of this, Whitgift reacted forcefully. Neither must the visible government of the church be conflated with Christ's invisible spiritual government, nor must the visible congregation be conflated with the elect:

> There are two kinds of government in the church, the one invisible, the other visible; the one spiritual, the other external. The invisible and spiritual government of the church is, when God by his Spirit, gifts, and ministry of his word, doth govern it, by ruling in the hearts and consciences of men, and directing them in all things necessary to everlasting life: this kind of government indeed is necessary to salvation, and it is in the church of the elect only. The visible and external government is that which is executed by man, and consisteth of external discipline, and visible ceremonies practised in that church, and over that church, that containeth in it both good and evil, which is usually called the visible church of Christ, and compared by Christ to "a field" wherein both "good seeds" and "tares were sown," and to "a net that gathered of all kind of fishes."[57]

Cartwright's conflation of the outward government of the church by ministers with Christ's own, Whitgift consistently decried as papist;[58] his perfectionist account of the visible congregation, he denounced as Anabaptist. This disjunc-

---

53. *SR* 171.6–11.
54. Lake, *Anglicans and Puritans?* 41.
55. *SR* 230.14–17.
56. *SR* 229.18–19.
57. *WW* I:183–84.
58. See section IV below for a more extensive discussion of Whitgift's and Cartwright's rival doctrines of the two kingdoms/two governments.

tion between visible and invisible appears throughout Whitgift's theology, and is indeed for him an essential bulwark of evangelical doctrine. We find this, for instance, in his treatment of vestments. The precisianists, of course, had argued that while it was all very well that the vestments and ceremonies were not actually being prescribed for papist reasons, why give the appearance of evil? To the common people, they looked papist, so should they not be done away with? Should the visible form of the church not be made, as much as possible, to conform to pure doctrine, which needed nothing of such outward trappings? Whitgift responds, on the contrary, that things indifferent must not be abrogated as soon as they are abused, for this will imply that they are not indifferent in fact, depriving ministers of the valuable teaching opportunity to instruct their congregations in this "necessary" doctrine. It is not lamentable that outward and inward do not correspond perfectly, for if they did so, this would in fact fail to root out superstition, which consists in attaching a higher spiritual value to outward things than rightly belongs to them.[59]

The clash between Cartwright and Whitgift here reflects one of the most deeply seated tensions in Protestant theology, and indeed perhaps in all Christian theology, often typified as the tension between Paul and James. On the one hand, faith alone freed the believer before God; on the other hand, faith must never remain alone, but must make itself visible in outward service to God. The tension between inward and outward in the doctrine of Christian liberty reflected this dialectic. Whitgift sought to do justice to Luther's emphasis on liberty of the mind in external things by minimizing the importance of outward ceremonies. For him, as John Coolidge summarized, "both Christian liberty and edification are matters of inward understanding. Together they describe an integrity of conscience maintained by a conscious disjunction between social gesture and inner meaning, between metaphor and sober sense."[60] And yet this suspicion toward precisianist attempts to make inward salvation outwardly visible resulted in a conformist retreat from the Reformation ideal of a reformed culture and worship, a church and community that visibly expressed its willing subjection to God's Word. Indeed, Peter Lake suggests that by the time we reach Richard Bancroft, Whitgift's successor as chief anti-Puritan polemicist in the 1580s and 1590s, "there was no room left . . . for any sort of active (and conventionally protestant) lay piety."[61]

---

59. *WW* II:43.
60. Coolidge, *Pauline Renaissance*, 46.
61. Lake, *Anglicans and Puritans?* 128.

III. The Logic of Precisianist Biblicism[62]

Private Judgment vs. Public Authority

Whitgift's disjunction between inward and outward, while certainly carrying good Lutheran credentials, tended merely to hold apart the clashing spheres of conscience and authority, rather than genuinely reconciling them. While Luther and Calvin both prescribed the law of charity as the guide for each individual Christian in navigating laws and duties in the civil kingdom, a law that could offer very different prescriptions for different individuals in different circumstances, many Protestants craved principles that could prescribe actions in advance with more certainty and regularity. As we have seen, many Puritans emphasized that even where Scripture did not provide detailed guidance, it offered general rules that should be followed in determining right and wrong conduct in the civil kingdom. In particular, four "rules" out of St. Paul were often singled out as regulative and always binding: (1) that none be offended (1 Cor. 10:32); (2) that all be done "in order and comeliness" (1 Cor. 14:40); (3) that all be done to edification (1 Cor. 14:26); (4) that all be done to the glory of God (Rom. 14:6–7).[63] Conformists, on the other hand, tended to make another rule out of St. Paul normative above all else: Romans 13:1. Ultimately, then, it could be said that both sides in fact agreed that the general rules of Scripture must guide the use of adiaphora, but they differed as to which general rules should take precedence.[64]

From Whitgift's standpoint, it was unthinkable that Paul could have intended these four rules to serve as principles that each individual could apply at his own discretion, since this would contradict Paul's injunctions to obey the prince in all indifferent matters (Romans 13).[65] The difference between

---

62. I had the misfortune to complete this book manuscript before the appearance of Daniel Eppley's fine study *Reading the Bible with Richard Hooker* (Minneapolis: Fortress, 2016). However, it covers many of the same themes as this section as well as many elements of Chapters Four and Five that follow, and I would commend it to readers interested in studying further Cartwright's and Hooker's different understandings of religious certainty and biblical interpretation.

63. Cartwright, *Replye*, 15 (*WW* I:195).

64. Daniel Eppley, *Defending Royal Supremacy and Discerning God's Will in Tudor England* (Aldershot, UK: Ashgate, 2007), 152: "Whitgift and Cartwright do not differ on the issue of *whether* scripture provides general guidelines to order adiaphora; they differ regarding *what* general guidelines scripture provides. The controversy is thus about the interpretation of the Bible, not the authority of the Bible."

65. Eppley, *Defending Royal Supremacy*, 154.

Whitgift and Cartwright at this point is thus more nuanced than many commentators have realized. Cartwright acknowledges that many, at least, of the matters under dispute are adiaphora, but insists that things indifferent in their own nature must be concretely used "as the circumstances of the times and persons, and profit or hurt of our brethren," require.[66] Whitgift agrees, but "with this proviso, that it is not every man's part in the church to judge and determine what the circumstance of the times and persons maketh profitable or hurtful (for then should we never be quiet), but theirs only to whom the government of the church is committed."[67] Like Parker before him, then, Whitgift has to insist that the criterion of edification can only be used as a yardstick for weighing potential courses of action *before* laws have been imposed. We ought to seek to avoid offending our brother, unless law directs us otherwise:

> but, being by lawful authority commanded to wear it, if I should refuse so to do, I should offend against the magistrate, and against God, who by his apostle hath given this commandment: *Omnis anima potestatibus, etc.*: "Let every soul be subject to the higher power, etc.;" which is to be understood in all things that are not against God. And therefore, if any man be offended with me in so doing, the offence is taken, it is not given.[68]

Confronted with such remarks, we might well conclude, with Patrick Collinson, that "to intimidate their presbyterian opponents, apologists for the ecclesiastical *status quo* erected a blank and uninviting wall bearing the single word Obedience."[69] Of course, as we have seen above in Chapter Two, it was possible to make this argument in such a way as to emphasize the priority of the law of charity, contending that violation of civil laws was always wrong because it would always be, as a matter of fact, a source of offence to other Christians. Whitgift considers nonconformity more certain to cause a brother to stumble than obedient use of corrupt ceremonies. But if there is an implicit appeal to such an empirical argument, then it would seem that Whitgift should allow for the possibility that in particular circumstances, nonconformity would be an appropriate action. Indeed, the Dutch articles, to which Whitgift expressly appealed in defense of his assertion that "things otherwise indifferent of themselves after a sort change their nature, when by some lawful

66. Cartwright, *Replye*, 52 (*WW* II:1).

67. *WW* II:3.

68. *WW* II:5.

69. Patrick Collinson, *The Religion of Protestants: The Church in English Society, 1559–1625* (Oxford: Clarendon, 1982), 12.

commandment they are either commanded or forbidden,"[70] had stipulated that laws must not be so tyrannically imposed that they do not admit of exceptions when such would not cause offense.[71] Whitgift indeed concedes as much in his *Answere*, summarizing from Bullinger and Gualter five conditions for the lawful requirement of ecclesiastical ceremonies, of which the fifth is "that men be not so tied unto them but that by occasion they may be omitted, so that it be without offence and contempt."[72] Unfortunately, Whitgift showed little disposition to expand on this concession either in his *Answere* or in his later tenure as archbishop of Canterbury, deeming no doubt that only the supreme magistrate could judge when omission was and was not "without offence."

Edification per Accidens

To be sure, Whitgift did not intend to absolutely reject Cartwright's four Pauline rules as important guides, especially the second and third, so long as they were interpreted according to the magistrate's judgment, rather than "every private man's":[73] "[I]f you object that they be not comely and decent, then I say unto you that it is your part, and the part of all those that be obedient, to submit yourselves to the judgment of those that be in authority."[74] For Whitgift, as for earlier conformists, "order and comeliness" meant considerations of civil order above all, which must outweigh Cartwright's more concrete liturgical concerns. This attentiveness to the needs of the peaceful administration of Elizabeth's state allowed Whitgift to brush aside almost any objection Cartwright could raise, from the papistical and superstitious nature of various ceremonies, to the lack of competent preachers, to the manifest corruptions in procedures of ecclesiastical administration. Moreover, while Whitgift was more than willing to grant the importance of "edification," the term was evacuated of almost any positive meaning beyond that of "order and comeliness," conceived again in terms of uniformity, civil order, and procedural efficiency. "Such lawes and orders as keep godly peace and unity in the church do edify; but the laws for apparel keep godly peace and unity in the church; ergo, they

---

70. *WW* I:208, II:5.

71. See article X in Appendix I.

72. John Whitgift, *An Answere to a certen libell intituled, An Admonition to Parliament* (London: Henrie Bynneman, 1573), 61. Reprinted in *Whitgift's Works*, ed. John Ayre (Cambridge: Parker Society, 1849–51), II:44.

73. Whitgift, *Answere*, 237 (*WW* II:50).

74. *WW* II:55.

edify."[75] Indeed, he will go so far as to make the *petitio principii* argument that, seeing as the ministry of the word and sacraments edifies, and by the queen's command, the wearing of vestments was necessary to minister the word and sacrament, the vestments now edified *per accidens*.[76]

However "mealy-mouthed"[77] this may sound, Whitgift actually felt theologically constrained to say no more than this, for nothing external should be said to edify of itself—"only the Holy Ghost on this sort doth edify by the ministry of the word."[78] This was good two-kingdoms doctrine; or would be, at any rate, if justification and edification were identical. When, on a couple of occasions in his argument, Whitgift attempts to go further than this, he runs up against the Protestant hesitancy to attach any definite spiritual value to liturgical ceremonies, and Cartwright is only too willing to alert Whitgift to his difficulty. When the latter suggests, quoting Vermigli in fact, that white vestments may signify that ministers are like angels, God's messengers, Cartwright seizes upon this, saying that if this were true, then he can no longer claim them as adiaphora: "[B]y this means [they] not only make it an ecclesiastical ceremony, but also a matter of conscience. For, if so be that the white apparel of the minister have any force either to move the people or the minister unto greater pureness, or to any other godliness whatsoever, then it is that which ought to be commanded, and to be obeyed of necessity."[79] Cartwright goes on, maintaining that if the church has power to attach such religious significations, then this is power to "institute new sacraments," a charge he repeats later in the argument when Whitgift hesitantly suggests an edifying signification for the use of a wedding ring.[80]

Thus fenced in by his own principles, it is little wonder that Whitgift proves so quick to fall back on bare magisterial authority to defend the established polity and ceremonies of the English church, or, despite his rejection of Cartwright's biblicism, to fall to protracted exegetical wrangling with Cartwright about the biblical precedent for some ceremony or other. Unable to clearly distinguish between different senses of "adiaphora," he does not know quite how to say how something soteriologically indifferent (that is, indifferent to *justification*) might still be useful for *sanctification,* or how to justify it as such when Scripture offers no clear guidance (making it epistemologically

---

75. *WW* II:61.

76. *WW* I:71, II:59.

77. Lake, *Anglicans and Puritans?* 164.

78. Whitgift, *Answere*, 238 (*WW* II:56).

79. Cartwright, *Replye*, 59 (*WW* II:64); see also *RSR* 228–30.

80. *WW* III:354.

indifferent). When Cartwright suggests that Whitgift is proposing *reason* as a standard for determining the value of disputed ceremonies, Whitgift refuses to take the bait, anxious of both common Protestant attacks on the authority of reason, and on the potentially democratic consequences of an appeal to reason.[81]

Against such an apparent resolution of conscience and authority in favor of the latter, Cartwright was insistent that religious duties, above all the duty to guard the conscience of a weaker brother, must outweigh all other considerations. In one of the few passages of his *Second Replie* where his chronic indignation rises to the pitch of eloquence, Cartwright characterizes Whitgift's position as, "that if all should be offended, that is to say perish and make shipwreck of conscience . . . yet we ought to do that which is commanded; the Magistrate being thereby lifted above the Lord." On the contrary, Cartwright asserts, it is "a flat commandment of the Holy Ghost that we abstain from things in their own nature indifferent if the weak brother should be offended," so that "no authority either off church or commonwealth can make it void." In a crystal-clear articulation of the threefold clash of loyalties we have observed (to God, to magistrate as putative guardian of the common good, and to neighbor as concrete demand of the common good), Cartwright declares,

> And where the magistrates commanding and our obedience ought to be squared out first by the love of God then off men, our brethren especially; this new carpenter, as one that frameth his squire [square] according to his timber, and not his timber according to the squire, will make our obedience to the civil Magistrate the rule of the love of God, and our brethren.[82]

It is at points such as this that Cartwright's argument is at its strongest, leading some to the conclusion that it is in fact the precisianist who is most concerned with the variable, circumstantial nature of adiaphora. John Coolidge will praise the precisianists' "dynamic" understanding of Christian liberty, in contrast to the flat and sterile doctrine of the conformist, arguing that the former is motivated by a positive vision of edification that drives him to seek the upbuilding of the neighbor and the church in all his actions.[83] Unfortunately, Cartwright does not rest content with asserting the supremacy of our duty to God's glory

---

81. M. E. C. Perrott, "Richard Hooker and the Problem of Authority in the Elizabethan Church," *Journal of Ecclesiastical History* 49, no. 1 (1998): 43–45.

82. *SR* 403.31–404.7.

83. See Coolidge, *Pauline Renaissance*, ch. 2; also Lake, *Moderate Puritans*, 2–3.

and our brethren's salvation over civil concerns. Indeed, how could he, after long battles in the Vestiarian controversies had ended indecisively, with conformists earnestly insisting that God's glory and the salvation of the brethren were not in fact at stake? A "dynamic" understanding of Christian liberty, in which the believer exercised his freedom by cultivating prudence in response to changing circumstances, seemed inadequate to the task. A more certain rule for resolving the doubtful conscience and adjudicating clashing loyalties was needed—Scripture.

"A Word of God for All Things We Have to Do"

"No man's authority . . . can bring any assurance unto the conscience,"[84] Cartwright concluded. Perhaps in "human sciences" the word of man carried "some small force" but "in divine matters [it] hath no force at all."[85] Of course, whether the matters in question were "divine matters" or "human sciences" was part of what was in question. Whitgift would concede that in divine matters, Scripture alone was our guide, but if the disputed orders and ceremonies were merely civil ordinances, Scripture did not necessarily have much to tell us. When pressed, then, Cartwright would go so far as to insist that in *all* actions of moral weight, Scripture was our guide: unless we "have the word of God go before us in all our actions . . . we cannot otherwise be assured that they please God."[86] The reasoning behind this claim was as follows: "But no man can glorify God in anything but by obedience; and there is no obedience but in respect of the commandment and word of God: therefore it followeth that the word of God directeth a man in all his actions."[87] Whitgift, breathless at such a declaration, answers that this would make not merely the matters in question, but all civil matters as well dependent on the Word, indeed, any action whatsoever, even "to take up a straw."[88] As we saw above, Cartwright happily swallows the *reductio*, acknowledging that the guidance of Scripture is needed for the taking up of a straw. Why? Because although a class of action may be indifferent in itself, any particular action takes on the moral quality of goodness or badness based on the *motive*, and the motive, says Cartwright, must always be a desire to please God; since, as he has already argued, no

84. *SR* 19.33–36.
85. *SR* 19.18–21.
86. *SR* 61.9–12.
87. Cartwright, *Replye*, 14 (*WW* I:190).
88. *WW* I:193.

man may be confident he pleases God except when acting in adherence to the Word, Scripture must in this sense go before us even in the most trivial of actions.[89] Cartwright has thus, under pressure to find some certain rule for guiding the Christian amidst doubtful and disputed moral decisions, come close to rendering the concept of moral indifference obsolete, and with it, the epistemological concept as well. Since no action is morally neutral, and since the Christian must have guidance in all moral matters, and since Scripture is the Christian's surest guide, Scripture must be taken to somehow pronounce positively or negatively on all matters.[90] Even the relative indifference of the adiaphora, it would seem, would have to come from the positive permission of the Word. Thus certainty is gained, but at the cost of both the peace of conscience and the exercise of prudence necessary to a true possession of Christian liberty.

And indeed, when Whitgift expresses concern on this score, Cartwright confirms that this is precisely his meaning: "For even those things that are indifferent, and may be done, have their freedom grounded off the word of God; so that unless the word of the Lord, either in general or especial words, had determined of the free use of them: there could have been no lawful use of them at all."[91] This is a remarkable transformation of the doctrine of adiaphora; no longer is scriptural silence regarding a matter *demonstrative* of its moral lawfulness, but it is *constitutive* of it, so that this silence is to be construed as a positive act of permission, without which the matter would have remained morally illicit.

The fundamental difference between the conformist and the precisianist, then,[92] is not merely that the precisianist considers that fewer matters have been left indifferent than the conformist does, although that is certainly the

89. *SR* 59–60.

90. An example of Cartwright's confusion on this question comes when he attacks Whitgift's notion of adiaphora as things "not commanded or expressed in the Scriptures" by pointing out that this would leave it indifferent whether we came to receive communion clothed or naked. Clearly this is not a matter indifferent, reasons Cartwright, so we clearly need a wider understanding of scriptural authority. See *WW* I:64, *SR* 24.

91. *SR* 59.8–13.

92. To be sure, we must use caution in essentializing "the precisianist," given the difficulty we noted at the beginning of this chapter in identifying a stable essence to the Puritan protest. However, neither Whitgift nor Hooker was being arbitrary in identifying Cartwright as the leading representative of the stream of aggressive Puritan and presbyterian opinion that most concerned them. To this extent, we may generalize from the logic of his biblicism, though with the additional caveat that of course he sometimes shies away from the apparent implications of that logic.

case; nor is it merely that the precisianist considers scriptural guidance on matters that are indifferent to be more detailed and constraining than the conformist does, although that is certainly the case; rather, it is that the precisianist considers all moral law whatsoever to be divine positive law. We may see what this difference of approach entails by considering the role of the Mosaic judicial laws in Cartwright's system. Whitgift, worrying that the precisianist principle of scriptural direction for every action would lead not merely to the abridgement of the magistrate's freedom over ecclesiastical matters, but over strictly civil matters as well, was met with a curious waffling on the part of his adversary. On the one hand, Cartwright and other precisianists would insist that as ministers of the gospel, they disclaimed all interest in merely civil and political matters, leaving those to the lawyers; moreover, they denied that the principles they advanced regarding ecclesiastical polity necessitated a similar reconfiguration of civil polity.[93] On the other hand, however, they could also assert that the laws of England ought to take the laws of Moses as their guide, and were to be condemned as unjust whenever they failed to do so.[94]

Paul Avis has drawn particular attention to this emphasis on the abiding validity of the Mosaic judicial laws for its idiosyncrasy among the Protestant reformers (with the exception of the Scots presbyterians, who were in this of a similar mind as their English brethren), showing that even where they used similar language, there was a compelling difference between a Calvin and a Cartwright on this issue.[95] The former, although much more emphatic about

93. See for instance *SR* xv.1–17, 228.11–22 (also A. F. Scott Pearson, *Church and State: Political Aspects of Sixteenth Century Puritanism* [Cambridge: Cambridge University Press, 1928], 2–5; Glenn Burgess, *British Political Thought: 1500–1660: The Politics of the Post-Reformation* [Basingstoke, UK: Palgrave Macmillan, 2009], 117–21). Indeed, they complained that it was their opponents who were guilty of ecclesiastical meddling in civil affairs (Walter Travers, *A Full and Plaine Declaration of Ecclesiasticall Discipline Owt Off the Word Off God / and Off the Declininge Off the Churche Off England From the Same* [Zurich: C. Froschauer, 1574], 78–84; Cartwright, *RSR* 151–70).

94. Cartwright, *Replye*, 22 (*WW* I:270); *SR* 95–118.

95. Paul D. L. Avis, "Moses and the Magistrate: A Study in the Rise of Protestant Legalism," *Ecclesiastical History* 149 (1975): 148–72. Though idiosyncratic, however, it proved remarkably influential on later Puritans, particularly in North America. See David VanDrunen, *Natural Law and the Two Kingdoms: A Study in the Development of Reformed Social Thought*, Emory University Studies in Law and Religion (Grand Rapids: Eerdmans, 2010), 230–33, for a discussion of a seventeenth-century theonomist, John Cotton; and see Steven Wedgeworth, "The Two Sons of Oil and the Limits of American Religious Dissent," *Journal of Law & Religion* 27, no. 1 (2011/2012): 141–61 for a nineteenth-century example, Samuel Wiley. Indeed, the legacy continues to have modern advocates, such as Greg Bahnsen, *Theonomy in Christian Ethics* (Phillipsburg, NJ: P&R Publishing, 1984).

the positive uses of the law than Luther was, took a fundamentally similar tack on the judicial laws. Luther believed that while the Ten Commandments summed up the natural law, the latter temporally and logically preceded this formal expression, and the same principle applied to the rest of the Mosaic laws. They were expressions and applications of natural law in a particular polity, and so, although their accuracy as a good application was, by virtue of its divine revelation, more assured than that of the law of Solon, it was not intrinsically more binding on us. Only inasmuch as our own circumstances were the same as those of the Hebrews should we expect our own judicial laws to be similar to theirs.[96] Calvin's argument is similar, viewing the natural principle of equity, perfected in the gospel principle of charity, to be instantiated in the Mosaic judicial laws, but to exist independently of them, so that it might and often should be instantiated quite differently in a contemporary Christian polity.[97] Cartwright, however, while he will use Calvin's term of the "general equity" of the law, understands this as something *posterior*, rather than *prior*, to the particular positive law, *extracted from* it, rather than *instantiated in* it. Accordingly there is some room for flexibility in application, but not a great deal:

> And as for the judicial law, forasmuch as there are some of them made in regard of the region they were given, and of the people to whom they were given, the prince and the magistrate, keeping the substance and equity of them (as it were the marrow), may change the circumstances of them, as the times and places and manners of the people shall require. But to say that any magistrate can save the life of blasphemers, contemptuous and stubborn idolaters, incestuous persons, and such like, which God by his judicial law hath commanded to be put to death, I do utterly deny.[98]

This is because, for Cartwright, according to Joan O'Donovan, "the particular command . . . is the perfect form of law because it 'leave[s] as little undetermined and without the compass of the law as can be.'"[99] Accord-

---

96. Avis, "Moses and the Magistrate," 153–55.

97. Avis, "Moses and the Magistrate," 163–64. See also the detailed treatment in Matthew Tuininga, *Calvin's Political Theology and the Public Engagement of the Church: Christ's Two Kingdoms* (Cambridge: CUP, forthcoming 2017), ch. 7.

98. Cartwright, *Replye*, 22 (*WW* I:270). See Pearson, *Church and State*, 108–9; Joan Lockwood O'Donovan, *Theology of Law and Authority in the English Reformation*, Emory University Studies in Law and Religion 1 (Atlanta: Scholars, 1991), 122–23 for a brief discussion.

99. J. O'Donovan, *Theology of Law and Authority in the English Reformation*, 122, quoting Cartwright, *SR* 94.6–7.

ingly, we ought never to rest content with a mere general moral intuition if a clear scriptural directive could be found; indeed, the latter was the only basis upon which the former could be valid. This conviction leads Cartwright to a preposterous dependence on scriptural proof texts at many points in his debate with Whitgift where mere common sense would have more than sufficed. For instance, when complaining that in the Prayer Book service, the minister cannot be clearly heard by the congregation when he stands at the far end of the chancel, Cartwright feels the need to allege a scriptural positive law for the principle, and resorts to Acts 1:15: "Peter stood up in the midst of the disciples." When Whitgift raises his eyebrows, Cartwright holds his ground: "The place of St. Luke is an unchangeable rule to teach that all that which is done in the church ought to be done where it may be best heard, for which cause I alleged it."[100] At another point, discussing the requirements for elders, he says "The Holy Ghost by Jethro prescribing what officers are to be chosen doth not only require that they should fear God, . . . be wise and valiant, but also requireth that they be trusty."[101] Jethro's counsel to his son-in-law can no longer be read merely as prudent counsel, the prudence of which ought to be obvious in similar situations, such as the choosing of church officers, but must appear as a specific prescription of the Holy Spirit, intended for use as a positive law for the church.

This style of reasoning permeates the writings of Cartwright, Travers, and other precisianists, and is undergirded by two syllogisms that we find frequently repeated. The first finds perhaps its most amusing expression when Whitgift queries the *Admonition*'s statement that in the Apostles' time, there was always a careful examination of communicants before they were permitted to receive the Supper—how, he asks, do they prove this in Scripture? "After this sort," replies Cartwright, "all things necessary were used in the churches of God in the apostles' times; but examination of those whose knowledge of the mystery of the gospel was not known or doubted of was a necessary thing; therefore it was used in the churches of God which were in the apostles' time."[102] Thus putative apostolic practice, even when not explicitly stated in Scripture, becomes canonical! It should not surprise us to find this sort of reasoning given the obsession with certainty that we discussed above; for the Christian convinced that he must please God in all actions, it was clear that the church *needed* detailed guidance in all its practices, and since God must

100. *RSR* 187.
101. Cartwright, *SR* 172.29–32.
102. Cartwright, *Replye*, 130 (*WW* 3:79).

love and favor his church, it stood to reason that he must have provided such guidance in Scripture. Moreover, since the most specific form of law was the most perfect, the more God loved his church, the more detailed legislation we should expect. Accordingly, we frequently find the following form of *a fortiori* syllogism:

> To prove that there is a word of God for all things we have to do: I alleged that otherwise our estate should be worse, than the estate of the Jews, which the *Ans*[*werer*] confesseth to have had "direction out of law, in the least thing they had to do." And when it is the virtue of a good law, to leave as little undetermined and without the compass off the law as can be: the A[nswerer] in imagining that we have no word for divers things wherein the Jews had particular direction: presupposeth greater perfection in the law, given unto the Jews, than in that which is left unto us. And that this is a principal virtue of the law may be seen . . . by that I have shewed, that a conscience well instructed and touched with the fear of God seeketh for the light off the word of God in the smallest actions.[103]

In a remarkable early passage of his *Full and Plaine Declaration*, outlining the scriptural plan of presbyterian polity, Walter Travers manages to combine both syllogisms side-by-side. God's care for his people, he says, is apparent in the precise and detailed legislation for the building of the tabernacle in the Old Testament; even though Scripture describes David and Solomon's changes to the worship and building of the temple without narrating God's prescription of them, we may safely conclude, given the obvious approval of their actions, that they would have only made such changes by express divine command. "And," concludes Travers, "how absurd and unreasonable a thing is it, than especially to think the love and care of God to be diminished towards his Church" that he would omit such express commands in the New Covenant?[104]

In their quest to safeguard Christian liberty, then, the precisianists have so hedged it in with unchangeable divine law that they have obscured it even more surely than Whitgift's cold call to submission. In either case, the believer is left with no room to deliberate about a course of action, and much to fear if he strays from the right path, but the cause for fear is rather greater in the precisianist paradigm, where failure to "walk exactly" could have eternal consequences. Yet this legalism threatens the same disastrous consequences for

---

103. *SR* 94.2–15.
104. Travers, *Full and Plaine Declaration*, 8.

civil polity as libertinism, charges Whitgift, for while they claim to be obedient to the civil magistrate as far as conscience allows, since they "in all things pretend the word of God and 'conscience,'" they "straiten the authority of the magistrate to [their] own purpose."[105] Moreover, by emphasizing that Christ's kingship takes visible form here on earth in the institutions of his church, and that Christ rules over these institutions as lawgiver and judge, the precisianist, far from resolving the clash of loyalties between these two kingdoms, ensured that it would come to an open conflict, a struggle between rulers temporal and spiritual.

IV. The Precisianist Rivalry of Church and State

Two Governments vs. Two Kingdoms

We turn in our final section to examine the implications of this precisianist variant of the two-kingdoms doctrine, in which the two kingdoms are clearly identified with the church on the one hand and the commonwealth on the other. Twenty years after the Admonition Controversy, Richard Bancroft neatly summed up presbyterian two-kingdoms doctrine and the dangers it posed:

> Cartwright and some others with him do affirm . . . that all Kings (as well heathen as Christian) receiving but one commission and equal authority immediately from God, have no more to do with the Church the one sort than the other, as being in no respect deputed for Church officers under Christ otherwise than if they bee good Kings, to maintain and defend it. And secondly, that as God hath appointed all Kings and Civil Magistrates his immediate Lieutenants for the government of the world in temporal causes, so Christ, as he is mediator, and governor of his Church, hath his immediate officers to rule in the Church under him, and those they say are no other, than Pastors, Doctors, and Elders, to whom they ascribe as large authority in causes Ecclesiastical.[106]

---

105. *WW* I:82–83.

106. Richard Bancroft, *A Survey of the Pretended Holy Discipline, Containing the Beginnings, Success, Parts, Proceedings, Authority, and Doctrine of It: With Some of the Manifold and Material Repugnances, Varieties, and Uncertainties in That Behalf* (London: Richard Hodgkinson, 1593), 256–57.

This pithy synopsis highlights the two great dangers of this doctrine as conformists saw it: secularism (for lack of a better word) and clericalism. The former danger Cartwright might have been quick to dismiss as one of Bancroft's slanders, although there was in fact some just cause for the criticism, as we shall see later on. The latter, however, he would have had no difficulty recognizing as his position, which conceived of "ecclesiastical governors" as occupying an equivalent place under God in the society of the church as civil governors did in the commonwealth.[107] Over the church as a visible institution, Christ exercised his "spiritual government" through his subordinate pastors.[108] For Whitgift, however, in this again hewing closer to Luther and other magisterial reformers such as Vermigli and even Calvin, this was a seriously confused use of the language of spiritual government. As we saw above, Whitgift defined the two kingdoms much more in terms of "two kinds of government . . . one invisible, the other visible; the one spiritual, the other external." The first was by the Spirit and the Word "ruling in the hearts and consciences of men, and directing them in all things necessary to everlasting life"; only this was necessary to salvation, and it was found "in the church of the elect only." The latter, however, "is that which is executed by man, and consisteth of external discipline, and visible ceremonies" in the visible church of Christ, the one "that containeth in it both good and evil."[109] By this definition, there were no subordinates in Christ's spiritual government; ministers of the gospel there were, to be sure, who outwardly assisted this spiritual ministry, but these ultimately held their office as part of Christ's external government, since Christ alone had the power to inwardly nourish the hearts of believers.

> In the spiritual government Christ is only the Prince, the King, the Judge, and in respect of him all other be subjects . . . Christ is "the only Head of the church," if by the head you understand that which giveth the body life, sense, and motion; for Christ only by his Spirit doth give life and

---

107. "And to note the distinction of these regiments civil and spiritual, the place unto the Thessa. is well alleged; for by the words, 'such as rule over you in the Lord,' the apostle doth put a difference between the civil and ecclesiastical regiment. For, albeit that godly civil magistrates do rule over us in the Lord, yet St. Paul . . . ascribeth that unto the ecclesiastical governors, because that, whereas the civil magistrate, beside his care for the salvation of the souls of his people, is occupied in procuring also the wealth and quietness of this life, the ecclesiastical governors have all their whole care set only upon that which pertaineth to the life to come" (Cartwright, *Replye*, 166 [*WW* III:417]).

108. *SR* 410.

109. *WW* I:183–84.

nutriment to his body: he only doth pour spiritual blessings into it, and doth inwardly direct and govern it.[110]

In the spiritual kingdom, clergy and laymen are all the same—passive recipients of the justifying grace of Christ. Rule and authority and hierarchy there must be in the church, to be sure, but all this must be understood as part of the external government. Given that the ministry served for the outward government of the visible society of professing believers, which is what a Christian commonwealth was, it seemed clear to Whitgift that the magistrate had every right to be part of, indeed, head of, this external government of the church.[111]

Cartwright professes astonishment at this set of distinctions so "full of disorder" and "nothing sound."[112] On the one hand, it divides what must be united—the inward and the outward aspects of the church's means of grace, both components of the "spiritual government" without qualification; on the other hand, it unites what must be divided—Christ's rule over the church and over the commonwealth. Whereas Whitgift will go so far as to say, "I make no difference betwixt a Christian commonwealth and the church of Christ; wonder you as much at it as you will."[113] Cartwright understands them as, in Scott Pearson's words, "two self-sufficient complete and distinct, but related, societies."[114] As distinct societies, they have different ends, different constitutions (for the church, a complete law-code given in Scripture, but not so for the state, Cartwright will insist, despite his occasional statements regarding the Mosaic judicials), different rulers, different political structures, different forms of coercion (excommunication vs. civil punishments),[115] and ultimately different heads as well.[116] This last remark may puzzle, since Cartwright describes both as governments under Christ, but in fact, when pressed, he will

110. *WW* II:84–85.

111. "I do not perceive why the magistrate may not as well be called the head of the church, that is, the chief governor of it in the external policy, as he is called the head of the people, and of the commonwealth" (*WW* II:85); "Because it hath also an outward and visible form, therefore it requireth an outward and visible government, which Christ doth execute as well by the civil magistrate, as he doth by the ecclesiastical minister" (*WW* III:419).

112. *SR* 409.32.

113. *WW* 3:313.

114. Pearson, *Church and State*, 10.

115. Pearson, *Church and State*, 111: "While the Puritans looked to the State to administer corporal punishment they held that the Church had a coercive jurisdiction of its own, according to which ecclesiastical penalties are imposed upon defaulters. The chief of these is excommunication." Cf. Cartwright, *RSR* 151–53.

116. *SR* 440–41.

insist that Christ occupies two totally distinct personas in his headships over these two kingdoms: the civil as he is "the son of God only before all worlds coequal with his father," as "creator and preserver of mankind," the other "as mediator between God and us," as "redeemer, and upholder of his church."[117]

As a result, it should not be too surprising that Whitgift and other conformists saw, as the inevitable consequence of such a personal separation of church and commonwealth, "an inevitable de-Christianizing of the secular political order," as Torrance Kirby puts it.[118] We witnessed this in the Bancroft passage above, and it turns up repeatedly throughout Whitgift's critiques of Cartwright. Whitgift accuses Cartwright of separating the church from the Christian commonwealth as thoroughly as he would separate "betwixt the church and a heathenish commonwealth that hath a persecuting and an unbelieving magistrate"; how, in Cartwright's model, does the church in England stand in any different relation to the commonwealth as "the church of Christ in Turcia"?[119] This too he sees as more evidence of presbyterian affinity with papal apologists, who argued "that Christian magistrates do govern, not in the respect they be Christians, but in the respect they be men; and that they govern Christians, not in that they be Christians, but in that they be men." This, Whitgift again fulminates, "is to give no more authority to a Christian magistrate in the church of Christ than to the great Turk."[120] According to precisianist political doctrine, he charges, political order serves merely for temporal purposes, and has no responsibility over divine matters. This he sees as a violation of the standard Protestant two-kingdoms insistence that "Christ came not to overthrow kinds of government and civil policy; neither doth the gospel dissolve kingdoms," which he takes to imply that the gospel takes nothing away from royal jurisdiction that belonged to it before the coming of Christ (and that includes the care of religion).[121] On the contrary, he quotes Wolfgang Musculus that it is pointless and impious to distinguish between "ecclesiastical and profane laws" in a Christian commonwealth, since "there is nothing in it that is profane, seeing it is a people holy to the Lord God, and the magistrate is holy and not profane."[122]

In this, Whitgift is somewhat reading between the lines of Cartwright, and extrapolating to conclusions Cartwright would deny. Certainly Cart-

117. *SR* 411.10–11, 416.36–417.1, 418.2, 417.2.
118. Kirby, *Richard Hooker's Doctrine of the Royal Supremacy*, 106.
119. *WW* III:296–97.
120. *WW* III:160.
121. *WW* III:192.
122. *WW* III:298. Cf. Lake, *Anglicans and Puritans?* 75–76.

wright's emphasis on the magistrate's duty to enforce Old Testament laws against heresy is proof enough that he did not see the office in thoroughly secular terms. Indeed, in the near term, the precisianists were determined to bring about their ecclesiastical reform by gaining the ear of Parliament and the queen, who could use their authority to sweep away the hated jurisdiction of the bishops and purify the church in accordance with the Word of God. However, given that Luther and Melanchthon had defended the magistrate's authority in the church on the basis of their doctrine of the universal priesthood and the prince's position as the *praecipuum membrum ecclesiae* ("foremost member of the church"),[123] any diminution of the doctrine of the universal priesthood would tend to reduce the magistrate to purely secular status. In point of fact, such a diminution was a key tendency of Cartwright's doctrine, one that troubled Whitgift even more than the danger of making the queen into no more than the Great Turk.

Licking the Dust at the Feet of the Church

Although we have spoken above of the threat of individual conscience to the magistrate's authority, the precisianists were not, in practice, all that interested in the authority of the individual believer to assert his interpretation of Scripture. As Peter Lake describes it, they "placed very severe restrictions on the workings of the individual conscience in confrontation with the word of God."[124] Indeed, their campaign against the mere public reading of the Word of God in place of preaching suggested that the unmediated Word alone was of little use for the believer.[125] Instead, they placed immense emphasis on the importance of a learned preaching ministry that could rightly interpret the Scriptures for the people. "In practice," observes Lake, "this rendered the average layman totally dependent on the minister."[126] In this respect, although certainly worthy of high honor, the prince was no different than the average layman, and was ultimately bound to submit his or her policy determinations to the judgment of church ministers. Cartwright, showing

---

123. See P. D. L. Avis, *The Church in the Theology of the Reformers* (Atlanta: John Knox, 1981), ch. 9.

124. Lake, *Moderate Puritans*, 90.

125. It was at this point that Richard Hooker was able to level one of his most blistering critiques of precisianist teaching as sub-Protestant in its denigration of the power of the Word. See V.19–22.

126. Lake, *Moderate Puritans*, 90.

even less-than-usual discretion in his choice of scriptural imagery to employ, declared,

> [C]ivil magistrates must govern [the church] according to the rules of God prescribed in his Word and that as they [nourish] so they be servants unto the church and as they rule in church so they must remember to subject themselves unto the church, to submit their scepters, to throw down their crowns, before the church, yea, as the prophet speaketh, to lick the dust of the feet of the church.[127]

Unfortunately, the church here is being conceived quite specifically in terms of the presbyterian ministers, lending weight to the conformist charge of a neo-papistical clerical tyranny.[128] The queen, to be sure, retains in theory her jurisdiction over all the matters of ecclesiastical polity that she currently governs, but it is a jurisdiction merely of enforcing laws, not of making laws, or if of making laws, doing so only upon the direction of her learned ministers. It is, as Whitgift and Bancroft insisted, *potestas facti non iuris*, which is the same as the ecclesiastical authority allowed to magistrates in papalist theory.[129] This is one charge that the precisianists simply could not escape, and their attempts to deny it simply damned them further. In his *Reply* to Bancroft, for instance, John Penry acknowledges that "we say that the true governors of the church are meetest to direct her majesty what laws and ceremonies are most lawful, expedient, and necessary, for the right government of the church." Put this way, the claim is rather innocuous, and not dissimilar from Hooker's later argument that it is only prudent for the queen to govern ecclesiastical matters by the counsel of her bishops. But Penry then asserts flatly, "[S]he [is] to establish nothing in the church, but that which the true ministers and true governors (if they may be had) shall show unto her to be according unto the word of God." Immediately Penry protests that this does not give ministers "power to enact laws, [for] we leave that authority unto her Majesty and the Parliament." However, they execute this authority only upon the direction of the ministers: "[H]er

---

127. Cartwright, *Replye*, 144 (*WW* III:189), quoting from Isaiah 49:23.

128. To be sure, the presbyterian system laid great stress on the importance of "*lay*-elders" as co-governors with the ministers, but in practice, rather than functioning as representatives of the laity at large, "the tendency in Calvinist churches was to progress (or regress?) from a lay to a clerical idea of the eldership" (Collinson, *Elizabethan Puritan Movement*, 299; see also pp. 108, 286–87).

129. *WW* III:297–313; Richard Bancroft, *A Sermon preached at Paules Crosse . . .* (London: E. B., 1588), 81–82. For a good overview of Elizabethan Catholic political thought, see Burgess, *British Political Thought*, 102–13.

majesty and the Parliament *are bound* to establish and erect amongst their subjects, all such laws and ceremonies, as the true ministers of the word, shall prove by the Scriptures of God, to be meet and necessary for the government of the temple, and house of the Lord, within this kingdom."[130]

Most scholars have in this at least readily acknowledged the justice of the queen's alarm at the precisianist threat.[131] Indeed, while they were almost always careful to qualify, as Penry does above, that it was only in ecclesiastical affairs that ministers wielded such interpretive authority, in practice this limitation would not have been so easy to maintain, especially given that the dividing line between what constituted "civil" and "ecclesiastical" affairs was so hotly debated. Ultimately, admits Scott Pearson, "the Cartwrightian scheme makes the Church governors, as the interpreters of God's will, the depositaries of conscience, and gives them the power to determine when obedience is due and the right to enforce it."[132] Cartwright cannot resist telling the magistrate that his religious duty extends to the continued enforcement of capital punishment against adultery, among other things—proof enough, perhaps, that Whitgift was not overly alarmist when he said that if the precisianist scheme won the day, the lawyers would have to abandon their trade and defer to the presbyterian clergy.[133]

V. Conclusion

In summary, the precisianist project to safeguard Christian liberty ran aground on a series of irresolvable contradictions. They seek to safeguard freedom with law, dissolving Luther's law/gospel dialectic, and accordingly in attempting to free the church from the bonds of political order so it may do its distinctive work, they make it into a petty imitation of political order. As Joan O'Donovan pithily describes it,

> Rather than seeking the principles of the church's discipleship, they seek a political constitution for it, erecting this structure into the vessel of salvation. As much as their papist enemies, they cast the city of God in the form of the earthly city, oblivious to the eschatological opposition of the two cit-

---

130. John Penry, *Briefe Discovery of the Untruthes . . .* (Edinburgh: Robert Waldegrave, 1589/90), 40. Italics mine.

131. See for example J. O'Donovan, *Theology of Law and Authority in the English Reformation*, 126.

132. Pearson, *Church and State*, 69.

133. *WW* I:273.

ies. Their undialectical concept of the church as a legally constituted polity brings it into inevitable rivalry and alignment with the secular polity.[134]

Worst of all, in seeking to free the conscience from being tyrannically bound by human authority, and providing it an assurance that the prince's will could not, they have merely inverted the conformist model of authority. Where the conformist denies to ministers the right to withhold assent from the interpretive decisions of the magistrate and the bishops, the precisianist denies to the magistrate and bishops the right to withhold assent from the interpretive decisions of the ministers. Both sides, seeking some definitive resolution to the adiaphora problem, have reached the point where the Protestant doctrine of Christian liberty in its full form is no longer usable. Some definitive sentence is necessary; an authoritative interpreter must be established, and all others must submit.

More than a battle over the prerogatives of episcopacy and presbytery, then, or over the Royal Supremacy understood primarily as a jurisdictional quarrel, the Admonition Controversy vividly illustrates the impasse at which conformists and precisianists both found themselves on the vexed question the Reformation had bequeathed—the relationship of conscience and authority, law and liberty. As the rhetoric became more and more strident through the 1580s, establishment leaders would abandon the task of persuading their opponents altogether, resorting to imprisonment, interrogation, and intimidation to break the back of the nascent Presbyterian organization. It would fall to Richard Hooker, however, to attempt to painfully unravel the knots in which both Cartwright and Whitgift had tied themselves, to offer the precisianist the assurance he lacked that he could please God and please his prince.

From the standpoint of our larger question about the clash of loyalties, and the difficulty of establishing "just bounds" between civil and ecclesiastical concerns, the result of precisianist two-kingdoms theory is sobering. Because Christian liberty in the ecclesial sphere is in fact a liberty only to follow precisely dictated laws, the church must dictate the terms of civil liberty to the state, requiring from the civil authority its subjection to honor such laws. This liberty, despite what might appear to be a proto-liberal "separation of church and state," provides little foundation for liberal pluralism, nor indeed any assurance that religious concerns will be kept out of politics (unless we assume, as some Presbyterian "spirituality of the church" advocates later would,[135] that

---

134. J. O'Donovan, *Theology of Law and Authority in the English Reformation*, 127.
135. See ch. 6 of VanDrunen's *Natural Law and the Two Kingdoms* for a good historical

Scripture happens to say very little on political topics). The stakes—the right ordering of Christ's kingdom on earth—are too high to allow such liberty. By lowering the stakes and taking more seriously the character of adiaphora, Hooker's attempt to harmonize loyalties also offers a more promising prospect for distinguishing them, and thus for a Christian liberty that sustains civil liberty.

---

treatment, and D. G. Hart's *Lost Soul of American Protestantism* (Lanham, MD: Rowman & Littlefield, 2002) and *A Secular Faith: Why Christianity Favors the Separation of Church and State* (Chicago: Ivan R. Dee, 2006) for a contemporary defense.

CHAPTER FOUR

Richard Hooker and the Freedom of a "Politic Society"

Between Legalism and Libertinism

Those things which the Law of God leaveth arbitrary and at liberty are all subject unto positive laws of men, which laws for the common benefit abridge particular men's liberty in such things as far as the rules of equity will suffer. This we must either maintain or else overturn the world and make every man his own commander.

Richard Hooker, *Lawes of Ecclesiasticall Politie* V.71.4

[If] all things lawful to be done are comprehended in the Scripture ... what shall the scripture be but a snare and a torment to weak consciences, filling them with infinite perplexities, scrupulosities, doubts insoluble, and extreme despaires?

Hooker, *Lawes* II.8.5–6

I. A Crisis of Christian Liberty

As we have seen in previous chapters, Luther's iconoclastic announcement of the "freedom of a Christian" in 1520 was powerful but dangerous, generating a conflict of loyalties to God and to human authority even as it tried to radically distinguish the two, and putting institutional and individual liberty on a collision course. Seeking an authority to adjudicate the conflict, precisianists tended to fall back upon the divine law of Scripture as an all-encompassing rule for Christian behavior, thus safeguarding in principle the liberty of the individual. Conformists, meanwhile, with a preference for institutional liberty that went right back to the Henrician phase of the English Reformation, minimized the scope of Scripture and offered instead human law as the decisive authority for the Christian life. Each solution, however, undermined in its own way the inward liberty of the justified conscience that was so central for Luther and the early Reformation.

The precisianist approach, as we have already seen, tended to replace the confident freedom of a conscience justified by faith with the wary submissiveness of a conscience seeking assurance through obedience to all the revealed words of God. The result was a legalistic trap, in which an ever more precise delineation of these commands was needed to provide the required assurance, but the demand of such a high standard of precision simply increased the opportunity for doubt. This apparent subjection of the conscience to a new bondage of works, together with their obvious threat to the institutional freedom of the Christian commonwealth to fashion its own polity, understandably elicited the charge of a neo-papalism from alarmed conformists.

The conformist approach, however, risked assimilating human law to divine, the will of the prince to the will of God, so thoroughly that the conscience had no freedom to dissent. Nor did most conformist apologists really escape the orbit of precisianist biblicism; they merely sought to confine it within a much smaller space, leaving a large vacuum to be filled by the royal authority which was itself commanded directly by Scripture.[1] Where Scripture did in fact command, it could not be gainsaid; where it did not, the magistrate's command could not be gainsaid. Although Cartwright contended that in justifying orders not contained in Scripture, Whitgift must be instead relying on "some star or light of reason"[2] as his standard for what should and shouldn't be done in the church, Whitgift would not take the bait; as Mark Perrott observes, he "never publicly affirmed or denied Cartwright's suggestion that his argument implied an assertion of rational authority and his attitude towards the role of human reason in the ordering of the Church remains unclear." As we have seen, Whitgift often proved very hesitant to explain why the magistrate found certain policies or ceremonies "edifying" or wise; emphasizing instead "the magistrate's freedom to establish indifferent orders as he saw fit."[3] By de-

---

1. As André Gazal has shown in ch. 8 of his *Scripture and Royal Supremacy in Tudor England: The Use of Old Testament Historical Narrative* (Lewiston, NY: Edwin Mellen, 2013), the standard conformist defense of royal supremacy during this period was divine right, resting on the same hermeneutic that the precisianists then deployed in favor of a divine-right presbyterianism.

2. *SR* 56.22.

3. M. E. C. Perrott, "Richard Hooker and the Problem of Authority in the Elizabethan Church," *Journal of Ecclesiastical History* 49, no. 1 (1998): 43–44. See also Peter Lake, *Angli-*

manding of the believer a blind obedience to orders that lacked clear rational justification, conformists could tend to overthrow the principle of voluntariety so central to early articulations of Christian liberty, rendering the conscience almost wholly passive before authority.[4]

I shall argue in the following three chapters that Richard Hooker constructs his argument in the *Lawes of Ecclesiasticall Politie* as (among other things) a response to this twofold crisis in the articulation of Christian liberty. With his sophisticated argument regarding the respective roles of natural, divine, and human law, he seeks, I shall suggest, to regain something akin to the original Lutheran dynamic of Christian liberty in its three dimensions (justification, voluntariety, and indifference), while attempting to stabilize the resulting tensions between individual and institutional liberty, and clarifying the nature and function of adiaphora in the Christian life and church polity.

The present chapter will seek to reconstruct his argument against the precisianist distortion of Christian liberty. He aligns himself with earlier conformists in seeking to defend the pole of institutional liberty in particular; however, he seeks to go further by demonstrating that the precianists undermine individual liberty of conscience as well by functionally removing the category of adiaphora. He thus seeks to get to the root of the conflict by disentangling the different senses of adiaphora and resituating the concept firmly in a soteriological context, as those things "not necessary to salvation." Moreover, in defending the institutional liberty of the English church-commonwealth to make laws for its common good, he resists the temptation to anchor the royal supremacy in divine law, using a version of the magisterial reformers' two-kingdoms doctrine to demonstrate the thoroughly human-law basis of ecclesiastical polity.[5]

---

cans and Puritans? Presbyterianism and English Conformist Thought from Whitgift to Hooker (London: Unwin Hyman, 1988), 39, and 119, 125, where Lake shows the same problem at work in later conformists such as John Bridges.

4. Of course, it would be unfair to exaggerate this tendency. After all, the conformists did not simply resort to bald coercion. On the contrary, they wrote lengthy tracts and treatises arguing against Puritanism and calling for conformity, and the very act of writing is an attempt to rationally persuade an intelligent reader. Nonetheless, as Lake has argued, they drew upon a rather thin arsenal of arguments for the purpose, and were quick to flee to the skirts of the magistrate for protection when they had run out of weapons (Lake, *Anglicans and Puritans?* 119).

5. It is worth noting how both sides in this dispute sought to defend the liberty of "the church"; where Puritans saw their opponents as enslaving the church to the state, conformists saw their opponents enslaving both church and state to a legalistic construal of Scripture. We often tend to view the controversy through Puritan eyes, as one between church and state, and

Chapter Five will then look more at how Hooker goes beyond a typical conformist argument, attempting to avoid the conformist tendency to trample on liberty of conscience, and seeking to offer a positive harmonization of his opponents' loyalties. This required that he, unlike Whitgift, assure their consciences and invite voluntary obedience by demonstrating the sound rational basis and the edifying character of the orders and ceremonies of the Church of England. The latter part of the chapter will show how Hooker seeks to achieve this without sacrificing his earlier emphasis on institutional liberty, by expounding his carefully constructed arguments about the role of corporate decision-making and the element of consent in English laws. By this means he seeks to argue that the freedom of subjects is not incommensurate with their willing subjection to the decisions of their representatives.

Where Chapter Five seeks to show how Hooker renders loyalty to the magistrate both rational and free, Chapter Six will show how it is a form of loyalty to Christ, who rules over both church and commonwealth. This sometimes-neglected aspect of Hooker's argument comprises his response to the dual threat of a secularizing or sacralizing conception of the state that we observed in Thomas Cartwright's political theology in Chapter Three. It also offers, perhaps, an alternative to the conundrums presented in Chapter One, in which the liberal state supposed to emerge from the Reformation seems to oscillate between a public neutrality that leaves religious conscience to its own quiet sphere, and a tumultuous forum in which conscientious zealots seek to enact their conceptions of the higher law. For Hooker, a modest civil state that restrains religious disputes in service to the public good is only possible in a polity that acknowledges the kingship of Christ. Whether or not his model remains compelling today, Hooker's clear sense of the harmony of nature and grace, and his careful application of an orthodox Christology and doctrine of the ascension offer an intriguing reconciliation of the purely natural and the distinctively Christian dimensions of the commonwealth.

---

might thus expect Hooker to set the question of the royal supremacy and the relative powers of civil and ecclesiastical authorities front-and-center in his argument. And yet it is in but one, and the last, of the "particular decisions" that Hooker undertakes to discuss, and plays no role in the "general meditations" of Books I–IV. The fundamental problem, for Hooker, is correctly characterizing the relationship between the two realms, *coram Deo* and *coram hominibus*; once he has shown that both civil and ecclesiastical polity belong in the latter, their specific administration is a comparatively secondary matter.

II. In Defense of Liberty

Unbinding the Church

When he comes to the end of Book III of the *Lawes*, having painstakingly traced the errors in precisianist claims about the kind of authority Scripture wields in the church, Hooker offers an admirably clear and succinct expression of what he considers to be the essential point at issue between the conformists and precisianists:

> The fault which we find with them is, that they overmuch abridge the Church of her power in these things [matters of order and ceremonies]. Whereupon they recharge us, as if in these things we gave the Church a liberty which hath no limits or bounds, as if all things which the name of discipline containeth, were at the Church's free choice. . . . So as the question is only how far the bounds of the Church's liberty do reach. (III.11.13; *FLE* 1:259.18–22, 260.13–15)

Cartwright and the precisianists, Hooker charges throughout, are in danger of so much abridging this liberty in favor of a legalistically construed biblical authority that they "overthrow such orders, laws, and constitutions in the Church, as depending thereupon if they should therefore be taken away, would peradventure leave neither face nor memory of Church to continue long in the world, the world especially being such as it now is" (II.7.1; *FLE* 1:175.9–13).

For Hooker, the problem with precisianism is a warped doctrine of Christian liberty that will assuredly destroy the liberty of the church (and along with it, the state and the individual). As we have seen already, the doctrine of Christian liberty declared that Scripture alone had authority over the conscience, and that therefore, no other authority outside Scripture could bind the believer. Given the original thrust of this doctrine as a weapon against papal authority, it is no wonder that it should tend to abridge the liberty of the church, pitting against it the freedom of the individual and the authority of Scripture. For Luther, and as we shall see for Hooker, this exclusive authority of Scripture chiefly concerned matters of faith and salvation, in "the spiritual kingdom" into which by definition no man could reach, thus averting (at least in theory) a clash with human institutions that remained suitably humble. But as some precisianists had made church discipline and ceremonies to be matters of faith and salvation, a clash was inevitable.

The problem this posed for the Church of England is revealed in a fascinating passage in Book V, where Hooker attacks Cartwright's argument that the church cannot ordain holy days because God, in ordaining the Sabbath, left believers at liberty on all other days. They contend, says Hooker, that it is not "more lawful for the Church to abridge any man of that liberty which God hath granted, than to take away the yoke which God hath laid upon them and to countermand what he doth expressly enjoin" (V.71.3; *FLE* 2:373.4–6). This, he argues, is anarchistic logic: "Which opinion, albeit applied here no farther than to this present cause, shaketh universally the fabric of government, tendeth to anarchy and mere confusion, dissolveth families, dissipateth colleges, corporations, armies, overthroweth kingdoms [and] Churches." On the contrary, Hooker avers that God has precisely defined our duties only in "things of the greatest weight," and has left us to our "own good discretion" only when we are "free from subjection to others." Whereas the precisians claimed that "every man is left to the freedom of his own mind in such things as are not either exacted or prohibited by the law of God," this is in fact to render void all human positive laws whatsoever (since such laws by definition govern those things which Scripture does not). To this disastrous logic he peremptorily answers:

> The plain contradictory whereunto is infallibly certain. Those things which the Law of God leaveth arbitrary and at liberty are all subject unto positive laws of men, which laws for the common benefit abridge particular men's liberty in such things as far as the rules of equities will suffer. This we must either maintain or else overturn the world and make every man his own commander. (V.71.4; *FLE* 2:374.7–11, 16, 21–22, 374.33–375.3)

Of course, the precisianists would have vigorously disputed this interpretation of their principle, insisting that they thus limited the power of human authority only with regard to "spiritual matters," and the public order of the church. In properly "civil" matters, they insisted that the magistrate remained free to bind by positive law on matters that Scripture left at liberty. However, Hooker is convinced that the underlying logic of their view tends to undermine this distinction (hence their willingness to argue that the magistrate remains bound in civil matters to the Mosaic judicial laws), especially as he is convinced that laws of ecclesiastical polity are of the same nature as those of civil polity.

This seeming libertinism, leaving the believer free in all things not prescribed by Scripture, disappeared into a stark legalism when combined with Cartwright's dictum that "[i]t is the virtue of a good law to leave as little as may be in the discretion of the judge."[6] On this basis he had concluded that Christ's love for the church ensured that he had given her the most detailed and comprehensive law.[7] Hooker objects that there is no point in saying that God *must have* blessed the church with detailed laws, when we face the simple empirical fact that he *has not*: "[I]t is manifest that our Lord and Saviour hath not by positive laws descended so far into particularities with us as Moses with them . . . [therefore] to us there should be freedom and liberty granted to make laws" (III.11.10; *FLE* 1:256.2–4, 7–9). Here then it is Hooker arguing that we are "left at liberty" when Scripture is silent; only the liberty is that of an institution to make laws, not of an individual to be free from law.

This curious dynamic between legalism and libertinism was a recurrent feature of the Reformation's search for a certain resolution to the clash of loyalties. This could only be found, it seemed, by resort to the certainty of the Word of God, thus expanding the sphere of loyalty to God and diminishing the sphere of loyalty to the magistrate. By asserting the rigid positivity and massive scope of biblical law, regulating in detail the conduct of a believer, the precisianist platform left the believer, it would seem, very little liberty before God. On the other hand, functioning as it does to obviate the need for human discretion or prudence, this divine law muscles out of the way all other forms of authority; since it leaves no matter in need of legislation untouched, we are to assume that no further legislation is permissible where it does not speak. The believer is thus left a great deal of liberty before man. By failing to distinguish the different planes on which the two loyalties operated, so that freedom of conscience before the one can coexist with submission before the latter, the precisianist has imagined the two to be competing for territory on the same plane, necessarily in conflict, and with the latter sure to give way before the superior claims of the former. Thus the assertion of Christian liberty strikes directly at the foundation of institutional liberty.

On the contrary, says Hooker, those things left uncommanded by divine law, being matters of adiaphora, are grants of liberty to political societies to frame positive laws "for the common benefit," not chains restricting them from any legislation. If we do not say this, then nothing is left to the authority of such institutions, but all to the individual or to Scripture—privately interpreted.[8] The result of this, Hooker is convinced, will be the crippling

---

6. *SR*, Appendix, i.21–22. See n. 13 in Chapter Three above.

7. *WW* I:264–67, II:90; Cartwright, *SR* 440.

8. In V.10.1 he asks, "[If] the Church did give every man license to follow what himself imagineth that God's Spirit doth reveal unto him, or what he supposeth that God is likely to have revealed to some special person whose virtues deserve to be highly esteemed, what other

of any capacity for corporate action, a reasonable concern, as Robert Eccle-shall acknowledges: while the effect of the precisianist doctrine was to permit any individual to challenge the established structure at any point he desired, no community could withstand some of its members undermining the social fabric simply because they disagreed with certain features of public policy.[9]

Hooker thus seeks to turn the burden of proof back against the precisianists. While they had insisted that, since all things in the church must be ordered according to the Word, the burden of proof was on the apologists for conformity to show scriptural justification for existing orders, he denies the premise, and thus establishes a presumption in favor of publicly enacted law against mere private dissent.[10] It is thus up to the precisianists to prove that the present order is positively wrong: "Surely the present form of Church-government which the laws of this land have established, is such, as no law of God, nor reason of man hath hitherto bene alleged of force sufficient to prove they do ill, who to the uttermost of their power withstand the alteration thereof" (Pref. I.1; *FLE* 1:2.17–21).

Unbinding the Conscience

But however convenient the doctrine of adiaphora may have been for shifting the burden of proof, Hooker's defense of it appears to have a deeper motiva-tion, recognizing that its denial erodes not merely institutional liberty, but individual liberty as well. One of Hooker's foremost and most clearly stated purposes in the *Lawes* is to offer reassurance to Christian consciences that may have been driven by precisianist teachings into a spirit of bondage, rather than freedom—undoing, in Hooker's mind, the gains of the Reformation.[11] We saw

---

effect could hereupon ensue, but the utter confusion of his Church under pretense of being taught, led, and guided by his spirit[?]" (*FLE* 2:46.22–28).

9. Robert Eccleshall, "Richard Hooker's Synthesis and the Problem of Allegiance," *Journal of the History of Ideas* 37, no. 1 (1976): 114.

10. Eccleshall, "Richard Hooker's Synthesis," 114. Cf. "We therefore crave . . . to have it granted, that where neither the evidence of any law divine, nor the strength of any invincible argument otherwise found out by the light of reason, nor any notable public inconvenience doth make against that which our own laws ecclesiastical have although but newly insti-tuted, for the ordering of these affaires, the very authority of the Church itself, at the least in such cases, may give so much credit to her own laws, as to make their sentence touching fitness and convenience weightier than any bare and naked conceit to the contrary" (V.8.5; *FLE* 2:40.24–33).

11. Perrott, "Problem of Authority," 38–39, 48–52. See also Barry G. Rasmussen, "The

in Chapter Three that precisianist biblicism stemmed from the very concern to assure the conscience, with Cartwright insisting that unless we "have the word of God go before us in all our actions . . . we cannot otherwise be assured that they please God."[12] In point of fact, however, the appeal to Scripture in all things had not necessarily served as a salve for uncertain consciences; on the contrary, it could have precisely the opposite effect, as Bozeman has shown in his *The Precisianist Strain*.[13] Hooker, accordingly, seeks to turn the tables on the precisians. If Scripture is to be our guide in everything, thus abrogating the law of nature, "what shall the scripture be but a snare and a torment to weak consciences, filling them with infinite perplexities, scrupulosities, doubts insoluble, and extreme despairs?" (II.8.6; *FLE* 1:190.16–19).

Accordingly, he dedicates Book II to addressing what he takes to be the chief point at issue in the precisianist protest: "For whereas God hath left sundry kinds of laws unto men, and by all those laws the actions of men are in some sort directed; they hold that one only law, the scripture, must be the rule to direct in all things, even so far as to the 'taking up of a rush or straw'" (II.1.2; *FLE* 1:145.10–14). As we saw in the previous chapter, it was Cartwright's argument that this must be the case if we were to have confidence of pleasing God. Hooker (aside from qualifying "all things" to only "actions which have in them vice or virtue," which does not include picking up straws) rejects this premise. Rather, he insists that although we might grant that Scripture does in some sense guide all moral actions, we are not bound to deduce our rule of action directly from Scripture, so long as it is "framed according to the law of reason," which being in harmony with Scripture, and embedded in it, will ensure that our action "may be deduced by some kind of consequence" from

Priority of God's Gracious Action in Richard Hooker's Hermeneutic," in *Richard Hooker and the English Reformation*, ed. W. J. Torrance Kirby (Dordrecht: Kluwer Academic Publishers, 2003), 12–14, for the argument that Hooker is responding to a perceived "Pelagianism" in his precisianist opponents.

12. *SR* 61.10–12.

13. See chs. 7 and 8 in Theodore Dwight Bozeman, *The Precisianist Strain* (Chapel Hill: University of North Carolina Press, 2004). It should be noted that Hooker's preoccupation with the subject of assurance extended beyond merely the moral dimension that we are focusing on here. In his surviving sermons from the 1580s, the issue of attaining assurance of saving faith is a prominent theme (see especially *A Learned and Comfortable Sermon of the Certaintie and Perpetuitie of Faith in the Elect*, in *FLE* 5:69–82), and has engaged the attention of several scholars (see for instance Egil Grislis, "The Assurance of Faith According to Hooker," in *Richard Hooker and the Construction of Christian Community*, ed. Arthur Stephen McGrade [Tempe, AZ: Medieval & Renaissance Texts & Studies, 1997], 237–50; and Deborah Shuger, "Faith and Assurance," in *A Companion to Richard Hooker*, ed. W. J. Torrance Kirby [Leiden: Brill, 2008], 221–50).

Scripture (II.1.2; *FLE* 1:145.19–20, 24–25, 27–28). We do not need explicit recourse to Scripture at every point to be confident of pleasing God.

This latter point highlights the key problem with precisianist biblicism that we identified in the last chapter: that it was not a matter of *how much* Scripture governed, but of *how* it governed, namely, in such a way as to abrogate the law of nature and the exercise of prudence. While interpreters have very often implied that the issue at stake between Hooker and the Puritans is one of the *scope* of scriptural authority[14] (and Hooker does occasionally use this sort of language[15]), this is clearly not quite accurate. Hooker freely grants here that Scripture does govern *all* moral actions, but insists that it is not our sole guide, but operates together with the law of reason, with which it is in harmony. Whereas for Cartwright it is essential that the believer not only act in conformity with Scripture, but be consciously guided by it and in submission to it at every point,[16] for Hooker it is adequate that we act in conformity with reason, this also being a law God has given us. Otherwise, it is hard to see how the doctrine of adiaphora remains intact:

> Whereas therefore they still argue that "wheresoever faith is wanting, there is sin," and "in every action not commanded, faith is wanting," *ergo*, "in every action not commanded, there is sin": I would demand of them, first for as much as the nature of things indifferent is neither to be commanded nor forbidden, but left free and arbitrary: how there can be anything indifferent, if for want of faith sin be committed, when anything not commanded is done. (II.4.3; *FLE* 1:153.30–154.5)

In response, Hooker insists, directly contra Cartwright's claims,[17] that adiaphora are those things *left* free by Scripture, not *made* free by Scripture; whereas

---

14. See for instance the discussions in H. C. Porter, "Hooker, the Tudor Constitution, and the *Via Media*," in *Studies in Richard Hooker: Essays Preliminary to an Edition of His Works*, ed. W. Speed Hill (Cleveland: Press of Case Western Reserve University, 1972), 104–7; Joan Lockwood O'Donovan, *Theology of Law and Authority in the English Reformation*, Emory University Studies in Law and Religion 1 (Atlanta: Scholars, 1991), 142–45; and Glenn Burgess, *British Political Thought: 1500–1660: The Politics of the Post-reformation* (Basingstoke, UK: Palgrave Macmillan, 2009), 131.

15. See for instance I.1.2 (*FLE* 1:145.6–10), I.1.4 (*FLE* 1:147.3–6), although in the larger context of both passages, it becomes clear that Hooker is more concerned with describing the *mode* of scriptural authority (operating conjointly with reason) than in limiting its scope.

16. Cartwright, *SR* 59–60; John S. Coolidge, *The Pauline Renaissance in England: Puritanism and the Bible* (Oxford: Clarendon, 1970), 11.

17. *SR* 59.9–13.

the Puritans say that "unless the word of the Lord had determined of the free use of them, there could have been no lawful use of them at all," in fact "it is not the Scriptures setting down such things as indifferent, but their *not setting down* as necessary that doth make them to be indifferent" (II.4.5; *FLE* 1:155.16–18). Such matters, while indifferent in themselves, are of course not indifferent in use, being still subject to the moral demands of concrete circumstances. Whereas Cartwright, seeking a certain rule to guide the believer in the edifying use of adiaphora, enlists Scripture, Hooker is concerned that this pious-sounding insistence will actually overturn the whole concept, since "[i]f scripture require me so to do, then is not the thing indifferent, because I must do what scripture requireth" (II.4.5; *FLE* 1:155.25–27). Since adiaphora are those things in which Scripture has not clearly bound us, we should not persist in seeking to wrest guidance from Scripture by dubious deduction, forcing Scripture to speak when it does not. Rather, we should feel free to rely on reason, prudence, or human authorities to make our decision.

Hooker goes on to explain why he considers this point so important:

> A hard case, that hereupon [determining an action by discretion, not Scripture] I should be justly condemned of sin. Nor let any man think, that following the judgement of natural discretion in such cases we can have no assurance that we please God. For to the author and God of our nature, how shall any operation proceeding in natural sort be in that respect unacceptable? The nature which himself hath given to work by, he cannot but be delighted with, when we exercise the same any way without commandment of his to the contrary. (II.4.5; *FLE* 1:155.30–156.2)

The doctrine of Christian liberty that is at stake, therefore, is not simply the liberty of the Christian church or the Christian magistrate; rather, it is, like Luther's, the freedom of a conscience that does not have to fear divine condemnation at every turn. Such liberty is not to be safeguarded by making Scripture the sole and exhaustive authority, but by using it in conformity with the nature God "hath given to work by."

III. Defining Adiaphora

Ambiguities

This discussion, however, highlights the difficulty in defining the concept of adiaphora, and the relationship between "indifference" from a moral standpoint and from a scriptural (or epistemological) standpoint. We have also seen above that Luther and others could employ the term from a soteriological standpoint, treating all things unnecessary to salvation as indifferent. A lack of precision in defining and relating these three contexts had dogged disputes between conformists and Puritans throughout the English reformation.

Within the context of moral philosophy, the concept of adiaphora had been a part of discussions regarding what sorts of human actions (leaving aside the complexity of defining an "action") were intrinsically good or evil, which were good or evil depending on intention, circumstance, and object (for which the word "indifferent" was sometimes used), and which were absolutely indifferent considered in themselves.[18] Related to this discussion was also the distinction of actions so good that we are morally obliged to perform them, and goods that are merely recommended, not required, treating the latter as in some sense adiaphorous.[19]

Distinct from this set of issues was the question of which actions had been prescribed or proscribed in Scripture, which was an epistemological question, distinguishing how we *know* whether an action is good or evil. Where Scripture has spoken, we have direct knowledge of the good and are obliged to act accordingly; where it has not, however, the good has been left underdetermined, and it is up to us to discern and apply it as we see fit. Of course, if this was merely an epistemological distinction, it did not mean that matters outside of Scripture were morally neutral (indifferent in our first sense), only that we had to use other means (reason or human law) to determine their morality. Nor, for that matter, did it mean that things commanded in Scripture were not, in themselves and apart from such command, morally indifferent; sometimes they were. In other words, not everything scripturally indifferent need be morally indifferent, and not everything morally indifferent need be scripturally indifferent. However, as we have seen, under pressure of demands to conform to unedifying ceremonies, precisianists such as Cartwright had increasingly lost sight of such a distinction.

Within the soteriological context, the concept of adiaphora had its home in Luther's doctrine of the "two realms" of Christian existence, which distin-

---

18. For a general background on this pre-Reformation usage of the concept of adiaphora, see Bernard J. Verkamp, *The Indifferent Mean: Adiaphorism in the English Reformation to 1554* (Athens: Ohio University Press, 1977), 21–26.

19. See for instance Hooker's distinction between the law of reason's "mandatory," "permissive," and "admonitory" declarations in I.8.8 (*FLE* 1:89.1–31), and Joyce's discussion of the same in A. J. Joyce, *Richard Hooker and Anglican Moral Theology* (Oxford: Oxford University Press, 2012), 177–78.

guished between the salvific "spiritual kingdom" of Christian existence *coram Deo* and the indifferent "temporal kingdom" *coram hominibus*. The former contained those things *necessary to salvation* (on the most minimal definition, passive faith merely, though with suitable qualifications, others could be added to this category); the latter contained those things *accessory to salvation* and thus of no ultimate significance for the Christian soul. Again, important as this way of putting things was for supporting the Protestant edifice of justification by faith, it sat somewhat uncomfortably with the other dimensions of the adiaphora concept. After all, just because lying to your brother does not exclude you from salvation does not mean that it is morally indifferent; nor, just because feeding the hungry cannot win heaven for you does not mean that there is no moral virtue in such a deed. And, as both these examples show, many deeds could be either commanded or forbidden in Scripture even if, on this soteriological definition, they were "not necessary."

We have noted how, faced with the need for certainty, many Protestants displayed an increasing tendency to develop the doctrine of Christian liberty from the starting point of *sola Scriptura* (as we saw later thinkers like Thornwell and VanDrunen doing as well), rather than *sola fide* (as Luther had clearly done), and thus a tendency to privilege the epistemological dimension of adiaphora. For the precisianists, convinced that God would not leave the Christian adrift without detailed moral guidance, this meant identifying the epistemological dimension with the moral, so that Scripture became the only rule to determine the moral goodness of an action, and very little could be considered adiaphora in the epistemological or moral sense. Moreover, by their intensified focus on sanctification, and on the need for the Christian to walk exactly in all the ways of Scripture, they risked collapsing the distinct soteriological sense into the first two, so that now matters formerly considered "accessory" were taken to be "matters of faith and salvation."

The other side of this was that conformist apologists, starting too from the second dimension but unable to see in Scripture the profusion of commands that the precisianists read there, could point to Scripture's formal silence on an issue and conclude thereby that the matter was in every meaningful sense indifferent—left up to essentially arbitrary human judgment, morally and soteriologically insignificant. Or else, still worse, they might exclusively emphasize the third dimension in order to foster a minimalistic quietism. If only a very few things were necessary to salvation, then everything else was essentially free for human authority to devise as it thought best—even if Scripture addressed other subjects, its commands here were not to be taken in any permanently binding sense, since these matters were adiaphorous and changeable. So Starkey could argue that the English people should concern themselves with little more than the Apostles' Creed; whatever else the authorities might see fit to legislate for the Church of England, they should happily consent to.[20] So Whitgift, in his more fatalistic moments, could imply that as the availability of right doctrine was the only prerequisite for God to call sinners to himself, it little mattered what other spiritual provision the Church of England offered.[21]

Hooker's Response

In seeking to "open, of what nature and force laws are, according unto their several kinds" (I.16.1; *FLE* 1:134.21–22), Hooker thus seeks to rightly distinguish these three dimensions, and define their relations to one another. This meant overcoming an exclusive reliance on the scriptural criterion, in which all matters of moral significance were addressed in Scripture, and in which "all the commandments of God . . . are needful for our salvation."[22] The way in which Scripture did and did not bind believers was to be assessed in relation to moral criteria of things that were good, evil, or indifferent in themselves, and soteriological criteria of what things were necessary to salvation, the revelation of which comprised "the principal intent of Scripture" (I.14.1; *FLE* 1:124.31).

To discern what role the moral dimension plays for Hooker, let us return to the two conditions he insisted on in response to Cartwright's claim that Scripture "must be the rule to direct in all things." First, this could only be so "within the compass of moral actions, actions which have in them vice or virtue." By this, Hooker suggests that there are some actions that are quite simply morally indifferent, and of course we should not expect Scripture to direct in such things.[23] But second, he insists that

20. Thomas Starkey, *Exhortation to Unitie and Obedience* (London, 1540; facsimile repr., Amsterdam: Theatrum Orbis Terrarum, 1972), 7v.

21. Lake, *Anglicans and Puritans?* 41; "The 'Anglican Moment'? Richard Hooker and the Ideological Watershed of the 1590s," in *Anglicanism and the Western Christian Tradition: Continuity, Change and the Search for Communion*, ed. Stephen Platten (Norwich, UK: Canterbury, 2003), 98.

22. Cartwright, *Replye*, 18 (*WW* I:231).

23. However, we should note that he later argues in II.8 that, inasmuch as all voluntary actions are directed toward an end, from which they take their moral character, "*all* actions of men endued with the use of reason are generally either good or evil" (II.8.1; *FLE* 1:186). To this extent, he would agree with Cartwright (and Augustine!) that all actions must be ordered toward the love of God, or else they are evil. The problem was that Cartwright had tried to

it sufficeth if such actions be framed according to the law of reason; the general axioms, rules, and principles of which law being so frequent in holy scripture, there is no let but in that regard even out of scripture such duties may be deduced by some kind of consequence . . . howbeit no man bound in such sort to deduce all his actions out of Scripture. (II.1.2; *FLE* 1:145.24–30)

This serves to render the determination of moral good, evil, or indifference epistemologically independent from Scripture (in principle, at least, though not always in practice, since the postlapsarian corruption of our reason often means that we will need to resort to Scripture). Clearly, it is not metaphysically independent, for he believes the moral substance of Scripture to be identical to that which the law of reason reveals; as he says at one point, "scripture is fraught even with laws of nature" (I.12.1; *FLE* 1:119.29), and we shall look more closely at this harmonious relationship in Chapter Six. But "the natural measure whereby to judge our doings, is the sentence of reason, determining and setting down what is good to be done. Which sentence is either mandatory, shewing what must be done; or else permissive, declaring only what may be done; or thirdly admonitory, opening what is the most convenient for us to do" (I.8.8; *FLE* 1:89.2–5).

The permissive sentence of reason, argued Hooker, may permit some things which are "free in their own nature and indifferent . . . left to our own discretion" (such as what kind of clothing to wear), until "some higher duty remove the indifferency that such things have in themselves." For instance, "if God himself have precisely abridged the same, by restraining us unto, or by barring us from some one or more things of many, which otherwise were in themselves altogether indifferent. Many fashions of Priestly attire there were, whereof Aaron and his sons might have had their free choice without sin, but that God expressly tied them unto one" (II.4.4; *FLE* 1:154.16–19, 23–28). The moral and epistemological criteria remain clearly distinct here, as the mere fact that God has limited our actions by positive command in Scripture does not change the fact that such things are indifferent in themselves. It is because such moral indifference is *antecedent* to the epistemological that we saw Hooker insisting, "it is not the Scripture's setting down such things as indifferent, but their *not setting down as necessary* that doth make them to be indifferent" (II.4.5; *FLE* 1:155.16–18)—in other words, Scripture does not

---

replace this wholly internal and circumstantial determination of goodness with a requirement of explicit outward conformity to Scripture.

have to first positively permit something for it to become indifferent. Thus he attacks the attempt to force Scripture to speak on matters where it simply does not, and he insists that we must take as our starting point not what we think Scripture *should* have said (because of its moral importance), but what it *has in fact* said: "When the question is whether God have delivered in scripture (as they affirm he hath) a complete particular immutable form of Church-polity, why take they that other both presumptuous and superfluous labour to prove he should have done it, there being no way in this case to prove the deed of God saving only by producing that evidence wherein he hath done it?" (III.11.21; *FLE* 1:269.12–17).

Brian Tierney has recently drawn attention to these passages as marking one of Hooker's most important contributions to the natural law tradition, specifically the idea of *permissive natural law*. Whereas Cartwright had required explicit scriptural permission to make something indifferent, and Whitgift had wavered when appealing to reason as a standard, Hooker forthrightly argued that reason could and should tell us when actions were not so good as to be required and not so evil as to be forbidden.

> A recurrent teaching that runs through Hooker's work held that we need to be guided by both the law of scripture and the law of reason, or law of nature, in following a Christian way of life; and at the core of the argument was the assertion that reason and nature can teach us not only what is demanded of us but also what is permitted.[24]

Although such a notion of permissive natural law had been explicitly formulated and defended by many of the medieval canonists, shows Tierney, it was curiously absent from Aquinas's account of natural law, which Hooker otherwise follows fairly closely. This is accordingly one point where, Tierney suggests, Hooker may have improved upon Aquinas by "making explicit what was implicit"[25] in the *Summa* regarding the relationship between moral law and human freedom.

Taken by itself, however, this line of argument would not seem to get Hooker very far in his polemic against the precisianists. He has rebutted the idea that merely because something is morally significant, it must be the subject of scriptural prescription, thus allowing that God may leave many matters

---

24. Brian Tierney, *Law and Liberty: The Idea of Permissive Natural Law, 1100–1800* (Washington, DC: Catholic University of America Press, 2014), 179.

25. Tierney, *Law and Liberty*, 179.

to human discretion. However, he has appeared to concede that, to the extent that Scripture *has* addressed the matter, it is no longer indifferent from the epistemological standpoint, and such discretion has been taken away from the church. This would appear to leave him the same difficulty as Whitgift, admitting that *if* Cartwright's exegesis was sound, then his claims for pres-byterianism *would* follow, and thus condemning himself to an interminable exegetical tug-of-war about what Scripture had and had not spoken to. Hooker thus seeks to provide a satisfactory argument as to why we should expect Scripture to address *some matters and not others*—why we should be *prima facie* skeptical of the claims that it has prescribed in detail matters like church polity, rather than leaving them indifferent. This argument involves bringing in the soteriological criterion.

Accordingly, he insists that in praising the sufficiency of Scripture, we define this in terms of "the sufficiency of scripture *unto the end for which it was instituted*" (I.14; *FLE* 1:124.27–28; italics mine). Although Scripture contains many things, "the principal intent of scripture is to deliver the laws of duties supernatural" (I.14.1; *FLE* 1:124.31–32), which he goes on to define as things "necessary to salvation."[26] Against the precisianist tendency to make Scripture the rule of all our actions, Hooker thus seeks to maintain Luther's emphasis on the gospel of justification as the heart of the Scriptures.[27] He returns to this concept at much more length in II.8, where, having spent seven chapters rebutting the precisianist construal of the scope of scriptural authority, he turns to elaborate his own account, synthesizing the moral, epistemological, and soteriological elements.

Having established that "all actions of men endued with the use of reason are generally either good or evil" (II.8.1; *FLE* 1:186.13), he proceeds to outline three different kinds of morally good action. First, while we might want to say that all actions are in some sense either good or evil, there are some things that are almost absolutely indifferent: "Some things are good, yet in so mean a degree of goodness, that men are only not disproved or disallowed of God for them," actions, we might assume, like "taking up a rush or straw," or even triv-ial matters of church order; in these actions "the very light of nature alone may

26. Richard Muller observes (*After Calvin: Studies in the Development of a Theological Tradition* [Oxford: Oxford University Press, 2003], 11) that this kind of distinction was becom-ing common in late-sixteenth-century Reformed discussions of the clarity and sufficiency of Scripture.

27. See for instance in *Freedom of a Christian*: "You may ask, 'What then is the Word of God, and how shall it be used, since there are so many words of God?' I answer: The Apostle explains this in Romans 1. The word is the gospel of God concerning his Son" (*LW* 31:346).

discover that which is so far forth in the sight of God allowable" (II.8.2; *FLE* 1:187.29–30). Second, on the other extreme, are those things not only allowed but "also required as necessary unto salvation, by way of direct immediate and proper necessity final, so that without performance of them we cannot by ordinary course be saved."[28] Here, "our chiefest direction is from scripture, for nature is no sufficient teacher what we should do that we may attain unto life everlasting. The [insufficiency] of the light of nature is by the light of scripture so fully and so perfectly herein supplied, that further light than this hath added there doth not need unto that end" (II.8.3; *FLE* 1:187.30–188.7). But in between these two is a third category, the sphere with which moral theology is usually concerned, those things we normally recognize as virtues or vices:

> Finally some things although not so required of necessity that to leave them undone excludeth from salvation, are notwithstanding of so great dignity and acceptation with God, that most ample reward in heaven is laid up for them. Hereof we have no commandment either in nature or scripture which doth exact them at our hands: yet those motives there are in both which draw most effectually our minds unto them. (II.8.4; *FLE* 1:188.7–13)[29]

In Hooker's second category, Scripture is our sole authority, and both clear and sufficient in directing us. If anything is necessary for salvation, we may be sure that it is included in Scripture, and we may be sure moreover that we could not have divined it on our own, without the aid of Scripture (though even here this does not mean that reason plays no instrumental role). Our task is but to carefully attend to and obey the testimony of Scripture; indeed, if we do otherwise, and import doctrines or duties from other authorities, we are sure to err, and in the end to overthrow the gospel. But clearly not all our Christian duties fall under this heading, not even everything of a "spiritual" nature; most fall under Hooker's first and third headings. There are many things useful for ordering the church and our Christian lives of which Scripture tells

---

28. It should be noted that Hooker, like Luther, would include here the observance of sacraments (see for instance V.57.3–4), thus complicating any attempt to simplistically map "things necessary" onto the "internal" and "things indifferent/accessory" onto the "external." However, Hooker is much more nuanced in his treatment of the necessity of sacraments than most of his interpreters. See my *Richard Hooker: A Companion to His Life and Work* (Eugene, OR: Cascade, 2015), ch. 11.

29. These range from the "cup of cold water" bestowed in Christ's name mentioned in Matt. 10:42 to the selling of possessions described in Acts 4:32–37.

us nothing clearly, and on which we may freely make use of reason. On other things, Scripture does give moral guidance, but on duties to which we are already bound by nature, such that reason may already provide adequate guidance. In such cases, we may make use of reason, and even when we seek to be guided by Scripture, we will recognize that the nature of such duties requires us to use prudence in applying Scripture to particular circumstances. Crucial here is Hooker's at first possibly perplexing distinction between "exacting at our hands" and "drawing our minds unto them"—it is possible for Scripture to direct our paths in a certain direction without prescribing specific actions in a binding way.

Hooker illustrates the difference with the helpful metaphor of the pathway in which the church is to walk. Without the articles of her creed and the sacraments, "the Church of God should not be able to measure out the length and the breadth of that way wherein forever she is to walk," and here she relies wholly on Scripture. Other things there are, however, "that are accessory hereunto," and "to alter them is no otherwise to change that way, than a path is changed by altering only the uppermost face thereof, which be it laid with gravel, or set with grass, or paved with stone, remaineth still the same path." In these things, "because discretion may teach the Church what is convenient, we hold not the Church further tied herein unto scripture, than that against scripture nothing be admitted in the Church, lest that path which ought always to be kept even, do thereby come to be overgrown with brambles and thorns" (III.3.3; *FLE* 1:211.9–23).

IV. The Variability of Divine Law: The Church as "Politic Society"

Hooker has thus attempted to establish a neat correlation between the realm of epistemological adiaphora (actions left free by Scripture) and of soteriological adiaphora (actions unnecessary to salvation). Those things necessary to salvation are fully revealed in Scripture; for those things accessory, "we have no commandment either in nature or in Scripture which doth exact them at our hands" (II.8.4; *FLE* 1:188.10–12). Yet still the precisianist may ask why we cannot simply reverse the equation, and insist that anything for which we do find a commandment in Scripture must then be considered "necessary to salvation"; indeed, this was just the sort of reasoning we encountered in Cartwright.[30] For Hooker, this is an unacceptable move, displacing the gospel

---

30. Cartwright, *Replye*, 14 (*WW* I:181). See also *SR* 5.

proclamation at the heart of Scripture by an unwholesome focus on peripheral matters. Hooker therefore has to show that in point of fact, when it comes to matters of polity, Scripture does not "exact them at our hands" in the way it does matters of faith. Rather than resorting to point-by-point confutation of disciplinarian proof texts, Hooker thus seeks to categorically redefine all matters of polity as by nature changeable, beyond the scope of divine law in the strict sense. This is why he is able to say that in such matters, "we hold not the Church further tied herein unto scripture, than that against scripture nothing be admitted in the Church." In other words, just because one can find a scriptural command for something, it does not necessarily continue to bind the church, if it can be shown to be by nature outside the soteriological realm of "things necessary to salvation."

Hooker mounts this argument in Book III, where he defends his conception of the church as a "politic society," subject to the same constraints of other human societies, and governed by changeable human laws, rather than unchangeable divine law.[31] As Cargill Thompson has argued, this conception ties together the whole argument of the *Lawes*, and renders Hooker's case coherent.[32] Yet Thompson's exposition leaves us unclear as to why Hooker might have expected this argument to be persuasive to his opponents, committed as they were to the idea that the church was a supernatural society ruled by Christ alone according to divine law. To them, Hooker's argument might seem like philosophical sleight-of-hand, cheating Scripture of authority even in those places where Hooker could not deny its clarity, in order to yield the desired result of a church establishment liberated to legislate as it desired. Accordingly, we must understand the theological foundation that undergirds Hooker's concept of the church as "politic society," which turns out to be an adaptation of Luther's "two kingdoms" doctrine that we have encountered before.[33]

This becomes clear right at the outset of Book III, which Hooker begins

---

31. Hooker first makes this identification in I.15.2, saying that "as it is a society" the church has "the selfsame original rounds which other politic societies have" (*FLE* 1:131.11–12).

32. Cargill Thompson, "Philosopher of the Politic Society: Richard Hooker as Political Thinker," in *Studies in Richard Hooker*, ed. W. Speed Hill, republished in W. D. J. Cargill Thompson, *Studies in the Reformation: Luther to Hooker*, ed. C. W. Dugmore (London: Athlone, 1980), 177–82.

33. Torrance Kirby has persuasively argued that "[t]he distinction of the two realms constitutes the pivotal link between Hooker's fundamental theological premises, on the one hand, and his ecclesiology and political theory, on the other. Indeed, this same pattern of thought permeates the argument of the Lawes and connects one stage of the discourse to another like a golden thread" (*Richard Hooker's Doctrine of the Royal Supremacy* [Leiden: Brill, 1990], 31).

with a systematic examination of "[w]hat the Church is, and in what respect laws of polity are thereunto necessarily required" (III.1; *FLE* 1:194.17–18). Here he draws on the classic Protestant distinction between the church visible and invisible, or in Hooker's language, "mystical."[34] The mystical church is apparent only to the eyes of faith,[35] and its membership known only to God.[36] The visible church, on the other hand, is a "sensibly known company" (III.1.3; *FLE* 1:195.26), identified by the "outward profession of those things, which supernaturally appertain to the very essence of Christianity, and are necessarily required in every particular Christian man" (III.1.4; *FLE* 1:196.8–11), viz., the creed and baptism. Torrance Kirby has argued that this distinction maps neatly onto the set of distinctions between the internal forum, *coram Deo*, and the external forum, *coram hominibus*, which is central to Luther's two-kingdoms doctrine:

> Just as the true believer was simultaneously "in heaven" (*coram Deo*) with Christ, saved, and totally justified, and "in earth" (*coram hominibus*) a sinner, gradually being sanctified; so also the Church has a twofold character—it too, one might say, is *simul justus et peccator*. In its primary and

34. For whatever reason, many scholars have been resistant to the idea that Hooker means by his distinction quite the same thing as the magisterial reformers did (see for instance William P. Haugaard, "Introduction to 'Books II, III & IV,'" in *FLE* 6[1]: 172–73, William H. Harrison, "The Church," in *A Companion to Richard Hooker*, ed. W. J. Torrance Kirby [Leiden: Brill, 2008], 306), with Peter Lake going so far as to insist that the purpose of Hooker's theology is to "conflate" the two (*Anglicans and Puritans?* 180–81), notwithstanding his forthright statements in III.1. This claim seems to stem from several misunderstandings. One simply concerns the term "mystical," which is hardly unique to Hooker in this context, and often functioned as a virtual synonym for "invisible" in the sixteenth century. Another is the contention that for Hooker, the "mystical" church is defined not so much in terms of predestination but in terms of the believer's invisible union with Christ. The same, however, could be said of Luther and Calvin. In point of fact, it would probably be more accurate to say that in certain respects, Hooker *radicalizes* the invisible-visible distinction, by renouncing any attempt to define which visible churches are "true churches" that properly embody the invisible church; outward profession of faith alone designates the boundaries of the visible church. See Paul D. L. Avis, "'The True Church' in Reformation Theology," *Scottish Journal of Theology* 30, no. 4 (1977): 341–45. See also my *Richard Hooker*, ch. 10.

35. "That Church of Christ which we properly term his body mystical, can be but one, neither can that one bee sensibly discerned by any man. . . . Only our minds by intellectual conceit are able to apprehend, that such a real body there is . . . a body mystical, because the mystery of their conjunction is removed altogether from sense" (III.1.2; *FLE* 1:194.27–195.3).

36. "They who are of this society have such marks and notes of distinction from all others, as are not object unto our sense" (III.1.2; *FLE* 1:195.9–10).

antecedent form the Church is placed altogether in the realm of total justice; in its secondary and derivative form, the Church has lost its divine character. Thus, for Luther the visible Church in the world is a natural, earthly institution, and therefore subject to human custom, tradition, and positive law.[37]

So it is that we find Hooker describing the mystical church in terms of the passivity of justification, which freely receives and rests on the promises of God by faith, and the visible church with the activity of sanctification,[38] which responds to grace, seeking to become more like Christ: "And as those everlasting promises of love, mercy, and blessedness belong to the mystical Church; even so on the other side when we read of any duty which the Church of God is bound unto, the Church whom this doth concern is a sensibly known company" (III.1.3; *FLE* 1:195.22–26). The former is *justus*, pure and righteous in the sight of God (III.1.2); the latter is *peccator*, a mixed company in which are many who are the very "imps and limbs of Satan" (III.1.7; *FLE* 1:198.22). Accordingly, as Hooker later explains when outlining his theology of worship, the outward visible church should be always striving toward a fuller correspondence with the inward mystical church: "That which inwardly each man should be, the Church outwardly ought to testify" (V.6.2; *FLE* 2:33.26–27). Moreover, to these two kingdoms correspond, as for Luther, two *regiments*, two different ways in which these two dimensions of the church are ruled: one in which Christ alone works "secretly, inwardly, and invisibly" as "that fountain, from whence the influence of heavenly grace distilleth," and the other "external and visible in the Church, exercised by men" (VIII.4.9; *FLE* 3:378.11–12, 377.19–20, 378.10).[39] Laws of church polity are those that govern the latter (III.1.14).

---

37. Kirby, *Richard Hooker's Doctrine of the Royal Supremacy*, 62. For Luther's treatment of the visible church as part of the civil kingdom, see John Witte Jr., *Law and Protestantism: The Legal Teachings of the Lutheran Reformation* (Cambridge and New York: Cambridge University Press, 2002), 7; F. Edward Cranz, *An Essay on the Development of Luther's Thought on Law, Justice, and Society* (Cambridge, MA: Harvard University Press, 1959), 144–45, 173–77; James M. Estes, *Peace, Order, and the Glory of God: Secular Authority and the Church in the Thought of Luther and Melanchthon, 1518–1559* (Leiden: Brill, 2005), 41, 66–67, 107–10.

38. Although some older scholarship questioned the orthodoxy of Hooker's understanding of the relationship of justification and sanctification in general, Kirby has argued that it is essentially that of Luther and Calvin (*Richard Hooker's Doctrine of the Royal Supremacy*, 41–59), a judgment that a careful recent study by Ranall Ingalls ("Sin and Grace," in *Companion to Richard Hooker*, 151–84) has by and large confirmed.

39. See Chapter Six, Sect. 5 below for fuller exposition of how this distinction functions in his account of the royal supremacy.

The outward, visible church, engaged in the process of sanctification, is Hooker's primary concern in the *Lawes*,[40] and Hooker is keen to oppose the disciplinarian tendency to spiritualize this visible church, thus attributing the perfection of the mystical church, *justus* in Christ, to the visible, still very much *peccator*. The result, as Kirby notes, "is a 'humanizing' of the church as an external, political organization, with the consequence that there is no longer a theological or metaphysical necessity for an 'essential' distinction to be drawn between ecclesiastical and civil power; both belong properly to the sphere of the 'politic society.'"[41] Hooker accordingly proceeds in the remainder of Book III to explain why church polity, as an external government of the visible church that does not belong to the realm of faith and salvation, is mutable like any other earthly government:

> There is no reason in the world wherefore we should esteem it as necessary always to do, as always to believe the same things; seeing every man knoweth that the matter of faith is constant, the matter contrariwise of action daily changeable, especially the matter of action belonging unto Church polity. . . . Which kind of laws (for as much as they are not in themselves necessary to salvation) may after they are made be also changed as the difference of times or places shall require. (III.10.7; *FLE* 1:244.21–245.7)

Hooker has thus provided a theological foundation for his claim in I.15.2 that the church, as a "politic society," functions within the sphere of human law. Therefore, to say that Scripture does not strictly bind us on these matters is in no way to demean or dismiss Scripture, but simply to understand that Scripture necessarily functions differently as the matter differs: immutably on matters that are *coram Deo*, and to some extent mutably on matters *coram*

---

40. See William H. Harrison, "Powers of Nature and Influences of Grace in Hooker's *Lawes*," in *Richard Hooker and the English Reformation*, 15–18.

41. W. J. Torrance Kirby, "From 'Generall Meditations' to 'Particular Decisions': The Augustinian Coherence of Richard Hooker's Political Theology," in *Law and Sovereignty in the Middle Ages and the Renaissance*, ed. Robert S. Sturges (Turnhout: Brepols, 2011), 62. As we shall see in Chapter Six, this "humanizing" does not mean a wholesale desacralization, taking place as it does within a Christological logic of what Kirby calls "an *ecclesiological* 'communication of idioms' between the mystical and institutional Churches, just as in Christology between the human and divine natures" so that for Hooker, there is "an explicitly divine basis for the human, positive laws and external institutions of the Church" (*Richard Hooker's Doctrine of the Royal Supremacy*, 76).

hominibus. This is in a way the central contention of the first three books of the *Lawes*, summarized in Hooker's pregnant statement of I.15.1: "Positive laws are either permanent or else changeable, *according as the matter itself is concerning which they were first made*" (*FLE* 1:130.26–28; italics mine). In the three concluding chapters of Book III, Hooker at last elaborates on this statement, delineating carefully how we may know when the church is given institutional liberty to legislate in the adiaphora, and when it is not.

In III.10, Hooker details four subcategories of positive law, and how long they continue in force. Some positive laws will state just how long they continue in force; many, however, will not. In the latter case, the only way for us to determine whether they are still in force is "by considering the nature and quality of such laws," which is to be judged "by the end for which it was made, and by the aptness of things therein prescribed to the same end" (III.10.1). This yields four categories: laws with unknown ends; laws with known permanent ends; laws with known temporary ends; and laws with permanent ends but impermanent matter.[42]

First are those laws whose end has simply not been disclosed to us by the lawmaker, and in which we are unable to divine it on our own. As an example, Hooker gives God's original command to Adam, not to eat of the tree of the knowledge of good and evil. We know it must have had a good reason, but not knowing what that reason was, we cannot be sure whether the command had permanent force or would have expired when certain conditions changed. When the end of the law is unknown, says Hooker, only the lawmaker has power to change the law; otherwise, we must assume it to be perpetually binding.

But what if we do know the end for which a law was instituted? Well, if that end is known to be permanent, then such laws are "also perpetual, unless they cease to be effectual unto that purpose for which they were at the first instituted" (III.10.1; *FLE* 1:240.16–18). The qualification here is a crucial one, distinguishing the second (permanent means to permanent end) and fourth (impermanent means to permanent end) subcategories of positive law, so it is worth paying attention to Hooker's elaboration: "[W]e cannot be ignorant, how sometimes that hath done great good, which afterwards, when time hath

---

42. For a similar set of distinctions applied to a similar question, see the fascinating treatise by Hooker's contemporary, Franciscus Junius, *The Mosaic Polity*, trans. Tom M. Rester, ed. Andrew M. McGinnis, Sources in Early Modern Economics, Ethics, and Law (1613; repr., Grand Rapids: Christian Library's Press, 2015), 71–96.

changeth the ancient course of things, doth grow to be either very hurtful, or not so greatly profitable and necessary" (III.10.1; *FLE* 1:240.21–24).

Before elaborating on this, Hooker turns to the third subcategory, positive laws with temporary ends: "Whether God be the author of laws by authorizing that power of men whereby they are made, or by delivering them made immediately from himself, by word only, or in writing also, or howsoever; notwithstanding the authority of their maker, the mutability of that end for which they are made doth also make them changeable" (III.10.2; *FLE* 1:240.27–32). Examples here include the ceremonial laws of the Old Testament, and even New Testament laws such as the decree of the Council of Jerusalem. These are laws made to serve temporary purposes, which expire when these purposes expire. Hooker is particularly insistent on this category because his Puritan opponents are arguing that the divine authority of the lawmaker should be sufficient proof that we have no right to change his laws—to do so would be to assert our authority above his. This argument rests on a fundamental confusion, and an inability to distinguish the different kinds and purposes of laws, says Hooker.

Those who concede this point, however, insist that any law with a permanent end must be unchangeable, considering any change to be "execrable pride and presumption, if so be the end and purpose for which God by that mean provideth be permanent." Specifically, his opponents argue that "if it be necessary always that the Church of Christ be governed, then doth the end for which God provided remain still, and therfore in those means which he by law did establish as being fittest unto that end, for us to alter any thing is to lift up ourselves against God and as it were to countermand him" (III.10.3; *FLE* 1:242.4–9). This too, however, manifests a crucial misunderstanding:

> [T]hey mark not that laws are instruments to rule by, and that instruments are not only to be framed according unto the general end for which they are provided, but even according unto that very particular, which riseth out of the matter whereon they have to work. The end wherefore laws were made may be permanent, and those laws nevertheless require some alteration, if there be any unfitness in the means which they prescribe as tending unto that end and purpose. (III.10.3; *FLE* 1:242.9–16)[43]

This thus leads him to discussion of the fourth category, laws with permanent ends but impermanent matter. The *end* of the law (e.g., "good order in

---

43. Cf. Thomas Aquinas, *ST* I–II q. 104 a. 3 ad. 2.

the church") is completely good, and remains as long as the world lasts, but the *matter* may change, so that a law formerly good ceases to be so, and must be altered so as to realize the original end in new circumstances. There is plenty of evidence for this happening in the Old Testament itself, and it is clear that many of the apostolic injunctions to the New Testament church, while their general aim remains constant, may require alteration when the church finds itself in new settings. To be sure, it will be hard to reach agreement about precisely which injunctions fall under this heading, but everyone will ultimately have to grant that some laws do.

> And therefore laws though both ordained of God himself, and the end for which they were ordained continuing, may notwithstanding cease, if by alteration of persons or times they be found unsufficient to attain unto that end. In which respect why may we not presume that God doth even call for such change or alteration, as the very condition of things themselves doth make necessary? (III.10.4; *FLE* 1:243.6–12)

Together, these distinctions establish a template for determining the proper scope of the church's liberty in adiaphora. By highlighting the soteriological function of Scripture as providing a "way that leadeth us from misery into bliss," a "way of supernatural duty . . . 'that ye believe in him whom he hath sent'" such that "without belief all other things are as nothing" (I.11.6; *FLE* 1:118.22–30), Hooker has given the doctrine of Christian liberty and adiaphora a clear compass. Whatever God commands in Scripture beyond the supernatural duties "necessary to salvation" are things soteriologically indifferent, and thus mutable to the extent that their object is mutable. Some are unchanging moral duties, but these coincide with the natural law, so that Scripture illuminates the weakness of fallen reason at this point. Once we move to the concrete realization of these moral duties in human law, we are in the realm of the mutable, where only a careful application of reason can determine to what extent scriptural teaching and precedent continue to bind. Accordingly, the category of epistemological adiaphora is reconfigured in terms of the soteriological and moral. If something is soteriologically indifferent—not necessary to salvation—it may still not be morally indifferent, but a perpetual duty of natural law (which will also be contained in Scripture either expressly or by deduction). If it is not such a perpetual duty, then it is morally indifferent, in the sense that its goodness or badness will depend on changeable circumstances, *whether or not Scripture addresses the matter*; Scripture may specify additional circumstances (e.g., when the high priest served in the Jewish temple, his clothing was not indifferent), but outside of these, it does not bind.

V. Implications

We thus find Hooker—in his resolute defense of the importance of things indifferent, of the liberty of the authorities to make binding judgments regarding their use, in his distinction of the two kingdoms in terms of two realms, and his clear positioning of the institutional structures and rituals of the visible church in the "civil kingdom," the realm of adiaphora—following closely in the footsteps of conformists such as Whitgift. But he is not merely repeating their arguments. On the contrary, Hooker has succeeded in providing a much clearer and more comprehensive account of what it means to be a "thing indifferent," so as to avoid the apparent fatalism that seemed to exhort dissenters to rest content that the gospel was preached and ask for no more. He has also supplied conformists with a powerful hermeneutical key for determining when and how Scripture dictates matters of church polity, rather than simply engaging in piecemeal exegetical wrangling. Moreover, he has taken the offensive against precisianist Puritans, attempting to show how it is their view which, by reintroducing a legalistic understanding of Scripture and the church, has overturned the Protestant commitment to Christian liberty. Hooker has thus accomplished the impressive feat of limiting the role of scriptural authority vis-à-vis ecclesiastical authority, while effectively positioning himself on the side of the Reformers and of Christian liberty, and refusing this honor to the precisianists. He has done this by focusing unswervingly on the distinction between the "two realms," which marks out Christian liberty before God, freedom from all earthly authority in bondage to Scripture alone, as something purely spiritual, in contrast with Christian existence in the world, in "politic societies" that wield authority by God's institution outside of Scripture.

By combining this "two realms" doctrine with a Thomistic division of the different kinds and functions of law, Hooker has arrived at a much more satisfying and consistent understanding of human law, both civil and ecclesiastical, than either his precisianist opponents or conformist predecessors. The church in its external and institutional form is a "politic society" subject to the same limits as any other human society. The ordering of the church, as of other societies, is thus a matter accessory to salvation, and consequently a matter on which we should not expect detailed scriptural guidance, and should not feel the need to justify every law directly from Scripture. Not only that, but concerning as they do those matters of human social life that are subject to great mutability by time, place, and circumstance, even divine positive law itself does not necessarily bind us to follow it to the letter. Scripture provides instruction and precedents in the government of both church and state, but how these instructions are to be applied and how far these precedents are to be followed, reason must judge, according to the particular circumstances of a politic society.[44] This, then, is the first step of his strategy for harmonizing loyalties to prince and to God: seeking to distinguish precisely between the proper scope for each.

This does leave us in considerable uncertainty within the outward realm, required to judge at every turn according to discretion and prudence—precisely what Cartwright considered the mark of a bad law. However, by recovering the soteriological center of Christian liberty Hooker seeks to reassure his readers that such uncertainty is acceptable outside the sphere of those things necessary to salvation. Indeed, it is unavoidable, and to demand certainty will simply be a snare and a torment to weak consciences, "filling them with infinite perplexities, scrupulosities, doubts insoluble, and extreme despairs" (II.8.6; *FLE* 1:190.16–19). Accordingly Hooker is not afraid to overturn the hermeneutic that had for decades helped undergird conformist defenses of royal supremacy—the authoritative examples of Old Testament rulers. The royal supremacy itself is defended on grounds of prudence and good order, that which is most suitable for government of civil and ecclesiastical polity in England as it now stands.[45] Hooker clearly believes that something like the royal supremacy will be best for most if not all Christian societies, but it is not in itself a matter of divine law. By tempering the zeal for absolute certainty in earthly matters, he has rehabilitated the usefulness of reason as a way of determining good and evil within the adiaphora. This sets the stage for the second step of Hooker's strategy for harmonizing loyalties, which we shall turn to now.

---

44. To be sure, Hooker hardly seeks to give reason unlimited discretion in such matters. In fact, Hooker closes his statement of these issues by recognizing that both sides agree that there are scriptural limits to the church's discretion; the question is just how extensive they are: "Besides, in the matter of external discipline or regiment itself, we do not deny but there are some things whereto the church is bound till the world's end. So as the question is only how far the bounds of the Church's liberty do reach" (III.11.13, *FLE* 1:260.11–15).

45. Gazal documents this hermeneutical turn, and the need for it given the failures of existing conformist polemics, in *Scripture and Royal Supremacy*, 495–519. See also Daniel Eppley, "Royal Supremacy," in *Companion to Richard Hooker*, 508–9.

CHAPTER FIVE

Harmonized Loyalties

....

Conscience, Reason, and Corporate Moral Agency

> In all things then are our consciences best resolved, and in most agreeable sort unto God and nature settled, when they are so far persuaded as those grounds of persuasion which are to be had will bear.
>
> Hooker, *Lawes* II.7.5

> A law is the deed of the whole body politic, whereof if ye judge your selves to be any part, then is the law even your deed also.
>
> Hooker, *Lawes*, Pref. 5.2

I. Conformism in Jeopardy: The Problem of Edification

Having seen in the previous chapter how Hooker sought to protect the doctrine of Christian liberty from the alternately libertine and legalistic logic of precisianism, we shall turn now to consider his attempts to correct a conformism that did not seem overly interested in the doctrine either. Where Luther's liberated conscience was busy and active, using its freedom indefatigably to seek out how the neighbor could be served in every circumstance, Whitgift's was by contrast a passive and quietist one, meekly accepting the greater wisdom of authority to determine what love demanded. The Puritan protest of the 1560s–1580s could thus claim to be carrying forward the legacy of Luther's insistence that Christian liberty is a freedom *for* the neighbor. This protest might have lacked the ring of authenticity by the legalistic form in which it was often lodged, but the Puritan challenge to conformists was often a reasonable one: prove that these "indifferent" ceremonies are edifying, and we will submit. Christian liberty, on this construction, could rightly be maintained in the midst of submission to law only if believers could recognize that the laws were good laws, laws that would build up the church, strengthen it, and make it grow in righteousness; only thus could law-obedience be sure to be an exercise of charity.

But Whitgift and other conformists proved decidedly shy when it came to answering whether "reason" served to justify the disputed rites, or how exactly they conduced to "edification"; indeed, it cannot be said that the conformist case had advanced very far, if at all, on this point, from Gardiner in 1536 to Bancroft in 1589. The reasons for this failure lie not in poor apologetic ability, but in the internal logic of conformism. Three problems in particular may be discerned. First, the terms in which the concept of adiaphora had often been couched rendered the whole discussion of "edification" in ceremonies extremely awkward. In Whitgift's strictly dualistic version of the two-kingdoms doctrine, a minimalistic account of "things necessary to salvation" faced off against a totally indifferent realm of outward ceremonies to which he hesitated to attribute any spiritual value. Accordingly, he and other conformists repeatedly shied away from attributing any concrete value to a particular ceremony aside from its contribution to *civil* order and decorum.[1] This public order simply *is* edification: as Whitgift put it, "Such laws and orders as keep godly peace and unity in the church do edify; but the laws for apparel keep godly peace and unity in the church; ergo, they edify."[2] Second, insofar as they did seek to establish the edifying value of the debated ceremonies, they were limited by the highly word-centered piety that they shared with their opponents, as Peter Lake shows repeatedly in *Anglicans and Puritans*.[3] For Whitgift, the preaching of the word, which is the instrument of conveying saving doctrine into the hearts of the elect, is the only kind of spiritual edification worth considering. Therefore, in Chapter Three we found him arguing, without any hint of disingenuousness, that the required vestments are edifying, not because of anything in them, but *per accidens*, because, by the queen's law, it is necessary to wear the vestments in order to preach, and to preach is to edify.[4]

Both of these points clearly entail a kind of circular reasoning: Why

---

1. See Peter Lake, *Anglicans and Puritans? Presbyterianism and English Conformist Thought from Whitgift to Hooker* (London: Unwin Hyman, 1988), 45–46, 123.

2. *WW* II:61.

3. Lake, *Anglicans and Puritans?* 39–40, 46–47, 123–25. See also John S. Coolidge, *Pauline Renaissance: Puritanism and the Bible* (Oxford: Clarendon, 1970), 44–46.

4. *WW* I.71.

require these orders and ceremonies? Because they are edifying. Why are they edifying? Because they are required. Clearly, if anything that establishes uniform civil order is thereby edifying, any ceremony that does so is as good as another, and there is no good reason for the particular ones that have been established, particularly if they were stumbling blocks to the weak. In the standard conformist defense, as Lake observes, "the ceremonies were . . . denied any directly religious function or significance. They were there because they were there and because order and uniformity and obedience were all good things in themselves the ordinary Christian should simply do what he or she was told."[5]

The conformists felt confident resting on such a weak rational case because, to their minds, the main point was not to make a rationally compelling case for the particular laws established.[6] Indeed, this was the crucial third constraint on how far they could go in demonstrating the edifying qualities of the disputed ceremonies: for most conformists, to go too far in mounting such a defense was already to concede the most subversive Puritan assumption—namely, that it should be up to each Christian, or at any rate each Christian minister, to decide for himself whether the established laws were beneficial for the church. We witnessed both Matthew Parker and John Whitgift's consternation at this idea in previous chapters. To concede this, to suggest that there might be an independent bar at which the case between conformist and Puritan could be tried, was to shake the very foundations of Tudor government. Mark Perrott argues that it was for this reason that, when Cartwright challenged Whitgift that the disputed ceremonies, not being found in Scripture, could only be defended by resort to reason, Whitgift refused to take the bait and provide such a defense. An appeal to reason might seem more likely to open a debate than close it, given that the deliverances of reason lacked certainty and specificity, and that reason was the common property of all; a defense based on reason could thus invite objection and disobedience from Englishmen convinced that reason told them otherwise.[7]

<hr/>

5. Lake, *Anglicans and Puritans?* 164.

6. Of course, the minimalism of the conformist defense should not be overstated. Most conformists were eager to rebut Puritan charges that the disputed ceremonies were in fact *unedifying* or downright offensive to conscientious believers, but beyond this, they were unlikely to go. The ceremonies were not unedifying, they would maintain, but when it came to showing that they were in fact positively edifying, Elizabeth's apologists became much more hesitant and equivocal. See for instance Matthew Parker, *Briefe Examination for the Tyme* . . . (London: Richard Iugge, 1566), 6r–9v.

7. M. E. C. Perrott, "Richard Hooker and the Problem of Authority in the Elizabethan Church," *Journal of Ecclesiastical History* 49, no. 1 (1998): 44–45.

Therefore, the standard conformist line was that private Christian citizens simply were not to concern themselves with all such questions regarding indifferent matters, and that they were indeed to assume that most matters were indifferent. By the time we reach Bancroft's 1589 Paul's Cross sermon, comments Peter Lake, "There was, in short, virtually no need for any active interest in doctrine on the part of the laity, since God had promised his church to enlighten the learned 'to whose godly determination in matters of question her dutiful children ought to submit themselves without any curious or willful contradiction.'"[8] Coupled with this rejection of any active inquiry or participation in religious questions on the part of subjects, we should perhaps not be surprised to find a similar passivity in conformist political theory. We find little or no attempt to bridge the gap between the liberty of individual and institution with an account of the subject's consensual participation in the government.[9] Accordingly, the conformist defense of institutional liberty could only be achieved at the expense of the individual subject.

Hooker to the Rescue?

The conformist case thus found itself in a weak and ambiguous position by the time Hooker took up his pen, despite the political defeat of the Puritans. Not only that, but it found itself having dangerously compromised the Protestant vision of faith as a "living, busy, active, mighty thing,"[10] animating a church full of Christians who exercised their spiritual freedom in eager, open-eyed, conscientious regard for one another; in its place, they threatened to substitute a form of the hated papist doctrine of "implicit faith," suitably transposed into the key of political religion.[11]

8. Lake, *Anglicans and Puritans?* 128.

9. Whitgift offers hints in this direction, noting almost as an afterthought, "I add that every private man's consent is in the consent of the church, as it is in the consent of the parliament; and therefore no man's liberty otherwise restrained than he hath consented to" (*WW* II:573), but he never develops this line of reasoning (cf. Lake, *Anglicans and Puritans?* 63). Although Lake errs in treating the strong divine-right theories of sovereignty among Elizabethan conformists as some new development, he is right to highlight the powerful role these played in their attempt to quash Puritan dissent (*Anglicans and Puritans?* 129–39).

10. Luther, *Preface to the Epistle of St. Paul to the Romans* (1546) in *LW* 35:370.

11. Lake concludes his discussion of conformism: "Thus by 1593 the conformist avant-garde (in the persons of Saravia and Bancroft) found itself teetering on the edge of religious quietism and political absolutism. Both tendencies had been apparent in Whitgift's reply to

It was one of Hooker's great accomplishments to attempt to reintroduce, even in the midst of defending conformity, an element of voluntary, rational, conscious acceptance of the established orders on the part of subjects. By this means, he seeks, while carefully distinguishing loyalties to God and to man (as we saw in Chapter Four), to harmonize these loyalties, so that the conscience may freely submit to, and indeed, positively esteem human laws as distinct from, yet consonant with, divine laws. And yet he must find a way to retrieve such willingness without encouraging open dissent and disobedience on the part of those who, having heard his rational case, continue to differ.[12] He must, in short, articulate a model of corporate rationality and corporate moral agency, of government exercised through consent, that will require his opponents' submission without destroying their freedom, offering a reconciliation of law and liberty. To be sure, he remains a man taking the authoritarian side in an authoritarian age, so there is a limit to how far we today feel like we can travel with him. However, as I will argue here and in the concluding chapter, Hooker's development of Christian freedom, and in particular his concern for the principle of voluntariety, bring us noticeably closer to modern ideals of civil liberty, consent, and active citizenship. As he writes in the opening of his *Sermon on the Nature of Pride,*

> The nature of man being much more delighted to be led than drawn, doth many times stubbornly resist authority when to persuasion it easily yieldeth. Whereupon the wisest lawmakers have endeavored always that those laws might seem most reasonable which they would have most inviolably kept. A law simply commanding or forbidding is but dead in comparison of that which expresseth the reason wherefore it doth the one or the other.[13]

The argument in this chapter will comprise five main sections. First, I will show that Hooker does in fact make it quite clear that he is appealing to the consciences of his opponents, seeking free and rational agreement in the truth, and that this is no mere charade. Second, I will look at the importance of his rehabilitation of probable reason, in place of elusive certainty, as a criterion of the goodness of laws and ceremonies, and how this differs from the legalism

---

Cartwright, but now in the works of his protégé Bancroft they seemed to have established a position of dominance" (*Anglicans and Puritans?* 139).

12. Perrott, "Problem of Authority," 45–46, 54–55.

13. *A Learned Sermon on the Nature of Pride* I (*FLE* 5:309.7–11).

typical of both precisianist and conformist thought. Third, I will illustrate his repeated concern for edification, his willingness to argue that many of the disputed ceremonies are of real concrete spiritual benefit to believers, and are not merely "there because they are there." Fourth, I will suggest how the above considerations relate to the doctrine of Christian liberty as expounded by early magisterial reformers, arguing that Hooker comes closer to doing justice to the multidimensional demands of this concept than do many of his predecessors and contemporaries. Finally, I will look at Hooker's understanding of corporate rationality, and his political theory of consent, to suggest how Hooker sustains this genuine concern for individual liberty within an overarching call to submit to those in authority—for Hooker, we exercise our individual freedom in and through exercising a corporate freedom which structures that individual freedom.

II. "To Resolve the Conscience": Hooker's Apologetic Strategy

When Hooker states in his Preface that "my whole endeavor is to resolve the conscience" (Pref. 7.1; 1:34.20–21), this is no mere rhetorical trope, but in fact a declaration of what we have identified as one of his central ambitions in the *Lawes*: to recover the doctrine of Christian liberty and reclaim the Puritans from the labyrinth of conscience in which they had enmeshed themselves. We argued in Chapter Three above that the logic of precisianist biblicism, although attempting to provide certainty for the troubled conscience, only burdened it further, and, as Hooker recognized, led it into "infinite perplexities, scrupulosities, doubts insoluble, and extreme despairs" (II.8.6; *FLE* 1:190.18–19). The Puritans had demanded assurance that their loyalty to the magistrate did not clash with their loyalty to God, that in obeying the one, they were also obeying the other, and, Hooker argues, they had sought such assurance in the wrong place. Accordingly he may honestly profess to be seeking not merely the *submission* of his opponents to the law of the realm, but their *liberation*: from a Bible again conceived as a law of condemnation and from a self-defeating quest for precise certainty of what the will of God demands.[14]

---

14. C. S. Lewis puts it well: "Though Hooker is not writing to defend the freedom of the individual, he is certainly writing to defend the freedom of Man from what he believes to be a false conception of supernatural authority" (*English Literature in the Sixteenth Century, Excluding Drama*, vol. 3 of *The Oxford History of English Literature* [Oxford: Clarendon, 1954], 453). See also chapter 7 of my book, *Richard Hooker: A Companion to His Life and Work* (Eugene, OR: Cascade, 2015) for a consideration of the importance of Hooker's sense of pastoral concern.

The attribution of such irenic motives to Hooker, however, has become increasingly controversial in recent decades. When Cargill Thompson in 1972 challenged the old image of Hooker as dispassionate philosopher, calmly weighing the Puritan protest in the scales of eternal wisdom, and noted that "Hooker was continually arguing to a brief," this reevaluation prompted subsequent Hooker scholars to give closer attention to his rhetorical devices and polemical agenda.[15] For some this has involved an almost gleeful deconstruction of the "judicious" and irenic Hooker, in order to show that Hooker could fight dirty too. In recent years, this reading has taken on heightened significance as part of an attempt to refute Torrance Kirby's reinterpretation of Hooker as an apologist for the magisterial Reformation, given Kirby's emphasis on Hooker's argument as an "irenical appeal"[16] to his opponents whose basic Reformed doctrine he shares.

We can observe both agendas at work in the fullest recent statement of Hooker the polemicist, chapter 3 of A. J. Joyce's *Richard Hooker and Anglican Moral Theology*, which she devotes to proving that Hooker was "unambiguously contemptuous" of the Puritans, and "was fully capable of the most waspish, acerbic, and irreverent assaults" upon them, so that "it is difficult to see how the kind of account that Kirby and Atkinson have attempted to give . . . can possibly be sustained."[17] Unfortunately, Joyce's argument depends on a false dichotomy between irenics and polemics, a questionable hermeneutic of suspicion, and a systematic inattention to Hooker's polemical context. Under the first heading, we may note that Joyce seems to treat the tasks of

15. Cargill Thompson, "Philosopher of the Politic Society: Richard Hooker as Political Thinker," in *Studies in Richard Hooker*, ed. W. Speed Hill, republished in W. D. J. Cargill Thompson, *Studies in the Reformation: Luther to Hooker*, ed. C. W. Dugmore (London: Athlone, 1980), 140. Among the most significant, though occasionally overreaching, contributions on this score have been Rudolph P. Almasy, "They Are and Are Not Elymas: The 1641 'Causes' Notes as Postscript to Richard Hooker's *Of the Lawes of Ecclesiasticall Politie*," in *Richard Hooker and the Construction of Christian Community*, ed. Arthur Stephen McGrade (Tempe, AZ: Medieval & Renaissance Texts & Studies, 1997), 183–202; Almasy, "Language and Exclusion in the First Book of Hooker's *Politie*," in *Richard Hooker and the English Reformation*, ed. W. J. Torrance Kirby (Dordrecht: Kluwer Academic Publishers, 2003), 227–42; and Brian Vickers, "Public and Private Rhetoric in Hooker's *Lawes*," in *Richard Hooker and the Construction of Christian Community*, 95–145.

16. W. J. Torrance Kirby, *Richard Hooker, Reformer and Platonist* (Aldershot, UK: Ashgate, 2005), x, 20; see also *Richard Hooker's Doctrine of the Royal Supremacy* (Leiden: Brill, 1990), 20.

17. A. J. Joyce, *Richard Hooker and Anglican Moral Theology* (Oxford: Oxford University Press, 2012), 47, 51, 63. For a fuller riposte to Joyce, see my essay "The Search for a Reformed Hooker," *Reformation & Renaissance Review* 16, no. 1 (2014): 74–78, and my *Richard Hooker*, ch. 5.

polemics and irenics as mutually exclusive, when it is quite clearly the case that polemical means, endeavoring to refute an opponent's errors, may serve an overall irenic cause, one that hopes to bring about reconciliation in the truth.[18] Indeed, part of her error here seems to stem from a misunderstanding of an "irenic" or "judicious" Hooker as one that would conform to modern canons of scholarly objectivity, avoiding any sign of passionate commitment to his cause, or a predetermined conviction as to what truth demanded.[19] Under the second heading, we discover an unwillingness to treat any passage in which Hooker professes respect or peaceable intentions toward his opponents as anything more than "a highly successful and persuasive literary device." By this means, Joyce insulates her reading against any possible counter-evidence, which must be always read as "laden with irony and sarcasm."[20] Finally, Joyce does not seem overly interested in whether, in Hooker's more polemical passages, the Puritans actually said what Hooker accused them of saying, singling out as an example of his "outrageous parody" a passage in which Hooker in fact closely paraphrases Cartwright's own words (and alerts us to the fact with a footnote!).[21]

Pace Joyce, we can only take the full measure of how Hooker's *Lawes* "marks a revolution in the art of controversy," as C. S. Lewis puts it,[22] by comparing it to the full-blown polemics of a contemporary like Bancroft, who was prepared to compass the overthrow of his opponent by fair means or foul. Indeed, it is notable that, unlike Bancroft, Hooker was no officially commissioned propagandist, but appears to have written primarily "to satisfy himself," with only indirect and limited support from the authorities.[23] Further, what we know

18. Avis captures this balance well in his review: "Hooker is a highly effective controversialist who knows how to manipulate his readers to gain his ends. That does not mean that he was not seeking a change of heart and mind, a genuine conversion of his opponents; only that he goes about it in a formidably effective way" (P. D. L. Avis, "Review of *A Companion to Richard Hooker*," *Ecclesiology* 8 [2012]: 416).

19. See for instance Joyce, *Richard Hooker and Anglican Moral Theology*, 60–61, 64.

20. Joyce, *Richard Hooker and Anglican Moral Theology*, 58.

21. Joyce, *Richard Hooker and Anglican Moral Theology*, 51. The passage in question is from V.22.7, where Hooker critiques Cartwright's teaching on the efficacy of sermons in *SR* 375.1–17.

22. Lewis, *English Literature*, 459.

23. Diarmaid MacCulloch, "Richard Hooker's Reputation," in *A Companion to Richard Hooker*, ed. W. J. Torrance Kirby (Leiden: Brill, 2008), 572. See also Deborah Shuger, "'Societie Supernaturall': The Imagined Community of Hooker's *Lawes*," in *Richard Hooker and the Construction of Christian Community*, 308–9; Patrick Collinson, "Richard Hooker and the Elizabethan Establishment," in *Richard Hooker and the Construction of Christian Community*,

of Hooker's life bears out his own statements in the Preface that he writes as one who, having once sympathized with many aspects of the Puritan cause, has now, upon further study and reflection, concluded that their complaints lack merit, and has come to genuinely admire and support the established church.[24] Accordingly, where Whitgift had prefaced his *Answere* and *Defence* with warnings addressed to the authorities, Hooker began his by directly addressing his adversaries, beseeching them, "as ye tender the peace and quietness of this church . . . regard not who it is which speaketh, but weigh only what is spoken" (Pref. 1.3; *FLE* 1:2.34–3.1). In short, we ought to take seriously Hooker's repeated insistence that "our endeavour is not so much to overthrow them with whom we contend, as to yield them just and reasonable causes of those things which, for want of due consideration heretofore, they misconceived" (V.1.1; *FLE* 2:16.18–21). This represents a significant shift from the posture of Whitgift and Bancroft, both of whom liked to accuse the Puritans of arrogance and sedition at every opportunity.[25] Hooker was convinced that their errors stem primarily from a failure in reasoning, a failure that patient persistence in good reasoning could repair.[26] Whereas for Whitgift and Bancroft, the key problem was disobedience, for Hooker, the key problem was lack of assurance, and so long as the Puritans lacked any assurance that the laws were good, simply insisting on obedience would do little good. Perrott contends, "Hooker did not seek blind obedience to church law simply by emphasising the necessity of blind obedience to magisterial authority but rather by seeking the subject's apprehension that laws grounded on the authority of reason were sound."[27] In this, Hooker displays a willingness to go beyond the mere negative argument in favor of

---

165–69. Indeed, as Lake has noted, Hooker's argument was scarcely an unqualified endorsement of the *status quo* (*Anglicans and Puritans?* 146, 225), and Collinson observes in his essay that "no other apologist of the Elizabethan *status quo* chose to be as critical as Hooker of the institution he was supposed to be defending" (171).

24. Pref. 1. For a good survey of Hooker's journey from a sort of Puritanism to the author of its most powerful rebuttal, see Collinson, "Elizabethan Establishment," 153–64.

25. See for instance *WW* I.76–82, II.73; Bancroft, *A Sermon preached at Paules Crosse . . .* (London: E. B., 1588). More extensively, Collinson's documentation of Bancroft's "conspiratorial obsession" (1) with the Puritan threat in *Richard Bancroft and Elizabethan Anti-Puritanism* (Cambridge: CUP, 2013) ought to provide counterpoint enough for anyone who imagines similar vituperation in Hooker's writings.

26. See for instance Pref. 9.1–2, *FLE* I.16.6; also Perrott, "Problem of Authority," 36–37. However, Rudolph Almasy suggests that by the end of his life, as he was finishing the *Lawes*, Hooker may have begun to despair of the possibility of persuasion, concluding that some Puritans were simply incorrigible in their opposition (see "Elymas").

27. Perrott, "Problem of Authority," 37.

conformity—that the disputed rites were *not repugnant* to Scripture—and to show positively that "we are led by great reason to observe them." A substantial part of this reason is *reason* itself, "sound and sincere judgment" (Pref. 7.1; *FLE* 1:34.17, 22). This may seem natural enough, but Perrott notes that it constitutes "a significant development in conformist thought."[28] Whereas Whitgift appeared very hesitant to appeal to the judgment seat of reason, Hooker sought to rehabilitate the "probable authority of reason in church affairs" as the "key to resolving the conscientious muddle that underpinned Puritan dissent."[29] Hooker would thus seek to justify both the goodness of law-obedience in general—the goodness of established authority and of submission to it—but also the goodness of the particular laws and authorities established in the Church of England. And for both, goodness meant rationality.[30]

III. "The Rule of Well-Doing": Rehabilitating Reason

Indeed, when we look at the role of rationality in Hooker's *Lawes*, we will readily perceive that his appeal to the Puritan conscience is not merely a political expedient, designed to better secure long-term obedience than would peremptory calls for unquestioning submission. On the contrary, it is deeply rooted in Hooker's whole conception of God, man, and creation.

We see this right at the outset of the famous discussion of Book I. Since

28. Perrott, "Problem of Authority," 37.

29. Perrott, "Problem of Authority," 51. To this extent, Kirby's emphasis upon "the core principles of the reformed doctrinal orthodoxy" (*Richard Hooker's Doctrine of the Royal Supremacy*, 20) as the means by which Hooker aims to bring agreement, may be somewhat misplaced, given the more central role played by his appeal to the shared capacity to reason (so Joyce argues, *Richard Hooker and Anglican Moral Theology*, 156). Nonetheless, Kirby is right that such an appeal would have hardly been effective, had not Hooker been able to show that the appeal to reason was circumscribed within Reformed limits. Of course, the 1599 critique of the *Lawes*, *A Christian Letter*, shows that not all were convinced of the compatibility of Hooker's view of reason with Reformed thought (see especially *FLE* 4:11–17, 64–71), and the question remains one of hot debate in modern scholarship.

30. To be sure, some recent scholars, such as Ethan Shagan in *The Rule of Moderation: Violence, Religion and the Politics of Restraint in Early Modern England* (Cambridge: Cambridge University Press, 2011), have argued otherwise, applying a Foucauldian hermeneutic of suspicion to Hooker's text and arriving at the conclusion that Hooker's argument amounts to an automatic justification of any human law as "*ipso facto* moderate no matter how violent or aggressive" (147). This argument, however, bypasses entirely the critical role of divine and natural law in Hooker's thought, which always stands in judgment over human law, even if Hooker is skeptical of private citizens' abilities to form such judgments.

in Hooker's sapiential theology God is the principle and pattern of all things, it is in God that we are to discern the basic structure of law and of action,[31] which Hooker describes as follows: "God therefore is a law both to himself, and to all other things besides. . . . God worketh nothing without cause. All those things which are done by him, have some end for which they are done: and the end for which they are done, is a reason of his will to do them" (I.2.3; *FLE* 1:60.17–23). Hooker is clearly no voluntarist—God acts not arbitrarily, but always for a determinate end; his action follows law, his action is always rational, and the structure of law therefore, and law-obedience, is fundamentally rational. But this is no denial of God's freedom: "Nor is the freedom of the will of God any whit abated, let or hindered by means of this, because the imposition of this law upon himself is his own free and voluntary act" (I.2.6; *FLE* 1:62.29–63.1). God's will remains free even as it follows law, for law that is rational, oriented toward its proper desired end, is the form of freedom, not its contradiction, a point that will play a key role in Hooker's account of human law as well. Obviously, we are not God, and only in God, the unconditioned source of being, can will and reason, law and freedom, perfectly inhere in one another. Nonetheless, we bear God's image, and by our intellectual and moral capacities aspire to conformity with him (I.5.3). Therefore, our wills are not arbitrary either, but rational, moved by the desire of goodness: "To choose is to will one thing before another. And to will is to bend our souls to the having or doing of that which they see to be good. Goodness is seen with the eye of the understanding. And the light of that eye, is reason. So that two principal fountains there are of human action, Knowledge and Will" (I.7.2; *FLE* 1:78.1–5). Human action, then, is always motivated by desire and our wills incline toward what we perceive to be good, to be "the more available to our bliss" (I.8.1; *FLE* 1:82.7).

Hooker's basic theology and anthropology, then, demand that if the Puritans are to be brought to genuinely choose obedience to the laws of the Church of England, it can only be by demonstrating to them that reason shows these laws to be "more available for their bliss." This, he argues, can be shown

---

31. See Kirby, *Richard Hooker, Reformer and Platonist*, 29–57; "Creation and Government: Eternal Law as the Fountain of Laws in Richard Hooker's Ecclesiastical Polity," in *Divine Creation in Ancient, Medieval, and Early Modern Thought*, ed. Michael Treschow, Willemien Otten, and Walter Hannam (Leiden: Brill, 2007), 405–23; "The Neo-Platonic Logic of Richard Hooker's Generic Division of Law," *Renaissance and Reformation* 22 (1998): 49–68; "From 'Generall Meditations' to 'Particular Decisions': The Augustinian Coherence of Richard Hooker's Political Theology," in *Law and Sovereignty in the Middle Ages and the Renaissance*, ed. Robert S. Sturges (Turnhout: Brepols, 2011), 47–53.

not only by recourse to Scripture, but to the law of nature, which is itself part of God's law. "Of all good things God himself is the Author and consequently an approver of them. The rule to discern when the actions of men are good, when they are such as they ought to be, is more ample and large than the law which God hath set particular down in his holy Word, the Scripture is but a part of that rule" (VII.11.10; *FLE* III.210.14–18). By this means, Hooker can give a broader foundation and a broader application to the conformist (and magisterial Protestant) commonplace that the just commands of the magistrate, derived from the rule of charity, are to be taken as the commands of God.[32] While it is true that all things in the church "ought to be of God," this may mean "of his own institution" *or* "with his approbation." All things that are well done (which includes all things in accord with the law of nature) have God's approbation, and are thus "of God," and so "if the rule of well-doing be more ample than the Scripture, what necessity is there, that everything which is of God, should be set down in holy Scripture?" (VII.11.10; *FLE* III.210.20–23).

Book I of the *Lawes* offers a beautiful picture of the world as the theater of God's glory and wisdom, revealing the law of his being in angels, in inanimate creation, in beasts, and in the rational operations of mankind, the creature that bears his image. Because of this, the exercise of reason is glorifying to God, it is a participation in divine wisdom and as such deserves our respect. Hooker cannot hide his impatience with the precisianists who "never use reason so willingly as to disgrace reason . . . as if the way to be ripe in faith, were to be raw in wit and judgement; as if reason were an enemy unto religion, childish simplicity the mother of Ghostly and divine wisdom" (III.8.4; *FLE* 1:221.28, 222.26–28). He accordingly spends much of Book II, chapter 7, and Book III, chapter 8 in an *apologia* for natural reason, declaring that "to detract from the dignity thereof were to injure even God himself, who being that light which none can approach unto, hath sent out these lights whereof

---

32. Matthew Parker quotes Bucer and Calvin to this effect in his *Briefe Examination*, 10r–10v: "'Whatsoever man shall decree, which by any means may make to the use of his neighbours, for that the same is derived from the rule of charity, as be laws civil, domestical statutes, ceremonies and rites which Christian men use, thereby to teach or hear God's word more commodiously, or to prayer, and about the Lord's Supper and Baptism, yea, and whatsoever shall be a furtherance to pass our life here more profitably and decently: that thing ought not to be esteemed as a tradition or precept of man, though by men it be commanded, but as the tradition or precept of God.' Thus far Doctor Bucer. With whom Master Calvin very well agreeth, saying: 'That which is part of decency commended unto us by the Apostle, though it be prescribed by man, is God's tradition, and not man's, as kneeling at solemn prayers and such like.'"

we are capable, even as so many sparks resembling the bright fountain from which they rise" (III.8.9; *FLE* 1:226.11–15). Total depravity undermines natural reason in many ways, to be sure, but does not render it incapable of useful knowledge within human and civil affairs. Hooker's two-kingdoms doctrine thus circumscribes his view of depravity (as it did for other Reformers such as Calvin and Vermigli),[33] and his careful establishment of matters of church polity as adiaphora, within the realm of the civil kingdom, is presupposed in his appeal to the usefulness of reason in such matters.

We would thus be wrong to imagine, as some have, that Hooker's argument is simply about raising the bar as to what reason is capable. It is equally a matter of lowering the bar of what constitutes sufficient assurance in moral and political actions.[34] Whereas the precisianists had sought absolute certainty (and thus, direct scriptural warrant) for all such actions, Hooker insisted that this was rarely to be had. While our minds of course always seek the greatest degree of confidence possible, and this is especially important in matters of faith and salvation, where we may not be satisfied with mere probabilities, we can hardly ask this of most affairs of human life (II.7.5). After pointing out all the situations in which human judgment is a dependable authority, he acknowledges that it cannot provide infallible assurance or override divine testimony. "Howbeit in defect of proof infallible, because the mind doth rather follow probable persuasions, than approve the things that have in them no likelihood of truth at all," we generally accept as a probable authority the testimony of learned men (II.7.5; *FLE* 1:180.29–32). This probable assurance should suffice in most cases, so that, contra Cartwright,[35] our consciences may be assured without direct guidance from Scripture: "[I]n all things then are our consciences best resolved, and in most agreeable sort unto God and nature settled, when they are so far persuaded as those grounds of persuasion which are to be had will bear." Indeed, to demand otherwise does not give greater assurance, but rather greater "perplexity":

> When bare and unbuilded conclusions are put into their minds, they finding not themselves to have thereof any great certainty, imagine that this proceedeth only from lack of faith, and that the spirit of God doth not

33. Cf. Calvin, *Institutes* II.2.13; Vermigli's introduction to *Commentary on Aristotle's Nicomachean Ethics*. See Kirby, "Richard Hooker's Theory of Natural Law in the Context of Reformation Theology," *Sixteenth Century Journal* 30, no. 3 (1999): 696–701.

34. Perrott, "Problem of Authority," 48–52.

35. As noted in ch. 3, he says that unless we "have the word of God go before us in all our actions . . . we cannot otherwise be assured that they please God" (*SR* 61).

work in them, as it doth in true believers; by this means their hearts are much troubled, they fall into anguish and perplexity: whereas the truth is, that how bold and confident soever we may be in words, when it cometh to the point of trial, such as the evidence is which the truth hath either in itself or through proof, such is the hearts assent thereunto, neither can it be stronger, being grounded as it should be. (II.7.5; *FLE* 1:180.5–20)

By this means, the precisianists have in fact succeeded in trapping Christian consciences again in fear, uncertain that they have pleased God, which is precisely the labyrinth from which Luther's reform had sought to liberate the conscience. Again, then, we find Hooker claiming to be freeing the consciences of precisianists from a bondage of doubt and restoring them to robust Christian liberty.[36] The insistence on scriptural proof, argues Perrott, had shackled the conscience by demanding an impossible level of perfect assurance in matters on which Scripture simply gave no unambiguous testimony.[37] By seeking clear scriptural justification even in matters essentially adiaphorous, they were chasing a mirage, and were bound to be disappointed. In response, Hooker grants that Scripture must be attentively listened to and carefully applied, but insists that in the inevitable absence of a clear directive for every particular circumstance, we should readily make use of the other sparks of divine wisdom with which God has showered us.

IV. "Stirred Up unto Reverence": The Recovery of Edification

Nowhere was this more important than in his treatment of the concept of edification, which had been so unsatisfactorily expounded by most conformists before Hooker. Whereas Cartwright and the precisianists, by virtue of their demand for "edification," required that even in matters of adiaphora, our ceremonies be framed in accord with Scripture (for how else could one know what is spiritually upbuilding?), Hooker argues that reason may play a role as well. And yet in doing so, Hooker was ready to meet the Puritan challenge head-on and demonstrate that the ceremonies contributed to more than mere social stability. This argument meant linking the realm of inward grace with that of outward ceremony, and hence required a very careful parsing of the relationship between the two kingdoms. In the course

36. Cf. II.4.5; II.8.6.
37. Perrott, "Problem of Authority," 51.

of Hooker's doctrine of edification, then, we will be able to clearly discern the fundamental contours of his theology of the two kingdoms and the relationship of nature and grace.

In the previous chapter, we saw how Hooker in Book III drew a sharp distinction between the civil and spiritual realms, and resolutely placed matters of church order and most questions of liturgy within the former. This would appear to condemn him to the same unsatisfying conformist line about edification—ceremonies edify insofar as they conduce to civil order and peace, but that is all. This distinction is indeed a key pillar of Hooker's argument, though even here, he seeks to provide a broader foundation for this claim, repeatedly expounding the benefits of beauty, dignity, and order in purely civil affairs. But he is also willing to go further. At the outset of Book IV, he offers a careful definition of "edification," one that will underlie his whole subsequent defense of English liturgical ceremonies:

> The end which is aimed at in setting down the outward form of all religious actions is the edification of the Church. Now men are edified, when either their understanding is taught somewhat whereof in such actions it behooveth all men to consider, or when their hearts are moved with any affection suitable thereunto, when their minds are in any sort stirred up unto that reverence, devotion, attention and due regard, which in those cases seemeth requisite. Because therefore unto this purpose not only speech but sundry sensible means besides have always been thought necessary, and especially those means which being object to the eye, the liveliest and the most apprehensive sense of all other, have in that respect seemed the fittest to make a deep and a strong impression. (IV.1.3; *FLE* 1:273.30–274.8)

In other words, unlike Whitgift, who reflected the Protestant suspicion of the senses in applying the language of edification only to the Word (so that vestments, for instance, edify only as prerequisites for preaching), Hooker argues that the senses *can* help to fix our minds and hearts on spiritual things. Peter Lake thinks we can scarcely overstate the significance of this claim, a move that marks Hooker out, he thinks, as the founder of Anglicanism:

> This was little short of the reclamation of the whole realm of symbolic action and ritual practice from the status of popish superstition to that of a necessary, indeed essential, means of communication and edification; a means, moreover, in many ways more effective than the unvarnished

word. The ceremonies, Hooker claimed, must have religious meanings. That was what they were for.[38]

Lake goes on to explain how for Hooker "the observances of the church, if suitably well chosen and decorous, could, through a series of correspondences, use the external realm of outward performance and ritual practice to affect the internal realm of men's minds and characters."[39] But if all this is so, it would seem to represent a repudiation of that very two-kingdoms distinction upon which the conformist case, and Hooker's claim to continuity with magisterial Protestantism, so depended. And indeed, Lake is among those who claims as much, viewing Hooker's maintenance of the visible-invisible church distinction as mere lip-service, when he really means to undermine it.[40] Can both Lake and Kirby be right, then? By carefully attending to Hooker's argument here, we may discover sufficient nuance to make a reconciliation possible, and in so doing, better grasp how Hooker understands these two kingdoms.

Of course, we have already seen that these two are not distinguished in terms of things "sacred" and "secular" in our modern sense. For Hooker especially, God is revealed and encountered in all the arenas of mundane civil existence; and conversely, sacred business cannot take place without using the trappings of external social and political forms. So it is that after having made the above declaration, Hooker appeals to nature and to the common practice of all ages in "public actions which are of weight whether they be civil and temporal or else spiritual and sacred" (IV.1.3; *FLE* 1:274.16–18). In other words, the outward means of moving our hearts to awe and devotion in worship are not fundamentally different from the outward means of moving our hearts to awe and devotion in other settings, such as art or politics.[41] Puritans and papists alike will no doubt balk at this, but Hooker is a realist. We are creatures of sense, and for any great occasion or purpose, our senses need to be impressed if our hearts and minds are to be. Nor is this merely incidental; it is part and parcel of Hooker's Dionysian cosmology.[42] Having provided examples of the necessary use of sensible ceremonies in affairs both civil and religious, he quotes Pseudo-Dionysius: "The sensible things which Religion hath hal-

38. Lake, *Anglicans and Puritans?* 165.
39. Lake, *Anglicans and Puritans?* 166.
40. Lake, *Anglicans and Puritans?* 180–81.
41. On the relationship between worship and the commonwealth in Hooker's thought, see Kirby, *Richard Hooker, Reformer and Platonist*, 101–4, 110–12.
42. Kirby, *Richard Hooker, Reformer and Platonist*, 31–32.

lowed, are resemblances framed according to things spiritually understood, whereunto they serve as a hand to lead and a guide to direct" (IV.1.3; *FLE* 1:275.21–24). However, when Whitgift had made the slightest moves in this direction, Cartwright had objected that this was "to institute new sacraments."[43]

Hooker thinks that this objection has misunderstood the key function of a sacrament. This is not to serve as a visible sign of invisible things (for such signs are everywhere in human affairs), or even as a visible sign of specifically spiritual things (for Hooker believes that every creature serves as such a sign of God's presence, manifesting the law of his being through its own law-like operations). Instead, "sacraments are those which are signs and tokens of some general promised grace, which always really descendeth from God unto the soul that duly receiveth them" (IV.1.4; *FLE* 1:276.14–16). The "general promise" of grace in the sacraments establishes in their case a *necessary* connection between the outward and inward, bringing the soul into direct relationship with God; not so with the signifying ceremonies he is occupied with in most of Books IV and V.[44]

We find Hooker's Dionysian theology of sign and edification elaborated in the introductory chapters of Book V. Hooker, however, is considerably more careful to maintain the two-kingdoms distinction, rightly understood, than Lake makes him out to be:

> There is an inward reasonable, and there is a solemn outward serviceable worship belonging unto God. Of the former kind are all manner of virtuous duties that each man in reason and conscience to God-ward oweth. Solemn and serviceable worship we name for distinction's sake, whatsoever belongeth to the Church or public society of God by way of external adoration. It is the later of these two whereupon our present question groweth. (V.4.3; *FLE* 2:31.7–14)

Every bit as much as Calvin, then, Hooker simultaneously maintains the importance of outward worship while distinguishing it clearly from the inward forum of the conscience.[45] Between these two, there should be close corre-

---

43. Cartwright, *Replye*, 159 (*WW* III:354). (As mentioned in Chapter Three, the particular context is Whitgift's appeal to the symbolic value of a wedding ring.)

44. David Neelands offers a good discussion of Hooker's sacramentology in "Christology and the Sacraments," in *A Companion to Richard Hooker*, ed. W. Torrance Kirby (Leiden: Brill, 2008), confirming him to be in basic accord with Reformed doctrine on these issues.

45. In *Institutes* IV.10.1–8, 27–32, Calvin offers a thorough discussion of the role of church laws for government and worship and their relation to the conscience, in which he

spondence and congruity, but never confusion. Hooker explains this relation-ship of correspondence with great care two chapters later, in a crucial passage:

> [I]f we affect him not far above and before all things, our religion hath not that inward perfection which it should have, neither do we indeed worship him as our God. That which inwardly each man should be, the Church outwardly ought to testify. And therefore the duties of our religion which are seen must be such as that affection which is unseen ought to be. Signs must resemble the things they signify. If religion bear the greatest sway in our hearts, our outward religious duties must show it, as far as the Church hath outward ability. Duties of religion performed by whole societies of men, ought to have in them according to our power a sensible excellency, correspondent to the majesty of him whom we worship. Yea then are the public duties of religion best ordered, when the militant Church doth resemble by sensible means, as it may in such cases, the hidden dignity and glory wherewith the Church triumphant in heaven is beautified. . . . Let our first demand be therefore, that in the external form of religion such things as are apparently, or can be sufficiently proved effectual and generally fit to set forward godliness, either as betokening the greatness of God, or as beseeming the dignity of religion, or as concurring with celestial impressions in the minds of men, may be reverently thought of. (V.6.1–2; *FLE* 2:33.23–34.20)

It is easy to see here why Torrance Kirby considers Hooker's Christology to serve as the template for his understanding of the church in its two realms of existence, with a "communication of attributes" establishing correspondence between the inward and outward realms,[46] conjoined as they are, but without

---

quite clearly avoids the regulative principle logic into which some English Calvinists were to fall. Church laws must not seek to prescribe the "true and necessary worship of God" as the papists have done (IV.10.6; 2:1184), so as "to bind souls inwardly before God" (IV.10.2; 2:1181); however, those done "for the sake of public decency" (IV.10.28; 2:1206) are both necessary and praiseworthy. Calvin's description of the purpose of such rites is substantially similar to that of Hooker, belying Lake's insistence on Hooker's fundamental novelty: "But decorum for us will be something so fitted to the reverence of the sacred mysteries that it may be a suitable exercise for devotion, or at least will serve as an appropriate adornment of the act. And this should not be fruitless but should indicate to believers with how great modesty, piety, and reverence they ought to treat sacred things. Now, ceremonies, to be exercises of piety, ought to lead us straight to Christ" (IV.10.29; 2:1206–7).

46. Kirby argues extensively in *Richard Hooker's Doctrine of the Royal Supremacy* that Hooker's Christology is central to his whole theological paradigm, and in particular, that the

confusion, in the act of worship. The worship of the visible church is a public religious duty, which is not to be confused with the true religion of the heart, but which must never be separated from it. Through this worship, the inward reality, the "hidden dignity and glory" of the church in the presence of God, is imperfectly imaged by sensible means. These sensible ceremonies "testify" to the truth, "signify" spiritual realities, "betoken" the greatness of God, and hence serve to "set forward godliness." In short, we might say, they serve toward *sanctification*, enlightening our hearts with better understanding of the truth, strengthening our faith, and forming our affections in the virtues of holiness. For Hooker, it appears, while ceremonies are *testimonies* to justifying grace, they cannot be said to convey it, to improve our standing in the eyes of God or merit his pleasure. Indeed, it is significant that Hooker always speaks of the beneficial effects of the ceremonies *towards us*, and never as rites in themselves pleasing to God. If this distinction is correct, then Hooker would seem, in the midst of this reclamation of ritual, to have maintained the essential Protestant protest against Rome, which revolved around the relationship of justifying and sanctifying grace, and condemned the proliferation of outward rites that were necessary to endear us to God. Thus, Lake leaves out all the important nuances in his assertion,

> This reappropriation of symbolic action from the papists was in turn based upon those graded hierarchies of desire, experience and law (outlined in book I) which led man Godwards and held the realms of reason and grace, nature and supernature firmly together. By exploiting and mirroring the correspondences and links between these two realms, symbol and ritual were able to play a central role in that process whereby the church led the believer toward union with God.[47]

The last phrase here represents an elision of justification and sanctification that Hooker would never make.[48] While the Dionysian logic of mediated ascent to

---

clear distinction of two natures that are personally united in Christ serves as a blueprint for the relationship between the two kingdoms (pp. 51–125, but see especially 51–58).

47. Lake, *Anglicans and Puritans?* 169. For more on the oversights in Lake's evaluation of Hooker's ecclesiology, see my *Richard Hooker*, ch. 11.

48. Hooker's doctrine of justification and sanctification has been the matter of some debate, with both Voak (Nigel Voak, *Richard Hooker and Reformed Theology: A Study of Reason, Will, and Grace* [Oxford: Oxford University Press, 2003], ch. 4) and Joyce (*Richard Hooker and Anglican Moral Theology*, ch. 6) suggesting that even if Hooker's statements in *A Learned Sermon on Justification* were thoroughly consonant with Reformed theology, his mature views

God does represent a significant thread in Hooker's theology, it does so only at the level of sanctification; on justification, Hooker's thought remains governed by an Augustinian sense of hypostatic disjunction between the two realms.[49] As such, the liturgy, for all its value and potential, never threatens to rise above the level of changeable adiaphora for Hooker; only its legal imposition, not its intrinsic merits, gives it any character of necessity.

Hooker's concept of liturgy and ceremony, then, despite being charged with spiritual significance, remains fundamentally within the domain of nature, a domain that remained shot through with God's presence, perhaps even "drenched with deity," as C. S. Lewis's fulsome description has it.[50] Hence Hooker's comfort with arguing from natural law, historical consensus, and civil analogues for the value of many of the disputed ceremonies. So, when it comes to vestments, Hooker will both take the traditional line, emphasizing their essentially civil function ("To solemn actions of royalty and justice their suitable ornaments are a beauty. Are they only in religion a stain?" [V.29.1; *FLE* 2:123.18–19]), and yet also point to a spiritual correspondence:

> as also for that it suiteth so fitly with that lightsome affection of joy, wherein God delighteth when his Saints praise him; and so lively resembleth the glory of the Saints in heaven, together with the beauty wherein Angels have appeared unto men . . . [fitting for] they which are to appear before men in the presence of God as Angels. (V.29.5; *FLE* 2:127.10–15)[51]

The train of thought that ties together Hooker's understanding of natural utility and spiritual edification appears perhaps most clearly in his treatment of music. He first eulogizes music as "[a] thing which delighteth all ages and beseemeth all states; a thing as seasonable in grief as in joy; as decent being

---

on the subject in the *Lawes* are not. Ranall Ingalls, in "Sin and Grace," however, offers a convincing defense of the continuity of Hooker's thought on justification both across his *corpus* and vis-à-vis earlier reformers. To be sure, Lake (and others following him) have argued that at least when it comes to his theology of *sacraments*, Hooker makes claims that resemble an *ex opere operato* account that ties divine grace necessarily to physical instruments. For my own careful rebuttal of such readings, see ch. 11 of my *Richard Hooker*.

49. See Torrance Kirby, *Richard Hooker, Reformer and Platonist*, 29–43, and "From Generall Meditations."

50. Lewis, *English Literature*, 459.

51. The comparison of the white vestments to angels is one that Vermigli (*A Briefe Examination*, 33v) and Whitgift (*Answere*, 239 [*WW* 2:63]) have already made.

added unto actions of greatest weight and solemnity, as being used when men most sequester themselves from action" (V.38.1; *FLE* 2:151.10–14). It is useful for all human affairs, but not merely as ornament; so deeply does music affect us that it can contribute to our moral formation: "In harmony the very image and character even of virtue and vice is perceived, the mind delighted with their resemblances and brought by having them often iterated into a love of the things themselves" (V.38.1; *FLE* 2:151.21–24). This being the case, what could be more suitable to aid our worship?

> The very harmony of sounds being framed in due sort and carried from the ear to the spiritual faculties of our souls is by a native puissance and efficacy greatly available to bring to a perfect temper whatsoever is there troubled. . . . In which considerations the Church of Christ doth likewise at this present day retain it as an ornament to Gods service, and an help to our own devotion. (V.38.1–2; *FLE* 2:152.5–8, 19–21)

Equally fascinating is Hooker's treatment of festival days. Whereas Whitgift had confined himself to insisting that "[t]he magistrate hath power and authority over his subjects in all external matters, and bodily affairs; wherefore he may call them from bodily labour or compel them unto it, as shall be thought to him most convenient,"[52] Hooker justifies them via an elaborate disquisition on the nature of time, and the rhythms of rest and action appropriate to all created beings. All nature, and even heathen peoples, therefore testify "that festival solemnities are a part of the public exercise of religion" (V.70.5; *FLE* 2:365.29–30), and besides, he adds, working his way through the church year holiday by holiday, they are of great importance to "keep us in perpetual remembrance" (V.70.8; *FLE* 2:367.19–20) of God's redeeming work. Therefore, "the very law of nature itself which all men confess to be God's law requireth in general no less the sanctification of times than of places, persons and things unto God's honor" (V.70.9; *FLE* 2:368.30–369.2).

For Hooker, then, the ceremonies of the church are simultaneously (though distinctly) civil, natural, and spiritual; there is no need to categorize them as simply one or the other. As civil institutions concerned with outward order, they take their force from the command of the magistrate, who has lawful authority over such matters. As institutions fitting according to the order of nature, they can be determined by reason, which serves to identify their value and to make them useful in their particular times and places. And

---

52. *WW* II.70.

as institutions tending toward the cultivation of spiritual virtue and reverence, they serve not merely to preserve public order, but for the dynamic upbuilding of the people of God that the precisianists had demanded. By means of such distinctions, Hooker offered the English church a way to speak of the edifying value of her ceremonies without crossing back into a Catholic ritualism that made them conduits of grace or tools for pleasing God. Although this argument could hardly settle all debate about what or was not in fact edifying, it at least established the terms within which such a debate could fruitfully be had.

V. "Freed from the Law's Yoke": Conscience and Christian Liberty

Let us pause to consider where the foregoing threads of argument bring us, as regards the central question of this book: How can the Christian's liberty to be loyal to God alone reconcile fully with the Christian's loyalty to the prince and need to obey human laws? At the outset of this chapter, we noted that for Luther, the believer must not become a mere passive subject, but should remain active even in the self-limitation of law-obedience, discerning the need of the neighbor or the community, discerning the goodness of the limitation that this need imposes, and willingly subordinating himself to this limitation. This emphasis proved very difficult to maintain, however, and many conformist thinkers were happy to let it fall by the wayside. Hooker, however, has given us several grounds for the recovery of such an active obedience. Christians are to obey laws out of a genuine conscientious assurance that such laws are well made, that "we are led by great reason to observe them" (Pref. 7.1; 1:34.17). In this, they do not in fact need to set aside concern for edification of the church, since Hooker is prepared to argue that by and large, the laws and ceremonies of the church of England are such as will conduce not only to the civil peace but to the spiritual upbuilding of the people of God. He is the more able to make this argument because he seeks to lower expectations somewhat, reminding his readers that no polity can be perfect, and any set of laws must do the best they can under difficult circumstances, having regard to the greater good of the whole, even though some individuals may feel inconvenienced thereby.[53]

---

53. Hooker makes this point in Bk. IV, addressing the Puritan concern that certain disputed ceremonies will cause offense to the weaker brother: "[W]e are not to look that the Church should change her public laws and ordinances, made according to that which is judged ordinarily, and commonly fittest for the whole, although it chance that for some particular men the same be found inconvenient; especially when there may be other remedy also against the sores of particular inconveniences" (IV.12.7; *FLE* 1:325.9–14).

Likewise, by lowering the bar for what constitutes sufficient assurance, he can reclaim ordinary reason as a basis for determining "the rule of well-doing" so that his hearers do not need the absolute certainty that comes from divine law before they can confidently conclude that they do well to observe the laws of England. Hooker's ideal listener, then, is one who is drawn, through perception of goodness and well-reasoned assurance of the right course of action, to conform his reason and will to the laws of England, yielding his free obedience.

All this suggests that in Hooker's exposition we may have at last found a more satisfactory solution to the relationship of law and freedom than that offered by his predecessors, who, as we saw in Chapter Two, wrestled with how the doctrine of Christian liberty related to the obligation to obey civil laws. The second pillar of the doctrine of Christian liberty, the principle of voluntariety, even if originally articulated with relation to the moral law of Scripture, seemed *a fortiori* to require some expression in relation to civil law, inasmuch as this was taken to be a specification of the moral law: "[C]onsciences observe the law not as if constrained by the necessity of the law," said Calvin, summarizing the doctrine, but "freed from the law's yoke they willingly obey God's will."[54] Melanchthon put it similarly: "[F]reedom does not consist in this, that we do not observe the law, but that we will and desire spontaneously and from the heart what the law demands."[55] Such willingness, acting in response to the will's positive embrace of an action as desirable, requires, negatively, freedom from coercion (in which fear motivates our action), and positively, understanding (through which the intellect grasps the action as desirable, and the will responds). The first pillar of the doctrine of Christian liberty helps provide the former, by driving fear out of the believer's heart; the latter is supplied by the reformers' concept of charity as a law that is instinctively grasped and willed by the regenerate heart: the believer discerns the neighbor's need as a demand of charity, and in recognizing it as such, wills to respond to it, obeying thereby the moral law "spontaneously."

Luther accordingly often characterizes civil obedience as the Christian's expression of charity, and Melanchthon and Calvin both show a propensity to develop an ethic of civil obedience informed by the principle of Romans 13:8: "Owe no one anything except to love one another."[56] However, in both, this is overshadowed by a heavy reliance on 13:1: "Let every person be subject to the

54. Calvin, *Institutes*, 1:836 [III.19.4].

55. Melanchthon, *Loci Communes* (1521 edition), in Wilhelm Pauck, ed., *Melanchthon and Bucer* (Louisville: Westminster John Knox, 1969), 123 (*CR* XXI:196).

56. See Melanchthon, *Loci Communes* (1521), in Pauck, *Melanchthon and Bucer*, 148–49 (*CR* XXI:223–25); Calvin, *Institutes*, 2:1183–84, 1199–1201 [IV.10.5, IV.10.21–22].

governing authorities. For there is no authority except from God, and those that exist have been instituted by God," which seems to demand peremptory law-obedience as matter of direct obedience to God. This might seem to relativize the role of the understanding, which need grasp only *who* makes the law, not why he makes it, or why it will further the common good. We have seen already how in some conformist literature, such a marginalization of the understanding was quite intentional. More seriously, however, the appeal to 13:1 might seem to bring fear back into the equation, threatening the conscience with God's displeasure, particularly depending on how one takes 13:5: "Therefore one must be in subjection, not only to avoid wrath but also for the sake of conscience."[57]

If conscience is, in Calvin's words, an "awareness which hales man before God's judgment,"[58] then to obey for the sake of conscience would appear to refer back to 13:1, suggesting in fact little difference between the two motives listed in 13:5. On the other hand, if conscience means something like "a conscientious regard for love of neighbor," then it invokes the considerations of 13:8, and indeed suggests that these considerations of love should ultimately supersede considerations of fear. Melanchthon suggests as much in the first edition of the *Loci Communes*: "If they command anything that is for the public good, we must obey them in accordance with Rom. 13:5: 'Therefore one must be subject, not only to avoid God's wrath, but also for the sake of conscience.' For love constrains us to fulfill all civil obligations."[59] This is gone, however, by the 1555 edition, where the passage is now glossed as reminding us that human laws "can bind us to eternal punishment."[60] In the 1541 *Moralis Philosophiae Epitome*, this darker tone heavily predominates, with Melanchthon taking the first motive of 13:5 to refer to human wrath and the second motive, "conscience," to refer to divine wrath: "And if we obey not, he saith that he will revenge it . . . with eternal torments after this life, except we do repent."[61] However, we saw above in Chapter Two that, when treating of ecclesiastical laws, Melanchthon still emphasizes that our obedience stems from the law of love, a conscious recognition that laws of order are necessary for the peace and edification of the church. Calvin, moreover, was emphatic that civil laws could

---

57. It should be noted that the opposition here between Rom. 13:1 and 13:8 is intended merely as a heuristic tool, not an exegetical point.

58. Calvin, *Institutes*, 1:848 [III.19.15].

59. Melanchthon, *Loci Communes* (1521), in Pauck, *Melanchthon and Bucer*, 148 (*CR* XXI:223).

60. Melanchthon, *Loci Communes* (1555), in Manschreck, 334.

61. Melanchthon, *Whether it be a mortall sinne*, 4–5 (*CR* XVI:10).

not be different from ecclesiastical laws in this respect and that neither "of themselves bind the conscience" in the way Melanchthon seems to describe.[62] However, Calvin leaves us in no doubt either that for those disposed to resist good laws, fear of God's wrath provides another motive: "Let no man deceive himself here. For since the magistrate cannot be resisted without God being resisted at the same time, even though it seems that an unarmed magistrate can be despised with impunity, still God is armed to avenge mightily this contempt toward himself."[63]

Although Hooker is of course equally persuaded that human authorities have been instituted by God, and that to disobey them is a way of disobeying God, he shows remarkably little interest in playing up this theme, or in emphasizing divine wrath as a motive to enforce his opponents' obedience. Indeed, unlike most early Protestant political theologians and particularly conformist polemicists, he hardly cites Romans 13 at all; the chief exception, a fragment of Book VIII, chapter 6, is so incongruous in tone that Keble took it to properly belong to an independent "Sermon on Civil Obedience," and to have been mistakenly appended to the *Lawes*.[64] The argument of this fragment does indeed at first follow the Melanchthonian line, using 13:1 to establish a direct link between obedience to God and obedience to his ministers, and then invoking 13:5 in a way that makes clear that conscience is consciousness of divine judgment for disobedience. However, the fragment breaks off with an abrupt and tantalizing shift of direction: "Disobedience therefore unto laws which are made by men is not a thing of so small account as some would make it. Howbeit too rigorous it were that the breach of every human law should be held a deadly sin.[65] A mean there is between these extremities, if so be we can find it out" (VIII.6.9; *FLE* 3.400.26–401.2).

Although Hooker, alas, never carries on to tell us what this "mean between extremities" is, the overall logic of the *Lawes* gives us a good sense of how Hooker understood the obligation of civil obedience. Indeed, his whole argument could be seen as an attempt to flesh out Matthew Parker's quotation from Martin Bucer: "Whatsoever man shall decree, which by any means may

---

62. Calvin, *Institutes*, 2:1183 [IV.10.5].

63. Calvin, *Institutes*, 2:1509–11 [IV.22–23].

64. See John Keble, ed., *The Works of that Learned and Judicious Divine Mr. Richard Hooker: with an Account of His Life and Death by Isaac Walton* (Oxford: Oxford University Press, 1836), 3:570.

65. As it had been, apparently, by Melanchthon. Mark Perrott recognizes this as proof of Hooker's desire to maintain the Protestant understanding of Christian liberty ("Problem of Authority," 59n91).

make to the use of his neighbours, for that the same is derived from the rule of charity . . . [and] that thing ought not to be esteemed as a tradition or precept of man, though by men it be commanded, but as the tradition or precept of God."[66] We are to perceive in civil law the law of God himself, but precisely *through*, rather than instead of, a rational grasp of that law as an instantiation of the law of charity. Conscientious obedience to the laws of England, for Hooker, would be obedience directed by right reason (well-formed probable judgments) and right will (well-formed desires). Hooker thus rejects the heteronomous legal voluntarism of a Whitgift that would seem to say, "Your prince's law is the command of God, therefore obey whether or not it appears rational"; rather, the logic is that the prince's law is the command of God precisely because it is rational, precisely because of its participation, indirectly through the participation of all mankind, in the divine wisdom. Likewise, Hooker rejects the heteronomous theological voluntarism of a Cartwright, in which the moral law gains its force simply from its expression in Scripture, summoning us to an obedience that bypasses our rational faculties. The law of God is presented not as a fearful command over against mankind, of which we are to stand in silent fear, but as the law of our own beings, so that to obey it (as mediated through human institutions) is indeed to obey our own selves, ourselves as we should be. To bring the Puritans to a truly Christian, truly Protestant obedience, then, Hooker saw that it was necessary to invite them to an obedience based on *understanding*. Hence the patient, architectonic structure of the *Lawes*, from "general meditations" to "particular decisions" (I.1.2; *FLE* 1:57.29, 32), in which the justification of any particular law cannot be made except by reference to its place in the whole scheme of God's creation and providence. Hooker accordingly defends the lengthy foundation-laying this method entails at the close of Book I:

> Lest therefore any man should marvel whereunto all these things tend, the drift and purpose of all is this, even to shew in what manner as every good and perfect gift, so this very gift of good and perfect laws is derived from the father of lights; to teach men a reason why just and reasonable laws are of so great force, of so great use in the world; and to inform their minds with some method of reducing the laws whereof there is present controversy unto their first original causes, that so it may be in every particular ordinance thereby the better discerned, whether the same be reasonable, just and righteous or no. (I.16.1; *FLE* 1:135.10–19)

66. Parker, *Briefe Examination*, 10r–10v.

Yet how does this attractive picture relate to the messy real world of Elizabethan England, in which not all laws seemed "reasonable, just, and righteous," and every individual of sound mind and charitable disposition did not find it equally easy to determine the fitness of laws and freely submit to them? Hooker may have given very good reasons to the Puritans why they should see the English church's ceremonies as good and edifying, reasons that he hoped would be compelling to the free and rational judgment of any Christian conscience, but he surely knew that many would still fail to see the light; and this indeed not only from obstinacy, but simply from difference of judgment. Indeed, immediately after the above passage, he admits, "Easier a great deal it is for men by law to be taught what they ought to do, than instructed how to judge as they should do of law" (I.16.2; *FLE* 1:135.30–32). What was to be done at the point where rational persuasion failed? For Whitgift and Bancroft, the answer was clear: the incorrigible must be coerced. Nor was Hooker any more convinced than most of his contemporaries that a policy of religious toleration was safe for the commonwealth. So Hooker would have to explain a way whereby, even in unconvinced submission to the judgment of another, the Christian subject could remain in an important sense free.

What this task required was an account of corporate moral agency, in which the reason and will of the individual were expressed in and through the action of the whole, as personified in the public authority. Some of the most profound statements of the Protestant doctrine of Christian liberty, Luther's *Freedom of a Christian* and Calvin's *Institutes* III.19, had explored the paradox that freedom need not be opposed to necessity. Our limitation in the sphere of external action, which we ought to accept freely as a self-limitation dictated by love of God and love of neighbor, is in fact the form through which we express and realize our freedom. Could this intuition be developed so as to provide a satisfactory synthesis of Christian liberty and civil obedience? Whereas the Calvinist resistance theorists developed the concept of political authority as the expression of the will of the people primarily in order to justify popular disobedience to that authority, for Hooker, the concept functions rather as a ground of obedience, an obedience in which he is convinced the Christian subject remains free and active, rather than disenfranchised and passive.

VI. "Even Your Deed Also": Corporate Rationality and Corporate Moral Agency

Certainly the way forward for such a synthesis was not straightforward. Indeed, there was a period of Hooker scholarship (during the 1950s–1960s) in which it was common to argue that Hooker had stumbled headlong into self-contradiction at this point. The argument went that, having articulated an essentially Thomist theology of law, in which law derived its authority from reason, Hooker found himself forced in Book VIII to retreat to a Marsilian voluntarism, in which law derived its force simply from the will of the sovereign—what Peter Munz went so far as to call a "Tudor Averroism."[67] Subsequent scholarship, including McGrade, Thompson, and Kirby,[68] have thoroughly rebutted these claims, demonstrating that they represent not only a mischaracterization of Hooker, but of Aquinas and Marsilius as well. Nonetheless, the question remains as to whether Hooker can really exploit all the conscience-salving potential of his emphasis on reason without undermining his fundamental objective as a conformist calling for unity and obedience.

Perrott summarizes the dilemma: "The problem for Hooker was that since he claimed that church laws were grounded on reason, his own argument allowed for the possibility of minority groups putting forward alternative suggestions to existing legislation on the basis of the same rational authority."[69] Therefore, he needed to limit "the subversive potential of such reliance on reason by subordinating subjective, private judgments of what is 'reasonable' to public determinations."[70] It is easy to see in this a certain disingenuity, as if Hooker merely gives with one hand in order to take away with the other. Eppley, indeed, argues that the functional conclusion of Hooker's argument is to systematically nullify every exercise of reason except that of the Crown-in-Parliament, before which no subject's reason can be considered valid.[71] Even if

---

67. This criticism is mounted by H. F. Kearney, in "Richard Hooker: A Reconstruction," *Cambridge Journal* 5 (1952): 300–311, and by Peter Munz, *The Place of Hooker in the History of Thought* (London: Routledge, 1952), 49–57.

68. A. S. McGrade, "The Coherence of Hooker's Polity: The Books on Power," *Journal of the History of Ideas* 24 (1963): 163–82; Thompson, "Philosopher of the Politic Society," 130–91; Kirby, "From Generall Meditations"; Kirby, "'Law Makes the King': Richard Hooker on Law and Princely Rule," in *A New Companion to English Renaissance Literature and Culture*, ed. Michael Hattaway (Malden, MA: Wiley-Blackwell, 2010), 1:274–88.

69. Perrott, "Problem of Authority," 54.

70. Daniel Eppley, *Defending Royal Supremacy and Discerning God's Will in Tudor England* (Aldershot, UK: Ashgate, 2007), 169.

71. Eppley, *Defending Royal Supremacy*, 182–203. Eppley argues that for Hooker, not only do the authorities have the right to establish rules in adiaphora, but indeed, only they are qualified to determine what constitutes an adiaphoron. And, since the disobedience of a subject must be grounded on a demonstrative, not merely probable reason, and a truly demonstrative reason would necessarily be recognized as such by the authorities, there can be no legitimate appeal by private persons against the authority of the Crown-in-Parliament. While Eppley's argument is ingenious, it relies on uncompromisingly forcing through syllogisms constructed

Eppley's argument succeeds, however, it would be cynical indeed to see this as Hooker's intention, given how much of his own argument in the *Lawes* would thereby be rendered obsolete. Perrott is surely correct to observe that "Hooker acknowledged the importance of conscientious integrity as an issue in church politics even when his argument was at its most staunchly conformist."[72]

Hooker's Constitutionalism

As we have seen, however, the same could hardly be said for Elizabethan conformism as a whole. In *Anglicans and Puritans*, Peter Lake identifies the authoritarian tendencies of conformist argument not only in their sterile doctrine of edification, but in their strong divine-right concepts of political authority. Lake errs, however, by treating this as a new development in response to Puritan pressure; in fact, Stephen Gardiner in the 1530s was every bit as much the royal absolutist as Whitgift and Bancroft, and for that matter, so was John Wycliffe in the 1380s. In his *Defence* against Cartwright, Whitgift once uses the argument that the laws of England involve the consent of the governed, and so the Puritans' liberty is in no respect being overridden: "I add that every private man's consent is in the consent of the church, as it is in the consent of the parliament; and therefore no man's liberty otherwise restrained than he hath consented unto."[73] But for him, this never implies that the ruled may withhold their consent from the sovereign, and in fact he repeatedly attacks the subversive potential of Puritan "popularity," which he saw in their teaching that ministers and elders must rule their congregations by consent of the multitude.[74] Although more constitutionalist versions of political theory had flourished alongside absolutism throughout the Tudor period, the rejection of a perceived Puritan commitment to popular government pushed most conformist divines decisively toward the latter. By 1593, Dutch emigrant Adrian Saravia, who had emerged as a leading conformist apologist, offered an uncompromising statement of divine-right absolutism, which was to become

---

from scattered statements of Hooker, syllogisms that seem to run counter to his own expressed intent. It is possible then that Eppley has discerned certain threads of inconsistency in Hooker, but unlikely that Hooker truly intends, as Eppley's argument suggests, to give to the English crown authority equivalent to the papal magisterium. Eppley's recent *Reading the Bible with Richard Hooker* (Minneapolis: Fortress, 2016) corrects this emphasis in chs. 3–4.

72. Perrott, "Problem of Authority," 54.

73. *WW* II:573.

74. Lake, *Anglicans and Puritans?* 60–64; see *WW* II:180–92.

the weapon of choice against pesky Puritan consciences a generation later, with disastrous results for church and commonwealth.[75] Lake therefore argues, not implausibly, that Hooker wrote not merely to provide yet another rejoinder to Puritanism, but also in an attempt to forestall the dangerous tendencies of such argument—to "sort out conformism," as he puts it.[76]

Lake thus lays great stress on Hooker's political theory of consent, as have a great many Hooker scholars. Hooker's consent, of course, is not that of Locke, as generations of Whig historians liked to think; his is a thoroughly medieval doctrine, one in which the "consent of the governed" does not necessarily entail an ongoing right of resistance, or the possibility that power might revert to individuals should they simply choose to withhold their consent.[77] A full treatment of Hooker's political theory—the origin of political power, the nature and locus of sovereignty, the relation of Crown and Parliament, and of Convocation, as the representative assembly of ecclesiastical polity, to both—is of course out of the question here, but thankfully it has been treated in depth by many excellent scholars.[78] Briefly, though, we may sketch Hooker's position in light of the above remarks about Romans 13. For many Protestant theologians, an appeal to Romans 13:1 was sufficient to establish the divine authorization of political authority. Without further reflection, however, on precisely how human authority related to divine, thorny problems were likely to arise. Did political power derive by immediate appointment of God, or indirectly, as a human ordinance made according to the light of nature, and hence with God's approval and by virtue of his wisdom? Too often the implication among

75. See Lake, *Anglicans and Puritans?* 135–39, engaging with Saravia's *De imperandi authoritate et christiana obedientia* (London: Barker, 1593).

76. Lake, *Anglicans and Puritans?* 139, 145–46.

77. F. J. Shirley, *Richard Hooker and Contemporary Political Ideas* (London: Published for the Church Historical Society by S.P.C.K, 1949), 93–104. For a full discussion of the right of resistance in the late sixteenth century, and Hooker's answer to it, see pp. 135–98. Cargill Thompson also treats these themes very adeptly in "Philosopher of the Politic Society," 159–71.

78. The most notable recent discussion, which has sought to breathe fresh air back into the old and now-deflated argument for Locke's dependence on Hooker, is Alexander Rosenthal's *Crown under Law: Richard Hooker, John Locke, and the Ascent of Modern Constitutionalism* (Plymouth, UK: Lexington Books, 2008). Although somewhat superficial (due in part to its scope), and not very reliable in its treatment of either Hooker's magisterial Reformed or English conformist predecessors, Rosenthal's core argument is persuasive, and his treatment of the themes mentioned here in ch. 3 of his book is one of the best available. See also Thompson, "Philosopher of the Politic Society," 159–91; Robert K. Faulkner, *Richard Hooker and the Politics of a Christian England* (Berkeley: University of California Press, 1981), 151–84; Daniel Eppley, "Royal Supremacy," in *Companion to Richard Hooker*, 503–34; and Lake, *Anglicans and Puritans?* 197–213.

early Protestant theologians was the former, which raised thorny questions in the 1550s and 1560s as monarchical opposition to reform heated up.[79] Many of the "monarchomachs" set out to reconfigure the logic of Protestant political thought so as to ground political power in the people and hence authorize armed resistance to tyrannical rulers.[80]

Naturally, in this context, it is easy to see why English conformists were so liable to shy away from the concept of consent as the origin of political authority. Hooker, however, insists, "[U]nto me it seemeth almost out of doubt and controversy that every independent multitude before any certain form of regiment established hath under Gods supreme authority full dominion over itself" (VIII.3.1; *FLE* 3:334.4-7). Therefore a king remains dependent on his people even when they make themselves dependent on him: "Original influence of power from the body into the King is cause of the Kings dependency in power upon the body. By dependency we mean subordination and subjection" (VIII.3.2; *FLE* 3:339.7-9).[81] Although this logic is not always embodied in appropriate constitutional forms, Hooker considers that in England it has been:

> where the people are in no subjection but such as willingly themselves have condescended unto for their own most behoof and security. In Kingdoms therefore of this quality the highest Governor hath indeed universal dominion, but with dependence upon that whole entire body over the several parts whereof he hath dominion so that it standeth for an axiom in this case. The King is *major singulis universis minor.* (VIII.3.2; *FLE* 3:336.23-337.1)

For Hooker, bodies politic are immortal, and therefore the consent embodied in their government does not have to be affirmed anew with the ac-

---

79. Interesting examples of Protestant attempts to rethink the meaning of Romans 13 appear in Christopher Goodman, *How superior powers oght to be obeyd of their subjects [. . .]* (1558; repr., New York: Columbia University Press, 1931), 110-19, and George Buchanan, *A Dialogue on the Law of Kingship Among the Scots,* ed. and trans. Roger A. Mason and Martin S. Smith (Aldershot, UK: Ashgate, 2004), 113-23.

80. The paradigmatic examples are of course Theodore Beza's *Of the Rights of Rulers* (1574) and the famous *Vindiciae Contra Tyrannos* (1579). For a full discussion of these and others, see Quentin Skinner, *Age of Reformation,* vol. 2 of *Foundations of Modern Political Thought* (Cambridge: Cambridge University Press, 1978), 189-348.

81. Of course, this conclusion would not follow if one had an alienative view of the transmission of political authority, such as we find in Hooker's contemporaries such as Bodin, and in its starkest form, in Hobbes. There, the initial act of consent serves simply to create the sovereign, who remains thereafter subordinate to God alone.

cession of each ruler; rather "the cause of dependency is in that first original conveyance" (VIII.3.2; *FLE* 3:338.28–339.1), so that the consent of our ancestors to be so governed is our own consent. Of course, just because the constitution reflects some past act of consent, it does not necessarily follow that the continuing work of government includes a mechanism for the ongoing expression of consent. Hooker again believes, however, that in England, Parliament (and Convocation) happily serve just such a role. Through these gatherings, not only does the government of England as such embody the consent of its people, but the particular laws passed also embody this consent.[82] "A law is the deed of the whole body politic" (Pref. 5.2; *FLE* 1.27.33–28.1), Hooker will declare.

This much has been treated at length by a great many Hooker scholars. However, it remains to show just how integral this concept of law-making by consent is to Hooker's broader project of establishing the appropriate balance of conscientious freedom and institutional freedom in the doctrine of Christian liberty. Mark Perrott has attempted this in outline, and I shall build on his argument here. So how does Hooker's stress on the use of reason in determining the goodness of law support, rather than undermine, his call for submission?

Government as a Corporate Exercise of Reason

The first thing to note is that when Hooker speaks of reason, he is of course not working within our modern post-Enlightenment mold. For Hooker, reason is not first and foremost something exercised by the individual (though we are each as individuals capable of exercising reason and called to do so) but something exercised collectively. This follows of course from Hooker's realist and participationist ontology—to reason is to participate in the law of reason that is implanted in human nature, the law by which human nature is directed. It is for this reason that Hooker, despite the Fall, will rest such confidence in the collective wisdom of mankind, when seeking to determine what the law of reason is. Although he grants that demonstrative reasoning from first causes (which can theoretically be done by an individual mind) is the surest way of determining the law of reason, he considers this very rare indeed (I.8.2). Much more often, the law will be determined by consulting "the general persuasion of all men" (I.8.3; *FLE* 1:83.18). Indeed, he will go so far as to say, "The general

82. Thompson, "Philosopher of the Politic Society," 171–72; VIII.2.7, 13.

and perpetual voice of men is as the sentence of God himself. For that which all men have at all times learned, nature herself must needs have taught; and God being the author of nature, her voice is but his instrument" (I.8.3; *FLE* 1:83.33–84.4).

It is for this reason that we find him repeatedly throughout the *Lawes* arguing by appeal to tradition. Of course, this was a common enough strategy in any of the debates of that period, even for the Puritans, who although eager to disparage the authority of mere men, even the church fathers, could not resist trying to line up a list of respected authorities on their side in their debates with conformists (an inconsistency Hooker was only too happy to point out to them).[83] In his interactions with Cartwright, Whitgift frequently cited the magisterial reformers and the testimony of the church fathers to bolster the credentials of his arguments, and to present the Puritans as arrogant and obstinate for setting their own feeble judgments against those of such lofty authorities. However, for Whitgift as for Cartwright, these appeals had something of an *ad hoc* character; both were happy to dismiss authorities with which they disagreed, and both tended to write off most of the medieval period as an era of apostasy to which no appeal could be made. Hooker, however, as a number of scholars have observed, was eager to resurrect a sense of continuity with the past, and was not ashamed to defend a particular ritual on the basis that the English church for many centuries (even centuries of "popery") had practiced it.[84] He elevated this respect for tradition to the level of principle: "Neither may we in this case lightly esteem what hath bene allowed as fit in the judgment of antiquity and by the long continued practice of the whole church, from which unnecessarily to swerve experience hath never yet found it safe" (V.7.1; *FLE* 2:34.24–27). Of course, it was not necessarily to church tradition alone that Hooker appealed, but to the common practice of mankind, whether this be instanced by the patriarchs, Old Testament kings, early Christian emperors, or even heathen peoples. This appears repeatedly in his justification of particular ceremonies in Book V, as we saw above in his discussion of holy days. For this reason, it is important to recognize that for Hooker at least, it is misleading to speak in terms of the Anglican "three-legged stool" of Scripture, reason, and tradition. This terminology fails to realize the extent to which for Hooker, the last of these is simply the second, considered diachronically, and to which the second is almost always to some extent understood corporately.[85]

---

83. II.7.8.
84. Lake, *Anglicans and Puritans?* 157.
85. See David Neelands, "Scripture, Reason, and 'Tradition,'" in *Richard Hooker and the*

At this point, however, our modern predispositions may be prone to mislead us again, as all this talk of appealing to the judgments of all men might seem a rather democratic proposition. But for Hooker, there is no question of putting every man's judgment on the same level. On the contrary, he repeatedly warns the Puritans against the danger of such democratization:

> [T]he matter, wherein ye think that ye see and imagine that your ways are sincere, is of far deeper consideration than any one amongst five hundred of you conceiveth. Let the vulgar sort amongst you know that there is not the least branch of the cause wherein they are so resolute, but to the trial of it a great deal more appertaineth than their conceit doth reach unto. I write not this in disgrace of the simplest that way given, but I would gladly they knew the nature of that cause wherein they think themselves thoroughly instructed and are not. (Pref. 3.3; 1:14.13–20)

The complexity of human affairs is such that "men of common capacity and but ordinary judgment are not able (for how should they?) to discern what things are fittest for each kind and state of regiment" (I.10.7; *FLE* 1:102.6–8). For this reason, Hooker's appeal to the authority of the "general and perpetual voice of mankind" and the authority of church tradition always privileges the judgment of those who, by reason of learning, age, and station, have a claim to be regarded as the wisest. Hence the weight he will put on the role of Convocation in determining the ecclesiastical laws that the prince will enforce.[86]

On these bases alone, Hooker can rest much of his appeal for individual consciences to submit themselves to the judgments embodied in the English laws. The reason of an individual cannot presume itself above that of so many and so wise minds, so the only rational course is to yield precedence to their judgments, which we may safely take to be the judgments of God. This alone ought to suffice to deflect the argument from Christian liberty, which claims that we must obey only the voice of God: "It is a loose and licentious opinion which the Anabaptists have embraced, holding that a Christian man's liberty is lost, and the soul which Christ hath redeemed unto himself injuriously drawn into servitude under the yoke of human power, if any law be now imposed besides the Gospel of Jesus Christ" (III.9.3; *FLE* 1:238.8–14), says Hooker in

---

Construction of Christian Community, 89–94, and Paul Avis, *In Search of Authority: Anglican Theological Method from the Reformation to the Enlightenment* (London: Bloomsbury, 2014), 117–20, for a good discussion of what Hooker's concept of tradition is and isn't.

86. See especially VIII.6.12–14.

a passage that sums up a great deal of the argument of the *Lawes*. They say we should be led by the light of the spirit, but since "the light of natural understanding, wit and reason is from God" we may trust that "the laws which the very heathens did gather to direct their actions by, so far forth as they proceeded from the light of nature, God himself doth acknowledge to have proceeded even from himself, and that he was the writer of them in the tables of their hearts." If this be so for heathens, all the more highly may we value laws "which have been made by his Saints, endued further with the heavenly grace of his spirit, and directed as much as might be with such instructions, as his sacred word doth yield." Once we discern human laws to be such, and cultivate "that dutiful regard which their dignity doth require: it will not greatly need, that we should be exhorted to live in obedience unto them" (III.9.3; *FLE* 1:238.25–26, 238.31–239.10).

Government as Corporate Agency

Nonetheless, we might still ask whether Hooker is not overstating his case when he says, "To them which ask why we thus hang our judgments on the Churches sleeve, I answer with Salomon, because 'two are better than one.' . . . The bare consent of the whole Church should itself in these things stop their mouths who living under it dare presume to bark against it" (V.8.3; *FLE* 2:39.14–16). After all, the "consent of the whole church" was precisely what was lacking, and had been for decades, as Puritans in the churches, among the gentry, and even in Parliament continued to oppose the judgments enshrined in law. Indeed, not just some few, but "thousands, yea and even of those amongst which divers are in public charge and authority," as Hooker would quote Cartwright in his Preface.[87] To this Hooker responds, in a crucially revealing sentence, "As though when public consent of the whole hath established anything, every man's judgement being thereunto compared, were not private, howsoever his calling be to some kind of public charge" (Pref. 6.6; *FLE* 1:34.3–6). The distinction drawn here is one key to Hooker's political thought, as well as that of many of his contemporaries, between *singulis* and *universis*,[88] citizens considered individually and considered as "the whole." Neither the number nor the status of dissenting voices counts against the "consent of the whole" inasmuch as this has been enshrined in law.

---

87. Pref. 6.6. The reference is to Cartwright, *RSR* 181.
88. See VIII.3.2 (*FLE* 3:337.1).

More, then, than merely an appeal to corporate rationality, to the wisdom found in tradition, underlies Hooker's argument for submission. Indeed, immediately after his remark in I.10 that laws must be made by wise men, he cautions, "Howbeit laws do not take their constraining force from the quality of such as devise them, but *from that power which doth give them the strength of laws*" (I.10.8; *FLE* 1:102.18–21). This power is *sovereignty*, the moral agency exercised by a collective through its authorized representatives, as he discusses at length in Book VIII. To be sure, laws thus made can be overturned, but only by the same exercise of corporate agency that created them, not by the dissent of individual members, no matter how numerous. "Laws that have been approved may be (no man doubteth) again repealed, and to that end also disputed against, by the authors thereof themselves. But this is when the whole doth deliberate what laws each part shall observe, and not when a part refuseth the laws which the whole hath orderly agreed upon" (Pref. 5.2; *FLE* 1:8.4–8). For Hooker, to speak of our "consent" to these laws is no mere metaphor, but an expression of the fact that we really do act not merely through our private wills, but through others:

> As in parliaments, councils, and the like assemblies, although we be not personally ourselves present, notwithstanding our assent is by reason of others agents there in our behalf. And what we do by others, no reason but that it should stand as our deed, no less effectually to bind us than if our selves had done it in person. (I.10.8; *FLE* 1:103.2–7)

As members of a body politic, our agency simply is constituted by our participation in this public action, and it is meaningless to pretend that we can exempt ourselves:

> [It is] unmeet that laws which being once solemnly established, are to exact obedience of all men, and to constrain thereunto, should so far stoop as to hold themselves in suspense from taking any effect upon you, till some disputer can persuade you to be obedient. *A law is the deed of the whole body politic, whereof if ye judge your selves to be any part, then is the law even your deed also.* (Pref. 5.2; *FLE* 1:27.30–28.2; italics mine)

This statement, though it comes at the beginning of the *Lawes*, could be considered the capstone of Hooker's argument. Here we have the logic of God's own action—a law to himself, completely free although bound to observe his eternal law, because this law is the most perfect expression of himself, and of rationality—mirrored in the logic of the human agent: we remain free even in being bound by law, because this law is our own rational action. This is Hooker's final argument; if all else fails, if the Puritan conscience refuses to see the edifying value of the laws, refuses to see their basis in the law of reason, refuses to defer to the judgment and wisdom of antiquity, persists in stubborn conviction that these laws are badly made, his obedience is still, Hooker maintains, congruent with Christian liberty because he is simply obeying himself.

Of course, we will have some concerns about this line of argument. To what extremity could this go? Perhaps the particular laws that Hooker defends really were fairly reasonable, but could the same logic be applied to underwrite meek acquiescence to true tyranny and injustice? Many scholars have noted that Hooker specifically holds back from offering any doctrine of political resistance,[89] although it has been less often noted that he equally holds back from altogether dismissing such doctrines.[90] Certainly, he grants, no man ought to obey an unjust law: "Not that I judge it a thing allowable for men to observe those laws which in their hearts they are steadfastly persuaded to be against the law of God" (Pref. 6.6; 1:33.12–14). But he continues, "[Y]our persuasion in this case ye are all bound for the time to suspend, and in otherwise doing, ye offend against God by troubling his Church without any just or necessary cause. Be it that there are some reasons inducing you to think hardly of our laws. Are those reasons demonstrative, are they necessary, or but probabilities only?" A demonstrative argument, Hooker grants, "dischargeth . . . the conscience, and setteth it at full liberty." But where is this demonstrative argument? "But if the skilfullest amongst you can show that all the books ye have hitherto written be able to afford any one argument of this nature, let the instance be given" (Pref. 6.6; 1:33.14–22, 25–27). There will be times when the Christian must say with Luther, "Here I stand, I can do no other," but in the absence of an utterly compelling reason to disobey the laws, a *certainty* with which we are rarely privileged in civil affairs, the Puritans must be willing to suspend the judgments of their conscience in deference to the superior weight of probability that public consensus holds. Charity itself demands this, for whatever their concerns about the harm to be done by bad laws, they must surely recognize the greater harm that will be done by contentiousness and disobedience: "[O]f peace and quietness there is not any way possible, unless the probable voice of every entire society or body politic overrule all private of like nature in the same body" (Pref. 6.6; 1:34.6–9).

---

89. See for instance Rosenthal, *Crown under Law*, 123–26.
90. See VIII.9.2 (*FLE* 3:437.1–5).

VII. Conclusion

Throughout this chapter, we have seen how Hooker carefully constructs his defense of the institutional liberty of the Church of England and the commonwealth so as to preserve and enhance the doctrine of Christian liberty, particularly the principle of voluntariety. Having carefully distinguished loyalties to God and to prince, he does not leave them in opposition but attempts to bring them into harmony, by seeking to demonstrate that the prince's laws are particular obligations of the law of charity, for the upbuilding of the people. He accordingly articulates a much more positive understanding of edification, not merely as means to civil peace (though this is certainly important), but as aids to sanctification and the upbuilding of Christian community. He further invites his opponents to a positive use of reason as a way of discerning the goodness of laws and freely assenting to them. Lest such an appeal to reason, however, invite dissension and strife, he reminds them that reason is always a corporate enterprise, exercised in submission to tradition and to the judgment of the wise. Moreover, once this enterprise of corporate reasoning has concluded in the promulgation of law, he appeals to the consensual foundation of political authority and the Tudor Constitution to persuade his hearers that this law is "even your deed also," an expression of free action within the constraints imposed by the law of charity and concern for the common good. Even when obedience demands a suspension of private rational judgment, this too is a requirement of neighbor-love, since there will be "no end of contention without submission of both parts unto some definitive sentence" (Pref. 6; 1:29.21–22). As a vindication of the *probable* authority of reason, tradition, and human law, Hooker uses this defense to take the offensive against the Puritans' misguided demand for certainty, one that traps the conscience rather than freeing it.

One thing, however, is still lacking in our exposition: a detailed consideration of the authority of the Word of God in its relation to human law. Hooker has made quite clear that Christian liberty is determined first by justification and only second by submission to the laws of Scripture, that the Word of God is not to be a legalistic chain upon a Christian people. Yet any satisfactory harmonization of loyalties, to show human laws as consonant with the voice of God, will require him to give a fuller account of how this consonance is displayed in the commonwealth: Does the Word nonetheless have a public authority in the laws of a Christian commonwealth? It is to this that we turn in the next chapter.

CHAPTER SIX

The Soul of a Christian Commonwealth

....

Politics in Submission to the Word

> The works of supreme Dominion which have been since the first
> beginning wrought by the power of the Son of God are now most
> truly and properly the works of the Son of man. The *word* made
> *flesh* doth sit forever and reign as Sovereign *Lord* over all.
>
> Hooker, *Lawes* VIII.4.6

I. Introduction: A Secularizing Agenda?

In the past two chapters, we have sought to establish Hooker's concern for the
freedom of a Christian commonwealth, against an overreaching Puritan biblicism that might seem to shackle both the individual and the commonwealth.
We have argued that this can be understood as an effort to harmonize loyalties,
to demonstrate how good citizenship can cohere with good Christianity, how
rulers may be free to act without inappropriately impinging on their subjects'
freedom of conscience. In Chapter Four, we explored how the doctrine of
adiaphora and traditional Protestant teaching on Christian liberty grounded
Hooker's of the church. In Chapter Five, we showed how this freedom was not
simply a freedom for authorities to do however they pleased, but was bound
to rules of right reason, and must be used for edification; by this means, we
sought to show, the liberty of individual consciences was not trampled upon
by the commonwealth. However, we might be forgiven for wondering whether
the foregoing had sufficiently established the freedom of a *Christian* commonwealth, or whether this legislative liberty had not been gained at the expense
of biblical authority and subordination to Christ. Does Hooker's polity have
liberty *in* the Word, or liberty *from* the Word?

The question is clearly a crucial one for this book, given that we noted in Chapter One the possibility of attempting to solve the conflict of loyalties by liberating the "civil kingdom" from obedience to Scripture, as Rawlsian liberalism would seem to demand, or by arguing, as David VanDrunen does, that Scripture itself authorizes the liberty and neutrality of this realm. In this formulation of the two kingdoms, the line between them is drawn in such a way as to render the civil kingdom a strictly secular realm, neither concerning itself with the business of the church nor with any concern for the church as such. Scriptural authority, on this account, which we noted most starkly in the example of Southern Presbyterian James Henley Thornwell, was to be confined essentially to the spiritual kingdom of the institutional church, outside of which natural law and human law prevailed. In practice, of course, we saw that this separationism was question-begging, and subject to demolition by a more expansive conception of biblical law, like Cartwright's. Given the lines of continuity between Cartwright's formulation of biblical authority in the church and that of later *jure divino* Presbyterians like Thornwell, it is perhaps natural to enlist Hooker for an alternative formulation of the two kingdoms in which both kingdoms lie in the domain of the Word.

However, this might seem an odd move given the shape of our narrative thus far, in which it may have appeared to be the *Puritans* who have been seeking to extend the bounds of scriptural authority, and *Hooker* who has been laboring to confine Scripture within narrower limits, complaining that "whereas God hath left sundry kinds of laws unto men . . . they hold that one only law, the scripture, must be the rule to direct in all things" (II.1.2; *FLE* 1:145.10–13). Moreover, in our discussion of Hooker thus far, we have repeatedly emphasized the role of human law and of reason in the civil kingdom. Indeed, the discussion of the previous chapter, although couched in terms of "Christian liberty" and the "Christian conscience," might seem to be little more than a debate about the respective roles of private reason and public reason in a polity concerned essentially with maintaining civil order. In Chapter Four, we saw how Hooker used a soteriological definition of the two kingdoms to confine *sola Scriptura* within a range of narrow spiritual concern, leaving all other matters as adiaphora, subject to reason and positive law. Far from widening Scripture's scope so as to bring it to bear on the civil kingdom, Hooker might seem merely to have widened the scope of the civil kingdom over which Scripture did not exercise authority, so that even matters of church polity and liturgy were to be ruled by reason, not Scripture.

If anything, then, it seems that Hooker is the proponent of secularism, not the champion of the role of Scripture in public life. Indeed, in popular stereotypes, which are not always entirely disclaimed in the scholarly literature, we are likely to find a presentation of Puritans as rabid theonomists, eager to take *sola Scriptura* to its logical conclusion, countered by a moderate, *via media* Hooker who wishes to restore reason to a place of honor, and relegate Scripture to narrowly spiritual matters.[1] To many moderns, Hooker's invocation of natural law might suggest the embrace of a rationally acceptable, religiously neutral standard for moral and political life that can be embraced by all people of goodwill. Although we might chide him for defending the royal supremacy over the church, we might be prone to try to enlist Hooker as a proto-modern, wary of overtly religious claims in the public square. Indeed, as mentioned in the previous chapter, it was once fashionable to suggest, as Peter Munz did, that Hooker had offered an argument for a "Tudor Averroism" in which the realm of nature was detached from the realm of grace, and politics functioned as an autonomous secular order accountable to reason only, not revelation.[2]

Curiously, however, this does not seem to be at all how the Elizabethan conformists saw what was at stake. Far from defending the "de-Christianization of the secular political order," they lament it as one of the looming disasters that might ensue upon the adoption of the Puritan program. Thus we encountered Whitgift fulminating against Cartwright's sharp distinction between church and commonwealth on the basis that it makes the English commonwealth no more Christian than "the commonwealth of Turcia," and accusing Puritans of perpetuating a papist doctrine "that Christian magistrates do govern, not in the respect they be Christians, but in the respect they be men; and that they govern Christians, not in that they be Christians, but in that they be men."[3] On the contrary, Whitgift argued that in a Christian commonwealth, "there is nothing in it that is profane, seeing it is a people holy to the Lord God, and the magistrate is holy and not profane."[4] Nor is Hooker of a different opinion,

1. D. J. McGinn's discussion in *The Admonition Controversy* (New Brunswick, NJ: Rutgers University Press, 1949), 110–23, is a good example of a rather hostile and simplistic attack on Puritan biblicism; see H. C. Porter, "Hooker, the Tudor Constitution, and the *Via Media*," in *Studies in Richard Hooker: Essays Preliminary to an Edition of His Works*, ed. W. Speed Hill (Cleveland: Press of Case Western Reserve University, 1972), 103–7 for an example of the argument that Hooker abandoned the Reformed principle of *sola Scriptura* to make way for the authority of reason.

2. Peter Munz, *The Place of Hooker in the History of Thought* (London: Routledge, 1952), 49–57.

3. *WW* III:296–97.

4. *WW* III:298.

drawing similar comparisons with Rome and declaring, with one of the more colorful similes in the *Lawes*, "A gross error it is to think that regal power ought to serve for the good of the body and not of the soul, for men's temporal peace and not their eternal safety; as if God had ordained Kings for no other end and purpose but only to fat up men like hogs and to see that they have their mash" (VIII.3.5; *FLE* 3:352.20–25).

How can we make sense of this? How is it that Puritanism can be blamed both for overreaching biblicism and incipient secularism? Certainly, in both subjecting the civil office to the church's interpretation of biblical law, and insisting on a "separation perpetual and personal between the *Church* and the *Commonwealth*" (VIII.1.2; *FLE* 3:317.24–25),[5] their project was, as Joan O'Donovan has noted, "beset by irresolvable contradictions."[6] The difficulty, as we saw above in Chapter Three, was that the Puritan spiritual kingdom was too much like the civil kingdom for the two to effectively complement one another. Either they must jostle with one another for position, with, as the conformists saw it, potentially subversive implications, or they must be radically separated from one another to avoid intermeddling. VanDrunen, then, is unmistakably developing one thread of the Puritan two-kingdoms distinction in eschewing biblicism in the civil kingdom and erecting a high institutional wall of separation between church and state.

Whatever, then, we are to make of Richard Hooker's rehabilitation of reason and attack on precisianist biblicism, we would clearly mistake him if we thought he was interested in carving out a "secular" civil order in the modern sense. For Hooker, nothing is more natural than the care for religion, as Cargill Thompson notes in response to Peter Munz:

> At no point does Hooker come close to suggesting that the State is a purely secular institution, which is only concerned with the advancement of man's temporal well-being in the world. On the contrary, his political philosophy is founded on precisely the opposite assumption. For Hooker, it is the essence of all "politic societies" that they are concerned with the promotion of man's spiritual welfare and, therefore, with the advancement of religion.[7]

5. See the discussion in W. Torrance Kirby, *Richard Hooker's Doctrine of the Royal Supremacy* (Leiden: Brill, 1990), 106.

6. Joan Lockwood O'Donovan, *Theology of Law and Authority in the English Reformation*, Emory University Studies in Law and Religion 1 (Atlanta: Scholars, 1991), 127.

7. Cargill Thompson, "Philosopher of the Politic Society: Richard Hooker as Politi-

Hooker, then, is seeking to defend the "freedom of a *Christian* common-wealth," and we have not rightly understood what is at stake between him and the Puritans if we have not understood the centrality of this *Christian* identity.

C. S. Lewis, in his splendid treatment of Hooker in *English Literature in the Sixteenth Century*, insists on this point, rebutting head-on the charge that, whatever Hooker's purported intent, "the unconscious tendency of his mind was to secularise." On the contrary, says Lewis,

> there could be no deeper mistake. Few model universes are more filled— one might say, more drenched—with Deity than his. "All things that are of God" (and only sin is not) "have God in them and he them in himself likewise" yet "their substance and his wholly differeth" (V.56.5). God is unspeakably transcendent; but also unspeakably immanent. It is this conviction which enables Hooker, with no anxiety, to resist any inaccurate claim that is made for revelation against reason, Grace against Nature, the spiritual against the secular.[8]

Among recent interpreters, Torrance Kirby has been particularly eager to advance this harmonious picture of Hooker's thought, repeatedly citing Lewis's memorable phrase, "drenched with deity," and elaborating Lewis's essentially neo-Platonic reading of Hooker's model of the universe. In a series of recent writings, Kirby has drawn attention to Hooker's image of the eternal law "in the bosom of God in himself" as the original unity from which the whole order of creation and redemption proceeds and in which it participates, describing natural law and divine law as "the two most essential moments in the self-mediating operation of the one eternal law."[9]

This primordial unity and mutual dependence of natural law and divine law ensure a similar mutual dependence of reason and Scripture:

> For Hooker the sapiential theologian, claims regarding the respective authorities of Scripture and Reason are not to be construed in binary opposition, in "zero-sum" fashion. Rather he views these two sources as

---

cal Thinker," in *Studies in Richard Hooker*, ed. W. Speed Hill, republished in W. D. J. Cargill Thompson, *Studies in the Reformation: Luther to Hooker*, ed. C. W. Dugmore (London: Athlone, 1980), 189.

8. C. S. Lewis, *English Literature in the Sixteenth Century, Excluding Drama*, vol. 3 of *The Oxford History of English Literature* (Oxford: Clarendon, 1954), 459.

9. W. J. Torrance Kirby, *Richard Hooker, Reformer and Platonist* (Aldershot, UK: Ashgate, 2005), 43.

simultaneously both presupposing and participating in a higher, unifying principle which is present in both as a cause in its effects. Whereas "scripture alone" is to be followed in the formulation of the "rule of faith," reason, custom and human authority are necessary in order to avoid "infinite perplexities, scrupulosities, doubts insoluble and extreme despaires" in the external ordering of religion.[10]

On this account, the neo-Platonic concept of participation ensures the unity and theocentrism of Hooker's universe, and ensures that the heightened role of reason in Hooker's theology constitutes no threat to the authority of Scripture. However, it is easy to overstate the centrality of this concept in the *Lawes*, and indeed, it is perhaps telling that in his many writings on the subject, Kirby has generally appealed to the same quite limited selection of passages to provide evidence for this paradigm in Hooker's thought.[11]

Although most scholars, therefore, would agree with Kirby that nature and grace, reason and revelation are not in conflict in Hooker's thought, for many, this is not because of any mutual participation between the two, but because of a clearly defined separation of roles and spheres, in which each has its proper autonomy. Indeed, this concern is nothing new, but was voiced by Hooker's first critics, the anonymous authors of *A Christian Letter*, who sought to drive a wedge between Hooker and the magisterial reformers on the relation of faith and reason.[12] H. C. Porter argues that these were correct to see

10. Kirby, "The 'sundrie waies of Wisdom': Richard Hooker's sapiential theology," in *Oxford Handbook of the Early Modern Bible*, ed. Kevin Killeen (Oxford: Oxford University Press, 2015). Of course, it must also be noted that even in formulating the "rule of faith," reason is not absent. Hooker is clear that reason is the instrument by which we rightly distinguish the meaning of Scripture and distill it into doctrinal formulations: "Exclude the use of natural reasoning about the sense of holy scripture concerning the articles of our faith, and then that the scripture doth concern the articles of our faith who can assure us?" (III.8.16; *FLE* 1:233.15–18).

11. Kirby's arguments for a neo-Platonic paradigm in Hooker's thought can be found particularly in *Richard Hooker, Reformer and Platonist*, 29–56; "From 'Generall Meditations' to 'Particular Decisions': The Augustinian Coherence of Richard Hooker's Political Theology," in *Law and Sovereignty in the Middle Ages and the Renaissance*, Arizona Studies in the Middle Ages and the Renaissance 28, ed. Robert S. Sturges (Turnhout: Brepols, 2011); "The Neo-Platonic Logic of Hooker's Generic Division of Law," *Renaissance and Reformation* 22 (1998): 49–68; and "'Law Makes the King': Richard Hooker on Law and Princely Rule," in *A New Companion to English Renaissance Literature and Culture*, ed. Michael Hattaway (Malden, MA: Wiley-Blackwell, 2010), 1:274–80.

12. *A Christian Letter of certaine English Protestants* (1599), in *FLE* 4:11–17, 64–71; see also discussion in Kirby, *Richard Hooker, Reformer and Platonist*, 13–15.

his work as "a celebration of 'our natural faculty of reason'"[13] that relativized the Reformation teaching of *sola Scriptura*.[14] Peter Lake, likewise, is pleased to observe Hooker's emphasis on "the independent exercise of human rational faculties."[15] Joan O'Donovan, on the other hand, laments such an emphasis, but concurs: "In breaking down the puritan opposition of God's eternally valid decrees to the blind and transient dictates of man's depraved rationality, Hooker retained a separation of reason and revelation that works to the advantage of reason's autonomy and jurisdiction."[16] Indeed, she suggests, Hooker is less interested in a mutual autonomy, than in an autonomy for reason that will result in its superiority to Scripture:

> [T]he authority of Scriptural revelation is everywhere bounded by reason's own assured authority; reason disposes of divinely revealed truth according to its invariable principles and operations, without itself apparently being at the disposal of faith's immediate and certain knowledge, without itself being demonstrably directed and empowered in its work by the Holy Spirit.[17]

Although always a recurrent theme, debates about the relative authority of reason and revelation in Hooker's thought have intensified in the past decade, with Nigel Voak in particular insistently arguing for Hooker's departure from Reformed orthodoxy on this point, and Torrance Kirby just as insistently maintaining the contrary.[18]

13. Porter, "Tudor Constitution," 103.

14. A similar perspective is advanced by Lee Gibbs, in his "Introduction to Book I," *FLE* 6(1): 118–20.

15. Peter Lake, *Anglicans and Puritans? Presbyterianism and English Conformist Thought from Whitgift to Hooker* (London: Unwin Hyman, 1988), 153.

16. J. O'Donovan, *Theology of Law and Authority in the English Reformation*, 145.

17. J. O'Donovan, *Theology of Law and Authority in the English Reformation*, 145.

18. Voak, while conceding that the old *via media* portrayal of Hooker is untenable, and he must be read as an essentially Reformed thinker, has assertively argued in his *Richard Hooker and Reformed Theology: A Study of Reason, Will, and Grace* (Oxford: Oxford University Press, 2003) that Hooker nonetheless crucially departs from a Reformed consensus at key points, including many of the same issues listed by *A Christian Letter* (such as the authentication of Scripture, the reliability of reason, and freedom of the will). Kirby's initial response to Voak suggested that his arguments were unoriginal and similarly tainted by a Puritan interpretation of what Reformed theology was all about (Kirby, "Review: *Richard Hooker and Reformed Theology: A Study of Reason, Will, and Grace*," *Sixteenth Century Journal* 36, no. 1 [2005]: 261–63). Kirby's retort here might be fortified by considering Richard Muller's remarks on the general endorsement among the Reformed orthodox of an "instrumental function" of

Although certainly distinct from the question of the role of religion in the political order, these issues are clearly related. If natural law, and reason's capacity to apply it in human affairs, are essentially autonomous, then so, might we conclude, is the civil state, in which revealed religion plays a marginal role at best, and Scripture is hardly relevant to the business of governing. On this reading, all of Hooker's apologetics for the royal supremacy cynically dissolve into a mere Hobbesian defense of civil religion, in which Scripture may help buttress the magistrate's authority, but will never really call him to account. On the other hand, if we stress that Scripture and reason "presuppose and participate in a higher, unifying principle," then it is much easier to take seriously Hooker's insistence on the dependence not only of religion on the commonwealth, but of the commonwealth on religion, and indeed, quite specifically, on the Bible.

We might appear then to be confronted with a straightforward question about the relationship of reason and revelation in Hooker's political theology: Does Hooker seek to reverse the *sola gratia* of the Reformation and rehabilitate the role of an "autonomous" natural reason, upon which an "autonomous" natural political state is constructed? Or does Hooker seek to emphasize the dependence of all things on God—both reason and Scripture, both spiritual and civil affairs? To frame the question this way, however, is entirely too vague.[19] In the sixteenth century, it was never a question of whether all things, the secular powers included, depended on God. Whatever one meant by the two kingdoms, one thing at least was clear: these were *God's* two kingdoms.

---

reason in theology, only not a "principal function" (*After Calvin*, 79).However, in a subsequent article, "Richard Hooker and the Principle of Sola Scriptura" (*Journal of Theological Studies* 59, no. 1 [April 2008]: 96–139), Voak has sharpened his attack at just this point, arguing that at least on the particular issue of the self-authentication of Scripture, Hooker implicitly grants reason principal authority by rejecting the Reformed doctrine of *autopistos*, putting him outside of Reformed bounds. Kirby remains unconvinced (see "Sundry waies of Wisdom"), though a much more convincing response to Voak on this point can be found in Andrew Fulford's essay, "'A Truth Infallible': Richard Hooker and Reformed Orthodoxy on Autopistos," in *Richard Hooker and Reformed Orthodoxy*, ed. Scott Kindred-Barnes and W. Bradford Littlejohn (Göttingen: Vandenhoeck & Ruprecht, 2017), 203–20.Regardless, however, of how this debate is settled, it concerns only the way in which our minds are brought to an initial acknowledgment of Scripture's authority, not the subsequent relationship between the faithful exercise of reason and faithful attention to the word of Scripture, which is our concern here.

19. So, for instance, Glenn Baker sets out to demonstrate the latter answer—the dependence of all things on God in Hooker's theology—in a lengthy but maddeningly vague study, "Richard Hooker and Writing God into Polemic and Piety" (unpublished PhD dissertation, University of Leicester, 2007).

To say that he ruled over one by natural law, rather than by Scripture, did not necessarily mean that it was "secular" in the modern sense, since natural law was understood as proceeding from God, or promulgated by God.[20] Likewise, reason was a gift of God, one whose effective functioning depended on him; to speak of reason as "autonomous" could thus only be a relative statement. For this reason, debates about precisely how much "autonomy" or "dependence" could be attributed to the civil kingdom, or to natural law, or to reason, require enormous nuance, and in Hooker's case, involve consideration of almost every aspect of his theology.

Hooker himself frames the problem here as one of "exact distinguishing" between nature and grace, and "observing what they have in common and what peculiar"; the want of this, declared Hooker in his *A Learned Sermon on the Nature of Pride*, "hath been the cause of the greatest part of that confusion whereof Christianity at this day laboureth."[21] To say that Hooker's own understanding can be described by the common Thomistic formulation, "grace does not destroy nature, it perfects it,"[22] might seem to get us nowhere, given the ubiquity of this formula among theologians from Aquinas right down to the present.[23] However, if we pursue this formula within the context

20. See for instance E. J. Hutchinson's rejoinder to Merio Scattola on this point with reference to the thought of the Danish theologian and jurist Niels Hemmingsen, whose thought has a number of parallels to Hooker ("Divine Law, Naturally: *Lex Naturae* and the Decalogue in Two Works of Niels Hemmingsen," in *For Law and for Liberty: Essays on the Trans-Atlantic Legacy of Protestant Political Thought*, ed. W. Bradford Littlejohn, Proceedings of the Third Annual Convivium Irenicum (Moscow, ID: Davenant, 2016); cf. also E. J. Hutchinson and Korey D. Maas, "Introduction" to Niels Hemmingsen, "On the Law of Nature in the Three States of Life," *Journal of Markets and Morality* 17, no. 2 [Fall 2014]: 619–46).

21. Hooker, *A Learned Sermon on the Nature of Pride*, in *FLE* 5:313.19–23.

22. This Thomistic formulation is applied to Hooker by W. David Neelands in "Hooker on Scripture, Reason, and Tradition," in *Richard Hooker and the Construction of Christian Community*, ed. Arthur Stephen McGrade (Tempe, AZ: Medieval & Renaissance Texts & Studies, 1997), 80: "For Hooker, as for Thomas, grace does not destroy but perfects nature, and Scripture does not obliterate but perfects reason. 'Supernaturall endowements are an advancement, they are no extinguishment of that nature whereto they are given' [V.55.6]. Grace being the beginning of glory in us, the same pattern is also claimed, by Thomas, for the relation of nature and glory: 'nature is not done away, but perfected, by glory.' Hooker frequently adopts the thesis that grace perfects nature. Less frequently, but equally clearly, he extends this to the stronger thesis, that glory is a perfection of nature." Neelands's whole discussion of this issue (pp. 76–91) offers a fantastic summary of the relevant material in Books I–III of the *Lawes*. See also Ranall Ingalls, who argues convincingly in "Sin and Grace" that this Thomistic formulation is in no way at odds with an Augustinian and broadly Reformed soteriology.

23. Indeed, H. C. Porter, whom we have met already at a rather different end of the

of Hooker's political-theological polemic, we may find that it sheds some important light on the nature of his quarrel with Cartwright's two-kingdoms theology.

Disciplinarian Puritans such as Cartwright, we saw, had reified the two kingdoms in such a way that the spiritual kingdom might appear to have all the relevant features of the civil—an independent, self-governing social body, its own rulers and autonomous sphere of jurisdiction, and above all, a detailed, almost exhaustive code of positive law to govern its polity. The church, in short, appeared to be little short of a new political institution alongside the kingdoms of the world, which implied that the kingdom of grace in fact replaces the kingdoms of nature. This was why, for all their protestations of loyalty to the crown, the Puritans could be perceived as Anabaptistic or papalist, threatening to overthrow the civil kingdom altogether. If divine positive law had established a divine constitutional polity, why bother with a merely human?

Against the implication that the church was a sort of supernatural political community that could exist alongside or in place of natural political community, Hooker wanted to maintain that Christian political community must be natural political community perfected by grace. That is to say, he insisted that grace enabled political community to achieve its natural potential, to function rightly within its own limitations, and to point beyond itself to the operations of grace that transcended those limitations. The supernatural law of Scripture, then, must not "clean have abrogated . . . the law of nature" (II.8.6; *FLE* 1:190.11), as it seemed to do in Puritanism. Rather, Hooker would insist that regarding matters of the civil kingdom, Scripture would serve to enrich, illuminate, clarify, and apply the law of nature, straightening and sharpening a bent and blunt tool, but not replacing it.[24]

---

spectrum from Neelands (who presents a thoroughly Protestant Hooker), uses the same formulation (and the same attribution of a "Thomistic" standpoint) to describe his understanding of Hooker's theology of nature and grace. Given the contemporary malleability of this dictum since its *ressourcement* by the *nouvelle théologie*, we must discern its meaning by attending to its concrete deployment. It is worth noting, however, that we can at least say, *contra* Porter and other incautious claims, the mere use of this formula hardly entailed any departure from magisterial Protestantism. Cf., for example, Franciscus Junius's explicit adoption of this formula in his *De Politiae Mosis Observatione* (exactly contemporary with Hooker's *Lawes*), 12 (*The Mosaic Polity*, trans. Tom M. Rester, ed. Andrew M. McGinnis, Sources in Early Modern Economics, Ethics, and Law [1613; repr., Grand Rapids: Christian Library's Press, 2015], 38).

24. Hooker's approach here is remarkably similar to that of his contemporary Junius, who would write, "And therefore with respect to the laws by which nature itself is preserved and renewed, grace restores those that have been lost, renews those that have been corrupted, and teaches those that are unknown" (*De Politiae*, 12; *Mosaic Polity*, 38; see further Littlejohn,

This understanding of nature and grace laid the groundwork for his vision of a Christian commonwealth, and informed his answer to the second key question that will occupy us in this chapter: In what sense is Christ the king over the two kingdoms? This question leads us into the realm of Christology, an area of theology that might seem at first quite alien to the very practical and political questions we have before us, but has in fact regularly been a touchstone of Christian political thought. This should not strike us as surprising, in fact, given the frequency with which Christ is spoken of in the language of "kingship" throughout Scripture. However, what precisely was the extent of his kingdom? As just mentioned above, most anyone in the sixteenth century could maintain that political rule was delegated by God, and in some sense mediated his rule to mankind. The civil kingdom, in this sense, was not thoroughly secular, because it was bound to creational norms, was accountable to God the Creator, and bore witness to him. However, to say that political rule was "creational" was not yet to say it was Christian. It is no coincidence that as early modernity moved increasingly toward a secular, autonomous mode of politics, it shifted its accent from the kingship of Christ the Redeemer to the kingship of God the Creator.[25] The latter seemed quite distant and removed; the former was too close for comfort. A political theology lacking Christological content, then, it could be safely assumed, was one in which the natural tools of human reason might need little illumination by Holy Scripture in order to govern rightly.

So it is intriguing to note that David VanDrunen, in developing his natural law/two-kingdoms schema, lays great stress on the doctrine of dual mediatorship, whereby, he argues, Christ mediates over the spiritual kingdom—the church—as man, as incarnate Redeemer; but over the civil kingdom only as eternal God and Creator.[26] From this doctrine, VanDrunen quite explicitly

---

"Cutting Through the Fog in the Channel: Hooker, Junius, and a Reformed Theology of Law," in *Richard Hooker and Reformed Orthodoxy*, 221–40).

25. The Christological model of kingship is clearly the dominant one at the outset of the great period of High Medieval political theology, as we see in writers like the "Norman Anonymous" (ca. 1100; see Ernst Kantorowicz, *The King's Two Bodies: A Study in Mediaeval Political Theology* [Princeton: Princeton University Press, 1957], 42–86; Oliver O'Donovan and Joan Lockwood O'Donovan, eds., *From Irenaeus to Grotius: A Sourcebook in Christian Political Thought, 100–1625* [Grand Rapids: Eerdmans, 1999], 250–60), but the shift is already apparent in anti-papalist writers like John of Paris (1250–1306; see *From Irenaeus to Grotius*, 398–405) and is complete when we reach chs. 31–32 of Hobbes's *Leviathan*, where it is the "kingdom of God," the sovereign lawgiver, that provides the paradigm for earthly kingship.

26. "Christ rules the one kingdom as *eternal God, as the agent of creation and providence, and over all creatures*. Christ rules the other kingdom as *the incarnate God-man, as*

derives the conclusion that the political order has no specifically Christian identity or Christian concerns; it is concerned simply with maintaining the order of creation, not with being renewed in light of redemption.[27] Few of his arguments, it turns out, are more directly relevant to the dispute between Hooker and the Puritans, for in his *Second Replie to the Answer*, Cartwright develops precisely this doctrine in order to underwrite the same basic agenda. Of course, Cartwright does not draw the sweeping secularizing implications from it that VanDrunen does, but the immediate target of critique—the magistrate's care for religion—and the immediate goal—the establishment of an independent visible kingdom of Christ in the church—are the same.

To this argument of Cartwright's, Hooker directly responds in an electrifying though widely neglected section of Book VIII, arguing that *Jesus Christ the Redeemer* rules over the earthly kingdom, which is thus accountable to witness to the order of redemption. This claim might seem at first quite shocking to those accustomed to see in Hooker the great opponent of theocracy, and champion of natural law. If the civil kingdom exists to witness to the order of redemption, what becomes of Hooker's steadfast insistence on the natural law as the chief rule for understanding and ruling the civil kingdom? As we shall see, however, this objection would presuppose the very disjunction of nature and grace that Hooker refuses.

The argument of this chapter will thus have something of the shape of a pyramid, laying some broad foundations and then building more focused layers of argument, until we reach at the pinnacle a sketch of Hooker's view

---

the agent of redemption, and *over the church*. The latter kingdom is redemptive, the former is nonredemptive. The latter is exclusive, the former is inclusive" (David VanDrunen, *Natural Law and the Two Kingdoms: A Study in the Development of Reformed Social Thought*, Emory University Studies in Law and Religion [Grand Rapids: Eerdmans, 2010], 177). For further discussion, see *Natural Law and the Two Kingdoms*, 75–76, 176–83, 313–14, 341–44.

27. See especially such passages as "Reformed orthodox theologians also recognized Christ's continuing distinct identities as creator/sustainer and as redeemer and developed this idea . . . [by] tying it specifically to the two-kingdoms doctrine. As they grounded natural law in the covenant of works, and hence in creation rather than in redemption, so they also grounded the civil kingdom in creation rather than redemption" (VanDrunen, *Natural Law and the Two Kingdoms*, 182); and "to defend the idea of the 'Christianization' of the common grace realm because it is the work of 'Christ,' is to confuse categories and language. . . . If the Son of God creates in a different capacity from his capacity as redeemer, then he does not create as 'Christ' and the terrain of common grace, grounded in the creation order, is not 'Christian,' no matter how noble it becomes" (314); see also VanDrunen's intriguing interaction with Barth on this issue on pp. 341–44, where he fails to see the force of Barth's objections to such a creation/redemption dichotomy.

of the religious responsibilities of the Christian ruler, and the authority of Scripture in a Christian polity. Section II will survey the general principles of Hooker's understanding of nature and grace as it relates to his taxonomy of laws, natural and divine, and section III will survey the relation of nature and grace in his carefully nuanced Christology. Section IV will show how this Christology informs his understanding of Christ's rule over church and commonwealth, in opposition to Cartwright (and by extension, VanDrunen). Sections V and VI will then bring all of these points together to show how Hooker both ties grace intimately to the natural life of the commonwealth, and yet leaves considerable freedom for the way in which this relationship is concretely realized in particular polities.

II. "Natural Desire Cannot Utterly Be Frustrate": Natural and Divine Law in Hooker's Theology

Let us then turn to consider more carefully the teleological relation of nature and grace in Hooker's theology. We have noted above Torrance Kirby's proposal that Hooker's theology be described in terms of the neo-Platonic pattern of a *processio* and *reditus*: the procession of all things outward from the unity that is God, differentiating according to their creaturely plurality, and the return of all things to God, their differences harmonized in a deeper unity that they have by participation in God.[28] Whether or not we accept the distinctively neo-Platonic features of this scheme, it provides an admirable rubric for discerning the movement of Hooker's thought on nature and grace, natural law and divine law, and eventually, as we shall see, divine law and human law. To use John Perry's terms, Hooker's thought begins by first carefully distinguishing the just bounds of different kinds of law, before seeking to reunite them in a symbiotic harmony.

We see the initial outward movement of procession and distinction in Hooker's famous generic division of law in Book I, which reflects Hooker's deep familiarity with Thomas Aquinas and the scholastic tradition, and supplies the systematic foundation for his theology. This has been very carefully described by many scholars, so our summary here can be quite brief.[29]

---

28. See especially "Law Makes the King," "From General Meditations," and "The Neoplatonic Logic."

29. See especially Cargill Thompson, "Philosopher of the 'Politic Society,'" 150–60; J. O'Donovan, *Theology of Law and Authority in the English Reformation*, 137–42; Kirby, "Reason and Law," in *A Companion to Richard Hooker*, ed. W. J. Torrance Kirby (Leiden: Brill, 2008),

Hooker begins his *apologia* not with the divine law of Scripture, as a Puritan might, or the laws of England, as a conformist might be tempted to, but with the primordial source from which both ultimately derive, "the eternal law," which "is laid up in the bosom of God." Indeed, God himself operates according to this law, for law is intrinsic to being itself:

> All things that are have some operation not violent or casual. Neither doth anything ever begin to exercise the same without some foreconceived end for which it worketh. And the end which it worketh for is not obtained, unless the work be also fit to obtain it by. For unto every end every operation will not serve. That which doth appoint the form and measure of working, the same we term a *Law*. (I.2.1; *FLE* 1:58.22–29)[30]

In the case of God, we do not say that the eternal law governs his being, but that his being *is* this law (I.2.2), a law that encompasses every kind of law, inasmuch as God's operations encompass all that is; it is "that order which God before all ages hath set down with himself, for himself to do all things

---

251–71; and most thoroughly and systematically, though not without some problems, F. J. Shirley, *Richard Hooker and Contemporary Political Ideas* (London: Published for the Church Historical Society by S.P.C.K, 1949), 71–92. Alexander Rosenthal gives particular attention to the Thomistic roots of Hooker's theory of law (*Crown under Law: Richard Hooker, John Locke, and the Ascent of Modern Constitutionalism* [Plymouth, UK: Lexington Books, 2008], 49–61), although Nigel Voak has played the contrarian, arguing in ch. 1 of *Richard Hooker and Reformed Theology* that on a number of key points, Hooker is more Scotist than Thomist. In any case, it has been common for some scholars to suggest that Hooker's dependence on Aquinas and the medieval scholastics sets him at odds with Reformed theology (some of the most forceful arguments on this score can be found in A. J. Joyce, *Richard Hooker and Anglican Moral Theology* (Oxford: Oxford University Press, 2012), 150–56, and Rosenthal, *Crown under Law*, 61–72). This betrays, however, an ignorance about the extent to which Thomistic and scholastic ideas were used by leading Reformed theologians such as Vermigli and Zanchi (see John Patrick Donnelly, *Calvinism and Scholasticism in Vermigli's Doctrine of Man and Grace* [Leiden: Brill, 1976], and "Calvinist Thomism," *Viator* 7 [1976]: 441–55; these studies are particularly useful for rebutting Lee Gibbs's spurious claim, of which Rosenthal makes a great deal, that whereas Hooker "stands predominantly within the medieval rationalist and realist tradition . . . the magisterial Protestant Reformers . . . stand squarely in the camp of the medieval voluntarists and nominalists" [*FLE* 6:103]; see also Arvin Vos, *Aquinas, Calvin, and Contemporary Protestant Thought* [Grand Rapids: Eerdmans, 1985]). For the fullest reevaluation of this issue, see Paul Dominiak, "Hooker, Scholasticism, Thomism, and Reformed Orthodoxy," in *Richard Hooker and Reformed Orthodoxy*, 101–26. Throughout the following exposition, I will use the footnotes to highlight the extent to which Hooker's theory of law shares key features not only with Aquinas, but also with Reformed predecessors and contemporaries.

30. Cf. Aquinas, *ST* II–I q. 90 a. 1.

by" (I.2.6; *FLE* 1:63.2–3).[31] Here Hooker introduces a distinction unique to his exposition, notably departing from Aquinas by describing this order as the "first law eternal"; the "second," on the other hand, is "that which with himself he [God] hath set down as expedient to be kept by all his creatures" (I.3.1; *FLE* 1:63.8–9). By this distinction, he seeks to steer clear of voluntarism by emphasizing the lawlikeness and rationality of God's eternal decrees, but at the same time to preserve a sharp Creator/creature distinction, by showing that although united in God, these decrees from our creaturely standpoint remain distinct from his revealed will, and thus inscrutable to us.[32]

Having safeguarded the inscrutability of the first, Hooker turns his exclusive attention in what follows to the second, which although one in itself, unfolds itself in different forms according to its different agents. Hooker summarizes succinctly:

> That part of it which ordereth natural agents, we call usually *nature's* law: that which Angels do clearly behold, and without any swerving observe is a law *celestial* and heavenly: the law of *reason* that which bindeth creatures reasonable in the world, and with which by reason they may most plainly perceive themselves bound; that which bindeth them, and is not known but by special revelation from God, *Divine* law; *human* law that which out of the law either of reason or of God, men probably gathering to be expedient, they make it a law. (I.3.1; *FLE* 1:63.17–26)

Hooker has relatively little to say about the *celestial* law, and although it is quite interesting that Hooker chooses again to depart from Aquinas in distinguishing "nature's law," which governs involuntary actions, from the "law of reason," which governs voluntary actions (i.e., those of human beings specifically), we need not dwell on the distinction here.[33] Both are contained in what the

---

31. Cf. Aquinas, *ST* II–1 q. 91 a. 1.

32. Torrance Kirby lays great stress on this distinction in his interpretation of Hooker, suggesting that "the crucial consequence of this gathering together of the various species of law within a second eternal law is to diminish the overall significance of the hierarchical *dispositio* as the primary mode of mediation between the divine source of law and the finite, created order of laws. In place of the Thomist logic of a gradual, hierarchical disposition of the species of law, Hooker's positing of the second eternal law sets up an Augustinian 'hypostatic' relation between the Creator/ Eternal Law and creature/manifold determinate species of law" ("From Generall Meditations," 51; see pp. 50–55 for a full discussion). In my essay "Hooker, Junius, and a Reformed Theology of Law," I suggest that a similar distinction is implicit in Franciscus Junius's formulation of the "eternal law" (*Mosaic Polity*, 41–43), paralleling his influential distinction of "archetypal" and "ectypal" theology.

33. While also considering the difference from Aquinas here to be of little significance,

Thomist tradition has called the "natural law," and Hooker's almost exclusive interest in what follows is with the latter part, "the law of reason," governing as it does moral actions. Just as "nature's law" guides irrational creatures to their appointed end and perfection, their unique form of participation in divine goodness, so does the law of reason guide mankind, only that we are uniquely called to reflect on, discern, and actively pursue the goodness proper to our natures. Man thus seeks not only after the perfections proper to all creatures, but to further perfections: "[S]uch as are not for any other cause, than for knowledge itself desired . . . [through which] by proceeding in the knowledge of truth and by growing in the exercise of virtue, man amongst the creatures of this inferior world, aspireth to the greatest conformity with God" (I.5.3; *FLE* 1:73.31–74.3).

By recognizing those goods that constitute the perfection of our nature and gaining experience in pursuing them, we derive maxims and axioms as a guide to right conduct. Of course, these are not always easy to discern, since there are a multitude of possible goods to choose from, and we often choose a less over a greater, or a faulty route to a genuine good. Nevertheless, "There is not that good which concerneth us, but it hath evidence enough for itself, if reason were diligent to search it out" (I.7.7; *FLE* 1:80.29–31). Therefore, although Hooker has no illusions about the power and prevalence of widely engrained error, he does not believe that it can ever become universal. Universal consensus, then, must be taken as a token of truth, indeed, "as the sentence of God himself. For that which all men have at all times learned, nature herself must needs have taught; and God being the author of nature, her voice is but his instrument" (I.8.3; *FLE* 1:84.1–4). Natural reason, Hooker believes, following Romans 1, can perceive the being, power, and fatherhood of God, and can deduce thereby such rules as "That in all things we go about his aide is by prayer to be craved, That he cannot have sufficient honour done unto him, but the utmost of that we can do to honour him we must" (I.8.7; *FLE* 1:87.21–23).[34] The latter of these, he says, is the same as the first great commandment that Jesus gives us—that we must love God with all our hearts. Moreover, by discerning the natural equality of all humans, we will necessarily recognize that one cannot expect to receive any greater good from one's fellows than that

---

Rosenthal notes that Hooker may well have derived this distinction from the Henrician jurist Christopher St. Germain's *Doctor and Student* (*Crown under Law*, 55–56).

34. Hooker is quoting here from Plato's *Timaeus* 27c and Aristotle's *Nicomachean Ethics* 1163b. Cf. Peter Martyr Vermigli, *Philosophical Works: On the Relation of Philosophy and Theology*, trans. and ed. Joseph C. McClelland, The Peter Martyr Library 4 (Kirksville, MO: Truman State University Press, 1996), 18–22.

which one gives unto them, and can expect to suffer from them in proportion to that which one causes them to suffer; this leads to the principle of the second great commandment, that we must love our neighbors as ourselves.[35]

Before treating of "the divine law," as we might expect him to, Hooker follows his discussion of the law of reason with a discussion of human law, reflecting his Aristotelian conviction that the latter is the chief means by which the general principles of the former are rendered concrete. Human law thus exists to remedy a deficiency in the law of reason, its lack of precision, since disagreement becomes more and more likely the more we descend from the general to the particular, as well as the fact that the law of reason does not usually serve as a sufficient motivation toward virtue.[36] Human law is more than mere rational deliberation about what the law of reason requires in relation to a concrete problem; deliberation can do no more than provide maxims of prudent action for private individuals. Human law has a necessarily *political* dimension; it is law promulgated and in some sense enforced for a community of men and women bound together by compact, by representatives authorized to act on behalf of the whole. It is thus within the context of his discussion of human law in Book I, chapter 10, that Hooker lays down the general foundations of his political theory, which we have had cause to touch on already in the preceding chapter.

Human laws, says Hooker, may be either *mixedly* or *merely* human.[37] In the former, human law rectifies the sloth of our intellects and the stubbornness of our wills, which prevent us from obeying that which reason already commands of us: "[T]he matter whereunto it bindeth, is the same which reason necessarily doth require at our hands, and from the law of reason it differeth in the manner of binding only . . . by virtue of human law [men] become constrainable, and if they outwardly transgress, punishable" (I.10.10; *FLE* 1:106.2–7). The latter, encompassing such things as laws of inheritance, represent an improvisation in matters where the law of reason has not already bound us necessarily to one or another course of action: "[T]he matter of them is anything which reason doth but probably teach to be fit and convenient, so that till such time as law hath passed amongst men about it, of itself it bindeth no man" (I.10.10; *FLE* 1:106.8–10).[38] Within this section, Hooker draws attention to a fact that is central to his argument throughout

---

35. Cf. Girolamo Zanchi, "On the Law in General," trans. Jeffrey J. Veenstra in *Journal of Markets and Morality* 6, no. 1 (Spring 2003): 320.

36. Cf. Aquinas *ST* II–I q. 94 a. 4, q. 95 a. 1; Zanchi, "On the Law in General," 22.

37. Cf. Junius, *Mosaic Polity*, 55–57.

38. Cf. Aquinas *ST* q. 95 a. 2; Zanchi, "On the Law in General," 23–24.

the *Lawes*: the vast diversity, and constant mutability, of human societies and circumstances. This diversity calls for great variety in the proper forms of human law, notwithstanding the original unity of its principles in the law of reason: "[T]he sundry particular ends whereunto the different disposition of that subject or matter, for which laws are provided, causeth them to have especial respect in making laws. . . . [O]ne kind of laws cannot serve for all kinds of regiment" (I.10.9; *FLE* 1:103.30–32, 104.15–16). This will be true even of *mixedly* human laws, which are simply applications of necessary principles of the law of reason—although the principle may be the same, the best way to apply the principle and achieve its desired end will differ depending on circumstances.

Divine Law, the Perfection of Nature

What, then, of divine law? We might be forgiven at this point for imagining that Hooker has indeed provided us with a robust naturalism, attributing an autonomy and self-sufficiency to the law of reason (and its applications in the form of human law) that would leave little need for revelation within this-worldly affairs. Indeed, by insisting that the law of reason includes the principles of the two great commandments—honoring God and loving our fellow man—we might ask what need we have of divine law at all. Of course, Hooker does take care to maintain, even within his exposition of the law of reason, that our reasons are at all times dependent upon "perpetual aid and concurrence of that supreme cause of all things" (I.8.11; *FLE* 1:92.26–27) for their effective operation, aid that can be withdrawn at any point if we give God just cause. However, this proviso, while important in ruling out Deistic forms of rationalism, offers few limitations on how far reason might proceed even in sacred matters. Much more, then, will need to be said to satisfy our questions about the scope of reason and the need for revelation. Thankfully, Hooker unfolds his answer to these questions in a sophisticated argument that occupies chapters 11 and 12 of Book I.

In this argument, he establishes three things: First, nature and reason cannot be autonomous in the sense of encompassing their own end; nature cannot be considered a self-enclosed compartment, nor can reason be satisfied merely with the task of investigating creation. This much should be clear already from Hooker's inclusion of the first great commandment as one of the prescriptions of the law of reason; however, he will have much more to say in support of this claim in chapter 11, insisting that man's final end is one beyond nature: God.[39] Second, nature and reason cannot be autonomous in the sense of being capable, on their own, of reaching their final, supernatural end. On this point, Hooker is particularly nuanced, attributing most of this incapacity to the reality of sin, but acknowledging a dependence on divine grace even in the state of innocence. Third, nature and reason cannot be autonomous even in the sense of being perfectly adequate to the task of discerning and reaching man's natural ends, without use of revelation. Let us investigate each of these three points in turn.

Hooker begins chapter 11 by returning to his statements early in chapter 5, where he introduced the law of reason, saying that it was the way in which man sought the unique goodness proper to his nature. Everything created, he says, must have not merely particular goods, but a final good, "our sovereign *good* or *blessedness* that wherein the highest degree of all our perfection consisteth, that which being once attained unto there can rest nothing further to be desired" (I.11.1; *FLE* 1:111.2–4). Indeed, when we look at created goods, we see how they each serve not as goods in themselves, but as instruments unto some higher good, and lest there be an infinite regress, "something there must be desired for itself simply and for no other" (I.11.1; *FLE* 1:111.24–25). For animals, mere continuance in being is an end in itself, but not for man. For man, as the highest order of being,

> doth seek a triple perfection: first, a sensual, consisting in those things which very life itself requireth as necessary supplements, or as beauties and ornaments thereof; then an intellectual, consisting in those things which none underneath man is either capable of or acquainted with; lastly a spiritual and divine, consisting in those things whereunto we tend by supernatural means here, but cannot here attain unto them. (I.11.4; *FLE* 1:114.18–25)

This last, the "spiritual and divine" good, must be infinite, for it is that final good "which is desired altogether for itself," a desire that would be evil if bestowed on anything finite (I.11.2; *FLE* 1:112.3–4).

So what is this final spiritual good, this supernatural end? It is union with God, the only infinite good and the object of our desire: "Then are we

---

39. The importance of this claim—a Thomistic one, as Neelands notes ("Scripture, Reason, and Tradition," 83)—to Hooker's theology is immense. Robert K. Faulkner declares, "All important peculiarities of Hooker's ethics are traceable to this final end external to man as he knows himself" (*Richard Hooker and the Politics of a Christian England* [Berkeley: University of California Press, 1981], 77).

happy therefore when fully we enjoy God, as an object wherein the powers of our souls are satisfied even with everlasting delight: so that although we be men, yet by being unto God united we live as it were the life of God" (I.11.2; *FLE* 1:112.17–20). Hooker goes on to specify further this condition of blessedness: it must be "according unto every power and faculty of our minds apt to receive so glorious an object"—"both by understanding and will"; it must be perpetual, a perpetuity that cannot proceed from any natural necessity within us, but "from the will of God, which doth both freely perfect our nature in so high a degree, and continue it so perfected" (I.11.3; *FLE* 1:113.7–9, 26–27).

Now this desire for supernatural happiness, Hooker is at pains to establish, is itself *natural*, for all men have it. It is not in our power *not* to desire this, he says. Therefore, being naturally desired, it must in some sense be within natural capacity since "[i]t is an axiom of nature that natural desire cannot utterly be frustrate" (I.11.4; *FLE* 1:115.15–16). So man's reason is not enclosed within the bounds of creation, but naturally transcends these bounds, by desiring and striving unto the supernatural end of union with God.[40] If natural desire, then, is not "frustrate," is natural reason capable on its own of achieving this end?

Certainly not as man now finds himself, which brings us to Hooker's second argument. For "this last and highest estate of perfection whereof we speak is received of men in the nature of a reward" (I.11.5; *FLE* 1:115.25–26), for works of obedience to the Creator. This would have been Adam's path to perfection and bliss had he not fallen. However, Hooker is careful to qualify here that we do not speak of this reward in terms of strict justice, as something that God *owed* to man, but "by the rule of that justice which best beseemeth him [God], namely the justice of one that requireth nothing mincingly, but all with pressed and heaped and over-enlarged measure" (I.11.5; *FLE* 1:117.25–27), and the perpetual continuance of that blessedness infinitely transcends mere natural justice. In any case, however, says Hooker, this is beside the point, for Adam failed, and what man now living can present his works, such as they are, before the throne of the Almighty as worthy of his favor? "There resteth therefore either no way unto salvation, or if any, then surely a way which is

---

40. Hooker's Aristotelian line of argument in these paragraphs resembles that of Aquinas in *ST* II–I q. 1 and q. 3, a. 1. But see also Vermigli, *Commentary on Aristotle's Nicomachean Ethics*, ed. Emidio Campi and Joseph C. McClelland, The Peter Martyr Library 9 (Kirksville, MO: Truman State University Press, 2006), 21–41. For a comparison of Vermigli and Thomas on this point, see Eric Parker, "A Christian and Reformed Doctrine of Right Practical Reason: An Examination of Thomistic Themes in Peter Martyr Vermigli's Commentary on Aristotle's Nicomachean Ethics" (unpublished M.A. dissertation, Reformed Theological Seminary [Jackson, MS], 2009), 102–17.

supernatural, a way which could never have entered into the heart of man as much as once to conceive or imagine, if God himself had not revealed it extraordinarily" (I.11.5; *FLE* 1:116.4–7). Thankfully for us, this latter is the case, and God has revealed a means, transcending any capacity of reason, whereby we might be granted this highest end of our desire.

The supernatural duties thereby revealed are faith, hope, and charity, and are not merely beyond natural capacity to do, but even to know. Hooker thus describes these as supernatural "both in respect of the manner of delivering them," coming to us by divine revelation, "and also in regard of the things delivered, which are such as have not in nature any cause from which they flow." As matters beyond the scope of nature, they are "by the voluntary appointment of God ordained . . . to rectify nature's obliquity withal" (I.11.6; *FLE* 1:119.18–24).

This reference to the rectification of "nature's obliquity" merits closer consideration, and leads us to Hooker's third argument. Thus far, we might be excused for understanding Hooker to say that fallen nature falls short only of encompassing its naturally desired supernatural end, but not of merely natural ends. On this reading, the revelation of divine law would serve merely to establish supernatural duties, which would serve merely to lead us to God, while reason remained perfectly adequate to guide us in natural, civil duties toward our fellow man. Certainly Hooker has already said a great deal in praise of reason's ability to guide us in such endeavors, and will continue to say a great deal throughout the *Lawes*. After all, God's wisdom comes to us in many ways—from "the sacred books of Scripture; . . . by the glorious works of nature; . . . by spiritual influence; . . . by worldly experience and practise"—all of which are to be respected and valued in their particular place: "We may not so in any one special kind admire her that we disgrace her in any other, but let all her ways be according unto their place and degree adored" (II.1.4; *FLE* 1:148.4–6). However, Hooker does not in fact think that the law of reason has no use of scriptural illumination within the realm of natural duties. Nor does he think the converse, which proceeds from the same misunderstanding: that the supernatural law, being once delivered, can serve as a substitute for the law of reason (the conclusion that the precisianists implied).

Rather, he declares at the outset of chapter 12, "When supernatural duties are necessarily exacted, natural are not rejected as needless. The law of God therefore is though principally delivered for instruction in the one, yet fraught with precepts of the other also. *The Scripture is fraught even with laws of Nature*" (I.12.1; *FLE* 1:119.26–29; italics mine). In redirecting us to our final end, Scripture cannot but redirect us also with respect to our finite ends, since these are ultimately oriented toward that final end of union with God. If we ought to pursue finite goods with a view toward possession of God as highest good, then our disorientation from our final end, as a result of sin, cannot but distort our grasp of finite ends. Consequently, the reorientation provided by revelation will set us back on our natural path and illuminate that path again for us.

We may thus distinguish "supernatural law" from the standpoint of *origin* and *object*. Inasmuch as divine law reveals supernatural duties, it is, as Hooker has just said, supernatural both in respect of its origin (we could not know it but by special revelation) and in respect of its object (it concerns those duties that comprise our supernatural path to our final end). However, divine law also reveals natural duties; in these it is supernatural in respect of origin, but not of object.[41] Hooker accordingly seeks throughout the *Lawes* to maintain the principle of *sola Scriptura* within the arena of supernatural duties, while insisting that Scripture and the law of reason can be mutually interpreting in the arena of natural duties. Let us then look more closely at how Hooker describes the inadequacies within the law of reason, and the cause for divine law's restatement of certain of them.

The Limits of Reason

Although Hooker is often thought to be dismissive of the effects of the Fall,[42] and inattentive to the limitations within the law of reason, in fact,

---

41. This same distinction, only implicit in Aquinas's treatment in the *Summa*, is also explicitly made by Junius in his *Mosaic Polity*, 69 (see also my essay, "Cutting through the Fog in the Channel: Hooker, Junius, and a Reformed Theology of Law," in *Richard Hooker and Reformed Orthodoxy*, 221–40).

42. Peter Lake speaks for many when he declares, "[C]ompared to the views of other Protestants, Hooker's vision of sin . . . seemed almost benign" (*Anglicans and Puritans?* 150). See also Egil Grislis, "Scriptural Hermeneutics," in *Companion to Richard Hooker*, 297–99 for an attempt to distinguish between Reason I (unfallen reason), Reason II (fallen reason), and Reason III (redeemed reason) in Hooker's thought. While the proper distinctions are there, Grislis believes, they are not always made clear: "At times in praising Reason I, he seemed to ignore his own comments on the corrosive influence on Reason II by original or actual sin" (297–98). However, as even Joyce acknowledges, Hooker was quite unambiguous about total depravity in his earlier works (*Richard Hooker and Anglican Moral Theology*, 92–93), perhaps varying his emphasis here in the *Lawes* based on the polemical context (p. 97). It also bears emphasizing that Hooker's Reformed predecessors were not always so dour about the capacity of human reason as often portrayed. Vermigli, for instance, was capable of considerable optimism, as we see throughout his *Commentary on the Nicomachean Ethics* (see also Donnelly, *Calvinism and Scholasticism*, 44–48). Even Calvin often spoke much more positively regarding

he is careful to enumerate these limitations not once but twice within these chapters. In chapter 8, where he provides his first survey of the law of reason, he qualifies its capabilities with three caveats. First, he says, it is not that the principles of the law of reason are in fact known to all men, but that they are such that "being proposed no man can reject [them] as unreasonable and unjust" and such that "any man (having natural perfection of wit, and ripeness of judgment) may by labour and travail find out" (I.8.9; *FLE* 1:90.16–17). They are in themselves knowable by all men, but that does not mean that a lack of such labor and travail may not leave many in ignorance of them. He returns to this theme in I.12, saying that for this reason, the divine law's "applying of them unto cases particular is not without most singular use and profit many ways for men's instruction" (I.12.1; *FLE* 1:120.10–12).[43] And when we are vexed with doubt as to whether we have determined and applied the law of reason correctly, the clear divine authority of these specific pronouncements is a great help to us. Hooker considers this a limitation of "sincere" (i.e., unfallen), not "depraved" nature, though sin exacerbates this considerably, so that "concerning the duty which nature's law doth require at the hands of men in a number of things particular, so far hath the natural understanding even of sundry whole nations bene darkened, that they have not discerned no not gross iniquity to be sin" (I.12.2; *FLE* 1:120.22–121.2).

Indeed, this is because of a second limitation that sin particularly introduces, that of "lewd and wicked custom," which, "beginning perhaps at the first amongst few, afterwards spreading into greater multitudes, and so continuing from time to time, may be of force even in plain things to smother the light of natural understanding" (I.8.11; *FLE* 1:91.30–33). By this means, it would seem, many of the key principles of the law of reason could become thoroughly obscured by sinful man. Related to this is Hooker's discussion of our fallen propensity "to fawn upon ourselves, and to be ignorant as much as may be of our own deformities" (I.12.2; *FLE* 1:121.2–4), so that we need to be told where our faults are and how they are to be fixed. Our nature has been distorted by sin, but that very sin keeps us from so much as recognizing the deformity; hence divine law comes to our aid and points it out to us. An example of this is the Sermon on the Mount, where Jesus reveals even secret concupiscence to

---

human nature post-Fall than he is generally known for doing (see William J. Bouwsma, *John Calvin: A Sixteenth Century Portrait* [Oxford: Oxford University Press, 1988], 142).

43. Hooker's remarks here, and indeed most of what he says about the value of divine law, closely approximate Aquinas's in *ST* II-I q. 91 a. 4.

be sin, where we might have deceived ourselves into imagining that the natural law required only outward purity (I.12.2).

The third qualification we have already mentioned: that the faculty of reason always depends upon the "aid and concurrence" of God, which, should we "cause God in his justice to withdraw," then we can expect only the darkness described in Romans 1, "even men endued with the light of reason notwith-standing 'in the vanity of their mind, having their cogitations darkened, and being strangers from the life of God through the ignorance which is in them, because of the hardness of their hearts'" (I.8.11; *FLE* 1:92.27–93.1).[44] After the Fall, then, although God continues to extend enough of his favor to most men to enable them to discern some knowledge of moral laws, their grasp is no longer clear and reliable, particularly when we move beyond natural law's first principles to second-order deductions. Hence, there seems to be the need for a supplementary source of revelation that will pierce through the self-imposed darkness of sin.

For all these reasons, then, we may be immensely grateful to God for providing in Scripture not merely a guide to the path of salvation, but con-siderable instruction in natural moral duties as well. Hooker summarizes the relationship of natural and divine law at the end of Book I:

> The law of reason doth somewhat direct men how to honour God as their Creator, but how to glorify God in such sort as is required, to the end he may be an everlasting Saviour, this we are taught by divine law, which law both ascertaineth the truth and supplieth unto us the want of that other law. So that in moral actions, divine law helpeth exceedingly the law of reason to guide man's life, but in supernatural it alone guideth. (I.16.5; *FLE* 1:139.4–10)

Indeed, such is the unity of the law of nature, and so extensive is Scripture's republication of it, that Hooker will happily admit that, in principle, one *could* derive a complete rule of moral action from Scripture. So where is his differ-ence from Cartwright?

It is first metaphysical, in his different answer to the *Euthyphro* dilemma: that things are commanded by God in Scripture because good, not good be-

---

44. Nigel Voak has argued for understanding this "aid and concurrence" in terms of the Reformed doctrine of common grace, which helps to make sense of how Hooker can hold together total depravity and relative optimism about fallen human capabilities (*Richard Hooker and Reformed Theology*, 100–112).

cause commanded. This leads him to conclude that although in the order of knowing the good, Scripture may sometimes precede nature, this is neither necessary nor always expedient: "[I]t sufficeth if such [moral] actions be framed according to the law of reason; the general axioms, rules, and principles of which law being so frequent in holy scripture, there is no let but in that regard, even out of scripture such duties may be deduced by some kind of consequence" (II.1.2; *FLE* 1:145.24–28). Indeed, as Hooker will go on to sketch in chapter 15, the divine law of Scripture also contains a good deal of positive law corresponding to "human law"—that is to say, particular applications of natural law (whether that be known naturally or by aid of Scripture) for the needs of particular human communities. Both the civil laws of the Old Testament, and a variety of New Testament commands for the order of the church, he argues, fall under this heading.[45] Hooker then also differs from Cartwright in that he understands these divine commands to function as human laws, and thus to be, despite their supernatural origin, mutable in respect of their object; as applications of laws of reason, they may be re-specified by reason should circumstances change. In the final section of this chapter, when summarizing the role of Scripture in guiding human law, we will return to consider in more detail how Hooker distinguishes the various categories of divine positive law.

Hooker's recapitulation at the conclusion of chapter 12 admirably summarizes the three points we have established in this section, the triple dependence of nature on the supernatural:

> We see, therefore, that our sovereign good is desired naturally; that God the author of that natural desire had appointed natural means whereby to fulfil it; that man having utterly disabled his nature unto those means hath had other revealed from God, and hath received from heaven a law to teach him how that which is desired naturally must now supernaturally be attained; finally we see that because those later [the supernatural] exclude not the former [the natural] quite and clean as unnecessary, therefore together with such supernatural duties as could not possibly have been otherwise known to the world, the same law that teacheth them, teacheth also with them such natural duties as could not by light of nature easily have bene known. (I.12.3; *FLE* 1:121.29–122.5)

---

45. Cf. Aquinas, ST II–I q. 104 a. 3 (see also William S. Brewbaker III, "The Bible as Law Book? Thomas Aquinas on the Juridical Uses of Scripture," *Rutgers Journal of Law and Religion* 12, no. 76 [Fall 2010]: 102–5); Vermigli, *Commentary on Aristotle's Nicomachean Ethics*, 58–59; Junius, *Mosaic Polity*, 60–70.

III. "An Associate of Deity": Hooker's Christology

Readers of Hooker have too often been tempted to read the *Lawes* from the outside in, highlighting Book I, with its sweeping, magisterial survey of law in general, and Book VIII, with its readily recognizable concerns such as royal supremacy and its obvious contributions to political theory.[46] Books II through VII, and especially the massive Book V, can too easily appear as tiresome and arcane quibbling about long-forgotten disputes. However, there is something to be said for reading the *Lawes* from the inside out, seeing the discussion of Christology in the middle of Book V as the linchpin and beating heart of the whole work. Indeed, given the space and care that Hooker devotes to this question of systematic theology, in the midst of a discussion of disputed liturgical practices, it is surprising that it has not received more attention. Torrance Kirby, however, has again done us great service in his *Richard Hooker's Doctrine of the Royal Supremacy*, arguing for the centrality of the Christological "paradigm" in underpinning the logical structure of the *Lawes*.[47]

This basic paradigm, we shall find, follows the logic of nature and grace just sketched above. In the Incarnation of the Word, our natural human desire for union with God is met; in him, the final end for humanity is brought to pass, but in a form beyond nature's own capacity. In Jesus Christ, we see that, in devising a supernatural means for mankind's return to God, God did not leave nature behind; rather, nature is preserved whole, and indeed, restored to a perfect condition, in the Incarnation. Grace does not destroy nature, but perfects it. The Incarnation thus follows Hooker's *processio/reditus* pattern, and the logic of distinguishing and differentiating in order to harmonize and unify appears in his Christological exposition. Hooker is keen to emphasize that the perfections that are bestowed on Christ's human nature by its union with the Word, while constituting an advancement, do not constitute an advancement beyond the human or the natural human condition; human nature is enriched in a manner suited to its creaturely capacity. In other words, correspondent with what we saw above regarding Scripture and the natural law, the Incarna-

---

46. This tendency has, alas, been intensified by the fact that the only quality edition of Hooker's *Lawes* readily available in paperback is McGrade's Cambridge Texts in the History of Political Thought edition (Cambridge: Cambridge University Press, 1989), which includes only the Preface, Book I, and Book VIII.

47. Kirby notes that Lionel Thornton observed in 1924 "that the section of the *Lawes* dealing with Christology 'is like a central tower' around which the whole argument of the treatise is constructed" (*Richard Hooker, Reformer and Platonist*, 91, quoting L. S. Thornton, *Richard Hooker: A Study of His Theology* [London: Society for Promoting Christian Knowledge, 1924], 54).

tion does not merely offer the introduction of a new divine element, entirely beyond nature; it simultaneously renews, restores, and elevates nature, without compromising its identity as nature. This conviction, as we shall see, plays a very important role in Hooker's political theology.

Under these three headings, then—the personal union of humanity with divinity, the continued distinction of human and divine natures, and the perfection of human nature within the bounds of its natural capacity—we may summarize the basic arguments of Hooker's investigation of Christology. The discussion of Christology proper occupies chapters 51–55 of Book V of the *Lawes*, and in it, Hooker seeks to thread the needle of orthodoxy, avoiding both the Eutychian temptation to so fuse the two natures within the one divine-human person that their separate natural properties are merged, exchanged, or confused, and the Nestorian temptation to completely bracket off the natures from one another, so that Jesus's actions in the flesh cannot really be predicated of the divine Son. These fifth-century disputes, after relative dormancy in the Middle Ages, had been resurrected as part of the fierce Lutheran-Reformed polemics on the subject of the Eucharist. Many Lutheran theologians, seeking to establish a basis for the ubiquity of Christ's incarnate body, argued that by a "communication of attributes," divine properties were transferred to or merged with the human. To the Reformed, this doctrine, as well as Catholic sacramental teaching, threatened a Eutychian confusion of the two natures of Christ, and their predication of a communication of attributes was rigorously circumscribed with an emphasis on the continuing integrity of each nature. Naturally, this prompted accusations of Nestorianism from their opponents. Although, as so often throughout the *Lawes*, Hooker leaves these debates and interlocutors below the surface of the text, his treatment of Christology clearly represents an attempt to offer a persuasive and balanced Reformed Christology that meets Lutheran objections but also attempts to establish as much common ground as possible on the disputed question of ubiquity. However, for the sake of space, I will generally confine myself to highlighting those elements that will be of significance in Hooker's revisitation of Christology in Book VIII.

The burden of chapter 51 is to establish that it is truly the divine person of the eternal Word that has become incarnate in Christ Jesus, and that in this union, he has not left behind his divine nature, so that "undoubtedly even the nature of God itself in the only person of the Son is incarnate, and hath taken to itself flesh" (V.51.2; *FLE* 2:210.13–14).[48] He then asks why it is that

48. In one of the few recent discussions of Hooker's Christology (though it occupies only four pages), David Neelands summarizes Hooker's as a Cyrilline Christology: "Christ

redemption should have taken place by such an extraordinary means—why should the eternal Word himself be the agent of our salvation? He answers this question in terms very reminiscent of Athanasius's renowned *De Incarnatione*, highlighting the relationship between creation and redemption: "It seemeth a thing unconsonant that the world should honor any other as the Savior but him whom it honoreth as the creator of the world . . . it became therefore him by whom all things are, to be the way of salvation to all, that the institution and restitution of the world might be both wrought by one hand" (V.51.3; *FLE* 2:210.18–20, 211.6–9). This tight link between the redeeming work of God and his original creating work is one of the ways in which Hooker highlights that the Incarnation represents the perfection, not the eclipse, of nature.

Hooker then proceeds in the next two chapters to carefully analyze the hypostatic union, first focusing on the personal unity between the two natures, which enables us to speak truly, and not merely metaphorically, of a *communicatio idiomatum*, whereby we predicate human actions of the divine, and divine of the human. "For as much therefore as Christ hath no personal subsistence but one whereby we acknowledge him to have been eternally the Son of God, we must of necessity apply to the person of the Son of God even that which is spoken of Christ according to his human nature." This enables Hooker to affirm in the strongest terms against Nestorianism "that no person was born of the Virgin but the Son of God, no person but the Son of God baptized, the Son of God condemned, the Son of God and no other person crucified" (V.52.3; *FLE* 2:215.6–9). But it also means, as Hooker will have occasion to emphasize shortly, that the works of divinity may now also be predicated of

---

is divine; Christ *has* human nature" ("Christology and the Sacraments," in *A Companion to Richard Hooker*, ed. W. Torrance Kirby [Leiden: Brill, 2008], 371). He notes that some, notably Ronald Bayne (*Of the Laws of Ecclesiastical Polity, The Fifth Book* [London: Macmillan, 1902], cix), have seen in this a sympathy with Luther rather than the putatively more Antiochene or even semi-Nestorian Reformed tradition (371–72). Gunnar Hillerdal's highly tendentious reading of Hooker's Christology in chapter 5 of his *Reason and Revelation in Richard Hooker* (Lund: CWK Gleerup, 1962) is perhaps the starkest version of this claim. However, the difference is one of emphasis at most. See François Wendel, *Calvin* (New York: Harper & Row, 1963), 220–25 for a comparison of Calvin's Christology with Luther's, and Kirby, *Richard Hooker's Doctrine of the Royal Supremacy*, 111–17 for a correlation of Hooker's Christology with that of Calvin's. Indeed, a comparison of Hooker's Christological exposition with that of Reformed stalwart Girolamo Zanchi in ch. 11 of his *De Religione Christiana Fides—Confession of the Christian Religion*, ed. Luca Baschera and Christian Moser (Leiden: Brill, 2007), 1:199–229 (see also his *Observations* on ch. 11 in 2:535–51, and his *Appendix* to ch. 11, 2:635–57) reveals them to be in agreement on every point of substance, and should put to rest any assumption that "Cyrilline" and Reformed Christologies are incompatible.

the fully human person Jesus Christ. Almost immediately, however, he moves on to qualify these strong statements of unity, insisting that the conjunction of natures involves

> no abolishment of natural properties appertaining to either substance, no transition or transmigration thereof out of one substance into another, finally no such mutual infusion as really causeth the same natural operations or properties to be made common unto both substances, but whatsoever is natural to deity the same remaineth in Christ uncommunicated unto his manhood. (V.53.1; *FLE* 2:216.23–28)

Thus, while we may speak of the divine doing human actions, and the human divine actions, we must subsequently clarify, explaining that the one person acts in each by virtue of the nature to which such actions are proper. To speak with precision, then, some things Christ does as God, others as man, others as both conjointly. Hooker thus proposes as a rule for deciding all doubts "that of both natures there is a *cooperation* often, an *association* always, but never any mutual *participation* whereby the properties of the one are infused into the other" (V.53.3; *FLE* 2:218.30–219.3). By virtue of this distinction, Hooker's concern is not so much to preserve the divine nature from the stain of finitude or passibility (as this doctrine is often criticized for doing), but to preserve the full integrity of the human nature. He wants to avoid any implication that Christ's human nature is anything other than fully human, that it is merged with his divinity in such a way as to be swallowed up in it or essentially changed: "We may not therefore imagine that the properties of the weaker nature have vanished with the presence of the more glorious, and have bene therein swallowed up as in a gulf" (V.53.2; *FLE* 2:217.18–21). Here, as throughout his theology, we see his concern to preserve the full integrity of nature even as it is graced.

However, Hooker does not want to rule out any influence upon the human nature, as if in the Incarnation, God simply attached himself to humanity without humanity being in any way altered thereby. On the contrary, by virtue of the Incarnation, Christ's "human nature hath had the honor of union with deity bestowed upon it . . . [and] by means thereof sundry eminent graces have flowed as effects from deity in to that nature which is coupled with it" (V.54.1; *FLE* 2:220.24–27). These graces, Hooker emphasizes, although focused on the particular human being Jesus, are given to human nature as a whole, since Christ has assumed "that *nature* which is common to all" (V.52.3; *FLE* 2:213.21); but again, this "gracing" of nature somehow does not "denature"

nature: "The very cause of his taking upon him our nature was to change it, to better the quality and to advance the condition thereof, although in no sort to abolish the substance which he took, nor to infuse into it the natural forces and properties of his deity" (V.54.5; *FLE* 2:223.16–20). Hooker goes on to elaborate this statement with many careful qualifications. The properties of human nature, he says, are not "so much altered, as not to stay within those limits which our substance is bordered withal" (V.54.5; *FLE* 2:223.25–27)—the advancement that occurs is one that is within the potentiality of man's nature. Clearly, Hooker can make this claim because of his insistence back in Book I that the supernatural end of union with God is one that is naturally desired, and one we are naturally capable of receiving.

In what does this advancement consist? Hooker will distinguish the "grace of union" from the "grace of unction," and in the cases of both, he is careful to qualify that the full graces obviously belong uniquely to the man Jesus Christ, that "man with whom deity is personally joined" (V.54.5; *FLE* 2:224.12); although we have been made sharers with him in them. By virtue of the former grace, human nature is taken up into the history of God, and made to share in all the honors and activities pertaining properly to the Logos: "[T]o be the way, the truth and the life; to be the wisdom, righteousness, sanctification, resurrection . . . [are] true of Christ even in that he is man. . . . [W]e cannot now conceive how God should without man either exercise divine power or receive the glory of divine praise. For man is in both an associate of Deity" (V.54.5; *FLE* 2:224.5–6, 11, 16–18). By virtue of the latter, Christ's human nature was made capable of operations beyond the ordinary power of human nature. Hooker qualifies this, however, by saying that it receives "all such perfections as the same is any way apt to receive" (V.54.6; *FLE* 2:225.1–2)—that is to say, with the elevated perfections that human nature is somehow predisposed to receive, that human nature can receive without going beyond what it means to be human. On this basis, he will exclude the Lutheran doctrine of ubiquity, as positing a "perfection" of human nature that goes quite beyond the capacities of human nature, so as to overturn that nature entirely, for "[s]upernatural endowments are an advancement, they are no extinguishment of that nature to which they are given" (V.55.6; *FLE* 2:230.28–29). However, Hooker clearly is prepared to argue that human nature is destined for, capable of, a greater perfection than that which it had at the beginning, and that in Christ, this perfection is reached.

IV. The Reign of the Son of Man

Now, what does all this have to do with political theology, with the nature of a Christian commonwealth? Judging by most expositions of Hooker's political thought, we would have to conclude, "Not much."[49] This oversight, however, is quite remarkable when we consider that Hooker himself makes the application quite directly and explicitly in Book VIII, chapter 4. For Hooker, the royal supremacy, and indeed, the whole identity of a Christian commonwealth, rests firmly on a Christological foundation. In establishing this foundation, he responds directly to Cartwright's invocation of Christology, one that was to represent a prominent theme in some streams of Reformed political theology, as VanDrunen has argued in *Natural Law and the Two Kingdoms*.

There VanDrunen lays great weight on what he calls the Reformed doctrine of the "two mediatorships," a doctrine forcefully asserted by Cartwright in his engagement with Whitgift, and common among both English Puritans and Scottish Covenanters. As articulated by many Reformed theologians, and recently well summarized by John Bolt, the doctrine seems a natural implication of the *extra Calvinisticum*, the Reformed insistence that Christ remained, in his divine nature, present always and everywhere *etiam extra carnem*—"even outside the flesh":

> As mediator, the divine Logos is not limited to his incarnate form even after the incarnation. He was mediator of creation prior to his incarnation and as mediator continues to sustain creation independent of his mediatorial work as reconciler of creation in the incarnation, death, resurrection, and ascension of Jesus of Nazareth.[50]

This distinction may be a useful heuristic device, but it runs into trouble when forced to bear too much ontological and ethical weight, as in expositions like Cartwright's, an approach that VanDrunen appears to follow in his *Natural Law and the Two Kingdoms*. At its worst it can suggest a permanent disjunction between the order of creation and the order of redemption, a dis-

---

49. Torrance Kirby is the notable exception, arguing in *Richard Hooker's Doctrine of the Royal Supremacy* (Leiden: Brill, 1990) that "the Chalcedonian formula and the systematic theology which developed from it are at the heart of Hooker's thinking and provide it with its essential coherence . . . the Christological 'paradigm' is the indispensable key to an interpretation of Hooker's defence of the union of Church and Commonwealth" (24–25).

50. John Bolt, "Church and World: A Trinitarian Perspective," *Calvin Theological Journal* 18, no. 1 (April 1983): 30.

junction found within the person of Christ himself. The result is not merely the Nestorianizing impulse of which the Reformed were often accused, but an abstraction of the work of redemption from the creation it is meant to redeem. This comes into particularly sharp focus in the doctrine of the ascension, on which VanDrunen asserts that the glorified and ascended Christ continues to execute his divine and human offices simultaneously and separately.[51] This doctrine of two separate kingships of Christ clearly underwrites a version of the two-kingdoms doctrine that sharply walls off the political and cultural sphere from the ecclesiastical and spiritual.[52]

However, Hooker emphasizes that the personal unity of the Incarnate Word ensures that creation and redemption can hold together as two works of the same agent and that these are not two unrelated works, but the latter renews the former and brings it to perfection. By distinguishing the two works, then, we do not necessarily underwrite any strict separation of church and state, of the norms of redemption from the norms of creation. Such separation depends on resisting any *communicatio idiomatum* whereby the human acts of the work of redemption can be predicated of the eternal Word and the divine acts of creation and governing creation can be predicated of the Son of man. VanDrunen thus asks us to separate out these two "capacities": "The Son of God rules the temporal kingdom as an eternal member of the Divine Trinity but does not rule it in his capacity as the incarnate mediator/ redeemer."[53] The rejection of the *communicatio* becomes more explicit in VanDrunen's language of "distinct identities"[54] within the incarnate Word,

---

51. VanDrunen, *Natural Law and the Two Kingdoms*, 75, 182. However, VanDrunen has quietly backed away from his most problematic formulations here in his more recent book, *Living in God's Two Kingdoms: A Biblical Vision for Christianity and Culture* (Wheaton, IL: Crossway, 2010), 118: "The Lord Jesus Christ rules all things. . . . So how does Christ now rule the many institutions and communities of this world other than the church? The answer is that he rules them through *the Noahic covenant*, for they are institutions and communities of the common kingdom. They operate according to the same basic principles and purposes as before Christ's first coming. What is different is that God now rules them through the incarnate Lord Jesus, the last Adam who has entered into the glory of the world-to-come."

52. Such is VanDrunen's announced intention in *Natural Law and the Two Kingdoms*. See David McKay, "From Popery to Principle: Covenanters and the Kingship of Christ," in *The Faith Once Delivered: Essays in Honor of Dr. D. Wayne Spear*, ed. Anthony T. Selvaggio (Phillipsburg, NJ: P&R Publishing, 2007), 135–50, for an account of how this same two-mediators distinction was used to undergird a similarly strict two-kingdoms separation in seventeenth-century Scotland.

53. VanDrunen, *Natural Law and the Two Kingdoms*, 181.

54. VanDrunen, *Natural Law and the Two Kingdoms*, 182.

such that we cannot rightly name him as "Christ" if referring to his creative and sustaining role:

> To distinguish between the Son as creator and the Son as redeemer entails that the title of "Christ" belongs only to the latter . . . in his special mission of becoming incarnate for the particular work of saving his people. The Son redeemed the world, but did not create the world, as the Messiah, the Christ. . . . If the Son of God creates in a different capacity from his capacity as redeemer, then he does not create as "Christ," and the terrain of common grace, grounded in the creation order, is not "Christian," no matter how noble it becomes.[55]

Distant as these Christological concerns may seem from politics, Cartwright's debates with Whitgift reveal him drawing very similar implications from such a doctrine. In his debate with Whitgift over the relationship of the two kingdoms, Cartwright developed an account of the two mediatorships, which he pursues at some length in his *Second Replie*. In attacking Whitgift's account of the civil and spiritual kingdoms, Cartwright argues that "it confoundeth and shuffleth together the authority of our Saviour Christ as he is the son off God only before all worlds coequal with his father [his authority over kingdoms]: with that which he hath given off his father and which he exerciseth in respect he is mediator between God and us [his authority over the church]."[56] Further on, he explains,

> Let it be considered first that our Saviour Christ is in one respect creator, and preserver of mankind, in another redeemer, and upholder of his church. For he created once and preserveth daily as God coequal with his Father, and Holy Spirit, but he both redeemed once, and daily gathereth his church, as mediator of God and man, in which respect even yet in his infinite glory he enjoyeth, he is, and shall be under his Father, and Holy Ghost, until having put down all rule and power, he shall render the kingdom to his father. Secondly it is to be considered, that as our Saviour Christ doth these in diverse respects: so he doth them by diverse means. To wit that as God simply he hath ordained certain means to serve his providence in the preservation of mankind; so as God and man, he hath ordained other certain, for the gathering, and keeping of his church. These

55. VanDrunen, *Natural Law and the Two Kingdoms*, 313–14.
56. *SR* 411.8–13.

grounds laid, it is to be considered, whether the exercise of the sword by the magistrate, come from our Saviour Christ preserver of mankind, wherein he is coequal to his father, or as mediator of his church, wherein he is inferior.[57]

In these passages, Cartwright is attempting to assert a Christological basis for a separate government of church and state. These institutions, says Cartwright, serve to provide for the ongoing work of redemption, and the ongoing government of creation, respectively. Accordingly, they are not simply under the government of Jesus Christ in the same way, and cannot be mixed together. In particular, Cartwright's point here is to insist that we cannot speak of a human head of the church, because the church already has a human head, Christ Jesus, who answers to God. As governor of the church, "our Saviour Christ himself hath a superior, which is his father." However, Cartwright does want to allow for human heads of state, and thus argues that these are subordinated to Christ only as he is God: "[I]n the government of kingdoms . . . he hath no superior, but immediate authority with his father."[58] Torrance Kirby explains that for Cartwright, "Christ has a *double* role or function as the 'God-man.' On the one hand, he is the source of all authority in the secular political order by virtue of his being the Son of God; on the other hand, he exercises ultimate power as head of his body, the church, through his Manhood."[59] With two distinct heads, then, the civil and spiritual kingdoms function in Cartwright's account as two distinct, personally separated bodies.

VanDrunen cites Samuel Rutherford advancing a similar, though perhaps even more starkly stated account, insisting that because the temporal kingdom is under "God the creator" and the spiritual under "Christ the redeemer," it follows that civil magistrates are "not subordinate to Christ as mediator and head of the Church" and are not "the ambassadors of Christ" but "the deputy of God as the God of order, and as the creator."[60]

Lurking behind this sort of account is the specter of Nestorianism, the implication that we must treat the Incarnate God-Man as a separate agent from the eternal Word, and must strictly avoid predicating of the one functions

---

57. *SR* 416.36–417.17.

58. *SR* 411.15–18.

59. Kirby, *Richard Hooker's Doctrine of the Royal Supremacy*, 104.

60. VanDrunen, *Natural Law and the Two Kingdoms*, 181, quoting from Samuel Rutherford, *The Divine Right of Church Government and Excommunication* (London: John Field for Christopher Meredith, 1646), 510–11.

carried out by the other. Hooker is alive to this danger, and also to its larger consequences, recognizing that, in Kirby's words, "such a separation within the source of authority, and its consequent 'personal' separation of the civil from the ecclesiastical community implies an inevitable de-Christianising of the secular political order."[61] Accordingly, he responds to Cartwright's claims from the *Second Replie* in a masterful stretch of argument in VIII.4.6, drawing on the Christological principles laid down already in Book V.

He begins, "As Christ being Lord or Head over all doth by virtue of that Sovereignty rule all, so he hath no more a superior in governing his Church than in exercising sovereign Dominion upon the rest of the world besides." On this basis, he will argue "that all authority as well civil as Ecclesiastical is subordinate unto his" (*FLE* 3:363.26–27). One cannot, as Cartwright does, separate Christ's kingship over the church as man from his divine kingship. Hooker constructs his argument carefully, beginning with the eternal Son's sharing in the rule of God the Father:

> That which the Father doth work as *Lord* and *King* over all he worketh not without but by the son who through coeternal generation receiveth of the Father that power which the Father hath of himself. And for that cause our *Saviour's* words concerning his own Dominion are, "To me all power both in heaven and earth is given." The Father by the son both did create and doth guide all. (3:364.7–14)

So far, VanDrunen and Cartwright would probably concur—the second person of the Trinity, by virtue of his divinity derived from the Father, is Creator and Ruler of all things. However, Hooker insists at this point on the *communicatio idiomatum*:

> [T]here is no necessity that all things spoken of Christ should agree unto him either as God or else as man, but some things as he is the consubstantial word of God, some things as he is that word incarnate. The works of supreme Dominion which have been since the first beginning wrought by the power of the Son of God are now most truly and properly the works of the Son of man. The *word* made *flesh* doth sit forever and reign as Sovereign *Lord* over all. (3:364.23–365.4)[62]

61. Kirby, *Richard Hooker's Doctrine of the Royal Supremacy*, 106.
62. Zanchi would support Hooker, rather than VanDrunen here, asserting in his *De religione Christiana fides*, 217–19: "[W]hatsoever Christ is or doeth according to the divine nature,

Indeed, at stake here is not merely the doctrine of the incarnation—by virtue of which divine agency can be predicated of Jesus of Nazareth—but the doctrine of the ascension, by virtue of which the man Jesus Christ has been elevated, in his human nature, to kingship at the right hand of God over all his works. Whereas VanDrunen asserts, and Cartwright implies, a version of the *extra Calvinisticum* that permanently sunders the human being Jesus Christ from the lordship exercised by the divine Son,[63] Hooker insists that all that the Son worked as God he works now also as man, and what the Son works as man, he now does by divine power: "And yet the dominion whereunto he was in his human nature lifted up is not without divine power exercised. It is by divine power that the Son of man, who sitteth in heaven, doth work as *King* and *Lord* upon us which are on earth" (3:367.10–14).[64] The two natures, in short, are united in one agency, one dominion, a dominion over not only the church, but all creation.

It is thus as both God and man that Christ rules over his church, and as both God and man that he rules over the kingdoms of this world. The basis of all earthly government is not merely from God the Creator, but now also through the God-man, the Redeemer, who as man sits on the throne at the right hand of God, as redeemer of the world exercises his rule over creation. All that the Son has and does by virtue of divinity, his humanity is made sharer in, and all that Jesus Christ has and does by virtue of his humanity, the divinity

---

that same whole Christ, the Son of man, may be said to be or to do. And again, whatsoever Christ doth or suffereth according to his human nature, that same whole Christ, the Son of God, God himself, is said in the holy scriptures to bee, to do and to suffer. . . . Yea, Christ the mediator according to his humanity never did or doeth anything, wherein his divinity did not or doth not work together, and he never performed anything according to his divinity, whereunto his humanity was not assisting or consenting."

63. For a helpful analysis of this *extra Calvinisticum* in its original theological context, see E. D. Willis, *Calvin's Catholic Christology: The Function of the So-Called Extra Calvinisticum in Calvin's Theology* (Leiden: Brill, 1966).

64. This is stated even more clearly back in Hooker's Christological discussion in Bk. V, which he is clearly drawing on at this point: "[T]hat deity of Christ which before our Lord's incarnation wrought all things without man doth now work nothing wherein the nature which it hath assumed is either absent from it or idle. Christ *as man* hath all power both in heaven and earth given him. He hath *as man not as God only* supreme dominion over quick and dead. For so much his ascension into heaven and his session at the right hand of God do import. . . . Session at the right hand of God is the actual exercise of that regency and dominion wherein the manhood of Christ is joined and matched with the deity of the Son of God. . . . *This government [over all creation] therefore he exerciseth both as God and as man*, as God by essential presence with all things, as man by cooperation with that which essentially is present" (V.55.8; *FLE* 2:232.16–22, 233.12–14, 28–30; italics mine).

is made sharer in. This, Hooker has argued, is simply the orthodox doctrine of the incarnation. One cannot then say that as divine Son, the Word exercises a dominion in which the man Christ Jesus has no part, or that as redeeming man, Christ exercises an office in which the divine Son has no part. Rather, all things on heaven and earth are made subject to the Word made flesh. For that reason, to return to the terms introduced earlier in this chapter, there is no part of the natural order that has not been united to, and perfected in, the order of grace.

Just as the implications of Cartwright's semi-Nestorian move for political theology are profound, so the implications of Hooker's response supply him with a strong foundation not merely for his defense of the royal supremacy, but more generally, for his account of the Christian commonwealth. Civil magistrates hold their authority derivatively from God through Christ, and thus are accountable to Christ for the outward protection of his kingdom.[65] Because we cannot sever Christ's redemptive work from his work of creating and governing, it follows that magistrates are responsible not merely for preserving the created order of human society, and witnessing to God's rule over it, but also for encouraging the redemption of society, and witnessing to the kingship of Christ the Redeemer. For Hooker, this is not a denial of his clear insistence on the integrity of the natural order, and of natural law as a means for governing this order. Rather, as we have seen, he has maintained throughout that human nature seeks its proper fulfillment in union with God, a union that is perfectly exhibited in the glorified and ascended Christ. Now that this *natural* end has been achieved by virtue of supernatural grace in the incarnation, resurrection, and ascension of Christ, one cannot speak of the natural order without reference to its rightful king, Christ the Redeemer. In him, human nature has not been destroyed, nor transformed into something else; rather, it has been restored from its fallen condition, and advanced to a higher perfection, a perfection not beyond nature but proper to it. Accordingly, the political order, while falling within the realm of nature, is not unaffected by the work of Christ; it cannot carry on as though it existed only under the banner of a generic deity. Rather, it is subject to the God-man who sits now in heaven as king and judge. By the same token, natural law cannot do without the revelation of Christ and his Word, despite having its roots in creation rather than redemption.

In the following two sections, we shall synthesize all these points to show how Hooker situates the role of religion, both natural and revealed, in the com-

---

65. VIII.4.6 (*FLE* 3:369.1–24).

monwealth, how he explains the duty of the magistrate to care for the souls of his subjects, and what role Scripture can play in framing human law. We shall once more witness the pattern of *processio/reditus*, of distinguishing and harmonizing, as Hooker seeks to knit together the two kingdoms under the kingship of Christ, but does not confuse the work of prince and priest, confining the magistrate's role to the external protection and nourishment of the church.

V. The Soul of a Christian Commonwealth

Throughout this chapter, we have repeatedly called attention to Hooker's application of the dictum *grace does not destroy nature, but perfects it*. Nowhere is this more true than his treatment of the role of religion in the commonwealth. We will recall already from Chapter Five that Hooker understands public religion as a natural and civil phenomenon, not as exclusively Christian or spiritual. Of course, this did not mean it was a mere simulacrum of the spiritual; rather, as we saw with his discussion of liturgy, although achieving its effect through natural and outward instruments, Christian worship can serve as a real pathway toward our growth in grace. The key point, however, was that the civil kingdom, in addition to being concerned with all the mundane concerns of public order, economic prosperity, and outward protection that characterize our modern conception of the domain of politics, was also properly a religious order; it existed under God, toward God, and animated and structured by worship.

Given what we have seen in Chapter Five, and in section II of this chapter, it is not hard to see why this should be the case. Human nature is not satisfied with mere finite, earthly ends, but constantly seeks a happiness beyond the bounds of temporal existence, a happiness to be found in God. This restless longing for God, which subordinates and orders all other desires, will always, thinks Hooker, be reflected in the life of human society, which will always establish some kind of religious devotion at the heart of its public life. Because of the centrality and ultimacy of this religious devotion, worship is not merely of value for its own sake, but serves as an anchor for the public life of the community, guaranteeing unity around a common object of love, and reverent esteem for the magistrates who are the guardians of this common life. At the outset of Book V, Hooker describes religion as "the highest of all cares appertaining to public regiment," especially "for the force which religion hath, to qualify all sorts of men, and to make them in public affairs the more serviceable, governors the apter to rule with conscience, inferiors for conscience sake the willinger to obey." In short, "[I]f the course of politic affairs cannot in any good sort go forward without fit instruments, and that which fitteth them be their virtues, let polity acknowledge itself indebted to religion, godliness being the chiefest top and wellspring of all true virtues, even as God is of all good things." Hooker then goes on to outline how religion helps preserve and perfect each of the four cardinal virtues, to the great benefit of the commonwealth, going so far as to say, regarding the greatest of the cardinal virtues, "So natural is the union of Religion with Justice, that we may boldly deny there is either, where both are not" (V.1.2; *FLE* 2:16.26–17.13).

Hooker will return to this argument early in Book VIII, where he constructs his defense of the Royal Supremacy on two chief pillars. The first is the personal identity of the visible church (being an outward society of those who profess the faith—see Chapter Four above) and the commonwealth in Elizabethan England. The other, however, is the natural responsibility of commonwealths for religious concerns:

> [F]or of every politic society that being true which Aristotle hath, namely, "that the scope thereof is not simply to live, nor the duty so much to provide for life as for means of living well," and that even as the soul is the worthier part of man, so human societies are much more to care for that which tendeth properly unto the soul's estate than for such temporal things as this life doth stand in need of. Other proof there needs none to shew that as by all men "the kingdom of God is first to be sought for": So in all commonwealths things spiritual ought above temporal to be provided for. And of things spiritual the chiefest is *Religion*. (VIII.1.4; *FLE* 3:321.7–17)

As André Gazal has noted, this represents a dramatic hermeneutical shift from the prevailing apologetic strategy of English defenders of the Royal Supremacy.[66] Although Hooker will cite scriptural precedents for the *cura religionis*, ultimately it is a duty of natural, not divine law.

---

66. André Gazal, *Scripture and Royal Supremacy in Tudor England: The Use of Old Testament Historical Narrative* (Lewiston, NY: Edwin Mellen, 2013), 495–519. However, as I have argued in "More than a Swineherd: Hooker, Vermigli, and the Aristotelian Defense of the Royal Supremacy," *Renaissance and Reformation Review* 15, no. 1 (2014): 78–93, a very similar line of reasoning had been employed by Peter Martyr Vermigli in his defense of the royal supremacy four decades before. See also Matthew Tuininga, *Calvin's Political Theology and the Public Engagement of the Church: Christ's Two Kingdoms* (Cambridge: CUP, forthcoming 2017), ch. 6, for a similar contention about Calvin's argument in favor of the magistrate's (for him, more restricted) *cura religionis*.

From all this, however, it might appear that Hooker has been so eager to demonstrate nature's receptivity to the supernatural, religion's integral place in the commonwealth, that he has perhaps naturalized religion altogether, reducing Christianity to a mere prop of political order. He anticipates this objection in V.1 and V.2, attacking both atheists, who conclude from the "politic use of religion . . . that religion itself is a mere politic device" (V.2.3; *FLE* 2:25.25–26), and skeptics, who suggest that if religion as such benefits the commonwealth, it doesn't much matter "of what sort our religion be" (V.1.3; *FLE* 2:19.23). Against these objections, he takes care to argue that on the contrary, it is not merely religion, but *true* religion, after which all men instinctively seek, and that finding the true religion, Christianity, makes a great difference, both in this life, and in that which is to come. He has no hesitation in recognizing the many virtues and benefits that flowed from heathen religion, as "certain sparks of the light of truth intermingled with the darkness of error" (V.1.5; *FLE* 2:22.20–21), but he maintains nonetheless that "the purer and perfecter our religion is, the worthier effects it hath in them who steadfastly and sincerely embrace it" (V.1.4; *FLE* 2:21.28–29).

Hooker thus develops his account of public religion under his overarching logic of nature and grace. The desire for and worship of God is natural to man, and indeed, so central to human nature that it serves to ground and orient the other virtues, and is a mainstay of civil polity. Fallen as man is, however, this religious devotion is tainted with "heaps of manifold repugnant errors" (V.1.3; *FLE* 2:21.25–26), on account of which we desperately need the gracious revelation of true religion. This true religion, then, serves not only to set us on the path to everlasting life, which the false religions cannot even begin to do, but also reorients our temporal existence, crowning the natural virtues with a perfection beyond the capacity of false religion, and enabling a more harmonious life together in civil society. For all these reasons, Hooker can argue for the Christian magistrate's overarching concern for the spiritual well-being of his subjects, which is found only in their redemption by Christ; for in this rests their ultimate good, to which they are naturally oriented, and from it flows all subsidiary goods that will ensure a peaceful and virtuous life for the commonwealth. On Hooker's definition, then, the church, considered as an external, visible society, is a commonwealth ordered toward the true religion:

> [T]he care of religion being common unto all *Societies* politic, such *Societies* as do embrace the true religion, have the name of the *Church* given them for distinction from the rest; so that every body politic hath some

religion, but the *Church* that religion, which is only true. Truth of religion is that proper difference whereby a *Church* is distinguished from other politic societies of men. (VIII.1.2; *FLE* 3:318.15–21)

He concludes, therefore, attacking what he perceives as the disastrous implications of the presbyterian separation of church and commonwealth, "A gross error it is to think that regal power ought to serve for the good of the body and not of the soul, for men's temporal peace and not their eternal safety; as if God had ordained Kings for no other end and purpose but only to fat up men like hogs and to see that they have their mash." To be sure, it does not belong to kings "to lead men unto salvation" either inwardly by "secret, invisible, and ghostly regiment" (as Christ only can do), or by "the external administration of things belonging to priestly order," the word and sacraments; but there is "no cause in the world to think them uncapable of supreme authority in the outward government which disposeth the affairs of religion so far forth as the same are disposable by human authority" (VIII.3.5; *FLE* 3:352.20–31).

This passage highlights at the same time Hooker's haste to qualify what he envisions by the magisterial care for religion. After all, if the prince is responsible for the good of his subjects, and their highest good is to be found in union with God, then does this not make the prince the *pontifex maximus*, both priest and king, arbiter of his subjects' eternal destiny as much as their temporal? Certainly, in some of the ambitiously caesaropapist declarations of the Henrician era, these implications would not have been far from the surface. Hooker protects himself against these excesses by two sets of distinctions. The first, of which we have already seen a good deal, is his two-kingdoms doctrine, which we see here in his qualification that "secret, invisible and ghostly regiment" belongs to Christ alone, as he works the salvation of believers by his Spirit invisibly in human hearts. External means he might use to ready the soil and water the sapling, but only he could plant the seed of spiritual life. No human servant can usurp his kingship here; they can only point to it: "The Headship which we give unto Kings is altogether visibly exercised and ordereth only the external frame of the Church's affairs here amongst us, so that it plainly differeth from Christ's even in very nature and kind" (VIII.4.5; *FLE* 3:362.26–363.2).

The second distinction further subdivides the realm of the "external frame of the Church's affairs." Although all the external affairs of the church are subject to positive law, we know from our discussion in Chapter Four above that not all scriptural positive laws are mutable, and among them are those that sever the powers of *order* and *jurisdiction* (preaching, administering the sacraments, ordination, etc.), which only clergy may properly bear, from that of *dominion*, which the supreme magistrate must bear as the repository of sovereignty and the deputy of Christ in the civil kingdom.[67] While insisting that church and commonwealth are one society, he is careful to preserve a diversity of roles and duties within this society. But precisely because of the personal unity of this society, he resists the implication that "they that are of the one can neither appoint, nor execute in part the duties which belong unto them which are of the other" (VIII.1.2; *FLE* 3:318.8–10). On the contrary, throughout his argument for the royal supremacy, he maintains that the monarch, by virtue of his office as supreme judge of all causes within his realm, ought in England to have final (though not sole) authority for correcting faults within the church, and directing her various offices toward the good of the whole.[68]

By virtue of these distinctions, Hooker tries to resolve the ambiguity inherent in the Puritans' constant insistence that the affairs of the visible church are "spiritual" and hence belong to Christ's "spiritual kingdom"; he is willing to accede to this language, so long as it be qualified rightly, distinguishing, as above in his discussion of laws, between the object and the mode of government:

> To make things therefore so plain that henceforth a Child's capacity may serve rightly to conceive our meaning, we make the *Spiritual* regiment of *Christ* to be generally that whereby his *Church* is ruled and governed in things spiritual. Of this general we make two distinct kinds, the one invisibly exercised by *Christ* himself in his own person, the other outwardly administered by them whom *Christ* doth allow to be the *Rulers* and guiders of his *Church*. (VIII.4.9; *FLE* 3:377.3–10)

This outward administration of the "spiritual regiment" is "external and visible . . . exercised by men" (VIII.4.9; *FLE* 3:378.10), and therefore subject to, though distinct from, the human dominion of the magistrate in the civil regiment, which encompasses the entire commonwealth in both its spiritual and temporal concerns.[69]

---

67. VIII.3.3 (*FLE* 3:346). He defines the power of dominion in VIII.2.1: "[T]hey have authority to command even in matters of Christian Religion, and that there is no higher, nor greater, that can in those causes overcommand them, where they are placed to reign as Kings" (*FLE* 3:332.12–15); however, as in their dominion over purely secular affairs, the extent and terms of this dominion are limited by both human and divine law.

68. VIII.3.4 (*FLE* 3:349–50).

69. Hooker elaborates these several distinctions with relation to his arguments about

VI. Scripture as a Rule for the Christian Commonwealth

As Christ's rulers and guides over his church, which is to say, in Hooker's terms, over a political society oriented toward the true religion, by what rule ought Christian princes to govern—by natural law or by Scripture? While it is common to imagine that the reformers' insistence on *sola Scriptura* precluded a serious appeal to natural law, even in political life, we have seen enough to realize that this was far from the case. VanDrunen is right at least to recognize that the two-kingdoms doctrine, for Protestant leaders such as Luther and Calvin, meant that Scripture was not primarily concerned with offering a blueprint for political life, and sources of natural reason could be safely consulted in this sphere. As we have also seen, however, the imprecision this left in judging what laws were appropriate, particularly on the vexed question of church-state relations, drove many Protestants to "precisianism," in which Scripture was taken to provide very clear criteria of what government should do or of what it should not do. The result was a classic example of the "clash of loyalties," in which believers found their duty to God at odds with their duty to the prince.

Hooker's harmonization of these loyalties therefore involves, as we have seen, a harmonization of natural and divine law, an insistence that Christian princes must govern by both, mediated, of course, through human law. We will recall above Hooker's programmatic summary of the relation between the "law of reason" and "divine law":

the headship of Christ. In the spiritual regiment properly so-called, Christ alone is head, "neither can any other Creature in that sense and meaning be termed *Head* besides him, because it importeth the conduct and governor of our Souls, by the hand of that blessed *Spirit*, wherewith we are sealed and marked, as being peculiarly His." However, "As for the power of administering those things in the *Church* of *Christ* which power we call the power of order, it is indeed both spiritual and *His*; *Spiritual*, because such duties properly concern the *Spirit*, *His* because by Him it was instituted, howbeit neither *Spiritual* as that which is inwardly and invisibly exercised nor *His*, as that which *He* himself in person doth exercise. Again that power of dominion which is indeed the pointe of this *Controversy* and doth also belong to the second kind of *Spiritual regiment*, namely unto that regiment which is external and visible, this likewise being *Spiritual* in regard of the matter about which it dealeth . . . must notwithstanding be distinguished also from that power whereby he himself in person administereth the former kind of his own spiritual regiment because he himself in person doth not administer this. We do not therefore vainly imagine but truly and rightly discern a power external and visible in the *Church* exercised by men and severed in nature from that *spiritual* power of Christ's own regiment, which power is termed *spiritual* because it worketh secretly inwardly and invisibly; *His*, because none doth or can it personally exercise, either besides or together with him" (VIII.4.10; *FLE* 3:377.13–16, 377.22–378.14).

> The law of reason doth somewhat direct men how to honour God as their Creator, but how to glorify God in such sort as is required, to the end he may be an everlasting Saviour, this we are taught by divine law, which law both ascertaineth the truth and supplieth unto us the want of that other law. So that in moral actions, divine law helpeth exceedingly the law of reason to guide man's life, but in supernatural it alone guideth. (I.16.5; *FLE* 1:139.3–10)

It is the realm of "moral actions" that politics is to govern, and for this realm, we have been given the gift of the law of reason, and the capacity to apply it in the form of human laws (both mixedly and merely human) to the needs of particular societies. But as the law of reason admonishes the prince of the paramount importance of religion to an ordered and moral society, and of not merely religion, but the true religion, then revelation about this religion cannot but be essential for good government. Scripture, as we have seen, not only teaches us new duties, but clarifies, illuminates, and applies those duties that we already had by the law of reason. For this reason, in establishing the best human laws to govern a Christian society, "partly scripture and partly reason must teach us to discern" (III.9.1; *FLE* 1:236.8). Indeed, so thoroughly do these two complement one another in this task that Hooker will all but equate the two:

> [A]s a man liveth joined with others in common society, and belongeth unto the outward politic body of the *Church* albeit the said law of nature and scripture have in this respect also made manifest the things that are of the greatest necessity; nevertheless by reason of new occasions still arising which the *Church* having care of souls must take order for as need requireth, hereby it cometh to pass, that there is and ever will be great use even of human laws and ordinances deducted by way of discourse as conclusions from the former divine and natural, serving for principles thereunto. (VIII.6.4; *FLE* 3:389.12–21)

Although when it comes to laws of civil polity, Hooker has given us little guidance as to how this deduction might proceed (this not being the immediate point at debate with the Puritans), he gives us a very thorough treatment of the relation of "conclusions" and "principles" in the establishment of laws of ecclesiastical polity in III.9–11. Scripture, he says, gives us three kinds of direction: examples, laws natural (which is to say, restatements of principles contained in the law of reason), and laws positive. Examples, he says, "can but direct as precedents only"; natural laws such that "in all things we must forever do according unto them"; and positive laws, "that against them in no case we may do anything, as long as the will of God is that they should remain in force." For each of these, reason is still needed:

> Howbeit when scripture doth yield us precedents, how far forth they are to be followed; when it giveth natural laws, what particular order is thereunto most agreeable; when positive, which way to make laws unrepugnant unto them; yea though all these should want, yet what kind of ordinances would be most for that good of the Church which is aimed at, all this must be by reason found out. (III.9.1; *FLE* 1:236.12–21)

Clearly enough, these three forms of direction apply not only to ecclesiastical polity, but to civil polity as well—in Scripture, we find many examples of political rule and temporal laws, we find also the restatement of natural laws such as those found in the second table of the Decalogue, and we find a great many positive laws, at least in the Old Testament.

These positive laws, often designated as the "judicial laws" (as contrasted with the "moral" and "ceremonial" laws of the Old Testament) can be discerned by the fact that they are laws in which the *end* (public order, justice, peace, etc.) is permanent—at any rate, permanent until the eschaton—but in which the *matter* (the circumstances upon which the laws are brought to bear) is changeable.[70] Hooker is not unaware that some of his Puritan adversaries are of the view that even Old Testament judicial laws remain binding; this rests, he says, on two misunderstandings: that the divine authority of the lawmaker renders a law unchangeable, and that any law with a permanent end must be unchangeable, as if that "which he by law did establish as being fittest unto that end, for us to alter any thing is to lift up ourselves against God and as it were to countermand him" (III.10.3; *FLE* 1:242.6–9).

To this Hooker replies, as we have seen above in Chapter Four,

> [T]hey mark not that laws are instruments to rule by, and that instruments are not only to be framed according unto the general end for which they are provided, but even according unto that very particular, which riseth

---

70. Hooker's discussion of these laws is closely paralleled by the much more extensive treatment of Franciscus Junius in *The Mosaic Polity*, trans. Tom M. Rester, ed. Andrew M. McGinnis, Sources in Early Modern Economics, Ethics, and Law (1613; repr., Grand Rapids: Christian Library's Press, 2015); see especially pp. 60–70.

out of the matter whereon they have to work. The end wherefore laws were made may be permanent, and those laws nevertheless require some alteration, if there be any unfitness in the means which they prescribe as tending unto that end and purpose. (III.10.3; *FLE* 1:242.9–16)

In other words, the ever-changing character of human social and political life ensures that the presence of positive laws in Scripture will never obviate the need for careful rational reflection (making use of the law of reason) on which laws are most appropriate for a particular society. But this in no way renders Scripture irrelevant to the task. We must still diligently seek to understand the general end provided for in biblical laws, and ensure that that same end is met in our own legislation (a process of exegesis and application that Hooker will repeatedly undertake in Books V–VIII of the *Lawes*, explaining how various Old Testament laws are and are not relevant to the task of framing a godly order for the Church of England). Moreover, we must learn from scriptural examples as well as positive laws. Finally, we must submit absolutely to scriptural natural laws, so that "in all things we must forever do according unto them," and, where necessary, enact laws that specify them and bind us to follow them in particular contexts.

VII. Conclusion

We have seen in this chapter how Hooker's nuanced understanding of nature and grace as always distinct yet harmonious underlies his entire political theology. Nature has its own proper end and mode of operation, and yet is perfected by union with a supernatural end, in which it participates, according to a finite mode, in operations beyond its capability. For Hooker, this paradigm finds its fullest expression in the person and work of Christ, in whom the Word has taken up human nature and made it an "associate of Deity" without abolishing its humanity. By this union, Jesus Christ is made, even as man, a sharer in God's reign over nations, and both churches and nations must acknowledge this kingship. In doing so, however, we have seen that they merely "perfect" that to which they are already drawn by nature—namely, a commonwealth ordered around public religion. In specifying the graced form of this natural duty, the laws and narratives of Scripture are an essential resource for lawmakers, and yet one that must be adapted to the times, places, and circumstances of particular commonwealths, "framed unto that very particular whereon they have to work."

All of this requires a far more subtle and supple sense both of how law operates, and how Scripture norms our crafting and discernment of laws, than Cartwright's precisianist dictum that "it is the virtue of a good law to leave as little as may be in the discretion of the judge." For Hooker, on the contrary, a good judge is indispensable, as is a wide scope for the exercise of prudence. Such is the rich variety and ceaseless change in the realm of mortal affairs, especially when political societies are involved, that no lawbook, be it ever so elaborate and detailed, can provide sufficient instruction. Consciences are not to be satisfied by false claims to provide certainty beyond what the nature of the matter in question can yield, but by inclining themselves "which way greatest probability leadeth," which will often mean resort to arguments from reason and consensus. Hooker's rehabilitation of reason does not then represent, as some interpreters would have it, an enthronement of reason as the source of a certainty and exhaustive knowledge that Scripture is incapable of providing. Instead, it represents his conviction that all knowledge of ethical and political duties is provisional and more inferential than deductive, limited by the mutability of human affairs. Rather than seeking in vain to resolve all uncertainties in advance, then, we must learn the art of living with uncertainty, the art of living in a culture of persuasion,[71] by the virtue of prudence.

Hooker's commitment to such a culture of persuasion makes him a likelier candidate for a precursor of modern liberalism than we might think, given his simultaneous commitment to a culture that confesses Christ's kingship. In the conclusion that follows, I will draw together the complex threads of argument that we have surveyed to suggest why Hooker's synthesis of law and liberty, theology and politics, can still challenge us today.

---

71. The term "culture of persuasion" comes from Andrew Pettegree's *Reformation and the Culture of Persuasion* (Cambridge: Cambridge University Press, 2005), though my use of it is informed primarily by Torrance Kirby's work (see for instance *Paul's Cross and the Culture of Persuasion in England, 1520–1640*, ed. W. J. Torrance Kirby and P. G. Stanwood [Leiden: Brill, 2014]).

CHAPTER SEVEN

"The Truth Will Set You Free"

The Peril and Promise of Christian Liberty

> We must receive ourselves from outside ourselves, addressed by a
> summons which evokes that correspondence of existence to being.
> "Where the Spirit of the Lord is, there is liberty" (2 Cor. 3:17).
>
> Oliver O'Donovan, *Desire of the Nations*[1]

I. A Reprise of the Argument

This book began with an apparently straightforward question: How might we
go about "transferring" the spiritual liberty promised to the justified believer
from the inward forum of conscience to the outward forum of civil society;
by what means was this liberty before God to be rendered into a liberty
before human authority? After all, such a transfer seemed quite evidently to
have happened, as a matter of historical record. Protestantism proclaimed
the freedom of the conscience from papal authority, and to be consistent,
they had to proclaim the freedom of the conscience also from all earthly
authorities, and with it, in due course, the freedom of the conscientious
believer to serve his or her God as he or she felt called to do. By this means,
Protestantism served as a midwife of the separation of church and state, the
distinction of the "just bounds" of their authority that was to resolve the
conflict of loyalties to God and to man. This narrative, however, founders
on the rocks of Calvin's strict warning about these two liberties that "when
the one is considered, we should call off our minds, and not allow them to

---

1. Oliver O'Donovan, *Desire of the Nations: Rediscovering the Roots of Political Theology*
(Cambridge: Cambridge University Press, 1996), 252.

think of the other,"[2] and the fact that, to most if not all Protestant reformers, the link between Christian liberty and civil liberty was not remotely obvious. As we have seen, most defended a *denial* of civil liberty in religious matters precisely on the basis of the doctrine of Christian liberty.

This could be done, as we saw, one of two ways. The freedom of a Christian could be understood as a radically inward and spiritual freedom, such that it was not compromised by substantial regulations of outward conduct by public authorities (whether in church or state) intent on maintaining institutional freedom and order. Alternately, the Christian's freedom could be emphasized as a freedom *to obey God*, a freedom that demanded externalization and public recognition. Such public recognition was not merely the granting of a right for the faithful to worship as they pleased, but a demand that such true worship be established and defended; if obedience to God was really at stake, kings too must yield their scepters to his law. The former was the policy of adiaphorists or conformists, confident that most of the external practice of Protestant religion was left to human discretion, and uniformity being better than disorder, that meant magistratical discretion. The latter was the policy of precisianists, confident that since most of the external practice of religion was prescribed by God, rulers must prescribe it also, even if that meant yielding much of their authority to the ministers. It has often been supposed that the former policy was repressive and medieval, the latter liberating and proto-modern. And indeed, we suggested in Chapter One that it was perhaps proto-modern in the sense of paving the way for liberty of the activist conscience, determined to reshape society in obedience to a higher law, but not especially conducive to the kind of liberal pluralism that many have wanted to credit to Calvinism, Puritanism, and their heirs. At the same time, by locating the institutional church as the site of the transformed society, such a program could tend to secularize the now-ancillary civil government as an accidental by-product of its sacred ambitions. The division of labor, however, would necessarily remain an unstable one.

But that wasn't all. In Chapters Two and Three, we also saw that not only did both of these approaches to "freedom of conscience" fail to provide much of a route to the modern notion of religious freedom, but they also seemed unable to do justice even to Luther's original clarion call for Christian liberty. Fundamentally inward though his idea of liberty was, it also demanded outward expression as the justified conscience poured out its gratitude in a free display of love for the neighbor. Many adiaphorists, to be sure, argued

2. Calvin, *Institutes*, 1:847 [III.19.15].

that civil peace and uniformity *was* a way of showing love to the neighbor, so that magistratical regulations were no more an imposition on Christian liberty in religious ceremonies as in purely civil matters. Given the high stakes, however—the risk that tender consciences would be led to perdition by apparently superstitious ceremonies—this line seemed weak, and freedom for the neighbor seemed to demand freedom to resist the law. In the face of such threats to conscience, it was no wonder that the second option, which looked to God's law rather than man's to determine the appropriate exercise of our freedom, rapidly gained ground in Elizabethan England. But of course, if God had commanded so many matters of polity and liturgy, it would be rash indeed to disobey him; to do so would be to invite both personal and national judgment. If the stakes had seemed high before, they were even higher now, and ordinary Christians and monarchs alike must submit their judgments and conduct to the exegesis of the precisianist presbyters. Such a policy was even less conducive to generating freedom for edification in the face of persistent disagreements about what edification required; worse, with so much focus on "exact precise severity," it threatened to reintroduce fear into the heart of the believer's relationship with God, from whence Luther had sought to exorcise it by his initial reforming protest.

Our survey of Richard Hooker sought to shed fresh light on his theology as an attempt to unravel these knots of conscience, rejecting the precisianist position as a threat to both the freedom of a Christian man and the freedom of a Christian commonwealth, but trying at the same time to improve upon the flimsy and authoritarian adiaphorist position. Assailing the precisianist position as one that "shaketh universally the fabric of government" and at the same time posed a "torment to weak consciences," he still recognized that they could only be brought to submit to England's ecclesiastical legislation if they could be shown a way to harmonize their loyalties, that is, shown a convincing theological case for dropping their scruples. Hence Hooker's careful investigation of the nature and function of Scripture, and the nature of the visible church, which we surveyed in Chapter Four. Moreover, such a harmonization of loyalties would remain merely abstract and theoretical unless it could be shown that the laws in question really did serve as means to edify the Christian people, that obeying them was a way of loving the neighbor rather than causing her to stumble. Of course, he also had to show that one did not have to rely on Scripture alone in making such judgments; reason was a legitimate and valuable tool for discerning what was and what was not wise and edifying in both civil matters and religious ceremonies. Finally, given that all such arguments would remain contentious and merely probabilistic, he had to make a convincing case for the lawfulness of an individual Christian suspending his judgment and swallowing his scruples to defer to the public determinations of law. The need to make this case led him to some penetrating statements on the relationship of freedom of conscience and submission to law. All of these arguments we surveyed in Chapter Five.

This still left one important question unresolved: the identity of the Christian commonwealth that was thus to be freed for corporate action. Hooker was determined to steer a course between the two unstable poles that he discerned in the precisianist platform. The freedom of a Christian commonwealth required genuine freedom of action to pursue new means to flourishing in ever-changing circumstances, so he could not accept any theonomic imposition of biblical law upon English society. At the same time, the freedom of a *Christian* commonwealth required that it be free to render corporate obedience to the King of all nations, Christ, so he could not accept Cartwright's Nestorian bifurcation of social life into the sphere of the Creator (the state) and the sphere of the Redeemer (the church). Intriguing as this final argument was, it might well have seemed to confirm the suspicion of most moderns that the conformist position was repressive and medieval, light-years away from the achievements of liberal pluralism. Hooker may, perhaps, have achieved a remarkable harmonization of freedom of conscience and freedom of commonwealth, but only so long as both terms in the equation were unambiguously Christian. Any extension to a broader liberty of conscience in a religiously plural age appears far out of reach, and thus Hooker's political-theological achievement remains, like the Great Pyramid, an impressive historical artifact, but one that has long outlived its usefulness.

We would thus appear to be left with a firm negative to our original question: there is no way to transfer the spiritual liberty of the justified believer that Luther and Calvin proclaimed to the realm of the civil liberties we have all come to hold dear, and which we consider the bedrock of any free society. If we want to do homage to the architects of liberalism, we should stick with Locke, Mill, and other such thinkers who have impeccable credentials as political theorists, not theologians.

In this short concluding chapter, I am not about to try to reverse course and seek to lay out a full case for the opposite conclusion, paving the way from Luther to Rawls brick by brick. However, I will suggest that the doctrine of Christian liberty we find outlined in Luther's proclamation of the freedom of a Christian man, and expanded in Hooker's defense of the freedom of a Christian commonwealth, offers both a cogent and compelling theory of individual liberty, and a promising foundation for political liberty.

Before we can fully appreciate the value of this theory, however, it may be helpful to take stock again of the profound tension between modern liberal conceptions of liberty and those implicit in the claims of Christian theology.

II. Two Concepts of Liberty

Berlin's Critique of "Positive Freedom"

Perhaps one of the most influential formulations of the idea of liberty among contemporary political theorists remains that of Isaiah Berlin, who with his 1958 lecture, "Two Concepts of Liberty," sought to distinguish the Western "liberal" conception of liberty from rival accounts that tended, he thought, toward totalitarianism. The first he called the "idea of negative liberty," the latter "positive liberty." The first designates "the area within which the subject . . . is or should be left to do or be what he is able to do or be, without interference by other persons." The second, on the other hand, concerns "the source of control or interference that can determine someone to do, or be, this rather than that."[3] The first, in short, concerns primarily the *world*, the objective field of action opened before us; the second concerns the *agent*, the subjective source of action. For the former, why I act is irrelevant; it is entirely up to me whether I act for good reasons, bad reasons, or no reasons, so long as my range of possible actions not be foreclosed by outside agents. For the latter, however, such internal conditions of action are all-important. Berlin explains, "I wish my life and decisions to depend on myself, not on external forces of whatever kind. I wish to be the instrument of my own, not of other men's, acts of will. I wish to be a subject, not an object; to be moved by reasons, by conscious purposes, which are my own, not by causes which affect me, as it were, from outside."[4] To act thoughtlessly or in response to enslaving passions is clearly not, on such an account, to be properly free. From this latter standpoint, the contraction of the external field of action need deal no fatal blows to my freedom; I can be free within my own soul so long as I am guided by reason and truth.

Berlin is certainly willing to acknowledge the many tensions that afflict the negative conception of liberty; he is no naïve libertarian idealist. Clearly an indefinite extension of my field of action cannot coexist with the indefinite

---

3. Isaiah Berlin, "Two Concepts of Liberty," in *Liberty: Incorporating Four Essays on Liberty*, ed. Henry Hardy (Oxford: Oxford University Press, 2002), 169.

4. Berlin, "Two Concepts," 178.

extension of every other individual's field of action. Accordingly, "the freedom of some must at times be curtailed to secure the freedom of others,"[5] and the task of liberal governments, committed to safeguarding this conception of freedom, must be one of constantly refereeing and renegotiating between competing wishes and claims, trying to draw the boundaries of action in such a way as to preserve the greatest freedom for the greatest number. However, despite these acknowledgments, Berlin was clearly far more worried by the dangers he saw hiding in the positive conception of liberty. By saying that true liberty consisted in self-mastery, and this meant the rule of the reason (the "true self") over the passions, the adherents of positive liberty, he argued, could readily justify the subjection of irrational individuals to those true free men who lived according to reason. And since they could at the same time say that true liberty (life according to reason) was in no way affected by the constriction of external freedom of action, the most crushing repression could somehow be justified as an expression of freedom. Berlin's portrait of totalitarianism masked as freedom seems at times tendentious and overly alarmist, but one must remember that he wrote in the shadow of the Soviet menace and the recent rise and fall of the Third Reich. Such movements, he argued, were natural outgrowths of a doctrinaire commitment to the idea of positive liberty.

However oversimplistic his framework, Berlin's analysis retains great influence in Western liberal societies, or at least, the worries and impulses that drove him still drive most of us today. Chastened by experiments in totalitarianism, Western liberal societies have preferred to embrace the messiness and anti-perfectionism of "negative liberty" over the idealism of positive liberty. Seeking to justify this stance, which Berlin himself was honest enough to grant was something of a historical novelty only a couple of centuries old, moderns have liked to tell themselves stories about the genesis of modern freedoms in Reformation ideas of "freedom of conscience" (among other narratives). This, of course, is what we called the "quietist" idea of freedom of conscience, the one that just wants to be left alone with space to worship whomever or whatever it wants, corresponding roughly to Berlin's "negative" liberty much as the "activist" idea of freedom of conscience chronicled by Walzer and Voegelin roughly equates to Berlin's "positive liberty." Inasmuch as this book has offered a critique of the precisianist form of positive liberty (eloquently summarized by Thomas Cartwright: "[T]he greatest liberty and freedom of Christians is to serve the Lord according to his revealed will, and in all things to hang upon his

5. Berlin, "Two Concepts," 173.

mouth"[6]) as prone toward individual and political repression, it might seem to agree in part with Berlin's assessment. And yet any attentive reader will surely have noticed that when it came to rival views on adiaphora, conformists like Hooker also seem to fit squarely within Berlin's description of positive liberty, arguing that the restriction of outward freedom of action by the public authorities could coexist with the Christian's true inward freedom of conscience. Perhaps many of their opponents failed to sustain a real commitment to external liberty either, hemming it in with divine law and church discipline, but some at least claimed to appeal to a conception not unlike Berlin's negative liberty, demanding that all things left free by Scripture be left free by authorities. Does Hooker's theory of liberty, with its sharp disjunctions of inward and outward, its disconcerting insistence that the individual's obedience to law is simply obedience to himself,[7] and its overtones of theocracy, not make common cause with totalitarianism after all, as its Puritan opponents claimed down through the centuries?

The question must be faced squarely. And yet, if Hooker's view is suspect from a modern liberal standpoint, it must be admitted with equal frankness that so is that of Christianity down through the ages. Consider again the statement of Cartwright just quoted; stripped from its somewhat legalistic Cartwrightean context, what good Christian thinker could really disagree? Surely the greatest liberty of a Christian *is* "to serve the Lord according to his revealed will"? One needs no historical survey to make the point. Many contemporary Christian theologians have singled out the modern ideal of negative liberty for fierce criticism, and posited a Christian conception of freedom that is much more like Berlin's "positive liberty."

Theological Critiques of "Negative Freedom"

In his *Atheist Delusions*, David Bentley Hart goes so far as to argue that the great apostasy of modernity lies in its concept of freedom, its abandonment of the Christian (which was also, he notes, the classical) understanding that freedom was about being true to one's nature and proper end, not simply about the removal of every external impediment to one's actions. Modernity, indeed, says Hart, has gone to the extreme of regarding every consideration,

---

6. *SR* 442.30–32.

7. To be sure, Hooker does not primarily argue, as those Berlin most critiques, by appealing to a "true self" argument, but to a theory of representation.

every objective value outside of the abstract individual will as an "external impediment," and hence is committed to a kind of nihilism:

> Modernity's highest ideal—its special understanding of personal autonomy—requires us to place our trust in an original absence underlying all of reality, a fertile void in which all things are possible, from which arises no impediment to our wills, and before which we may consequently choose to make of ourselves what we choose. We trust, that is to say, that there is no substantial criterion by which to judge our choices that stands higher than the unquestioned good of free choice itself, and that therefore all judgment, divine no less than human, is in some sense an infringement upon our freedom.[8]

In the classical understanding, says Hart,

> true freedom was understood as something inseparable from one's nature: to be truly free, that is to say, was to be at liberty to realize one's proper "essence" and so flourish as the kind of being one was . . . true human freedom is emancipation from whatever constrains us from living the life of rational virtue, or from experiencing the full fruition of our nature; and among the things that constrain us are our own untutored passions, our willful surrender to momentary impulses, our own foolish or wicked *choices*.[9]

As is his wont, Hart tends to almost wholly elide the Christian with the classical understanding here, passing from Plato's description of the Form of the Good as the sun that transfixes our gaze so that we are less and less able to look on lesser realities, to Augustine's notion of our highest freedom as being *non posse peccare*—"unable to sin." This, he says, is "a condition that reflects the infinite goodness of God, who, because nothing can hinder him in the perfect realization of his own nature, is 'incapable' of evil and so is infinitely free."[10]

We have drawn a similar parallel already in this study between Hooker's understanding of divine freedom self-bound in the eternal law as a paradigm and the law-bound freedom of human societies. On the other hand, few things

---

8. David Bentley Hart, *Atheist Delusions: The Christian Revolution and Its Fashionable Enemies* (New Haven: Yale University Press, 2009), 21.

9. Hart, *Atheist Delusions*, 24.

10. Hart, *Atheist Delusions*, 25.

occupy Hooker's attention so much as the profound indeterminacy of human law, a function of the fact that we and our societies, unlike God, constantly change. While Hooker would thus agree with Hart that too much purely external freedom undermines true freedom, by making it easy for us to lose sight of our proper end, he does not seem inclined to such a wholesale embrace of Berlin's pole of "positive freedom."

Richard Bauckham mounts a similar, but more nuanced, line of argument in his *God and the Crisis of Freedom*, contrasting what he calls the "modern libertarian idea of freedom" with the Christian idea. Today, he says, "freedom is felt to be opposed to all limits. Freedom means the ability to determine oneself however one wishes by making any choices without restriction." This, he argues, is essentially idolatrous, offering a "myth of humanity's godlike freedom."[11] His critique is not just theological, though, but also political. Perhaps Berlin, writing in 1958, could dismiss as manageable the conflicts sure to arise within an essentially individualistic and agonistic conception of freedom, but several decades down the line, their destructive effects on society are becoming ever clearer. Bauckham argues that, although seemingly well suited for a pluralistic society, the libertarian idea of freedom, "by renouncing all public values except individual freedom of choice, aggravates the difficulties of a pluralistic society. It contributes to the decay of public values and discourages the emergence of public values."[12] Worse, by portraying all outward limits on my freedom of action as shackles, it has encouraged the atrophying not merely of political authority, but of the wide range of social bonds that make human life worth living (Bauckham mentions burgeoning divorce rates as one consequence).[13]

Since late industrial capitalism has succeeded, it would seem, at producing a limitless supply of consumer goods, our hunger for directionless freedom has expressed itself above all in consumption run amok, with ultimately disastrous consequences for a world that is, despite all appearances, stubbornly finite:

> The consumer is persuaded to see himself or herself as an autonomous individual mastering the world by money, transcending limits by achieving an ever higher standard of living and enjoying endless novelty. But this

11. Richard Bauckham, *God and the Crisis of Freedom: Biblical and Contemporary Perspectives* (Louisville: Westminster John Knox, 2002), 33.

12. Bauckham, *God and the Crisis of Freedom*, 29.

13. Bauckham, *God and the Crisis of Freedom*, 34.

freedom, such as it is, is bought at a very high price. . . . [I]t is my freedom at the expense of nature and future generations. . . . We cannot reject limits without destroying the creation on which we depend.[14]

In response to this destructive embrace of negative freedom, Bauckham sketches a rich and attractive vision of a Christian account of freedom. Although several points from his exposition invite comparison with the themes explored in this book, we will pause to highlight just one of particular significance. In contrast to Hart, Bauckham argues for the necessity of limits, not as an expression of our imitation of God's own perfection, but more plausibly, on account of our finitude: "[H]uman freedom is not the absolute self-determination of God but the freedom of finite creatures, given us to be exercised within limits."[15] As the specification of our distinctive identity as human creatures, our natural limits ought to be accepted as a *gift* that enables us to be ourselves, rather than a chain that prevents us from self-realization. Developing a theme that will be familiar to us from the political theology of both Luther and the Henrician reformers, Bauckham argues that it is by charity that we can express our freedom—a freedom for others—in the midst of accepting limits: "What we need to grasp is that limits need not be opposed to freedom. They need not restrict freedom but can enable true freedom."[16]

Bauckham first applies this insight within matters of economy and ecology, but he develops it further within a theological context. Clearly our relationship to God as well is defined by limits, the limits of the moral law and numerous biblical commands with which God regulates our freedom. Like Cartwright, though, Bauckham insists that this kind of limit is the highest form of our freedom, at least, if rightly understood and accepted. "When I love God and freely make God's will my own, I am not forfeiting my freedom but fulfilling it. God's will is not the will of another in any ordinary sense. It is the moral truth of all reality. To conform ourselves freely to that truth is also to conform to the inner law of our own created being."[17]

In *Resurrection and Moral Order*, Oliver O'Donovan develops an account of freedom along similar lines to Bauckham, though with greater methodological rigor and precision. From O'Donovan's standpoint, something like

14. Bauckham, *God and the Crisis of Freedom*, 36.
15. Bauckham, *God and the Crisis of Freedom*, 38–39.
16. Bauckham, *God and the Crisis of Freedom*, 45.
17. Bauckham, *God and the Crisis of Freedom*, 46.

Berlin's concept of negative freedom is not simply potentially hazardous for society, and thus the worse of two coherent alternative conceptions. Rather, only one conception is fully coherent, the one that is much closer to Berlin's "positive freedom":

> In saying that someone is free, we are saying something about the person himself and not about his circumstances. Freedom is "potency" rather than "possibility." External constraints may vastly limit our possibilities without touching our "freedom" in this sense. Nothing could be more misleading than the popular philosophy that freedom is constituted by the absence of limits.[18]

O'Donovan's observation here is essentially a sharpening of Bauckham's point about finitude. If we literally had *no limits*, then all possibilities of action would be equally compelling, which is to say they would all be equally uncompelling. There would be no reason to ever choose one course of action over another, and thus we would either fall victim to total paralysis of will, or else be capable of nothing but random lurches in one direction or another, which, being unsusceptible of any rational account, would not rise to the level of human action at all. Therefore, it is precisely the presence of limits that makes possible reasons for action, and therefore makes possible meaningful human choice. This does not necessarily mean that we should conclude "the more limits, the more freedom," but it certainly means that we would be foolish to conclude the opposite.

> There is, to be sure, a truth which it intends to recognize, which is that the "potency" of freedom requires "possibility" as its object. For freedom is exercised in the cancellation of all possibilities in a given situation by the decision to actualize one of them; if there were no possibilities, there could be no room for freedom. Nevertheless, there do not have to be many. . . . Where the popular philosophy becomes so misleading is in its suggestion that we can maximize freedom by multiplying the number of possibilities open to us. For if possibilities are to be meaningful for free choice, they must be well-defined by structures of limit. The indefinite multiplication of options can only have the effect of taking the determination of the future out of the competence of choice, and so out of the

---

18. Oliver O'Donovan, *Resurrection and Moral Order: An Outline for Evangelical Ethics* (Grand Rapids: Eerdmans, 1986), 107.

category of meaningful possibility for freedom. . . . Decision depends upon existing limits and imposes new ones.[19]

It is for this reason that O'Donovan will speak of authority as "the objective correlate of freedom," a theme he returns to again and again throughout his work. Authority "is what we encounter in the world which makes it meaningful for us to act."[20] Since we are by nature social creatures, the freedom that authority enables is above all a freedom to act in ordered relation to others, "the realization of individual powers within social forms."[21] Accordingly, as Hooker realized much more fully than Luther had, the freedom of society and of the individual go hand-in-hand. The crisis of Luther's Reformation was that it had upended the social forms that had constituted the framework for the exercise of freedom, however oppressive they were, in Western Europe. The result was the danger both of individual and social unfreedom:

But we can be deprived of the structures of communication within which we have learned to act, and so we can find ourselves hurled into a vacuum in which we do not know how to realize ourselves effectively. . . . But what we can say of the individual in these circumstances, we can say equally of the society. It is not free unless it can sustain the forms that make for its members' freedom.[22]

19. O'Donovan, *Resurrection and Moral Order*, 107–8.
20. O'Donovan, *Resurrection and Moral Order*, 122.
21. Oliver O'Donovan, *The Ways of Judgment* (Grand Rapids: Eerdmans, 2005), 68.
22. O'Donovan, *Ways of Judgment*, 67. In his recent *Up with Authority: Why We Need Authority to Flourish as Human Beings* (Edinburgh: T&T Clark, 2010), Victor Austin expands upon O'Donovan's insights with the aid of philosopher Yves Simon to argue that this is the very reason why political authority is good and necessary even without the Fall. The growth of positive freedom, the virtue and power of the members of society to achieve their ends, results in an increase of the range of possibilities for action opened up to each member. Without authority to specify a common course of action in the midst of myriad possibilities, the potencies of each member of the society will fall short of full realization. This is why authority is necessary to a society. For if growth in virtue and excellence, in potency and knowledge, does not result in a limiting of our choices but instead effectively multiplies them, then reason and good will alone will be inadequate to make necessary determinations among the multiple possibilities for human flourishing. Those determinations, therefore, will have to be made by authority. This is authority's essential function. According to Simon, if it is to flourish a society needs to have steady action in pursuit of the common good. But if there are a "plurality of genuine means" that may be used for that common good, then unanimity based upon reason and good will cannot be "a *sufficient* method of steadily procuring unity of action." Hence there must be authority, "'*[t]he power in charge of unifying common action through rules binding for*

The narrative that we traced in Chapters Two and Three displayed sixteenth-century England's profound struggles to restore "the structures of communication" that would make social action meaningful once again in the wake of the great dismantling that had occurred between 1533 and 1558. For Puritans, the best way to restore such structures was clearly to turn to the same book that had inspired the dismantling of the old ones: Holy Scripture. Within its dense web of laws, men such as Cartwright argued, England could find the key to renewed flourishing of every class of society in every sphere of action. Their conformist opponents were naturally hesitant about this turn, fearing that continued reformation would lead to deformation of the English church and state. Their preference was to restore the structures of communication by relying on the other battering ram that had dissolved the old structures in the 1530s: royal power. Richard Hooker, as we have seen, did not quite embrace either pole, formulating a complex theory of authority that involved nature, Scripture, and human law working together to maximize the freedom of a Christian commonwealth, and with it, hopefully, the freedom of its members.

III. Two Concepts of Christian Liberty

We are not quite ready yet, though, to summarize the merits of Hooker's theory. First, let us return our attention to the specifically theological dimension of freedom, a subject on which O'Donovan too has a great deal to say. In one key passage, in the *Desire of the Nations*, he describes Christian freedom in terms very like Bauckham's:

> We discover we are free when we are commanded by that authority which commands us according to the law of our being, disclosing the secrets of the heart. There is no freedom except when what we are, and do, corresponds to what has been given to us to be and to do. "Given to us," because the law of our being does assert itself spontaneously merely by virtue of our existing. We must receive ourselves from outside ourselves, addressed by a summons which evokes that correspondence of existence to being. "Where the Spirit of the Lord is, there is liberty" (2 Cor. 3:17).[23]

---

all'" (26; quoting Yves Simon, *A General Theory of Authority* [1952; Notre Dame: University of Notre Dame Press, 1980], 48). Austin's account, I would argue, represents an excellent contemporary application of the insights we gleaned in Hooker's account of corporate moral agency in Chapter Five.

23. O'Donovan, *Desire of the Nations*, 252.

Once again we have the appeal to the notion of an inner "law of our being," a law from which we have been alienated by sin, and to which the divine command returns us. To obey God, then, is to obey our true selves, our selves as we were meant to be and will one day be, and thus to be freer than any earthly authority (or lack of authority) could make us. Hart, Bauckham, and O'Donovan, despite differences of exposition, seem to be at one in proclaiming that for the Christian, as for the virtuous pagan, true freedom lies in obedience, a call to obedience softened by the argument that it is really an obedience not to some alien authority, but to one's better self. The notion seems to be Berlin's "positive liberty" in a nutshell, and although Berlin worried particularly about the ways in which secular ideologies would co-opt such a notion for tyrannical ends, why should religious ideologies be any better? If Hart, Bauckham, and O'Donovan are right, couldn't a religious zealot seek to impose the "true freedom" of "hanging upon God's mouth" on an unwilling people and call it liberation? Wasn't this, in fact, what Hooker worried that Cartwright and his allies sought to do? And if so, was Hooker's conception different enough to keep us from having similar concerns about his commonwealth under Christ?

It is at this point that we must get more precise about the notion of evangelical liberty. It is not the case, as Hart imagined, that the Christian understanding of freedom can be so readily assimilated to the classical notion. The quote from O'Donovan should make the difference clear: "We must receive ourselves from outside ourselves." Whereas the pagan concept of freedom revolves around the idea of self-mastery, the Christian concept centers on self-renunciation. The ideal pagan was one who, through the practice of virtue, triumphed over his passions and lived in obedience to reason, obedience to his better self. Christianity, however, would insist that even this freedom was bondage, because it was inevitably tainted by sin. Only when we relinquished this striving for self-mastery, and instead acknowledged that we are not our own but Christ's could we be truly free. Perfect freedom then is to be a bondservant of Christ, as St. Paul will put it. This clearly takes us off in a direction radically different from Berlin's notion of "positive liberty," and, I will suggest, offers us a way beyond its nagging worries about totalitarianism.

To gain greater clarity on this point, in light of the insights we have gained throughout this study, it is worth returning to an ambiguity in the notion of adiaphora that I have highlighted a few times: between an essentially "soteriological" and an "epistemological" construal of the notion. On the former, which was closer to Luther's original formulation, the doctrine of justification by faith alone provided the main orientation; all outward things were indifferent to salvation inasmuch as, apart from true faith, they were of no benefit for the Christian. On the latter, which we saw increasingly taking hold as the Reformation progressed, the doctrine of Scripture alone provided the main orientation; anything commanded or forbidden in Scripture was binding, anything not so commanded or forbidden was indifferent. In practice, of course, neither conception could wholly do without the other, but they were rarely fully coordinated or integrated.

From these two, we may generalize two distinct understandings of Christian liberty, which we may call the *material doctrine* (based as it is on justification *sola fide*, the so-called "material principle" of the Reformation), and the *formal doctrine* (based as it is on *sola Scriptura*, the "formal principle"). Let us first analyze the latter, and some of the problems to which it arises, by using O'Donovan's terminology of *potency* and *possibility*.

The Formal Doctrine of Christian Liberty and Its Limitations

On the formal doctrine, Christian liberty came to be seen primarily as a positive freedom to obey God's will, and a negative freedom to act as we desired beyond the bounds of God's revealed will. The bounds of Scripture defined the boundary between these two types of freedom. Within the domain of what Scripture commanded, we were bound to obey; there was no freedom in the sense of *possibility*, the power to choose between a variety of options. However, there was freedom in the sense of *potency*; the Christian is enabled, by God's grace, to fulfill all these commands, and desires to do so. In successfully doing that which we desire to do, we experience delight in doing so, in doing the will of the true authority. Outside of what Scripture commands, we have freedom of possibility, to choose among whatever options we want, because these are "indifferent."

This way of conceiving things created difficulties within both domains, as well as at the boundary between them. This boundary, after all, of *what Scripture commands*, proved extraordinarily difficult to pin down. The formal doctrine has thus tended to oscillate between a kind of legalism and a kind of antinomianism. If the arms of Scripture are very long, embracing almost all of Christian life, then our only freedom is the freedom to obey, a freedom of potency, maybe, but not of possibility. If the arms of Scripture are short, leaving most of life unregulated, then our freedom is mostly only the freedom of possibility.

We witnessed this dialectic at work in the immediate aftermath of the Reformation, as the same impulse that gave rise to various forms of libertinism could also sustain the strictest legalism. The principle—divine law is our only law—was the same; the only difference lay in hermeneutics and exegesis. Nor was this a uniquely sixteenth-century problem. We have argued that David VanDrunen's account of the Reformed two-kingdoms doctrine fails as a foundation for liberal politics because it is subject to this unstable dialectic. One group of adherents, such as Thornwell and the nineteenth-century Southern "spirituality of the church" advocates, may for cultural reasons conclude that Scripture has little to say to the pressing political issues of the day, and hence leaves open a wide sphere of civic adiaphora. However, there is little in their fundamental principles to prevent another generation from demanding radical political reform in obedience to the Word of God.

Within modern evangelicalism, committed above all to affirming the authority of Scripture, a predilection for the formal doctrine of Christian liberty has manifested itself, generating interminable disputes between legalist and libertine wings of the evangelical movement. As with earlier Puritan disruptions, the tension manifests itself both in evangelical politics, characterized by a sharp rift between activists and quietists, and in matters of personal morality. For instance, when it comes to sexual morality, many evangelical Christians (particularly those who self-identify as "fundamentalist") have sought to navigate the myriad of temptations in this area by erecting detailed regulations surrounding any interaction between the sexes, and have insisted that these rules are no more than the direct application of scriptural teaching and precedents. Consider for instance the "biblical courtship" movement, which although sometimes modest enough to present general biblical principles of wisdom in seeking a marriage partner, sometimes seeks to present Mosaic judicial laws and social customs as still binding on the church today.[24] On the other hand, many other evangelicals, eager to demonstrate their relevance to contemporary culture, write marriage how-to books filled with guidance on the latest sexual fads, pointing out that nowhere are these directly condemned in Scripture, and so the only criterion for their practice is each couple's preferences.[25] Both sides, however, proclaim their commitment to the doctrines

---

24. See Joshua Harris, *Boy Meets Girl: Say Hello to Courtship* (Colorado Springs: Multnomah, 2005), for a moderate formulation, and Doug Wilson, *Her Hand in Marriage* (Moscow, ID: Canon, 1997), for a somewhat more theonomic approach, though still more moderate than some in the movement.

25. Mark and Grace Driscoll's controversial *Real Marriage: The Truth about Sex, Friendship, and Life Together* (Nashville: Thomas Nelson, 2012) provides a prominent example. The Driscolls' confusion is apparent right at the outset of chapter 10, when they turn to address sexual questions. They begin by quoting 1 Corinthians 6:12: "All things are lawful for me, but

of Christian liberty and *sola Scriptura,* authorizing constraints when they are convinced the Bible itself has done so, and happily taking a laissez-faire approach in other matters.

Aside from this intrinsic instability, there is a deeper difficulty with this formal doctrine of Christian liberty, and with Cartwright's statement that "the greatest liberty and freedom of Christians is to serve the Lord according to his revealed will, and in all things to hang upon his mouth."[26] In fact, there are three key difficulties that emerge in Cartwright's account of Christian liberty.

First of all, our free service of God ought to be the freedom of liberated sons, not of slaves; it ought to proceed from the confidence of a justified conscience. In other words, such obedience to the revealed will of God must be the response to a declaration that we *have been set free,* rather than the means by which we seek freedom. If it is the latter, then uncertainty and fear enter into the equation, and nothing is so contrary to the concept of freedom as that of fear; in fact, coercion is best defined as inducing action through the power of fear. An obedience that does not proceed from the assurance that God is well pleased, must seek to use such obedience to gain his pleasure and to avoid his wrath. While precisianists never denied justification by faith, we have noted that they certainly shifted the emphasis. The result is the distorted motivation in Cartwright's statement, that unless we "have the word of God go before us in all our actions . . . we cannot otherwise be assured that they please God."[27] We observed the sharp contrast between the logic of this statement and that of Luther: "If he finds his heart confident that it pleases God, then the work is good . . . [and] faith alone makes all other works good."[28] The proclamation of evangelical liberty began with the certainty that whoever lived by faith had assurance that God was pleased with him, whereas the precisianist appeal to Scripture arose out of a demand to attain such assurance, resolving the uncertainty of conscience through precise guidance. Hooker, reasserting the centrality of justification by faith alone, sought to demote again the status of

---

all things are not helpful. All things are lawful for me, but I will not be brought under the power of any" (178), and then immediately propose a threefold rubric for Christian sexual morality: (1) Is it lawful? (2) Is it helpful? (3) Is it enslaving? Obviously, if they were really taking 1 Corinthians 6:12 at face value, the first question would be needless, because it would always already be answered affirmatively. In point of fact, they do manage to always answer it affirmatively in this chapter, but only on the basis of demonstrating biblical silence or explicit permission on the matter.

26. *SR* 442.30–32.
27. *SR* 61.9–12.
28. *LW* 44:25.

adiaphora so that they might not become a burden unto the conscience. Our conduct in adiaphora still mattered, but as things indifferent, they fell within the realm of probability and hence our consciences might be adequately assured that they pleased God by resorting to the moral law within them, and to the prudential application of scriptural norms.

The lack of attention to such a moral law within is the second difficulty to which this "formal doctrine" is prone. Although never denying the natural law as such, precisianists clearly enthroned divine positive law as the paradigmatic form of law, rendering natural law secondary and perhaps unworthy to be considered law in the fullest sense. Since the essence of law was in command, and its perfection in precision, the concept of an innate but imprecise moral disposition hardly appealed to Puritans such as Cartwright. No wonder, then, that they were prone to make Scripture the only rule of moral action, suggesting that even things indifferent could only be so by the positive command of Scripture. The precisianist conception of God's will, then, remained irreducibly heteronomous. For Cartwright, despite his insistence that it is "the greatest liberty . . . to serve the Lord according to his revealed will," we have no sense that this will has ever been revealed internally, and hence no hint of O'Donovan and Bauckham's notion of "the inner law of our own created being." Hooker, however, by his recovery of the natural law tradition (one which the leading Protestant reformers had not rejected, but which had lost some of its richness and centrality in most Protestant churches), decisively reconfigured the paradigm for understanding God's will. Although the extrinsic gift of justification was necessary for us to rediscover a right sense of the will of God, the believer did not encounter this will merely as a command from without, but as an impulse from within. For Hooker, then, it was clear that obedience to God was realization of freedom as *potency*, freedom to be ourselves most fully; the precisianist might do lip-service to this idea, but could provide less convincing ground for it.

However, the final difficulty leads us in a different direction, requiring us to revisit our rough correlation of Christian liberty with Berlin's positive liberty, or O'Donovan's *potency*. Both Bauckham and O'Donovan elsewhere argue, in fact, that a full-fledged doctrine of liberty will require both dimensions.[29] Why? Well, if freedom consists in the cultivation of a mature agency, it should be clear that agency is unlikely to flourish in the absence of any possibility, any scope for action. We noted that a situation of pure possibility

---

29. O'Donovan, *Desire of the Nations*, 254; Bauckham, *God and the Crisis of Freedom*, 23–24.

would create moral paralysis, for there would never be any reason to choose one thing rather than another. However, a situation with but one possibility, the course clearly dictated by reason, would hardly teach us the art of prudent decision-making, which is essential to mature moral agency. To be sure, we should not wholly discount the value of such situations.[30] Even when there is only one right road to take, there are still many different attitudes we might adopt in taking it; to learn the discipline of cheerfully accepting necessity is the great virtue of fortitude. But a single virtue is not the whole of virtue, and prudence has been called the mother of all the rest. We saw the importance of this virtue in Luther's formulation of Christian liberty; the believer exercises his freedom for the neighbor by learning when to boldly confront Pharisaism and superstition, and when to tread softly to protect tender consciences.

We also saw, of course, that such a summons to uncertainty was decidedly unsettling to Luther's successors. Hence the emergence of the precisianist preference for resolving uncertain consciences with the clear (so they insisted) guidance of Scripture. They sought to find in the word of God the certainty that seemed to be lacking in all other sources of authority, and hence saw its perfection chiefly in its precision (recall Cartwright's dictum, "It is the virtue of a good law to leave as little as may be in the discretion of the judge"[31]). The goal of Scripture, in this understanding, was to take out of human hands any need for exercising interpretive discretion (although as we have seen, this being impossible, the practical effect was to put all such interpretive discretion in the hands of the presbyterian ministers). Scripture was to be made always and everywhere active, so that the believer could be, before it, wholly passive. This, however, served again to render the believer's obedience slavish, rather than free. Bauckham notes that the slave's obedience is *blind*, unlike the Christian's: "Like Jesus himself in obedience to his Father, his friends know the aim his commandments have in view, and they accept that aim."[32] This is another way of saying that Cartwright's concept of obedience is one that fails to render the believer a fully moral agent, which is central, on O'Donovan's account, to evangelical liberty:

> The Spirit evokes our free response as moral agents to the reality of redemption. . . . He confirms and restores us as moral agents, which is to say,

---

30. See the excellent discussion in Oliver O'Donovan, *Finding and Seeking: Ethics as Theology*, vol. 2 (Grand Rapids: Eerdmans, 2014), 183–84.

31. *SR*, Appendix, i.21–22.

32. Bauckham, *God and the Crisis of Freedom*, 86.

as the subjects of our actions. . . . It is this freedom that makes Christian ethics meaningful, and indeed demands it. For freedom is the character of one who participates in the order of creation by knowledge and action. That man is free implies that he can know and act; thus moral enquiry is a meaningful undertaking for him.[33]

Central to the proper expression of Christian freedom is the maturity of sonship by which we think the thoughts of our Father, by which we understand the end at which his commands aim, and are thus invited to actively apply that end to the circumstances in which we find ourselves. We are all invited to exercise the discretion of the judge, the virtue of prudence, perfected by faith as the virtue of charity. It is this, I have argued, to which Richard Hooker summoned the believer by his forceful emphasis on the immense variety of circumstances in which the believer is called upon to apply the will of God, his rehabilitation of probable reason as a tool for making such applications, and his constant distinction between the *end* of a law and its particular form.

If some uncertainty and possibility, some scope for decision-making, is necessary for the cultivation of individual prudence, it is surely all the more important at the level of societies and institutions. Again, Cartwright's maxim, "It is the virtue of a good law to leave as little as may be in the discretion of the judge," identifies the problem for us, and indeed even more pointedly than it did with respect to liberty of conscience. For the referent of the word "judge" here is of course a political authority, and by this statement Cartwright dramatically limits the scope within which rulers and judges can wield such authority. If it is the essence of human law, as Hooker argues, to improvise as changing circumstances dictate, discarding laws that have become no longer effective unto their intended purposes, and crafting new structures in their place (although with a wary and conservative eye on tradition, to be sure), then *discretion* is precisely what must be left to the judge and lawmaker. Of course, it was often the contention of the precisianists that the tight constraints of divine law apply only to the church, and not to the civil authorities. However, their tendency to overstep this boundary-line should not surprise us; after all, if good law is defined by its narrow precision, then natural law can only be a rather shabby, second-rate sort of law, the sort of thing you would only want to base human law on in very trivial matters. This mindset, accordingly, tends to generate a situation in which the Christian's loyalty to civil authorities will either be challenged by the claims of the church, which insist upon divine law

---

33. O'Donovan, *Resurrection and Moral Order*, 106–7.

as the standard for humans, or marginalized as something of relatively little significance beside the much more important ecclesiastical sphere.

The Material Doctrine of Christian Liberty and Its Promise

All of this suggests that we might do well to look to the *material doctrine* of Christian liberty as offering in some respects a better route forward for political theology. The material doctrine self-consciously takes justification by faith as its starting point, and from this derives the principles of voluntariety and indifference. Such an approach, as we see explicitly with Luther and, I would argue, implicitly with Hooker, understands that the chief freedom worth having is the freedom that consists in freedom from fear, and that the greatest fear of all is the fear of God's wrath. Christian liberty thus consists, first and foremost, in the assurance of forgiveness, in the experience that God is well pleased with oneself. And if God be for us, who can be against us? Here we see clearly what is missing in David Bentley Hart's equation of the Christian understanding of liberty with that of classical paganism. In both cases, to be sure, freedom is understood as *posse non peccare*—as "being able not to sin," the mastery of self that follows the purging of all enslaving passions. But for Christianity, and particularly for Protestants, no amount of individual effort can succeed in purging such passions; for a divided and depraved self, self-mastery is always a losing aspiration. Again, in O'Donovan's words, "We must receive ourselves from outside ourselves," if we are to truly be free. Hence the Reformation's almost obsessive emphasis on the *alien* righteousness of Christ as the ground of the believer's identity. We are only freed to be ourselves because we *are not our own*, and are thus freed from fruitless striving and fear of failure. From this standpoint of confidence, the Christian is liberated from the motivation of fear in all her actions, and receives instead the motivation of love: "Perfect love casts out fear."[34] The liberty of a Christian that begins in justification, then, issues forth in love of God and love of neighbor, a free desire to serve them.

This freedom faces both limit and possibility, and charity dictates the response in both cases. In the face of limit, which is to say the moral law, Christian liberty engenders the principle of voluntariety, which is a willing embrace of that limit for the sake of love of God who has placed it there. Moreover, confident in God's good pleasure toward her, the Christian perceives these

34. 1 John 4:18 ESV.

limits not as artificial constraints, but as there precisely for her good, as laws that enable her to be who she is meant to be. The law outside of her answers to the law of charity within her, directing her as to the form of her obedience to God. Beginning in faith, such law-obedience never risks collapsing into the fearful legalism that we have seen above. It enables an experience of freedom as fulfillment, and it invites the believer into the maturity of sonship, perceiving the heart of God and seeking to imitate it in her own actions, rather than simply obeying commands blindly. In the face of possibility, which is to say the contingent circumstances in which the will of God meets the believer, Christian liberty engenders the principle of indifference. Indifference here does not designate the mere negative possibility that we saw above that is directed to no object. Rather, freedom here is directed toward the object of love of neighbor; it is thus a freedom to improvise as this love seems to demand, untrammeled by fear. It consists in the prudent application of the will of God which the believer has come to discern in the concrete circumstances into which God has called the believer. Invited to exercise maturity as a free agent, the believer displays the fruits of this maturity in his love of neighbor.

It is worth returning at this point to a pregnant passage in Ted Smith's *Weird John Brown* that we paused to reflect on in the introductory chapter. There Smith argued against what Charles Taylor calls "code fetishism," which has much in common with the formal doctrine of Christian liberty that we have seen here. If the free conscience defines its freedom primarily in reference to its obedience to the higher law, and if this higher law is seen first and foremost as a solution to the uncertainty and imperfection of earthly laws, then a clash of laws and of loyalties is inevitable. The higher law is seen "as *the same kind of thing* as positive, earthly law. Such higher laws take the form of codes of obligations and prohibitions."[35] In response to this "code fetishism," preoccupied as it is with the imperative mood, Smith proposes a different understanding of the "higher law" in terms of an indicative mood.

> An imperative might be enforced, whether on someone else or on oneself. An indicative, on the other hand, just *is*. Such a higher law would need no more enforcement than the law of gravity. But the shift from imperative to indicative would not rob the higher law of its distinctly moral qualities. A higher law in the indicative mood would still give a picture of justice, a vision of relationships in the New Jerusalem. But it would not demand ac-

35. Ted A. Smith, *Weird John Brown: Divine Violence and the Limits of Ethics* (Stanford: Stanford University Press, 2015), 109.

tion to establish that city. Jesus does not give people a plan for bringing in the Kingdom of God but announces that the Kingdom is at hand. . . . The higher law, the new commandment, is not first of all a code that might be enforced. It is first of all a declaration of a change in the way things are.[36]

This change in the way things are, although not primarily a this-worldly reality, cannot help having a transformative effect on the structures and obligations of earthly life.

> The indicative of the higher law is not present as a simple description; it is present through its negation of earthly law. It breaks the structures of obligation of earthly laws not just by proposing better content for those laws but by declaring an indicative of fulfillment that undoes the absolute quality of the whole category of earthly law. The divine violence of the higher law relativizes not just every particular "ought" and "should" but the whole imperative mood. The proclamation that the Kingdom of God is at hand does not bring with it a new set of imperatives, for such imperatives would betray the gift they announce. The proclamation of the Reign of God instead relativizes the full spectrum of people's obligations. Because the Kingdom is at hand, obligations to Caesar, to families, and even to one's own life lose the sheen of absoluteness. And because the sign of the Kingdom is the cross, new obligations do not arise to fill the little gaps left by the old. In the cross Jesus does not squeeze himself into Caesar's throne. He does not just offer a new and improved edition of Roman law. In the cross Jesus relativizes not just particular claims to authority but the whole category of earthly law. The indicative of the higher law breaks the absolute hold of every earthly imperative without establishing new ones in their place.[37]

There is obvious resonance here between Smith's preference for the indicative over the imperative and Luther's doctrine of forensic justification, in which the believer's salvation does not begin with any change in what the believer does, but in a new statement about who the believer *is*. It is from this radical emphasis on the already-accomplished reign of Christ in the believer that Luther could seem to so thoroughly relativize every other matter of the Christian life as indifferent. And although Hooker seeks to carefully qualify

36. Smith, *Weird John Brown*, 117–18.
37. Smith, *Weird John Brown*, 118.

the doctrine of indifference here, the emphasis remains: it is precisely because of the unshakeable certainty of the gospel of justification which Scripture announces that we can rest secure even in the face of the profound uncertainties of the moral life, and Scripture's lack of exhaustive specificity in this realm.

IV. The Politics of Evangelical Liberty

Smith, however, has wider horizons in view. The indicative, for him, is also a statement about the reign of Christ in the world, over peoples and nations. It is this indicative—that the kingdom of God is at hand, even in its present invisibility—that "breaks the absolute hold of every earthly imperative." Let us turn, then, at last, to the properly political ramifications of the "material doctrine of Christian liberty" as we have expounded it in this book. Here we will find at last some ways in which the Reformation's proclamation of the freedom of a Christian points forward to the emergence of modern liberal politics, even while qualifying it in important respects. There are three themes I wish to highlight here, corresponding roughly to Chapters Four through Six above: the desacralization of earthly politics, the freedom of the citizen, and the acknowledgment of Christ's reign.

The Desacralization of Politics

First, then, let us consider the political implications of Smith's "indicative of fulfillment," which we have correlated to the centrality of the indicative in the gospel of justification. Such an emphasis generates a sharp distinction of morality and politics from soteriology, and while leaving civil rulers in their place, deprives them of any power to confer ultimate identity on their subjects or their realm. Or in O'Donovan's words, "The power that they exercise in defeating their enemies, the national possessions they safeguard, these are now rendered irrelevant by Christ's triumph."[38] This desacralization of political power was of course in the first place an achievement of Christianity generally,[39] but most medieval political theologies had muted this emphasis, and it was left to Protestantism to restate it in radicalized form. Thus, despite

---

38. O'Donovan, *Desire of the Nations*, 151.

39. See for instance Peter Leithart's excellent study, *Defending Constantine: The Twilight of an Empire and the Dawn of Christendom* (Downers Grove, IL: InterVarsity Academic, 2010).

Hooker's clear emphasis on the importance of political institutions, and indeed his reverence for the queen and other authorities, he shows that the believer can sit loosely with respect to them, knowing that his true identity and freedom is secured already by God, that he may face without fear the provisional structures of the civil kingdom as he navigates their ethical mazes. Indeed, one of the most striking features of Hooker's account of the royal supremacy in the church is his refusal to ground it in divine law, unlike most of his predecessors (although, as I have argued elsewhere, his argument is anticipated by Vermigli in important respects).[40] The magistrate's role in sacred matters, like the existence of festival days and various other ceremonies, is justified *not* in sacred terms but in the more mundane terms of natural religion and civil order.

In fact, as Eric Nelson has argued in *The Hebrew Republic*, this same line of reasoning underlay the gradual liberalization of Dutch and English politics during the seventeenth century. Defying modern stereotypes, Nelson shows that it was the *Erastians*, not free-churchers, who did the most to expand the domain of freedom of conscience in this period. "The turn toward toleration in Western Europe," says Nelson, "was primarily inspired by the religious conviction of the 'Biblical Century,' not by creeping secularization; and . . . it emerged to a very great extent out of the Erastian effort to unify church and state, not out of the desire to keep them separate."[41] Since they justified legal impositions in religious matters solely in terms of the needs of civic peace and order, rather than theological necessity, they were able to gradually reduce the number of such impositions. Indeed, after Erastus himself, Nelson begins this narrative with Hooker, showing that "For Hooker, as for Erastus, the *civil* character of all binding religious law argues for a narrowing of the range of cases in which religious matters should be legislated,"[42] and that this narrowing would only continue with seventeenth-century Dutch and English Erastian political theologians.

Indeed, from this standpoint, John Locke's seeming about-face in the 1670s and 1680s is not so dramatic as it may have seemed. In chapters 3 and 4 of his *Pretenses of Loyalty*, John Perry sheds fresh light on this transition from Locke as 1662 apologist for royally imposed religious uniformity to 1688

---

40. W. Bradford Littlejohn, "More than a Swineherd: Hooker, Vermigli, and the Aristotelian Defense of the Royal Supremacy," *Renaissance and Reformation Review* 15, no. 1 (2014): 78–93. See also Matthew Tuininga, *Calvin's Political Theology and the Public Engagement of the Church: Christ's Two Kingdoms* (Cambridge: CUP, forthcoming 2017), ch. 8.

41. Eric Nelson, *The Hebrew Republic: Jewish Sources and the Transformation of European Political Thought* (Cambridge, MA: Harvard University Press, 2010), 89.

42. Nelson, *Hebrew Republic*, 97.

apologist for toleration. Locke had always argued, Perry shows, in terms of the *civil*, rather than *religious*, function of ceremonies, convinced that civil peace and order were best served by uniformity of practice.[43] What changed was not this basic conviction, so much as a gradual persuasion that in point of fact, private freedom of practice in ceremonies could in fact be more conducive to civil peace. Of course, Locke recognized that this would only be the case for a populace that could indeed be convinced that the ceremonies in question were adiaphora, so that none would be alarmed by the diversity between neighboring churches. Hence the centrality of Locke's theological argument for the soteriological insignificance of the disputed practices in his *Letter Concerning Toleration*, an argument that parallels in important respects that of Hooker in Book III of the *Lawes*.[44]

Accordingly, if we focus our attention on Hooker's mingling of civil and ecclesiastical functions, seemingly anathema to modern liberal ideals (particularly as expressed in disestablishmentarian America), we are apt to miss the more important contribution of Protestant two-kingdoms theory. It consisted not in the ordering of human institutions per se, whether that be a Calvinist separation of church and state, or Hooker's defense of constitutional government,[45] but in the relation of all such institutions to their Lord. The two-kingdoms doctrine instilled in the Christian a sense of healthy detachment toward earthly loyalties, a healthy realism about what earthly institutions can accomplish, and offered consolation when they failed to achieve their lofty aims. It discouraged any attempt to make the kingdom of God a complete outward reality here and now by force, whether by holy war or holy law. In this doctrine, the authority of political institutions is quite limited: they may command the body, to the extent that the demands of civil order and justice require, but they cannot command the mind or the conscience. Each subject remains, in the last analysis, answerable to the Lord who made and redeemed him, not to his prince.

---

43. John Perry, *The Pretenses of Loyalty: Locke, Liberal Theory, and American Political Theology* (Oxford: Oxford University Press, 2011), 90–91. See also Jacqueline Rose, "John Locke, 'Matters Indifferent,' and the Restoration of the Church of England," *Historical Journal* 48, no. 3 (2005): 611.

44. See John Locke, *Letter Concerning Toleration*, ed. Mario Montuori (1689; repr., The Hague: Martinus Nijhoff, 1963), 23–27.

45. This, of course, is the point at which many Whig historians have claimed Hooker as antecedent for liberalism, an argument recently given an impressive new defense by Alexander Rosenthal in *Crown under Law: Richard Hooker, John Locke, and the Ascent of Modern Constitutionalism* (Plymouth, UK: Lexington Books, 2008), one that is, however, considerably weakened by its inattention to theological foundations.

The Freedom of the Citizen

This leads to our second point: the freedom of the citizen. It may have seemed that in various points in this book, Christian liberty has been interiorized to the point of being almost meaningless, a worry that this chapter's stress on freedom as *potency* has doubtless intensified. There is, we have seen, a radical interiority in the freedom of a Christian that, it would seem, remains wholly blind to the external embodiment of this freedom. This is particularly so in the Protestant doctrine of Christian freedom, in which the freedom of the Christian *coram Deo* can coexist with complete external bondage, and in which any claim to have achieved freedom in the earthly realm is illusory, since it is always tainted with the bondage of sin.

Understandably, this line of thinking has seemed unacceptable to many modern theologians. It appears to be a stance of complete political quietism, encouraging a dangerous complacency about injustice, inasmuch as it suggests that all that matters is the liberation of the soul from the bondage of sin, no matter how many physical chains remain. This is the doctrine, they will rant, that would preach the gospel to African slaves, while happily continuing the slave trade. This is the doctrine that upheld apartheid. They are no happier when they read it in St. Paul. Paul may have said that in Christ there is neither slave nor free, neither male nor female, and yet he betrayed his message (or perhaps, some other pseudo-Paul later on inserted a different message) by calling for slaves to obey their masters, calling for wives to submit to their husbands. The freedom of the gospel, on this reading, is empty and indeed oppressive if it does not involve a change in external relations, a real empowerment of individuals. The shrewder critics may even venture that this radical interiorization of freedom contributes in some way to the development of the modern autonomous subject, the concept of the naked unconditioned will that Hart identifies as the great modern heresy—that Luther, Kant, and modernity are all part of the same voluntarist line of development.

I have argued, however, in Chapter Five above that while Hooker accepts this essentially inward account of freedom, he nonetheless allows it to have potentially revolutionary political implications (even if he himself was naturally careful to downplay any such revolutionary potential). We noted there that one reason why John Whitgift had been so hesitant to accept Cartwright's charge that he based the goodness of established laws on some judgment of reason was his fear of the democratizing implications of such an admission. Some men might boast a better exercise of reason than others, but all possessed the faculty, and thus a law justified by appeal to reason could, in principle, be judged and contested by appeal to reason. It is precisely such judgment that Hooker allows and indeed invites, even while warning that clear proof of Scripture or demonstrative reason is needed to overturn laws founded on the probable reason of the whole body politic. Such merely mental freedom—the freedom to pass judgment on the rightness or wrongness of a law even while quietly submitting for the time being—might seem a feeble freedom indeed, but in fact few things are more powerful, as Bauckham argues:

> That the latter kind of freedom [inner freedom of spirit] is real and important can be seen, for example, in such extreme cases as Soviet dissidents in the Gulag, remaining free, in their thinking, of the system which oppresses them unbearably, or in the Christian martyrs under the Roman Empire, who could be regarded as the most truly free people of their time, in their refusal to let even the threat of death cow them into submission. Such freedom in and despite oppressive structures is not only real but essential to the cause of liberation *from* essential structures. It is only out of their inner liberation from the system that Russian dissidents can publicly protest against and hope to change the system. . . . It needed a Moses liberated by God from resignation to the irresistible power of Pharaoh to lead the people out of Egypt, and it needed the gradual psychological liberation of the people themselves to free them from Egypt even after their escape from Pharaoh's army.[46]

By the exercise of such critical intelligence, which as we have seen is one of Hooker's great themes, the citizen is rendered free even in the moment of obedience. Again, O'Donovan captures the essential insight that we have claimed for this doctrine of Christian liberty: "[S]overeignty properly belongs not to law but to truth, for only a perception of the truth can lead us to whole-hearted action. The marvel, we may say, is not that the community can demand conformity; the marvel is that conscience can secretly transcend that conformity and pass judgment upon it in the light of truth."[47] But of course, in passing such judgment and when necessarily challenging the sovereignty of law, the conscience presses inexorably beyond the bounds of interiority. While evangelical liberty must be understood as an inward, rather than outward, freedom, it cannot content itself with only inward expression, for the hope that sustains the free mind in the midst of oppression is the hope of a future

---

46. Bauckham, *God and the Crisis of Freedom*, 23–24.
47. O'Donovan, *Resurrection and Moral Order*, 131.

in which circumstances may change and outer freedom become a possibility: "The point is that real freedom cannot be confined to one dimension. Inner freedom cannot rest content with outer unfreedom, though it may have to suffer the contradiction in circumstances where outer freedom is unattainable."[48] Accordingly, in due time, Protestant jurists took the lead in constructing institutional forms for the expression of public consent or dissent, for enabling the judgment of each conscience to have a voice in the making of laws and sometimes even an exemption from their binding force.

This freedom of critical intelligence, although essentially epistemological, rests on the same soteriological foundation that we have emphasized. Justification confers on the individual a new unshakeable identity in relation to God that necessarily relativizes all earthly loyalties and sources of identity, even while maintaining their provisional role in the present age. Although this is first and foremost "a social reality, a new disposition of society around its supreme Lord which sets it loose from its traditional lords," says O'Donovan,

> individual liberty is not far away. For the implication of this new social reality is that the individual can no longer simply be carried within the social setting to which she or he was born; for that setting is under challenge from the new social centre. This requires she give herself to the service of the Lord within the new society, in defiance, if need be, of the old lords and societies that claim her. She emerges in differentiation from her family, tribe and nation, making decisions of discipleship which were not given her from within them.[49]

This emergence of the free individual, who receives her vocation from the Lord rather than from any earthly lord, in turn could not help but have transformative political implications. The success of early-modern liberal societies, says O'Donovan, lay in "the moment of self-abdication instilled by their monotheistic faith. Through that religious moment they directed their members to become critical moral intelligences, and taught them to see themselves as answerable directly to God."[50]

Of course, O'Donovan qualifies, "Modern liberalism is not yet ready to leap fully armed from the head that first conceived this thought. This is not yet 'freedom of conscience' in a generalized sense. It is 'evangelical liberty,' which is

---

48. Bauckham, *God and the Crisis of Freedom*, 24.
49. O'Donovan, *Desire of the Nations*, 254.
50. O'Donovan, *Ways of Judgment*, 76.

to say, the freedom freely to obey Christ."[51] This is a qualification to which we have returned again and again in this study. So long as the freedom of a Christian was understood quite specifically as the freedom of a *Christian*, not of any old individual who wanted to pursue his or her sense of meaning and ultimate reality, such freedom of conscience remained far off from a general liberal right to freedom of conscience. Indeed, for versions of the doctrine that emphasized rigorous obedience to Christ in the manifold laws he has prescribed, there might seem to be no room at all for the freedom for others to hold and act on erroneous beliefs, which is essential to any liberal theory of toleration. Yet in versions of the doctrine that encouraged a very capacious conception of adiaphora, such as Hooker's, a great deal of space was potentially opened up. When it came to what to believe, the state obviously could not bind the conscience; that, all the Reformers admitted, was simply an impossibility. When it came to how to act on that belief in love of neighbor, then, to the extent that most such actions were judged things indifferent, they could in principle be left up to individual judgment, to the extent that civil peace allowed. To be sure, Hooker himself judged that at his time, civil peace did not allow for much such freedom (and perhaps he was right, given the later chaos of the 1640s). But with little change to his underlying principles, later theorists could conclude that, where the public good was not threatened, individual freedom of judgment and practice could be granted a very long leash indeed. Thus, O'Donovan concludes,

> evangelical liberty has proved to be the foundation of a more generalized freedom, including a certain, not indefinite liberty for misguided and erroneous judgment. . . . Which is not to say that there is no such thing as evident and unarguable error . . . it is simply that [each person] has (*has*, not *is*) his own master, and his master is not the ruler who governs him in the order of civil society. There are some judgments that may be evident enough, but which do not fall to the ruler to make. The ruler has to establish a prima-facie interest in the implications for civil order before intervening between any man or woman and the God who commands. That is the correct way of stating the liberal doctrine which is often put misleadingly as "the separation of law and morality." There can be no separation of law and morality; but what there can be, and is, is a sphere of individual responsibility before God in which the public good is not immediately at stake.[52]

51. O'Donovan, *Desire of the Nations*, 255.
52. O'Donovan, *Desire of the Nations*, 255.

In short, I have argued that once all the proper definitions and qualifications have been made, there is a compelling case that the Protestant proclamation of evangelical liberty, and the attempts to clothe it in appropriate institutional forms by later theorists such as Hooker, *did* in fact lay the groundwork for the liberal freedoms that we cherish today.

The Acknowledgment of Christ's Kingship

We are thus left with perhaps the most pressing question of all. If this is true, as a descriptive matter, what does this mean in prescriptive terms? Do we need to continue to confess the Kingship of Christ, and the evangelical proclamation of his grace, in order to sustain something like the liberal order? Or are we dealing with something more like Wittgenstein's ladder, which we may safely throw away once we have scaled it? On the one hand, to speak of a liberal order sustained by Christian confession seems downright oxymoronic in contemporary pluralist discourse. And yet it is hard to see exactly how else one might sustain the all-important desacralization of political power discussed above. The modest pretensions of liberal politics depend on the conception of the political realm as relative, penultimate, and temporal. And yet, all these terms only make sense in relation to their opposites. Relative in relation to what if not the absolute? Penultimate in relation to what if not the ultimate? Temporal in relation to what if not the eternal? Edward Cranz's remarks at the conclusion of his magisterial 1959 exposition of Luther's two-kingdoms doctrine are striking in this regard:

> Indeed, from Luther's standpoint, we never find any true secularization apart from Christianity, for only Christianity teaches us not to "mix" the two realms, which the natural man cannot even distinguish. Apart from Christianity, what ought to be the world or reason or polity will always falsely claim to be more than the world, to be in some way a means of salvation, or a stage on the way to heaven or a "church."[53]

In other words, according to Luther, the proclamation of Christian liberty and its concomitant doctrine, the two kingdoms, is in fact the only way to avoid, in the long run, the sort of totalitarianism that Berlin feared in his exposition of positive liberty.

53. F. Edward Cranz, *An Essay on the Development of Luther's Thought on Law, Justice, and Society* (Cambridge, MA: Harvard University Press, 1959), 177.

Such claims are sharply debated in contemporary political theology. In John Witte's influential account of the emergence of liberalism out of the soil of the Reformation, *The Reformation of Rights*, we saw that Protestantism serves only as a "midwife"[54] of the broader conception of human rights that are so central to liberal society today. The metaphor is a telling one: a midwife, however important she is, is not even strictly essential to a birth, and certainly, once the child is out and growing, her role is done. Witte returns to the metaphor in his "Concluding Reflections" and although suggesting that this midwifing role is not a one-time thing—Christian ideas have served as midwives for the emergence of liberties at various key points in the development of modern society—he leaves behind the distinctiveness of Calvinism on which he has expended so much attention in his book to suddenly assert that any religious community can offer analogous resources for the generation of justice and freedom. Religion, he argues, must not be quite left behind, but no particular claims of any particular religion play a central role.[55]

On the other hand, another prominent Christian rights theorist, Nicholas Wolterstorff, despite beginning his influential *Justice: Rights and Wrongs* with a similar commitment to dialogical pluralism, confessed that he had reached a startling conclusion by the end: "I found myself led to conclude that there is no adequate secular grounding for human rights, and that it's unlikely there ever will be one; the only adequate grounding is a theistic grounding which holds that each and every human being bears the image of God and is equally loved by God."[56] Such a conclusion was seen as nothing less than an act of aggression by his secular interlocutor Jonathan Kahn,[57] a sign of how high the stakes are in this conversation: either you can have a Christian liberalism or you can have (perhaps) a secular liberalism, but you cannot very well have your cake and eat it too.

This sobering conclusion is highlighted in its own way by John Perry's excellent study *The Pretenses of Loyalty*. Throughout the book he shows the extent to which liberal theories of toleration, far from resting on timeless rational principles, rather emerged out of contingent historical theological

---

54. John E. Witte Jr., *Reformation of Rights: Law, Religion, and Human Rights in Early Modern Calvinism* (Cambridge: Cambridge University Press, 2007), 2.

55. Witte, *Reformation of Rights*, 338–39.

56. Nicholas Wolterstorff, "How Social Justice Got to Me and Why It Never Left," *Journal of the American Academy of Religion* 76, no. 3 (2008): 673.

57. Jonathan Kahn, "Nicholas Wolterstorff's Fear of the Secular," *The Immanent Frame* (February 22, 2009), http://blogs.ssrc.org/tif/2009/02/22/nicholas-wolterstorffs-fear-of-the-secular/ (accessed April 22, 2016).

commitments, without which any attempt to police the just bounds of religion and politics becomes immensely challenging at best. He thus concludes by raising the question of how we might respond in light of this: Are there contemporary models for taking seriously particular religious convictions as a foundation for sustainable pluralism? He identifies three options—"loyalty through cultural republicanism" (represented by Michael Novak and Richard John Neuhaus), "loyalty through ordered pluralism" (represented by Witte and Wolterstorff), and "loyalty through fidelity to conscience" (represented by Martha Nussbaum)—before identifying weaknesses in each and concluding that our best course through our present impasse is to relearn the art of rhetoric and persuasion.[58] We must regain faith in the possibility of public debates in which such conflicting visions of the good are made explicit, and in which persuasive reasoned speech can resolve such conflicts in part, and to the extent that they are not resolved, help us at least to agree on reasonable ways of managing them.

As a strategy for navigating the unprincipled pluralism in which we currently find ourselves, Perry's conclusion has much to commend it. As an enduring foundation for political order, it is less reassuring. For as Augustine famously asks, without common objects of love, how can a commonwealth endure? And if justice consists in the giving of each his due, how can a common commitment to justice endure unless the lord of all is given his due? The question remains unanswered in another great work of recent American political theology, Eric Gregory's *Politics and the Order of Love*. Despite his Augustinian commitments, Gregory resists any attempt to give public recognition to the love of God, deeming this an unacceptable transgression of the limitations of liberal order.[59] And yet he recognizes, with O'Donovan and other Augustinians, the advent of liberalism as an achievement of Christianity (and Augustinian Christianity in particular), which by its recognition of the provisional character of politics, and its incessant quest to do justice to every fellow-man, laid the foundations of liberal political order. This recognition, combined with his Augustinian contention that only the love of God can anchor the right order of neighbor-love, would seem to demand Augustine's conclusion that no truly loving liberal political order can long endure unless God is given his due. While Gregory rightly resists the idea that liberal order

58. Perry, *Pretenses of Loyalty*, ch. 7.

59. See particularly Eric Gregory, *Politics and the Order of Love: An Augustinian Ethic of Democratic Citizenship* (Chicago: University of Chicago Press, 2008), 145–46, where he critiques Oliver O'Donovan on this point.

cannot survive *at all* without explicit recognition of its normative (ultimately Christian) foundations,[60] he seems to too readily evade those who would press this objection. To be sure, one can do the right thing without knowing *why* it is the right thing, but not forever. Likewise, there is no doubt that the liberal order of neighbor-love can long survive without conscious public recognition of the love of God that orders it. But how long? A building whose foundations have been undermined can hold up for quite a while if it is well built, but at some point, it will start to crumble.

It is here that we return to the pregnant insights of Hooker's Christological politics. If Christ does indeed represent not merely a road to salvation, but the perfection of our human nature, the full fruition of all our natural ends, then the ends even of mundane political life are revealed to us in Christ. Revealed in a glimpse only, to be sure, never fully disclosed, for it is only in the resurrection and ascension of Christ that we see the culmination of human life as it was and is meant to be. Likewise, although all political authority derives from and depends on Christ as the Son of Man to whom all things on heaven and earth are subject, this sovereignty belongs to the ascended and presently absent Christ. There is thus no question of trying to enclose this sovereignty in earthly garb, to make the reign of Christ directly manifest in any human polity. Hooker's theology rejects any such theocratic aspirations at every point. He also takes with utmost seriousness the limited horizons of our present knowledge, and the intractable clay of fallen humanity with which we have to work. Both ensure that any attempt to fashion the human order of justice after our glimpses of divine justice will remain fragmentary, provisional, and subject to constant revision and renegotiation.

Moreover, and perhaps most importantly, the uniqueness and supremacy of Christ is no reason, for Hooker, to reject the political wisdom and competence of non-Christians. The fullness of human nature might be disclosed to us in Christ, but this graced nature does not destroy or utterly transform the mundane and fallen nature to which we currently look for guidance. Nor is the revelation of Christ our only access to the knowledge of God as Creator and Sustainer of this nature. The freedom of a Christian commonwealth, for Hooker, is a freedom that can be readily shared with, enjoyed with, and nourished by those who do not acknowledge Jesus as Lord (as indeed, he notes, a great number of professing English believers do not in fact). But it cannot, in the end, be sustained without the confession that Christ has set us free and thus he alone, and no earthly laws, can demand our ultimate loyalty.

60. Gregory, *Politics and the Order of Love*, 105.

Bibliography

Primary Sources

[Anon.] *A Christian Letter of certaine English Protestants . . . unto that Reverend and learned man . . . Mr. R. Hoo[. . .]*. Middelburg: Holland, 1599. In *The Folger Library Edition of the Works of Richard Hooker*, vol. 4: *Of the Lawes of Ecclesiasticall Politie: Attack and Response*. Edited by W. Speed Hill and John E. Booty. Cambridge, MA: Belknap Press of Harvard University Press, 1982.

Althusius, Johannes. *Politica Methodice Digesta* (1603). Reprinted as *The Politics of Johannes Althusius*. Translated and edited by Frederick S. Carney. London: Eyre & Spottiswoode, 1965.

Aquinas, Thomas. *Summa Theologiae*. Translated by the Fathers of the English Dominican Province. At New Advent, www.newadvent.org.

Bancroft, Richard. *Dangerous Positions and Proceedings, Published and Practised Within This Island of Britain, Under Pretence of Reformation, and for the Presbyterial Discipline. Collected and Set Forth by Richard Bancroft*. London: John Wolfe, 1593.

———. *A Sermon preached at Paules Crosse the 8. of Februarie, being the first Sunday in the Parleament, Anno. 1588. by Richard Bancroft D. of Divinitie, and Chaplaine to the right Honorable Sir Christopher Hatton Knight L. Chancelor of England*. London: E. B. [Edward Bollifant] for Gregorie Seton, 1588, i.e. 1589.

———. *A Survey of the Pretended Holy Discipline Containing the Beginnings, Success, Parts, Proceedings, Authority, and Doctrine of It: With Some of the Manifold and Material Repugnances, Varieties, and Uncertainties in That Behalf*. London: Richard Hodgkinson, 1593.

Bodin, Jean. *On Sovereignty: Four Chapters from the Six Books of the Commonwealth*. Translated and edited by Julian H. Franklin. Cambridge: Cambridge University Press, 1992.

Bucer, Martin. *De Regno Christi* (1550). Reprinted in *Melanchthon and Bucer*. Translated and edited by Wilhelm Pauck. Louisville: Westminster John Knox, 2006.

Buchanan, George. *A Dialogue on the Law of Kingship among the Scots: A Critical Edi-*

tion and Translation of George Buchanan's De Jure Regni Apud Scotos Dialogus. Translated and edited by Roger A. Mason and Martin S. Smith. Aldershot, UK: Ashgate, 2004.

Bullinger, Heinrich. *A Confutation of the Popes Bull Which Was Published More Than Two Yeres Agoe Against Elizabeth the Most Gracious Queene of England, Fraunce, and Ireland, and Against the Noble Realme of England Together with a Defence of the Sayd True Christian Queene, and of the Whole Realme of England. By Henry Bullinger the Elder.* London: Printed by Iohn Day dwelling ouer Aldersgate, 1572.

———. *The Decades of Henry Bullinger.* Edited for the Parker Society by Thomas Harding. 4 vols. Cambridge: Cambridge University Press, 1849–1852.

Calvin, John. *Commentary on the Epistles of Paul the Apostle to the Corinthians.* Translated by John Pringle. Grand Rapids: Baker, 1989.

———. *Institutes of the Christian Religion.* 2 volumes. Edited by John T. McNeill. Translated by Ford Lewis Battles. Louisville: Westminster John Knox, 1960.

———. *Treatises against the Anabaptists and Against the Libertines.* Edited by Benjamin Wirt Farley. Grand Rapids: Baker, 1982.

Cartwright, Thomas. *A Replye to an Answere Made of M. Doctor Whitgift . . . Agaynste the Admonition.* s.l., 1574. Reprinted in *Whitgift's Works.*

———. *The Reste of the Second Replie: Agaynst Master Doctor Whitgifts Second Answer Touching the Church Discipline.* Basel, 1577.

———. *The Second Replie of Thomas Cartwright: Agaynst Master Doctor Whitgifts Second Answer Touching the Church Discipline.* Heidelberg, 1575.

Eusebius. *Church History.* Translated by Arthur Cushman McGiffert. Accessed at New Advent, http://www.newadvent.org/fathers/2501.htm.

Frere, W. H., and C. E. Douglas, eds. *Obedience in Church and State: Three Political Tracts by Stephen Gardiner.* Translated and edited by Pierre Janelle. Cambridge: Cambridge University Press, 1930.

———. *Puritan Manifestoes: A Study of the Origin of the Puritan Revolt.* London: Society for Promoting Christian Knowledge, 1907.

Goodman, Christopher. *How superior powers oght to be obeyd of their subjects: and wherin they may lawfully by Gods Worde be disobeyed and resisted.* Geneva, 1558. Facsimile reprint. New York: Columbia University Press, 1931.

Hooker, Richard. *The Folger Library Edition of the Works of Richard Hooker,* vol. 1: *The Laws of Ecclesiastical Polity: Pref., Books I to IV.* Edited by W. Speed Hill and Georges Edelen. Cambridge, MA: Belknap Press of Harvard University Press, 1977.

———. *The Folger Library Edition of the Works of Richard Hooker,* vol. 2: *The Laws of Ecclesiastical Polity: Book V.* Edited by W. Speed Hill. Cambridge, MA: Belknap Press of Harvard University Press, 1977.

———. *The Folger Library Edition of the Works of Richard Hooker,* vol. 3: *The Laws of Ecclesiastical Polity: Books VI, VII, VIII.* Edited by W. Speed Hill and P. G. Stanwood. Cambridge, MA: Belknap Press of Harvard University Press, 1981.

———. *The Folger Library Edition of the Works of Richard Hooker,* vol. 4: *Of the Lawes of Ecclesiasticall Politie: Attack and Response.* Edited by W. Speed Hill and John E. Booty. Cambridge, MA: Belknap Press of Harvard University Press, 1982.

————. *The Folger Library Edition of the Works of Richard Hooker,* vol. 5: *Tractates and Sermons.* Edited by W. Speed Hill and Laetitia Yeandle. Cambridge, MA: Belknap Press of Harvard University Press, 1990.

————. *The Folger Library Edition of the Works of Richard Hooker,* vol. 6: *Of the Lawes of Ecclesiastical Politie, Books I–VIII: Introductions and Commentary.* Edited by W. Speed Hill. Binghamton, NY: Medieval & Renaissance Texts & Studies, 1993.

————. *The Works of that Learned and Judicious Divine Mr. Richard Hooker: with an Account of His Life and Death by Isaac Walton.* 3 vols. Edited by John Keble. Oxford: Oxford University Press, 1836.

Hooper, John. "Bishop Hooper's 'Notes to the King's Council' 3 October 1550." Edited by Constantin Hopf. *Journal of Theological Studies* 175–76 (1943): 194–99.

James VI and I. *King James VI and I: Political Writings.* Edited by J. P. Sommerville. Cambridge: Cambridge University Press, 1994.

Jewel, John. *An Apology of the Church of England* (1561). Edited by John E. Booty. Ithaca, NY, 1963.

Junius, Franciscus. *De Politiae Mosis Observatione.* Leiden: 1592.

————. *The Mosaic Polity.* Translated by Todd M. Rester. Edited by Andrew M. McGinnis. Sources in Early Modern Economics, Ethics, and Law. Grand Rapids: Christian's Library Press, 2015.

Knox, John. *On Rebellion.* Edited by Roger A. Mason. Cambridge: Cambridge University Press, 1994.

Locke, John. "First Tract on Government" (1660). In *Political Essays.* Edited by Mark Goldie. Cambridge: Cambridge University Press, 1997.

————. *Letter Concerning Toleration* (1689). Edited by Mario Montuori. The Hague: Martinus Nijhoff, 1963.

Luther, Martin. *On the Freedom of a Christian* (1520). Edited by Harold J. Grimm. In *Luther's Works: American Edition,* vol. 31: *Career of the Reformer I.* Edited by Jaroslav Pelikan and Helmut T. Lehmann. St. Louis: Concordia, and Philadelphia: Muhlenberg, 1955–.

————. *Preface to the Epistle to the Romans* (1546). Edited by E. Theodore Bachmann. In *Luther's Works: American Edition,* vol. 35: *Word and Sacrament I.* Edited by Jaroslav Pelikan and Helmut T. Lehmann. St. Louis: Concordia, and Philadelphia: Muhlenberg, 1955–.

————. *Theses Concerning Faith and Law* (1535). Edited by Harold J. Grimm. In *Luther's Works: American Edition,* vol. 35: *Career of the Reformer IV.* Edited by Jaroslav Pelikan and Helmut T. Lehmann. St. Louis: Concordia, and Philadelphia: Muhlenberg, 1955–.

————. *Treatise on Good Works* (1520). Translated by W. A. Lambert. Edited by James Atkinson. In *Luther's Works: American Edition,* vol. 44: *The Christian in Society I.* Edited by Jaroslav Pelikan and Helmut T. Lehmann. St. Louis: Concordia, and Philadelphia: Muhlenberg, 1955–.

Melanchthon, Philipp. *Loci Communes Theologici* (1521). Reprinted in *Melanchthon and Bucer.* Edited by Wilhelm Pauck. Translated by Lowell J. Satre. Louisville: Westminster John Knox, 2006.

————. *Melanchthon on Christian Doctrine: Loci Communes, 1555.* Translated and edited by Clyde L. Manschreck. New York: Oxford University Press, 1965.

————. *Opera Omnia.* In *Corpus Reformatorum.* Edited by C. B. Bretschneider and H. E. Bindseil. Halle and Brunswick: C. A. Schwetschke, 1834–.

————. *Whether it be a mortall sinne to transgresse civil lawes which be the commaundements of civill magistrates. The judgement of Philip Melancthon in his Epitome of morall Philosophie. The resolution of D. Henry Bullinger and D. Rod[olph] Gaulter, of D. Martin Bucer, and D. Peter Martyr, concerning thapparel of Ministers, and other indifferent things.* London: Richard Jugge, printer to the Queenes Maiestie, 1566.

————, et al. *De Rebus Adiaphoris: Epistola Concionatorum Hambergensium ad D. Philippum Melanthonem, et Responsio Eiusdem* (1549). In *A Collection of Articles, Injunctions, Canons, Orders, Ordinances, and Canons Ecclesiastical: With Other Publick Records of the Church of England, Chiefly in the Times of K. Edward VI., Q. Elizabeth, K. James, and K. Charles I.* Edited by Anthony Sparrow. London: Printed for Robert Cutler and Joseph Clarke, 1671.

De Mornay, Philippe Duplessis, or Hubert Languet. *Vindiciae Contra Tyrannos, Or, Concerning the Legitimate Power of a Prince Over the People, and of the People Over a Prince* (1579). Edited by George Garnett. Cambridge: Cambridge University Press, 1994.

Parker, Matthew, ed. (?). *A Briefe Examination for the Tyme, of a Certaine Declaration, Lately Put in Print in the Name and Defence of Certaine Ministers in London, Refusyng to Weare the Apparell Prescribed by the Lawes and Orders of the Realme: In the Ende Is Reported, the Iudgement of Two Notable Learned Fathers, M. Doctour Bucer, and M. Doctour Martir . . . Translated Out of the Originals, Written by Theyr Owne Handes, Purposely Debatyng This Controuersie.* London: Richarde Jugge, printer to the Queenes Maiestie, 1566.

————, ed. (?). *Whether It Be a Mortall Sinne to Transgresse Civil Lawes Which Be the Commaundementes of Civill Magistrates. The Iudgement of Philip Melancton in His Epitome of Morall Philosophie. The Resolution of D. Hen. Bullinger, and D. Rod. Gualter, of D. Martin Bucer, and D. Peter Martyr, Concernyng Thapparrel of Ministers, and Other Indifferent Thinges.* London: Richard Jugge, printer to the Queenes Maiestie, 1570.

Penry, John. *A Briefe Discovery of the Untruthes, and Slanders Against Reformation, and the favourers thereof, contained in D. Bancroft's Sermon [. . .].* Edinburgh: Robert Waldegrave, 1589/90.

Plato. *Apology.* In *The Dialogues of Plato.* Translated by B. Jowett. 2 vols. New York: Random House, 1937.

Ponet, John. *A Short Treatise of Politic Power* (London: 1556). Facsimile reprint. Amsterdam: Theatrum Orbis Terrarum, 1972.

Starkey, Thomas. *A Dialogue between Pole and Lupset.* Translated and edited by Thomas F. Mayer. London: Offices of the Royal Historical Society, University College London, 1989.

————. *Exhortation to Unitie and Obedience* (London: 1540). Facsimile reprint. Amsterdam: Theatrum Orbis Terrarum, 1973.

Thornwell, James Henley. *The Collected Writings of James Henley Thornwell*. 4 vols. Edited by B. M. Palmer. Richmond: Presbyterian Committee of Publication, 1873.

Travers, Walter. *A Full and Plaine Declaration of Ecclesiasticall Discipline Owt Off the Word Off God / and Off the Declininge Off the Churche Off England from the Same.* Zurich: C. Froschauer, 1574.

Vermigli, Pietro Martire. *Commentary on Aristotle's Nicomachean Ethics*. Edited by Emidio Campi and Joseph C. McClelland. The Peter Martyr Library 9. Kirksville, MO: Truman State University Press, 2006.

————. *The common places of the most famous and renowmed diuine Doctor Peter Martyr [. . .]*. Translated and edited by Anthonie Marten. London: Henry Denham & Henry Middleton, 1583.

————. *Philosophical Works: On the Relation of Philosophy and Theology*. Translated and edited by Joseph C. McClelland. The Peter Martyr Library 4. Kirksville, MO: Truman State University Press, 1996.

————. *The Political Thought of Peter Martyr Vermigli: Selected Texts and Commentary*. Edited by Robert M. Kingdon. Geneva: Librairie Droz, 1980.

Whitgift, John. *An Answere to a certen libell intitutled, An Admonition to Parliament*. London: Henrie Bynneman, 1573. Reprinted in *Whitgift's Works*.

————. *The Defense of the Aunswere to the Admonition: against the replie of T. C.* London: Henrie Bynneman, 1574. Reprinted in *Whitgift's Works*.

————. *Whitgift's Works*. Edited by John Ayre. 3 vols. Cambridge: Parker Society, 1849-51.

Zanchi, Girolamo. *De Religione Christiana Fides—Confession of the Christian Religion.* 2 vols. Edited by Luca Baschera and Christian Moser. Leiden: Brill, 2007.

————. "On the Law in General." Translated by Jeffrey J. Veenstra. *Journal of Markets and Morality* 6, no. 1 (Spring 2003): 305-98.

Secondary Sources

Almasy, Rudolph P. "The Elizabethan Church as Restoration: Notes on Richard Hooker's Rhetorical Strategy." *Renaissance and Reformation* 32, no. 4 (2009): 31-48.

————. "Language and Exclusion in the First Book of Hooker's *Politie*." In Kirby, ed., *Richard Hooker and the English Reformation*, 227-42.

————. "Rhetoric and Apologetics." In Kirby, ed., *A Companion to Richard Hooker*, 121-50.

————. "They Are and Are Not Elymas: The 1641 'Causes' Notes as Postscript to Richard Hooker's *Of the Lawes of Ecclesiasticall Politie*." In McGrade, ed., *Richard Hooker and the Construction of Christian Community*, 183-202.

Atkinson, Nigel. *Richard Hooker and the Authority of Scripture, Tradition and Reason: Reformed Theologian of the Church of England?* Carlisle, UK: Paternoster, 1997.

Austin, Victor. *Up with Authority: Why We Need Authority to Flourish as Human Beings.* Edinburgh: T&T Clark, 2010.

Avis, P. D. L. *Anglicanism and the Christian Church*. Edinburgh: T&T Clark, 2002.

———. *The Church in the Theology of the Reformers*. Atlanta: John Knox, 1981.

———. "Moses and the Magistrate: A Study in the Rise of Protestant Legalism." *Ecclesiastical History* 149 (1975): 148–72.

———. "Review of *A Companion to Richard Hooker*. Edited by Torrance Kirby." *Ecclesiology* 8 (2012): 416–20.

———. "Richard Hooker and John Calvin." *Journal of Ecclesiastical History* 32, no. 1 (1981): 19–28.

———. "The True Church in Reformation Theology." *Scottish Journal of Theology* 30, no. 4 (1977): 319–45.

Bahnsen, Greg. *Theonomy in Christian Ethics*. Phillipsburg, NJ: P&R Publishing, 1984.

Bainton, Roland. *Here I Stand: A Life of Martin Luther*. New York: Abingdon-Cokesbury, 1950.

Baker, Glenn. "Richard Hooker and Writing God into Polemic and Piety." PhD thesis, University of Leicester, 2007.

Baker, J. Wayne. "In Defense of Magisterial Discipline: Bullinger's *Tractatus de Excommunicatione* of 1568." In Gäbler and Herkenrath, eds., *Heinrich Bullinger, 1504–1575*, 141–59.

Balke, Willem. *Calvin and the Anabaptist Radicals*. Translated by William Heynen. Grand Rapids: Eerdmans, 1981.

Ballor, Jordan J. "Natural Law and Protestantism." *Christian Scholar's Review* 41, no. 2 (2012): 193–210.

———, and W. Bradford Littlejohn. "European Calvinism: Church Discipline." In Irene Dingel and Johannes Paulmann, eds., *European History Online* (EGO). Mainz: Institute of European History (IEG), 2013. http://www.ieg-ego.eu/en/threads/crossroads/religious-and-denominational-spaces/jordan-ballor-w-bradford-littlejohn-european-calvinism-church-discipline (accessed 24 May 2013).

Barrett, Matthew. "Review of *Living in God's Two Kingdoms: A Biblical Vision for Christianity and Culture*. By David VanDrunen." *Journal of Theological Studies* 62, no. 2 (2011): 817–21.

———. "Review of *Natural Law and the Two Kingdoms: A Study of the Development of Reformed Social Thought*. By David VanDrunen." *Journal of Theological Studies* 62, no. 1 (2011): 392–96.

Baschera, Luca. "Aristotle and Scholasticism." In Kirby, Campi, and James, eds., *A Companion to Peter Martyr Vermigli*, 133–60.

Bauckham, Richard. *The Bible in Politics: How to Read the Bible Politically*. Louisville: Westminster John Knox, 2011.

———. *God and the Crisis of Freedom: Biblical and Contemporary Perspectives*. Louisville: Westminster John Knox, 2002.

———. "Richard Hooker and John Calvin: A Comment." *Journal of Ecclesiastical History* 32, no. 1 (1981): 29–33.

Benedict, Philip. *Christ's Churches Purely Reformed: A Social History of Calvinism*. New Haven: Yale University Press, 2002.

Bibliography

Berlin, Isaiah. "Two Concepts of Liberty." In *Liberty: Incorporating Four Essays on Liberty*, ed. Henry Hardy, 166–217. Oxford: Oxford University Press, 2002.

Black, Joseph. "The Rhetoric of Reaction: The Martin Marprelate Tracts (1588–89), Anti-Martinism, and the Uses of Print in Early Modern England." *Sixteenth Century Journal* 28, no. 3 (1997): 707–25.

Black, J. William. "From Martin Bucer to Richard Baxter: 'Discipline' and Reformation in Sixteenth- and Seventeenth-Century England." *Church History* 70, no. 4 (2001): 644–73.

Bolt, John. "Church and World: A Trinitarian Perspective." *Calvin Theological Journal* 18, no. 1 (April 1983): 5–31.

Booty, John E. "Hooker and Anglicanism." In Hill, ed., *Studies in Richard Hooker*, 207–40.

Bouwsma, William J. "Hooker in the Context of European Cultural History." In McGrade, ed., *Richard Hooker and the Construction of Christian Community*, 41–58.

Bozeman, Theodore Dwight. *The Precisianist Strain: Disciplinary Religion & Antinomian Backlash in Puritanism to 1638*. Chapel Hill: University of North Carolina Press, 2004.

Brachlow, Stephen. *The Communion of Saints: Radical Puritan and Separatist Ecclesiology, 1570–1625*. Oxford: Oxford University Press, 1988.

Bremer, Francis J. *Puritanism: A Very Short Introduction*. Oxford: Oxford University Press, 2009.

Brewbaker, William S. III. "The Bible as Law Book? Thomas Aquinas on the Juridical Uses of Scripture." *Rutgers Journal of Law and Religion* 12, no. 76 (Fall 2010): 76–119.

Brydon, Michael A. *The Evolving Reputation of Richard Hooker: An Examination of Responses 1600–1714*. Oxford: Oxford University Press, 2006.

Burgess, Glenn. *British Political Thought, 1500–1660: The Politics of the Post-reformation*. Basingstoke, UK: Palgrave Macmillan, 2009.

Campi, Emidio. "John Calvin and Peter Martyr Vermigli: A Reassessment of Their Relationship." In Irene Dingel and Herman J. Selderhuis, eds., *Calvin und Calvinismus: Europäische Perspektiven*, 85–102. Göttingen: Vandenhoeck & Ruprecht, 2011.

———, ed. *Peter Martyr Vermigli: Humanism, Republicanism, Reformation*. Geneva: Librairie Droz, 2002.

Carson, D. A. *Christ and Culture Revisited*. Grand Rapids: Eerdmans, 2007.

Cavanaugh, William T. *Migrations of the Holy: God, State, and the Political Meaning of the Church*. Grand Rapids: Eerdmans, 2011.

———. *The Myth of Religious Violence: Secular Ideology and the Roots of Modern Conflict*. Oxford: Oxford University Press, 2009.

———. *Theopolitical Imagination*. London: T&T Clark, 2002.

Chadwick, Owen. "Richard Bancroft's Submission." *Journal of Ecclesiastical History* 3, no. 1 (1952): 58–73.

Christianson, Paul. "Reformers and the Church of England under Elizabeth I and the Early Stuarts." *Journal of Ecclesiastical History* 31, no. 4 (1980): 463–82.

Coffey, John, and Paul C. H. Lim. *The Cambridge Companion to Puritanism*. Cambridge: Cambridge University Press, 2008.

Collinson, Patrick. "Antipuritanism." In Coffey and Lim, eds., *The Cambridge Companion to Puritanism*, 19–33.

―――. *The Elizabethan Puritan Movement*. Berkeley: University of California Press, 1967.

―――. "The Fog in the Channel Clears: The Rediscovery of the Continental Dimension to the British Reformations." In *The Reception of the Continental Reformation in Britain*, ed. Polly Ha and Patrick Collinson, xxvii–xxxvii.

―――. *Godly People: Essays on English Protestantism and Puritanism*. London: Hambledon, 1983.

―――. "Hooker and the Elizabethan Establishment." In McGrade, ed., *Richard Hooker and the Construction of Christian Community*, 149–82.

―――. *The Religion of Protestants: The Church in English Society, 1559–1625*. Oxford: Clarendon, 1982.

―――. *Richard Bancroft and Elizabethan Anti-Puritanism*. Cambridge: Cambridge University Press, 2013.

Como, David. "Radical Puritanism." In Coffey and Lim, eds., *The Cambridge Companion to Puritanism*, 241–58.

Compier, Don H. "Hooker on the Authority of Scripture in Matters of Morality." In McGrade, ed., *Richard Hooker and the Construction of Christian Community*, 251–60.

Coolidge, John S. *The Pauline Renaissance in England: Puritanism and the Bible*. Oxford: Clarendon, 1970.

Cranz, F. Edward. *An Essay on the Development of Luther's Thought on Justice, Law and Society*. Cambridge, MA: Harvard University Press, 1959.

Cross, Claire. *The Royal Supremacy in the Elizabethan Church*. London: Allen & Unwin, 1969.

Dackson, Wendy. "Richard Hooker and American Religious Liberty." *Journal of Church and State* 41, no. 1 (1999): 117–34.

Davie, Martin. "Calvin's Influence on the Theology of the English Reformation." *Ecclesiology* 6, no. 3 (2010): 315–41.

Davies, E. T. *The Political Ideas of Richard Hooker*. New York: Octagon Books, 1972.

Davis, Charles Watterson. "'For Conformities Sake': How Richard Hooker Used Fuzzy Logic and Legal Rhetoric Against Political Extremes." In McGrade, ed., *Richard Hooker and the Construction of Christian Community*, 332–51.

Davis, G. Scott. "Doing What Comes Naturally: Recent Work on Thomas Aquinas and the New Natural Law Theory." *Religion* 31, no. 4 (2001): 407–33.

Davis, Kenneth R. "No Discipline, No Church: An Anabaptist Contribution to the Reformed Tradition." *Sixteenth Century Journal* 13, no. 4 (1982): 43–58.

Dixon, R. W. *History of the Church of England from the Abolition of the Roman Jurisdiction*. Vol. 6, *Elizabeth, A.D. 1564–1570*. Oxford: Clarendon, 1902.

Dominiak, Paul. "Hooker, Scholasticism, Thomism, and Reformed Orthodoxy." In Littlejohn and Kindred-Barnes, eds., *Richard Hooker and Reformed Orthodoxy*, 101–26.

Donnelly, John Patrick, SJ. *Calvinism and Scholasticism in Vermigli's Doctrine of Man and Grace*. Leiden: Brill, 1976.

―――. "Calvinist Thomism." *Viator* 7 (1976): 441–55.

———. "Peter Martyr Vermigli's Political Ethics." In Campi, ed., *Peter Martyr Vermigli: Humanism, Republicanism, Reformation*, 59–66.

———. "The Social and Ethical Thought of Peter Martyr Vermigli." In McClelland, ed., *Peter Martyr Vermigli and Italian Reform*, 107–20.

Driscoll, Mark and Grace. *Real Marriage: The Truth about Sex, Friendship, and Life Together*. Nashville: Thomas Nelson, 2012.

Duffield, G. E., and Ford Lewis Battles, eds. *John Calvin: A Collection of Distinguished Essays*. Abingdon (Berks.): Sutton Courtenay, 1966.

Durston, Christopher, and Jacqueline Eales. "Introduction: The Puritan Ethos, 1560–1700." In Christopher Durston and Jacqueline Eales, eds., *The Culture of English Puritanism: 1560-1700*, 1–31. New York: St. Martin's, 1996.

Eccleshall, Robert. "Richard Hooker's Synthesis and the Problem of Allegiance." *Journal of the History of Ideas* 37, no. 1 (1976): 111–24.

Edelen, Georges. "Hooker's Style." In Hill, ed., *Studies in Richard Hooker*, 241–78.

Eppley, Daniel. *Defending Royal Supremacy and Discerning God's Will in Tudor England*. Aldershot, UK: Ashgate, 2007.

———. *Reading the Bible with Richard Hooker*. Minneapolis: Fortress, 2016.

———. "Royal Supremacy." In Kirby, ed., *A Companion to Richard Hooker*, 503–34.

Estes, James M. *Peace, Order and the Glory of God: Secular Authority and the Church in the Thought of Luther and Melanchthon, 1518-1559*. Leiden: Brill, 2005.

Euler, Carrie. *Couriers of the Gospel: England and Zurich, 1531-1558*. Zurich: Theologischer Verlag, 2006.

Faulkner, Robert K. *Richard Hooker and the Politics of a Christian England*. Berkeley: University of California Press, 1981.

Fincham, Kenneth, and Peter Lake, eds. *Religious Politics in Post-reformation England: Essays in Honour of Nicholas Tyacke*. Woodbridge (Suffolk): Boydell, 2006.

Forsythe, Clarke D. *Politics for the Greatest Good: The Case for Prudence in the Public Square*. Downers Grove, IL: IVP Books, 2009.

Foxgrover, David, ed. *Calvin and the Church*. Grand Rapids: Published for the Calvin Studies Society by CRC Product Services, 2002.

Fulford, Andrew A. "'A Truth Infallible': Richard Hooker and Reformed Orthodoxy on Autopistos." In Littlejohn and Kindred-Barnes, eds., *Richard Hooker and Reformed Orthodoxy*, 203–20.

Gäbler, Ulrich, and Erland Herkenrath, eds. *Heinrich Bullinger, 1504-1575: Gesammelte Aufsätze zum 400. Todestag*. Zurich: Theologischer Verlag, 1975.

Gazal, André A. *Scripture and Royal Supremacy in Tudor England: The Use of Old Testament Historical Narrative*. Lewiston, NY: Edwin Mellen, 2013.

George, Robert P. *Natural Law Theory: Contemporary Essays*. Oxford: Oxford University Press, 1994.

Gibbs, Lee W. "Richard Hooker: Prophet of Anglicanism or English Magisterial Reformer?" *Anglican Theological Review* 84 (2002): 943–60.

———. "Richard Hooker's *Via Media* Doctrine of Scripture and Tradition." *Harvard Theological Review* 95, no. 2 (2002): 227–35.

Gordon, Bruce, and Emidio Campi, eds. *Architect of Reformation: An Introduction to Heinrich Bullinger, 1504–1575.* Grand Rapids: Baker Academic, 2004.

Grabill, Stephen J. *Rediscovering the Natural Law in Reformed Theological Ethics.* Emory University Studies in Law and Religion. Grand Rapids: Eerdmans, 2006.

Greaves, Richard L. "Concepts of Political Obedience in Late Tudor England: Conflicting Perspectives." *Journal of British Studies* 22, no. 1 (1982): 23–34.

Gregory, Eric. *Politics and the Order of Love: An Augustinian Ethic of Democratic Citizenship.* Chicago: University of Chicago Press, 2008.

Grislis, Egil. "The Assurance of Faith According to Richard Hooker." In McGrade, ed., *Richard Hooker and the Construction of Christian Community,* 237–50.

———. "The Hermeneutical Problem in Richard Hooker." In Hill, ed., *Studies in Richard Hooker,* 159–206.

———. "Scriptural Hermeneutics." In Kirby, ed., *A Companion to Richard Hooker,* 273–304.

Grudem, Wayne A. *Politics According to the Bible: A Comprehensive Resource for Understanding Modern Political Issues in Light of Scripture.* Grand Rapids: Zondervan, 2010.

Guggisberg, Hans R., and Gottfried G. Krodel, eds. *Die Reformation in Deutschland und Europa: Interpretationen und Debatten.* Gütersloh: Gütersloher Verlagshaus Gerd Mohn, 1993.

Ha, Polly, and Patrick Collinson, eds. *The Reception of Continental Reformation in Britain.* Proceedings of the British Academy 164. Oxford: Oxford University Press, 2010.

Hancock, Ralph C. *Calvin and the Foundations of Modern Politics.* Ithaca, NY: Cornell University Press, 1989.

Harris, Joshua. *Boy Meets Girl: Say Hello to Courtship.* Colorado Springs: Multnomah, 2005.

Harrison, William H. "The Church." In Kirby, ed., *A Companion to Richard Hooker,* 305–36.

———. "Powers of Nature and Influences of Grace in Hooker's *Lawes.*" In Kirby, ed., *Richard Hooker and the English Reformation,* 15–24.

Hart, David Bentley. *Atheist Delusions: The Christian Revolution and Its Fashionable Enemies.* New Haven: Yale University Press, 2009.

Hart, D. G. *From Billy Graham to Sarah Palin: Evangelicals and the Betrayal of American Conservatism.* Grand Rapids: Eerdmans, 2011.

———. *The Lost Soul of American Protestantism.* Lanham, MD: Rowman & Littlefield, 2002.

———. *A Secular Faith: Why Christianity Favors the Separation of Church and State.* Chicago: Ivan R. Dee, 2006.

Heckel, Johannes. *Lex Charitatis: A Juristic Disquisition on Law in the Theology of Martin Luther* (1953). Edited by Martin Heckel. Translated by Gottfried G. Krodel. Grand Rapids: Eerdmans, 2010.

Henreckson, David P. "Review of *Natural Law and the Two Kingdoms: A Study in the Development of Reformed Social Thought.* By David VanDrunen." *Journal of Church and State* 53, no. 1 (2011): 122–24.

Hill, W. Speed. "The Evolution of Hooker's *Laws of Ecclesiastical Polity*." In Hill, ed., *Studies in Richard Hooker*, 117–58.

———, ed. *Studies in Richard Hooker: Essays Preliminary to an Edition of His Works*. Cleveland: Press of Case Western Reserve University, 1972.

Hillerbrand, Hans Joachim, ed. *Oxford Encyclopedia of the Reformation*. Oxford: Oxford University Press, 1996.

Hodge, Charles. *Discussions in Church Polity*. New York: Charles Scribner's Sons, 1878.

Höpfl, Harro. *The Christian Polity of John Calvin*. Cambridge: Cambridge University Press, 1982.

Ingalls, Ranall. "Sin and Grace." In Kirby, ed., *A Companion to Richard Hooker*, 151–84.

James, Frank A., III, ed. *Peter Martyr Vermigli and the European Reformations: Semper Reformanda*. Leiden: Brill, 2004.

Jenkins, Gary. "Peter Martyr and the Church of England after 1558." In James, ed., *Peter Martyr Vermigli and the European Reformations*, 47–69.

Joyce, A. J. *Richard Hooker and Anglican Moral Theology*. Oxford: Oxford University Press, 2012.

Kahn, Jonathan. "Nicholas Wolterstorff's Fear of the Secular." *The Immanent Frame*, February 22, 2009. http://blogs.ssrc.org/tif/2009/02/22/nicholas-wolterstorffs-fear-of-the-secular/ (accessed April 22, 2016).

Kantorowicz, Ernst H. *The King's Two Bodies: A Study in Mediaeval Political Theology*. Princeton: Princeton University Press, 1957.

Keep, David J. "Bullinger's Defence of Queen Elizabeth." In *Heinrich Bullinger: 1504–75*, ed. Gäbler and Herkenrath, 231–41.

Kelly, Douglas F. *The Emergence of Liberty in the Modern World: The Influence of Calvin on Five Governments from the 16th through 18th Centuries*. Phillipsburg, NJ: P&R Publishing, 1992.

Kendall, R. T. *Calvin and English Calvinism to 1649*. Oxford: Oxford University Press, 1979.

Kernan, Dean. "Jurisdiction and the Keys." In Kirby, ed., *A Companion to Richard Hooker*, 435–80.

Kerr, Fergus. *After Aquinas: Versions of Thomism*. Malden, MA: Blackwell, 2002.

Kindred-Barnes, Scott. *Richard Hooker's Use of History in His Defense of Public Worship: His Anglican Critique of Calvin, Barrow, and the Puritans*. Lewiston, NY: Edwin Mellen, 2011.

Kingdon, Robert M. "The Church: Ideology or Institution." *Church History* 50, no. 1 (1981): 81–97.

———. "Ecclesiology: Exegesis and Discipline." In Kirby, Campi, and James, eds., *A Companion to Peter Martyr Vermigli*, 375–86.

———. "Peter Martyr Vermigli on Church Discipline." In Campi, ed., *Peter Martyr Vermigli: Humanism, Republicanism, Reformation*, 67–76.

———. "The Political Thought of Peter Martyr Vermigli." In McClelland, ed., *Peter Martyr Vermigli and Italian Reform*, 121–40.

Kirby, W. J. Torrance. "Angels Descending and Ascending: Hooker's Discourse on the

'Double Motion' of Common Prayer." In Kirby, ed., *Richard Hooker and the English Reformation*, 111–30.

———. "Calvin and the Public Sphere." In Richard R. Topping and John A. Vissers, eds., *Calvin@500: Theology, History, and Practice*, 52–66. Eugene, OR: Pickwick, 2011.

———. "The Civil Magistrate and the 'Cura Religionis': Heinrich Bullinger's Prophetical Office and the English Reformation." *Animus* 9 (2004): 25–36.

———. "Creation and Government: Eternal Law as the Fountain of Laws in Richard Hooker's Ecclesiastical Polity." In Michael Treschow, Willemien Otten, and Walter Hannam, eds., *Divine Creation in Ancient, Medieval, and Early Modern Thought: Essays Presented to the Rev'd Robert D. Crouse*, 405–23. Leiden: Brill, 2007.

———. "From 'Generall Meditations' to 'Particular Decisions': The Augustinian Coherence of Richard Hooker's Political Theology." In Robert S. Sturges, ed., *Law and Sovereignty in the Middle Ages and the Renaissance*, 41–63. Arizona Studies in the Middle Ages and the Renaissance 28. Turnhout: Brepols, 2011.

———. "Grace and Hierarchy: Richard Hooker's Two Platonisms." In Kirby, ed., *Richard Hooker and the English Reformation*, 25–40.

———. "'Law Makes the King': Richard Hooker on Law and Princely Rule." In Michael Hattaway, ed., *A New Companion to English Renaissance Literature and Culture* (2 vols.), 1:274–88. Malden, MA: Wiley-Blackwell, 2010.

———. "The Neo-Platonic Logic of Richard Hooker's Generic Division of Law." *Renaissance and Reformation* 22 (1998): 49–68.

———. "Peter Martyr Vermigli and Pope Boniface VIII: The Difference between Civil and Ecclesiastical Power." In James, ed., *Peter Martyr Vermigli and the European Reformations*, 291–304.

———. "Political Theology: The Godly Prince." In Kirby, Campi, and James, eds., *A Companion to Peter Martyr Vermigli*, 401–22.

———. "The Public Sermon: Paul's Cross and the Culture of Persuasion in England, 1534–1570." *Renaissance and Reformation* 31, no. 1 (2007): 3–19.

———. "Reason and Law." In Kirby, ed., *A Companion to Richard Hooker*, 251–72.

———. "Review of *Richard Hooker and Reformed Theology: A Study of Reason, Will, and Grace*. By Nigel Voak." *Sixteenth Century Journal* 36, no. 1 (2005): 261–63.

———. "Richard Hooker as an Apologist of the Magisterial Reformation in England." In McGrade, ed., *Richard Hooker and the Construction of Christian Community*, 219–33.

———. *Richard Hooker, Reformer and Platonist*. Aldershot, UK: Ashgate, 2005.

———. *Richard Hooker's Doctrine of the Royal Supremacy*. Leiden: Brill, 1990.

———. "Richard Hooker's Theory of Natural Law in the Context of Reformation Theology." *Sixteenth Century Journal* 30, no. 3 (1999): 681–703.

———. "The 'Sundrie Waies of Wisdom': Richard Hooker's Sapiential Theology." In Kevin Killeen, ed., *Oxford Handbook of the Bible in Early Modern England, 1530–1700*, 164–75. Oxford: Oxford University Press, 2015.

———. *The Zurich Connection and Tudor Political Theology*. Leiden: Brill, 2007.

———, ed. *A Companion to Richard Hooker*. Leiden: Brill, 2008.

————, ed. *Richard Hooker and the English Reformation*. Dordrecht: Kluwer Academic, 2003.

Kirby, W. J. Torrance, Emidio Campi, and Frank A. James III, eds. *A Companion to Peter Martyr Vermigli*. Leiden: Brill, 2009.

Kirby, W. J. Torrance, and P. G. Stanwood, eds. *Paul's Cross and the Culture of Persuasion in England, 1520-1640*. Leiden: Brill, 2014.

Kloosterman, Nelson D. "A Response to 'The Kingship of Christ Is Twofold': Natural Law and the Two Kingdoms in the Thought of Herman Bavinck by David VanDrunen." *Calvin Theological Journal* 45, no. 1 (2010): 165-76.

Knappen, Marshall. *Tudor Puritanism: A Chapter in the History of Idealism*. Chicago: University of Chicago Press, 1965.

Knox, S. J. *Walter Travers: Paragon of Elizabethan Puritanism*. London: Methuen, 1962.

Lake, Peter. "'The Anglican Moment?' Richard Hooker and the Ideological Watershed of the 1590s." In Stephen Platten, ed., *Anglicanism and the Western Christian Tradition: Continuity, Change and the Search for Communion*, 90-121. Norwich, UK: Canterbury, 2003.

————. *Anglicans and Puritans? Presbyterianism and English Conformist Thought from Whitgift to Hooker*. London: Unwin Hyman, 1988.

————. "Antipuritanism: The Structure of a Prejudice." In Fincham and Lake, eds., *Religious Politics in Post-Reformation England*, 80-97.

————. "Business as Usual? The Immediate Reception of Hooker's Ecclesiastical Polity." *Journal of Ecclesiastical History* 52, no. 3 (2001): 456-86.

————. "Calvinism and the English Church 1570-1635." *Past & Present* 114 (1987): 32-76.

————. "The Historiography of Puritanism." In Coffey and Lim, eds., *The Cambridge Companion to Puritanism*, 346-72.

————. "Introduction: Puritanism, Arminianism, and Nicholas Tyacke." In Fincham and Lake, eds., *Religious Politics in Post-Reformation England*, 1-15.

————. "The Laudian Style: Order, Uniformity, and the Pursuit of the Beauty of Holiness in the 1630s." In Kenneth Fincham, ed., *The Early Stuart Church: 1603-1642*, 161-85. Stanford: Stanford University Press, 1993.

————. *Moderate Puritans and the Elizabethan Church*. Cambridge: Cambridge University Press, 1982.

Lake, Peter, and Steven C. A. Pincus, eds. *The Politics of the Public Sphere in Early Modern England*. Manchester: Manchester University Press, 2007.

Lake, Peter, and Michael C. Questier, eds. *The Anti-Christ's Lewd Hat: Protestants, Papists and Players in Post-Reformation England*. New Haven: Yale University Press, 2002.

————. *Conformity and Orthodoxy in the English Church, c. 1560-1660*. Woodbridge (Suffolk): Boydell, 2000.

Leithart, Peter J. *Defending Constantine: The Twilight of an Empire and the Dawn of Christendom*. Downers Grove, IL: InterVarsity Academic, 2010.

Lewis, C. S. *English Literature in the Sixteenth Century, Excluding Drama*. Vol. 3 of *The Oxford History of English Literature*. Oxford: Clarendon, 1954.

Linch, Amy. "Community and Contention in Early Modern England." PhD dissertation, Rutgers, the State University of New Jersey, 2009.

Lindeboom, J. *Austin Friars: History of the Dutch Reformed Church in London, 1550–1950.* The Hague: Martinus Nijhoff, 1950.

Littlejohn, W. Bradford. "Bancroft v. Penry: Conscience and Authority in Elizabethan Polemics." In W. J. Torrance Kirby, ed., *A Companion to Paul's Cross.* Leiden: Brill, 2014.

———. "Cutting Through the Fog in the Channel: Hooker, Junius, and a Reformed Theology of Law." In Littlejohn and Kindred-Barnes, eds., *Richard Hooker and Reformed Orthodoxy,* 221–40.

———. "More than a Swineherd: Hooker, Vermigli, and the Aristotelian Defense of the Royal Supremacy." *Reformation and Renaissance Review* 15, no. 1 (2014): 78–93.

———. "Review of *Natural Law and the Two Kingdoms: A Study in the Development of Reformed Social Thought.* By David VanDrunen." *Scottish Bulletin of Evangelical Theology* 29, no. 1 (Spring 2011): 131–35.

———. *Richard Hooker: A Companion to His Life and Work.* Eugene, OR: Cascade, 2015.

———. "Search for a Reformed Hooker." *Reformation & Renaissance Review* 16, no. 1 (2014): 68–82.

———. "*Sola Scriptura* and the Public Square: Richard Hooker and a Protestant Paradigm for Political Engagement." In Neil Messer and Angus Paddison, eds., *The Bible: Culture, Community, and Society,* 209–22. London: Bloomsbury T&T Clark, 2013.

Littlejohn, W. Bradford, and Scott Kindred-Barnes. *Richard Hooker and Reformed Orthodoxy.* Göttingen: Vandenhoeck & Ruprecht, 2017.

Lowrie, Walter. *The Church and Its Organization in Primitive and Catholic Times: An Interpretation of Rudolph Sohm's Kirchenrecht, Volume 1.* New York: Longmans, 1904.

MacCulloch, Diarmaid. *The Later Reformation in England, 1547–1603.* Basingstoke, UK: Palgrave Macmillan, 2001.

———. "The Latitude of the Church of England." In Fincham and Lake, eds., *Religious Politics in Post-Reformation England,* 41–59.

———. *Reformation: Europe's House Divided, 1490–1700.* London: Allen Lane, 2003.

———. "Richard Hooker's Reputation." In Kirby, ed., *A Companion to Richard Hooker,* 563–610.

———. *Tudor Church Militant: Edward VI and the Protestant Reformation.* London: Allen Lane, 1999.

Manschreck, Clyde L. "The Role of Melanchthon in the Adiaphora Controversy." *Archiv für Reformationsgeschichte* 48 (1957): 165–81.

Marshall, Peter. "(Re)defining the English Reformation." *Journal of British Studies* 48, no. 3 (July 2009): 564–86.

Maruyama, Tadataka. *The Ecclesiology of Theodore Beza: The Reform of the True Church.* Geneva: Librairie Droz, 1978.

Mason, Roger A. *Kingship and the Commonweal: Political Thought in Renaissance and Reformation Scotland.* East Lothian, Scotland: Tuckwell, 1998.

Mayer, Thomas F. "Starkey and Melanchthon on Adiaphora: A Critique of W. Gordon Zeeveld." *Sixteenth Century Journal* 11, no. 1 (1980): 39–50.

―――. *Thomas Starkey and the Commonweal: Humanist Politics and Religion in the Reign of Henry VIII.* Cambridge: Cambridge University Press, 1989.

McCauliff, C. M. A. "Law as a Principle of Reform: Reflections from Sixteenth-Century England." *Rutgers Law Review* 40 (1987): 429–65.

McClelland, Joseph C., ed. *Peter Martyr Vermigli and Italian Reform.* Waterloo, ON: Wilfrid Laurier University Press, 1980.

―――. "Peter Martyr Vermigli: Scholastic or Humanist?" In McClelland, ed. *Peter Martyr Vermigli and Italian Reform,* 141–52.

McCoy, Richard C. *Alterations of State: Sacred Kingship in the English Reformation.* New York: Columbia University Press, 2002.

McGinn, D. J. *The Admonition Controversy.* New Brunswick, NJ: Rutgers University Press, 1949.

McGrade, Arthur Stephen, ed. *Richard Hooker and the Construction of Christian Community.* Tempe, AZ: Medieval & Renaissance Texts & Studies, 1997.

McGrath, Alister. *Christianity's Dangerous Idea: The Protestant Revolution—A History from the Sixteenth Century to the Twenty-First.* New York: HarperOne, 2007.

McKay, David. "From Popery to Principle: Covenanters and the Kingship of Christ." In Anthony T. Selvaggio, ed., *The Faith Once Delivered: Essays in Honor of Dr. D. Wayne Spear,* 135–69. Phillipsburg, NJ: P&R Publishing, 2007.

Milton, Anthony. "'Anglicanism' by Stealth: The Career and Influence of John Overall." In Fincham and Lake, eds., *Religious Politics in Post-Reformation England,* 159–76.

―――. "Puritanism and the Continental Reformed Churches." In Coffey and Lim, eds., *The Cambridge Companion to Puritanism,* 109–26.

Monahan, Arthur P. "Richard Hooker: Counter-Reformation Political Thinker." In McGrade, ed., *Richard Hooker and the Construction of Christian Community,* 203–18.

Moore, Susan Hardman. "New England's Reformation: 'Wee shall be as a Citty upon a Hill, the Eies of All People are upon Us.'" In Fincham and Lake, eds., *Religious Politics in Post-Reformation England,* 143–58.

Moots, Glenn. "Searching for Christian America." In *For Law and For Liberty: Essays on the Trans-Atlantic Legacy of Protestant Political Thought,* ed. W. Bradford Littlejohn. Proceedings of the Third Annual Convivium Irenicum. Moscow, ID: Davenant, 2016.

Morgan, Edmund S. *Visible Saints: The History of a Puritan Idea.* New York: New York University Press, 1963.

Morrissey, Mary. *Politics and the Paul's Cross Sermons, 1558–1642.* Oxford: Oxford University Press, 2011.

Mueller, William A. *Church and State in Luther and Calvin; A Comparative Study.* Nashville: Broadman, 1954.

Neale, Sir John. *Elizabeth I and Her Parliaments.* 2 vols. London: Jonathan Cape, 1957.

Neelands, W. David. "Christology and the Sacraments." In Kirby, ed., *A Companion to Richard Hooker,* 369–402.

―――. "Hooker on Scripture, Reason, and 'Tradition.'" In McGrade, ed., *Richard Hooker and the Construction of Christian Community,* 75–94.

―――. "Predestination." In Kirby, ed., *A Companion to Richard Hooker,* 185–220.

———. "Richard Hooker on the Identity of the Visible and Invisible Church." In Kirby, ed., *Richard Hooker and the English Reformation*, 99–110.

Nelson, Eric. *The Hebrew Republic: Jewish Sources and the Transformation of European Political Thought*. Cambridge, MA: Harvard University Press, 2010.

Nevin, John Williamson. "The Sect System." *Mercersburg Review* 1, no. 5 (1849): 482–539.

New, John F. H. *Anglican and Puritan: The Basis of Their Opposition, 1558–1640*. Stanford: Stanford University Press, 1964.

Nijenhuis, Willem. *Ecclesia Reformata: Studies on the Reformation*. 2 vols. Leiden: Brill, 1972.

Noll, Mark A. *America's God: From Jonathan Edwards to Abraham Lincoln*. Oxford: Oxford University Press, 2002.

O'Donovan, Joan Lockwood. "The Church of England and the Anglican Communion: A Timely Engagement with the National Church Tradition?" *Scottish Journal of Theology* 57, no. 3 (2004): 313–37.

———. *Theology of Law and Authority in the English Reformation*. Emory University Studies in Law and Religion 1. Atlanta: Scholars, 1991.

O'Donovan, Oliver. *The Desire of the Nations: Rediscovering the Roots of Political Theology*. Cambridge: Cambridge University Press, 1996.

———. *Finding and Seeking: Ethics as Theology*, vol. 2. Grand Rapids: Eerdmans, 2014.

———. *Resurrection and Moral Order: An Outline for Evangelical Ethics*. Grand Rapids: Eerdmans, 1986.

———. *The Ways of Judgment: The Bampton Lectures, 2003*. Grand Rapids: Eerdmans, 2005.

O'Donovan, Oliver, and Joan Lockwood O'Donovan, eds. *Bonds of Imperfection: Christian Politics, Past and Present*. Grand Rapids: Eerdmans, 2004.

———. *From Irenaeus to Grotius: A Sourcebook in Christian Political Thought, 100–1625*. Grand Rapids: Eerdmans, 1999.

Olson, Oliver K. *Matthias Flacius and the Survival of Luther's Reform*. Wiesbaden: Harrassowitz Verlag, 2002.

Parker, Eric. "A Christian and Reformed Doctrine of Right Practical Reason: An Examination of Thomistic Themes in Peter Martyr Vermigli's Commentary on Aristotle's Nicomachean Ethics." MA thesis, Reformed Theological Seminary, Jackson, MS, 2009.

Patterson, W. Brown. "Elizabethan Theological Polemics." In Kirby, ed., *A Companion to Richard Hooker*, 89–120.

———. "Richard Hooker on Ecumenical Relations: Conciliarism in the English Reformation." In McGrade, ed., *Richard Hooker and the Construction of Christian Community*, 283–303.

Pearson, A. F. Scott. *Church and State: Political Aspects of Sixteenth Century Puritanism*. Cambridge: Cambridge University Press, 1928.

———. *Thomas Cartwright and Elizabethan Puritanism, 1535–1603*. Gloucester, MA: Peter Smith, 1966.

Perrott, M. E. C. "Richard Hooker and the Problem of Authority in the Elizabethan Church." *Journal of Ecclesiastical History* 49, no. 1 (1998): 29–60.

Perry, John. *The Pretenses of Loyalty: Locke, Liberal Theory, and American Political Theology.* Oxford: Oxford University Press, 2011.

Pettegree, Andrew. *Reformation and the Culture of Persuasion.* Cambridge: Cambridge University Press, 2005.

Pink, Thomas. "Conscience and Coercion." *First Things* 225 (August 2012): 45–51.

———. "The Right to Religious Liberty and the Coercion of Belief: A Note on *Dignitatis Humanae*." In John Keown and Robert P. George, eds., *Reason, Morality, and Law: The Philosophy of John Finnis,* 427–42. Oxford: Oxford University Press, 2013.

Porter, H. C. "Hooker, the Tudor Constitution, and the Via Media." In Hill, ed., *Studies in Richard Hooker,* 77–116.

Porter, Jean. *Nature as Reason: A Thomistic Theory of the Natural Law.* Grand Rapids: Eerdmans, 2005.

———. *The Recovery of Virtue: The Relevance of Aquinas for Christian Ethics.* Louisville: Westminster John Knox, 1990.

Prestwich, Menna, ed. *International Calvinism, 1541–1715.* Oxford: Oxford University Press, 1985.

Primus, John. *The Vestments Controversy: An Historical Study of the Earliest Tensions within the Church of England in the Reigns of Edward VI and Elizabeth.* Kampen: J. H. Kok, 1960.

Pryor, C. Scott. "God's Bridle: John Calvin's Application of Natural Law." *Journal of Law and Religion* 22, no. 1 (2006): 225–54.

———. "Review of *Natural Law and the Two Kingdoms*. By David VanDrunen." *Journal of Law and Religion* 26, no. 2 (2011): 695–700.

Rasmussen, Barry G. "The Priority of God's Gracious Action in Richard Hooker's Hermeneutic." In Kirby, ed., *Richard Hooker and the English Reformation,* 3–14.

Reed, E. D. "Richard Hooker, Eternal Law and the Human Exercise of Authority." *Journal of Anglican Studies* 4, no. 2 (2006): 219–38.

Rodes, Robert. "Pluralist Christendom and the Christian Civil Magistrate." *Capital University Law Review* 8 (1979): 6–28.

Rose, Jacqueline. "John Locke, 'Matters Indifferent', and the Restoration of the Church of England." *Historical Journal* 48, no. 3 (2005): 601–21.

Rosenthal, Alexander S. *Crown under Law: Richard Hooker, John Locke, and the Ascent of Modern Constitutionalism.* Plymouth, UK: Lexington Books, 2008.

Russell, Andrea. "Richard Hooker: Beyond Certainty." PhD thesis, University of Nottingham, 2010.

Schreiner, Susan E. *Are You Alone Wise? The Search for Certainty in the Early Modern Era.* Oxford: Oxford University Press, 2011.

Secor, Philip B. *Richard Hooker: Prophet of Anglicanism.* Tunbridge Wells, UK: Burns & Oates, 1999.

Shagan, Ethan. *The Rule of Moderation: Violence, Religion and the Politics of Restraint in Early Modern England.* Cambridge: Cambridge University Press, 2011.

Shirley, F. J. *Richard Hooker and Contemporary Political Ideas.* London: Published for the Church Historical Society by S.P.C.K., 1949.

Shuger, Debora K. "Faith and Assurance." In Kirby, ed., *A Companion to Richard Hooker*, 221–50.

———. "'Societie Supernaturall': The Imagined Community of Hooker's *Lawes*." In McGrade, ed., *Richard Hooker and the Construction of Christian Community*, 307–30.

Skinner, Quentin. *Foundations of Modern Political Thought*. Vol. 2, *The Age of Reformation*. Cambridge: Cambridge University Press, 1978.

Smith, Edward O., Jr. "The Elizabethan Doctrine of the Prince as Reflected in the Sermons of the Episcopacy, 1559–1603." *Huntington Library Quarterly* 28, no. 1 (1964): 1–17.

Smith, James K. A. "Reforming Public Theology: Two Kingdoms or Two Cities?" *Calvin Theological Journal* 47 (2012): 122–37.

Smith, Ted A. *Weird John Brown: Divine Violence and the Limits of Ethics*. Stanford: Stanford University Press, 2015.

Spalding, James C. "The *Reformatio Legum Ecclesiasticarum* of 1552 and the Furthering of Discipline in England." *Church History* 39, no. 2 (1970): 162–71.

Springer, Michael S. *Restoring Christ's Church: John à Lasco and the Forma ac Ratio*. Aldershot, UK: Ashgate, 2007.

Stafford, J. K. "Scripture and the Generous Hermeneutic of Richard Hooker." *Anglican Theological Review* 84 (2002): 915–28.

Stevenson, William R. *Sovereign Grace: The Place and Significance of Christian Freedom in John Calvin's Political Thought*. Oxford: Oxford University Press, 1999.

Street, T. W. "John Calvin on Adiaphora: An Exposition." Unpublished PhD dissertation, Union Theological Seminary, NYC, 1954.

Strype, John. *Life and Acts of Archbishop Edmund Grindal*. 1710. Reprint, Oxford: Clarendon, 1821.

Sunshine, Glenn S. "Discipline as the Third Mark of the Church: Three Views." *Calvin Theological Journal* 33 (1998): 469–80.

Sykes, Norman. *Old Priest and New Presbyter: Episcopacy and Presbyterianism since the Reformation with Especial Relation to the Churches of England and Scotland*. Cambridge: Cambridge University Press, 1956.

Targoff, Ramie. "Performing Prayer in Hooker's Lawes: The Efficacy of Set Forms." In McGrade, ed., *Richard Hooker and the Construction of Christian Community*, 275–82.

Taylor, Charles. *A Secular Age*. Cambridge, MA: Belknap Press of Harvard University Press, 2007.

Tierney, Brian. *The Idea of Natural Rights: Studies on Natural Rights, Natural Law, and Church Law, 1150–1625*. Emory University Studies in Law and Religion. Atlanta: Scholars, 1997.

———. *Liberty and Law: The Idea of Permissive Natural Law, 1100–1800*. Studies in Medieval and Early Modern Canon Law 12. Washington, DC: Catholic University of America Press, 2014.

Thompson, W. D. J. Cargill. "The Philosopher of the 'Politic Society': Richard Hooker as Political Thinker." In Hill, ed., *Studies in Richard Hooker*, 3–76. Republished in W. D. J. Cargill Thompson, *Studies in the Reformation: Luther to Hooker*. Edited by C. W. Dugmore. London: Athlone, 1980.

———. *The Political Thought of Martin Luther*. Edited by Philip Broadhead. Brighton, UK: Harvester, 1984.

———. "A Reconsideration of Richard Bancroft's Paul's Cross Sermon of 9 February 1588/9." *Journal of Ecclesiastical History* 20, no. 2 (1969): 253–66.

———. *Studies in the Reformation: Luther to Hooker*. Edited by C. W. Dugmore. London: Athlone, 1980.

———. "The 'Two Kingdoms' and the 'Two Regiments': Some Problems of Luther's *Zwei-Reiche-Lehre*." *Journal of Theological Studies* 20, no. 1 (1969): 164–85.

Troxel, A. Craig. "Charles Hodge on Church Boards: A Case Study in Ecclesiology." *Westminster Theological Journal* 58 (1996): 183–207.

Tuininga, Matthew. *Calvin's Political Theology and the Public Engagement of the Church: Christ's Two Kingdoms*. Cambridge: Cambridge University Press, forthcoming 2017.

———. "Remembering the Two Kingdoms." *Christian Renewal* 30, no. 8 (Feb. 8, 2012).

Turrell, James F. "Uniformity and Common Prayer." In Kirby, ed., *A Companion to Richard Hooker*, 337–68.

VanderSchaaf, Mark E. "Archbishop Parker's Efforts toward a Bucerian Discipline in the Church of England." *Sixteenth Century Journal* 8, no. 1 (1977): 85–103.

VanDrunen, David. *A Biblical Case for Natural Law*. Grand Rapids: Acton Institute, 2006.

———. "Calvin, Kuyper, and 'Christian Culture.'" In R. Scott Clark and Joel E. Kim, eds., *Always Reformed: Essays in Honor of W. Robert Godfrey*. Escondido, CA: Westminster Seminary California, 2010.

———. "The Context of Natural Law: John Calvin's Doctrine of the Two Kingdoms." *Journal of Church and State* 46, no. 3 (2004): 503–25.

———. *Divine Covenants and Moral Order*. Grand Rapids: Eerdmans, 2014.

———. "The Importance of the Penultimate: Reformed Social Thought and the Contemporary Critiques of the Liberal Society." *Journal of Markets and Morality* 9, no. 2 (2006): 219–49.

———. "'The Kingship of Christ Is Twofold': Natural Law and the Two Kingdoms in the Thought of Herman Bavinck." *Calvin Theological Journal* 45, no. 1 (2010): 147–64.

———. *Living in God's Two Kingdoms: A Biblical Vision for Christianity and Culture*. Wheaton, IL: Crossway, 2010.

———. *Natural Law and the Two Kingdoms: A Study in the Development of Reformed Social Thought*. Emory University Studies in Law and Religion. Grand Rapids: Eerdmans, 2010.

———. "The Two Kingdoms Doctrine and the Relationship of Church and State in the Early Reformed Tradition." *Journal of Church and State* 49, no. 4 (2007): 743–66.

———. "The Use of Natural Law in Early Calvinist Resistance Theory." *Journal of Law and Religion* 21, no. 1 (2006): 143–67.

Van Gelderen, Martin. *The Political Thought of the Dutch Revolt, 1555–1590*. Ideas in Context 23. Cambridge: Cambridge University Press, 2002.

Venema, Cornelis. "The Restoration of All Things to Proper Order: An Assessment of the Two Kingdoms/Natural Law Interpretation of John Calvin's Public Theology." In Ryan C. McIlhenny, ed., *Kingdoms Apart: Engaging the Two Kingdoms Perspective*, 3–32. Phillipsburg, NJ: P&R Publishing, 2012.

Verkamp, Bernard J. *The Indifferent Mean: Adiaphorism in the English Reformation to 1554*. Athens: Ohio University Press, 1977.

———. "The Limits upon Adiaphoristic Freedom: Luther and Melanchthon." *Journal of Theological Studies* 36, no. 1 (1975): 52–76.

———. "The Zwinglians and Adiaphorism." *Church History* 42, no. 4 (1973): 486–504.

Vickers, Brian. "Public and Private Rhetoric in Hooker's *Lawes*." In McGrade, ed., *Richard Hooker and the Construction of Christian Community*, 95–145.

Voak, Nigel. *Richard Hooker and Reformed Theology: A Study of Reason, Will, and Grace*. Oxford: Oxford University Press, 2003.

———. "Richard Hooker and the Principle of Sola Scriptura." *Journal of Theological Studies* 59, no. 1 (2008): 96–139.

Voegelin, Eric. *The New Science of Politics: An Introduction*. 1952. Reprint, Chicago: University of Chicago Press, 1987.

Walhof, Darren. "The Accusations of Conscience and the Christian Polity in John Calvin's Political Thought." *History of Political Thought* 24, no. 3 (Autumn 2003): 397–414.

Walton, Robert C. "Henry Bullinger's Answer to John Jewel's Call for Help." In Gäbler and Herkenrath, eds., *Heinrich Bullinger: 1504–1575*, 245–56.

———. "The Institutionalization of the Reformation at Zurich." *Zwingliana* 8 (1972): 497–515.

———. *Zwingli's Theocracy*. Toronto: University of Toronto Press, 1967.

Walzer, Michael. *The Revolution of the Saints: A Study in the Origins of Radical Politics*. Cambridge, MA: Harvard University Press, 1965.

Wedgeworth, Steven. "The Two Sons of Oil and the Limits of American Religious Dissent." *Journal of Law & Religion* 27, no. 1 (2011/2012): 141–61.

Wendel, François. *Calvin: The Origins and Development of His Religious Thought*. Translated by Philip Mairet. New York: Harper & Row, 1963.

Westberg, Daniel. "Review of *Natural Law and the Two Kingdoms: A Study in the Development of Reformed Social Thought*. By David VanDrunen." *Studies in Christian Ethics* 24, no. 2 (2011): 260–62.

White, Peter. "The Rise of Arminianism Reconsidered." *Past and Present* 101 (1983): 34–54.

Williams, Rowan. "Hooker: Philosopher, Anglican, Contemporary." In McGrade, ed., *Richard Hooker and the Construction of Christian Community*, 369–83.

Wilson, Doug. *Her Hand in Marriage*. Moscow, ID: Canon, 1997.

Witte, John E., Jr. *Law and Protestantism: The Legal Teachings of the Lutheran Reformation*. Cambridge and New York: Cambridge University Press, 2002.

———. *The Reformation of Rights: Law, Religion, and Human Rights in Early Modern Calvinism*. Cambridge: Cambridge University Press, 2007.

Witte, John E., Jr., and Thomas C. Arthur. "The Three Uses of the Law: A Protestant Source of the Purposes of Capital Punishment?" *Journal of Law and Religion* 10 (1993–1994): 433–66.

Wolterstorff, Nicholas. "How Social Justice Got to Me and Why It Never Left." *Journal of the American Academy of Religion* 76, no. 3 (2008): 664–79.

Woodhouse, H. F. *The Doctrine of the Church in Anglican Theology 1547–1603*. London: Published for the Church Historical Society, 1954.

Bibliography

Wright, David F. *Martin Bucer: Reforming Church and Community.* Cambridge: Cambridge University Press, 1994.

Wright, R. J. "The Christian Lawmaker: The Contributions of the Covenant and Natural Law Traditions to a Revised Public Theology." PhD dissertation, Loyola University Chicago, 2008.

Wright, William J. *Martin Luther's Understanding of God's Two Kingdoms: A Response to the Challenge of Skepticism.* Grand Rapids: Baker Academic, 2010.

Zeeveld, W. Gordon. *Foundations of Tudor Policy.* Cambridge, MA: Harvard University Press, 1948.

Index

Index